Astro Cycles:

The Trader's Viewpoint

by

Larry Pesavento

TRADERS PRESS, INC.®
INCORPORATED
PO BOX 6206
GREENVILLE, SC 29606

Books and Gifts
for Investors and Traders

Acknowledgments

Special thanks and appreciation are extended to the following individuals from **Traders Press,** who played a part in revising the original edition of this book:

Allan McGill Dobson

Margaret Ros Hudson

Printed in the United States of America

ISBN: 0-934380-31-7

Published August 1996

TRADERS PRESS, INC.®
INCORPORATED
PO BOX 6206
GREENVILLE, SC 29606

Books and Gifts
for Investors and Traders

This book is dedicated to

BYRON G. TUCKER

Chicago, Illinois

Author's Note

"If you learn something and keep it to yourself--it is worthless."

Chinese proverb

You have purchased a book which presents an unusual approach to market timing. I would like to propose this most unusual offer to you. You may call or write me with any questions you may have regarding financial astrology. In return, I request that you not reproduce this book or any portion of it without my permission.

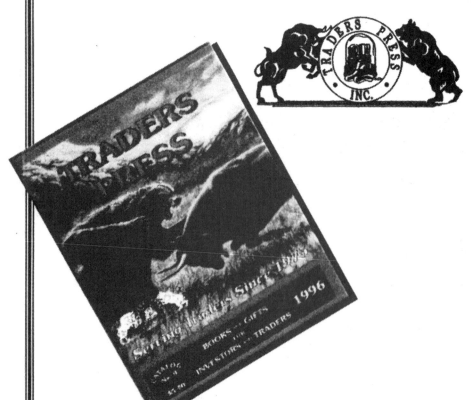

THE GREATEST WEAKNESS

I can give you the best rules in the world and the best methods for determining the position of a commodity, and then you can lose money on account of the human element, which is your greatest weakness. You will fail to **follow** rules. You will act on hope or fear instead of facts. You will delay. You will become **impatient**. You will act too quickly or you will delay too long in acting, thus **beating yourself** on account of your human weakness, then blaming it on the market. Remember that it is **your** mistakes that cause losses and not the action of the market or the manipulators. Therefore, strive to follow rules, or keep out of speculation, for you are doomed to failure.

If you will only study the weakness of human nature and see what fools these mortals be, you will find it easy to make profits by understanding the weakness of human nature and going against the public and doing opposite of what other people do. In other words, you buy near the bottom on knowledge and sell near the top on knowledge, while other people who just guess do the opposite. Time spent in the study of price, time and past market movements, will give you a rich reward.

W.D. Gann in
How to Make Profits in Commodities

Table of Contents

Table of Contents *(continued)*

List of Illustrations

List of Tables

List of Figures

List of Charts

List of Charts (continued)

Forward

When you finish studying this book you should be able to do the following:

1. Know how to use an ephemeris.
2. Identify key planetary aspects & know how to use them.
3. Know where to go for further information.
4. Identify important lunar turning points.
5. Refer to the appendix for key dates.

I have condensed years of personal research in astrology into a few ideas that will help you in timing the stock market and certain commodities. There is no "Holy Grail"--**at least I haven't found it**--but this will definitely put the probability of success in your favor.

I cannot over emphasize the importance of mental conditioning when trading the markets. Trading is 80% mental and 20% technical. You must learn to "master" yourself using a balanced mixture of courage and discipline.

Preface

The purpose of this book is two-fold. First is to introduce the skeptic to the uncanny harmonic nature of speculative markets. I do not know the mechanism of how or why it works the way that it does. However, I know what to do when I see the phenomenon unfolding. Thomas Edison once said "it was not necessary to understand how electricity worked but just that the lights came on when the switch was turned on." Second is to alert the market student as to the significant astrological events that are about to occur. The Appendix lists some of the major financial astrological events through 1989.

In these few pages you are going to be exposed to the summation of many years of study by three financial astrologers: the author, Larry Pesavento; Ruth Turner; and Jim Twentyman. Between the three of us, we reconstructed thousands of price and time patterns to determine the validity of planetary forecasting.

The man-hours and computer time involved with researching and testing these tenets was enormous. Two years of full-time study was only possible because of the spiritual and financial support of Byron Tucker, Jay Krosp, and Jim Twentyman among others. They were, at first, reluctant to see the results made public; but, after lengthy conversations, it became apparent that most people reading this will be too lazy to thoroughly analyze the material, disbelieve what they see, or some combination of the two.

I do not believe in the "Holy Grail" of trading systems. Placing probabilities in your favor is what the intelligent

speculator will try to achieve. Most speculators would prefer that someone else do the research that is necessary to test a market principle or tenet. This book has polarized longtime friends from different parts of the country to share our ideas and cumulative man-hours to test these tenets.

A word of caution should be inserted at this time. A very small segment of the mathematical mystery of the universe is presented in this book. The goal was to select certain phenomena that occur frequently in order for the "trader-speculator" to profit.

Upon completion of studying this book, I feel the reader will, at least, have "one of his eyes opened" when something significant is happening in the sky.

Acknowledgements

Ruth Miller and Jim Twentyman--Editorial comments

Laurel Beth Hobbs--Illustrations

The Latest Word--Word Processing & Editing

Beverly Smith--Typing and Moral Support

Byron Tucker--Forcing me to start and finish

Llewellyn Publications--Use of their diagrams

Commodity Perspective--Use of their charts.

Neil Michelsen and ACS Publications--Use of their ephemeris

Valliere's Natural Cycles Almanac 1988--Use of their charts

Lambert-Gann Publishing--Use of their graphs

Matrix Software--For developing "Blue Star"

LtCdr. David Williams--for his dedication to Financial Astrology

Pam Orth--Proofreading.

Introduction

One of the recollections of my first stock purchase was its name, Elastic Stop Nut. It was a tip from one of my fraternity brother's father. Tip takers become tip givers and I spread the word faster than Ivan Boesky; the difference was that I knew nothing, inside or outside. As fortune was smiling on me, the stock rose quickly and everyone that bought the stock on my advice was now asking me for another tip. It was the early 1960's and just about any stock you bought went higher. This was a classic example of a famous saying "Don't confuse brains with a bull market." In a mature bull market, investors are sniffing around for undervalued bargains and this was the era of the growth stock. Price earnings ratios of 30 to 1 were common.

This process continued through several stocks until the inevitable "Bear market raid" of 1966. Buying on margin is not much fun when prices suddenly drop. I soon realized that investing was more difficult than I had originally anticipated.

I was in graduate school at Indiana State University majoring in finance and marketing when I got my first taste of successful investing. One of my professors was a classic chartist and filled his office with graphs, oscillators and stock data. There was a huge weekly chart of silver that fascinated me the first time I went into his office. That chart was about to change my life, and you will see why.

Numbers have never scared me. Equations were another story. Seeing this weakness, my professor assigned my MBA thesis in probability theory. I had to mathematically prepare a

formula for beating the Las Vegas dice (crap) game. Knowing that it was impossible in the long run, I concentrated on beating the game in the short run. I developed a modified-Martingale betting system. The odds of the thrower hitting a seven on any throw of the dice were 6 "to" 1. The casinos paid 5 "for" 1, which mathematically is 4 "to" 1. This tacit difference in percentages is one of the reasons why the casinos are so plump and luxurious. I learned this lesson faster than any other. Professional gambling never interested me with the exception of poker, a game of skill that requires both good memory and patience: two notable characteristics of a successful speculator.

It was during one of my economics lectures that I heard of "Gresham's Law -- Bad money drives out good money." If the physical value of what the money was made of (i.e. gold or silver) becomes more valuable than its face value, it would be hoarded instead of being used as a medium of exchange. The year was 1965 and silver was freely traded at around $1.20 to $1.40 per ounce. It was illegal for U.S. citizens to own gold except in the form of rare numismatic gold coins. My economics instructor explained to us that the U.S. Treasury had been making dimes, quarters and half-dollars with 90% silver until 1964--A classic example of Gresham's law. He told us that once the price of silver started to rise, the coins that were 90% silver would be hoarded. He mentioned one other fact! The U.S. Treasury had outstanding paper bills that stated on the face "will pay to the bearer on demand in silver." They decided that anyone who wanted silver could present these bills to the Treasury and receive one ounce of

silver for each one dollar silver certificate. The window of opportunity to make a fast killing was now open! All anyone had to do was collect silver certificates at $1.00 each and wait to redeem them for silver at the mint. Our class studied this phenomenon and came to the conclusion that it was "the goose that laid the golden egg."

Over the next few months we put together a buying pool for silver certificates. We more than doubled our money in less that one year by taking the silver to Handy and Harmon for cash!

After graduate school, I moved to California and started a family and continued to follow the markets. It was 1970 and the commodity markets were staying in narrow trading ranges for months. We did not have the "exotic" financial futures that the traders of today can enjoy. Pork Bellies were about as exotic as one could expect.

I was concentrating in certain stocks and was not doing too well because the stock market had made a major top. Conti-commodity had been placing ads in the *Los Angeles Times* telling about the coming shortage in sugar. Roy Fassel was the manager of the L.A. office for Conti. Roy, is the best "pure" technical trader I have ever met. He is consistently profitable. At that time, Roy was very bullish on Wheat and his technical methods thoroughly impressed me. We began buying wheat and the higher it went the more excited I became. We didn't know until much later that the Russians were buying everything in sight that was <u>growing</u>. I was making money every month and my thirst for knowledge about this "<u>easy</u>" money was quenchless.

Dave Nelson was a veteran of 40 years in commodities and published an advisory service *Market Research Associates* in Pasadena, California. His office was next door to Earl Haddady and Jim Sibbett. Between these three men and Roy Fassel my initiation into the "technicians" society was complete.

Dave was **WILDLY** bullish on Soybeans! It was now late in 1971 and success had spoiled me. My speculative positions were increasing dramatically. To say my confidence level was high would be an understatement.

It should be mentioned that the people who were working or trading through Roy Fassel's office were quite special to the commodity business. Ed Horwitz the "premiere" legal expert in commodity law in the country, as well as a genius at campaign trading, used this office. Working and living with Roy was Rick **"Bid a Million"** Barnes of Barnes & Co. Rick was the broker for Goldman's Egg City. He left for Chicago in 1972 and has since amassed a huge fortune estimated to be hundreds of millions of dollars. Jay Krosp, one of my closest friends and supporters, made several million in Soybeans in 1977--sold out at the top and bought Jimmy Stewart's 11,000 acre ranch in Elko, Nevada. **He still owns the ranch!** Jim Twentyman knows more about the life and theories of W.D. Gann than **anyone-anywhere!** Several other people in that office went on to become members of the exchange or write commodity books. It was really a very special environment.

I started my entrance into technical analysis with the classic *Technical Analysis of Stock Trends* by Edwards and McGee.

Shortly after finishing this work I bought James Hurst's *The Profit Magic of Stock Transaction Timing*. He was giving seminars in San Francisco teaching the CycleTech method of trading commodities. There were quite a few famous people who attended this event: Walt Bressert of Hal Commodities, Phylliss Kahn of Gann World, John Hill of Commodity Research Institute among others. I studied his principles of harmonicity, syncronicity, periodicity, and half-span moving averages. It made a great deal of sense to me so I decided to try it in the market. **I could not lose!** It was now 1972 and all commodity markets were starting up. Inflation was rising, the Arabs raised the price of oil, and Nixon had taken the U.S. off the Gold standard.

My system of trading was to use the 12-18 day cycle lows to take advantage of buying opportunities. **Unbelievable**-- I was making more money in one month than my father would make in a year. I had a new house, several new cars, children's education fund and expensive clothes and jewelry. Humility did not have a place in my vocabulary. Then came the summer of 1974!

The previous year, soybeans had reached $12.90/bushel--sugar at 65 cents--wheat $6.00/bushel. The markets were very volatile and margins had been increased because of the higher prices. This did not concern me because I was long and had plenty of money.

The first price break came in early summer of 1974 but prices rallied back quickly. Then an interesting phenomenon happened. The markets would come down and make a 12 to 18 day cycle low and begin to rally. But the rally would only last a few days and

then fall quickly to the next cycle low. For the first time in three years, I was losing! **Enter the fall of 1974.**

By this time I had lost about half of my fortune. My confidence level was still high. I was long soybeans, soybean meal, and cattle. **The markets began to collapse in October**. Day after day they went lower for no apparent reason. **I did not use stops!** Finally, cattle started going down the limit every day. After four or five days of limit down moves, I was wiped out. All my trading capital was gone!

Lao Tse said "when the student is ready, the teacher will appear!" It was about this time that I met John Hill of Commodity Research Institute in Hendersonville, North Carolina. He began loaning me books to read and I started learning about technical analysis. Since I had no trading capital, I had to gain knowledge and I studied with **reckless abandon**. No trading--just reading and testing. The authors I studied are familiar to most of you: Elliott, Dunnigan, Wycoff, Babson, Williams, Tubbs, Chase, Longstreet, Gartley, Livermore, Gann, Taylor, Issac Newton and hundreds of others. I literally studied everything that I could find. I will always be grateful to John Hill of the Commodity Research Institute for aiding me in my search for knowledge. His library is an endless array of books and systems on trading.

By 1975, I had recovered emotionally, but not financially, from my 1974 loss. Jesse Livermore was right when he said that **"taking a big loss does damage to the soul."** Soybeans were rather quiet at the $5.00 per bushel level and most analysts were looking for lower prices. The reason escapes as to why I was so

bullish on soybeans but it was the right place to put risk capital. In a few short months I had accumulated about $70,000 in profits. I was spending most of my free time studying and trading the markets so I decided to become a stock and commodity broker. The next six years were very profitable, both from commissions and trading profits.

On my fortieth birthday, my wife asked me what I wanted most--my answer was to go to Chicago and trade as a local floor trader! It was 1982, and the foreign currencies and the treasury bills were the crowd favorites. I had leased an IMM seat from Lind-Waldock and proceeded to make money each month by trading on the "floor" for three weeks and in California for one week. It was during this stay in Chicago that I met Byron Tucker.

Byron was a floor trader with years of experience in the markets. He changed my life by coercing me into reading metaphysical books that I did not understand. **I still don't understand them!** However, I became strongly attracted to the writings of Confucius, Lao-Tsu, and Lao-Tse and eventually the Kabala. He is by any measurement a "true" friend and has supported and stood by me during the worst of times. This book would not be written if not for his encouragement.

There is one advantage of not having reserve capital and that is it allows one to do research. My interest in astrology started in 1977 while working as a broker at Drexel Burnham. A recently divorced elderly lady came into my office one afternoon and told me that she had been using astrology to trade silver. She asked if I would like to see her do it in real time trading--of course I said

yes. Her orders were unusual in that they were "time" orders. "Sell silver at 7:02 am on Monday--Cover short at 10:30 am Tuesday." Her accuracy rate was unbelievable! I continued to work with her for about two months via telephone.

One day when I called the lady for her order, I found the phone disconnected. She had moved and left no forwarding address. My efforts to locate her were unsuccessful. She had been living in Santa Monica and went into the Dean Witter office every morning to see how her silver was doing. My guess is that another broker or investor wanted her advice exclusively.

My next step was to reconstruct her trades "astrologically." That was not an easy task! I finally figured out that she **did not** trade when the moon was "void of course"--moving from one sign of the zodiac to another. This worked well until the vertical rise to $54.00 per ounce. Since that time it has yielded only fair results.

The spring of 1983 was the most significant turning point in my life. Unfortunately it was a turn-**down**. I was "bearish" on stocks in late April 1983. The Standard and Poor's 500 began trading at the Chicago Mercantile exchange in April 1982. It was an immediate success--**high volatility, low margin, good liquidity**!

My position consisted of approximately twenty short S & P June futures contracts and short eight 160 June calls. My trading plan was very specific and I had instituted warning signals if my assumptions were incorrect. As fortune would have it, the market started down and everything looked fine. Within a few days the market had recovered and my position was showing a small loss.

I had written notes to myself on what to expect and where my stops should be placed. Eight years had passed since I made a "fatal" market error. The next one turned out to be a dandy! One day that spring, the S&P 500 opened with a large gap and was quickly 500 points higher in a short time. I had this factor in my trading plan--it was a sign to cover shorts and go long. By not acting for several days, the lack of discipline cost me $100,000 plus the damage to my self-confidence.

Another cost involved in the lack of discipline was an "opportunity" cost. At the same time of my bearish position in stocks, I was very bullish on soybeans. My capital was depleted but more importantly I was emotionally drained. Soybeans soared $3.00 per bushel without me. I stopped trading for over a year and returned to California as a broker.

Meanwhile, I renewed contact with Ruth Miller, who had been an old friend of my family for over twenty years. She is a retired college professor now raising soybeans in Southern Illinois. One day several years ago she sent me a note in early summer: "October Soybean Oil will be trading at 13.80 on September 15th." I taped the note to my quote machine and waited until September. As September rolled around, I saw that Soybean Oil was getting very close to the 13.80 level. When I called Ruth, she was quite excited and said that she had found some very interesting astrological trading signals. I planned a trip to the Midwest to learn what she had discovered.

Spending a week with her opened my eyes about certain planetary configurations that put the probabilities of a successful

trade heavily weighted in <u>your</u> favor. Before starting to teach me what she had found she asked that I not divulge her "Corn" trading system. After she showed me the trade **I understood why!** This event pays the rent every month--and it has worked since corn started trading in the 1800's. Once she pointed out certain things to me I began to see the harmonic relationship of cycles and planets. Having the "Blue Star" program from Matrix Software enabled me to study many different ideas. You will find several of my worksheet charts in the book. They were included to illustrate the time involved in working with financial astrology.

It is my hope that after reading this book your interest in financial astrology will be awakened. You will have to read this book more than once to understand the unusual terminology in astrology and the concepts. If you will only follow the Venus-Uranus aspects presented here, it will return the cost of this book many times over.

Keep in mind that the most important **"tool"** in a technician's briefcase is--an eraser.

SECTION ONE:

OUR SOLAR SYSTEM

Section One:

Our Solar System

Astrology and Our Solar System

"Astrology is the Science of Life's Reactions to Planetary Vibrations."

Astrology, as the interpreter of Nature, shows that the world is conducted according to a well defined plan, that everything is arranged with wonderful order, clearly timed with marvelous precision and effected with unerring accuracy. Nothing happens by chance; there are no accidents in the divine plan; and in reality there is no discord, for nature recognized no distinctions and works only for progress through a refining process which sometimes destroys only to reconstruct with improvement. As students advance in the study of astrology they realize each in his place, according to an orderly or cosmic plan; with opportunities to produce certain results, but it remains for us to determine the quality of these results by refining our reactions to planetary influence.

Llewelyn George

In this book you are going to be exposed to some of the astronomical (aspects) of the solar system and the astrological (interpretation) of the houses and signs. There are several diagrams in the next few pages that will help you picture where we are and how things fit "harmonically" together. It will be necessary to be able to distinguish the planets, know the difference between a"house" and a "sign," and recognize when important aspects are forming. Most of this material was researched by "masters" much more adept than this author, but I have tried to put it together so that it may be used in trading. I owe a great deal of gratitude for the use of their graphs and charts. If credit was not acknowledged, it was done so without intent or malice.

I base my astro-cycle system on using an ephemeris. There are two ways of looking at our solar system, the geocentric method with the Earth as the center of the universe and the heliocentric method with the Sun at the center. This book will concentrate on the geocentric approach because I have found it to be most reliable from a trading standpoint. The earlier researchers such as Langham, Jensen, Butaney and others used the geocentric method. One could argue for years which is correct. Personally, I follow both but only make decisions based on the geocentric aspects (the only exception is the wheat market). Geocentric makes logical sense because the moon is such an accurate timer in many of the markets.

The reader will find diagrams that will be helpful to differentiate the planets, houses, signs, and certain solar and lunar phenomena.

PLANETARY ASPECTS

There are nine planets that revolve around the Sun: Mercury, Venus, Earth, Mars, Jupiter, Saturn, Uranus, Neptune and Pluto in that order. Most of the planetary aspects presented in this book will be geocentric (with Earth in the center). Aspects are the Geometric angles that exist between each planet. The next paragraph will explain why geocentric aspects are used as opposed to heliocentric aspects (Sun-centered).

Johann Kepler, the founder of modern astronomy, had this to say about the aspects: "An angle formed on the earth by the beams (rays) of two planets...A most unfailing experience of the excitement of the subliminal natures by the conjunction and aspects of the planets, has instructed and compelled my unwilling belief." Kepler went on to discuss why he used geocentric versus heliocentric aspects. He considered the earth as "a" center of influence and not exclusively "the" center of influence. As a trader, the geocentric aspects and lunar phenomena presented here will improve your timing.

A natal chart is directly concerned with the birth of a being (i.e. market). It is the planetary chart that exists at the exact moment, date, and place of birth. Natal astrology is one of the more difficult areas of financial astrology because it is subject to a wide range of interpretation. It was omitted from the book because of the complexity in presenting the material without confusing the reader. Geocentric aspects and lunar phenomena can stand alone as useful tools in market timing. The material was written to "Keep It Simple" as much as possible.

In the next few pages you will find several illustrations, diagrams and tables that will help the reader to grasp the concepts with relative ease. The section on houses and signs should be viewed as an overview. Once your interest in astrology intensifies you will make a transition into the interpretation of the zodiac.

OUR SOLAR SYSTEM

Relative Size of the Planets and Their Orbits

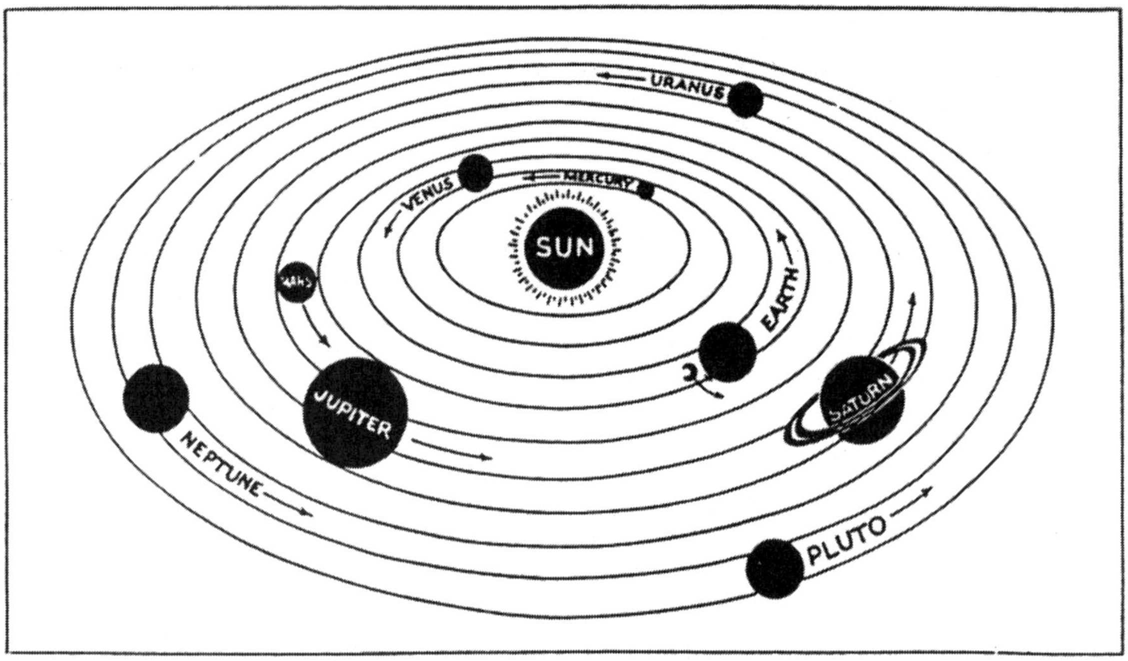

Planetary vibrations operate according to the grade of intelligence, whether it be through the seed, the animal or the human. The human has the advantage of being able to accept, modify, amplify, diminish or transform the effect of planetary vibrations through **conscious** exercise of his facilities. Man is free within the confines of Cosmic Law; the degree of freedom he manifests being largely dependent upon what **use** he makes of his intelligence. Hence the study of planetary aspects is important.

Llewellyn George in
A to Z Horoscope and Delineator
Llewellyn Publications

PLANETARY ASPECTS USED IN TRANSITS

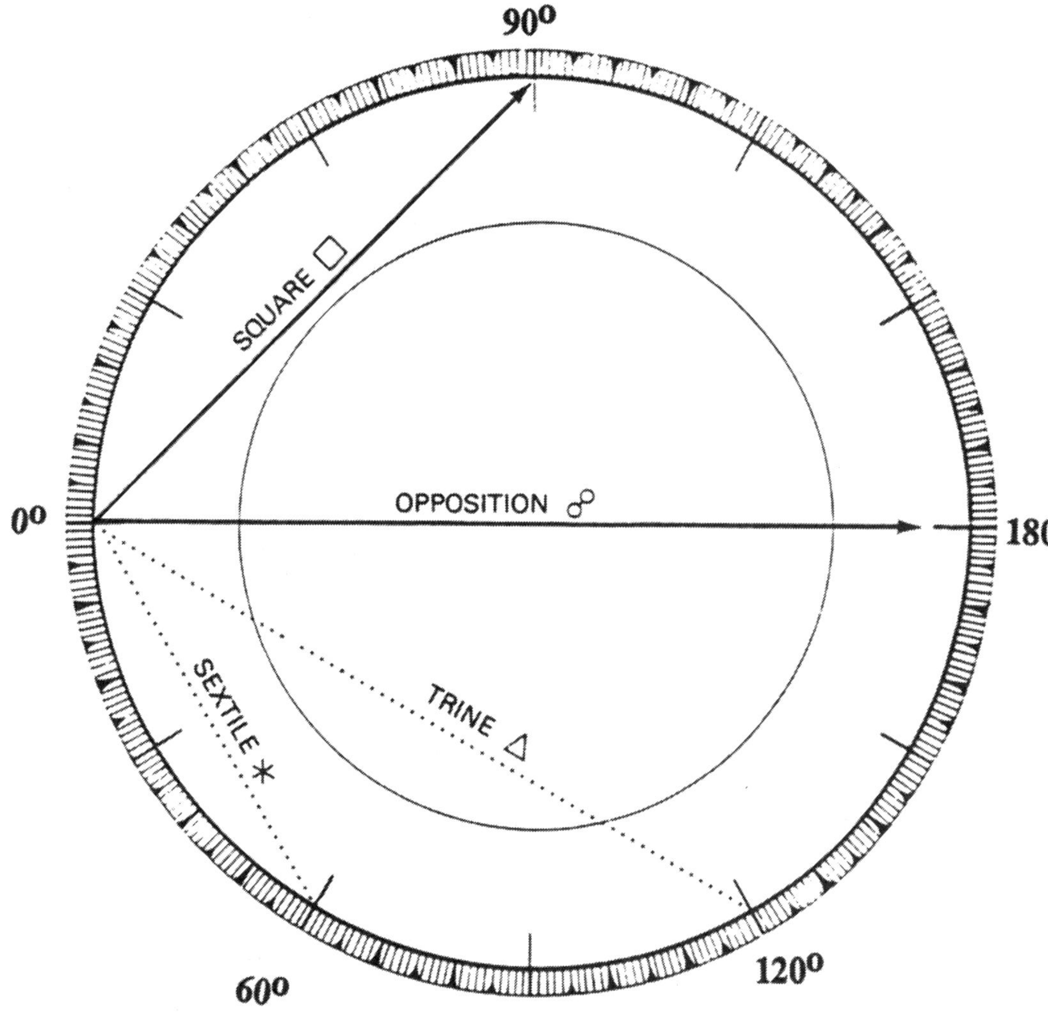

Conjunction 0°
Sextile 60°
Square 90°
Trine 120°
Opposition 180°

INTERPLANETARY SYNODICAL PERIODS

Mean Lengths in Tropical Years.

Mercury-Pluto	0.24	Sun-Jupiter*	1.09
Mercury-Neptune	0.24	Sun Venus	1.59
Mercury-Uranus	0.24	Mars-Pluto	1.89
Mercury-Saturn	0.24	Mars-Neptune	1.90
Mercury-Jupiter	0.24	Mars-Uranus	1.92
Mercury-Mars	0.27	Mars-Saturn	2.00
Sun-Mercury*	0.31	Sun-Mars*	2.13
Mercury-Venus	0.39	Mars-Jupiter	2.23
Venus-Pluto	0.61	Jupiter-Pluto	12.45
Venus-Neptune	0.61	Jupiter-Neptune	12.78
Venus-Uranus	0.61	Jupiter-Uranus	13.81
Venus-Saturn	0.62	Jupiter-Saturn	19.85
Venus-Jupiter	0.64	Saturn-Pluto	33.43
Venus Mars	0.91	Saturn-Neptune	35.86
Sun-Pluto	1.00	Saturn-Uranus	45.36
Sun-Neptune*	1.00	Uranus-Pluto	127.13
Sun-Uranus*	1.01	Uranus-Neptune	171.40
Sun-Saturn*	1.03	Neptune-Pluto	492.32

**Solar combinations in reality are those participated in by the earth*

A synodic period is the length of time two planets meet at conjunction (0°) and travel through sextile (60°), square (90°), trine (120°), opposition (180°) and back to conjunction again. The Venus-Uranus synodic period is .61 years or 225 days.

MAJOR ASPECTS

(Venus: ♀ Uranus: ♅)

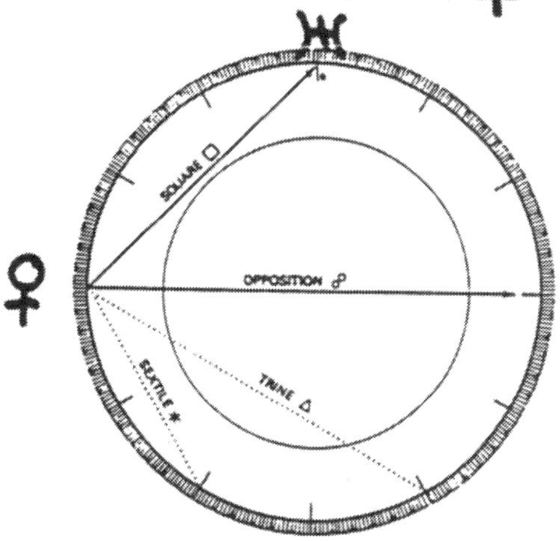

Square 90°

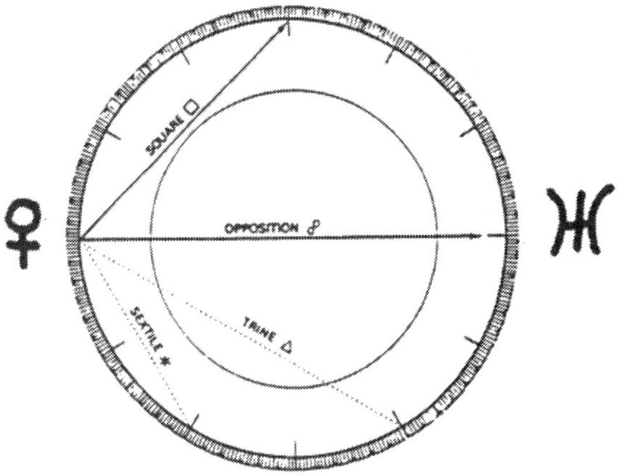

Opposition 180°

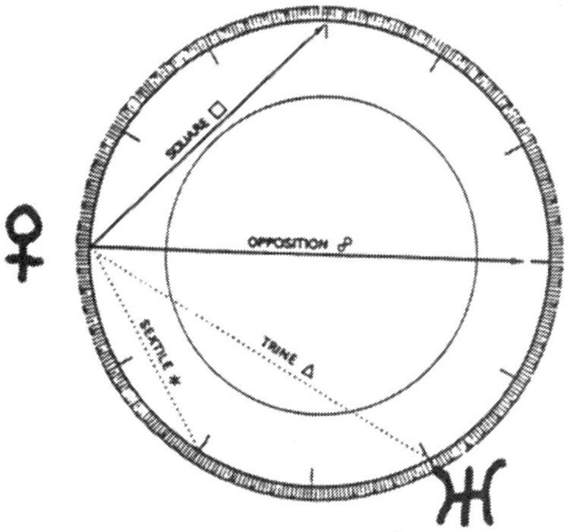

Trine 120°

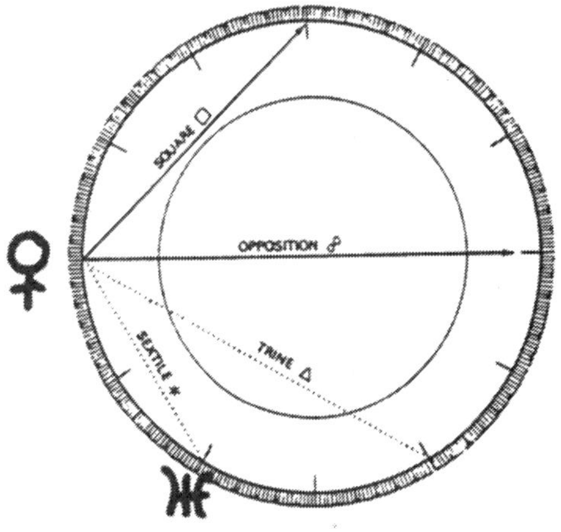

Sextile 60°

Conjunction 0°

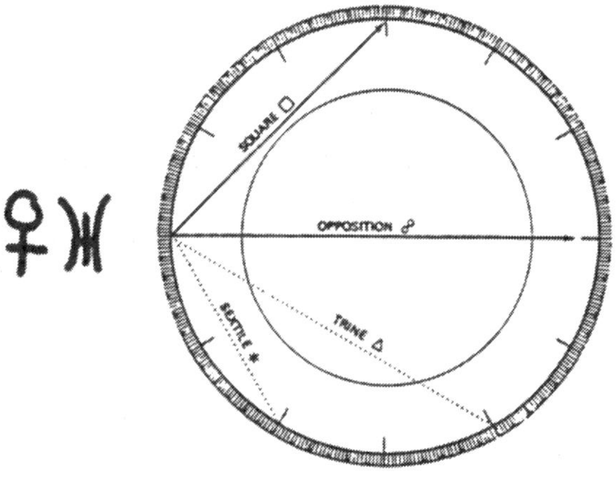

The Zodiac

There is an imaginary circle of space about 15 degrees wide in the heavens above the earth. It is the sun's apparent path that is called the ecliptic. The zodiacal circle is 360 degrees and is divided into 12 equal 30 degree segments. Each segment is called a sign. Although the zodiac is referred to as a circle it is actually elliptical. Every sign has its own influence.

The earth moves around the sun once each year to allow the sun to pass through each of the 12 signs in one year. A good source of how the signs affect prices is covered in *Astro Cycles in Speculative Markets* by Jensen, and *A to Z Horoscope Maker and Delineator* by Llewellyn.

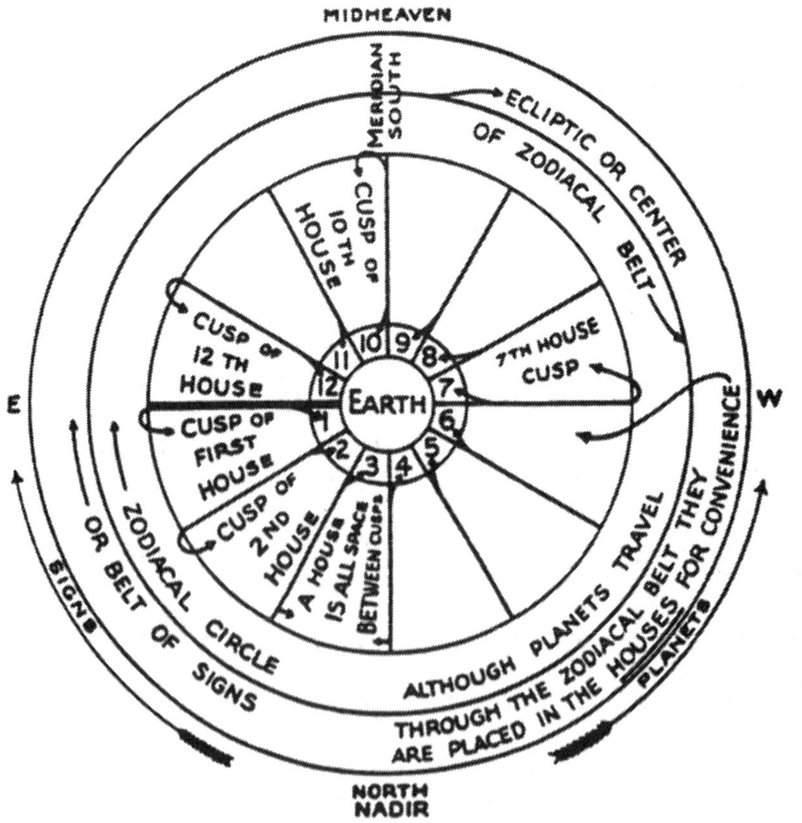

Changing Signs of the Zodiac

Each planet travels through each sign of this imaginary circle called the zodiac. The following is the approximate length of time that each planet stays in each of the twelve signs of the zodiac. These times vary depending on the retrograde motion of the individual planet.

Planet	Avg. time in Zodiac Sign
Moon	2 1/4 Days
Mercury	18 Days
Venus	23 Days
Sun	30 Days
Mars	46 Days
Jupiter	365 Days
Saturn	2 1/2 Years
Uranus	74 Years
Neptune	144 Years
Pluto	204 Years

The financial astrologer should be aware when planets change from one sign to another. Special attention must be given when several planets are all in the same house. An excellent example of this was August 1987! Five planets were in the sign of Leo as the stock market was making its top. The October low of 1974 in the stock market was accompanied by four planets in the sign of Virgo!

STANDARD ASTROLOGICAL SYMBOLS

THE ZODIACAL SIGNS

Symbol	Sign	Symbol	Sign
♈	Aries	♎	Libra
♉	Taurus	♏	Scorpio
♊	Gemini	♐	Sagittarius
♋	Cancer	♑	Capricorn
♌	Leo	♒	Aquarius
♍	Virgo	♓	Pisces

THE RELATION OF SIGNS AND HOUSES

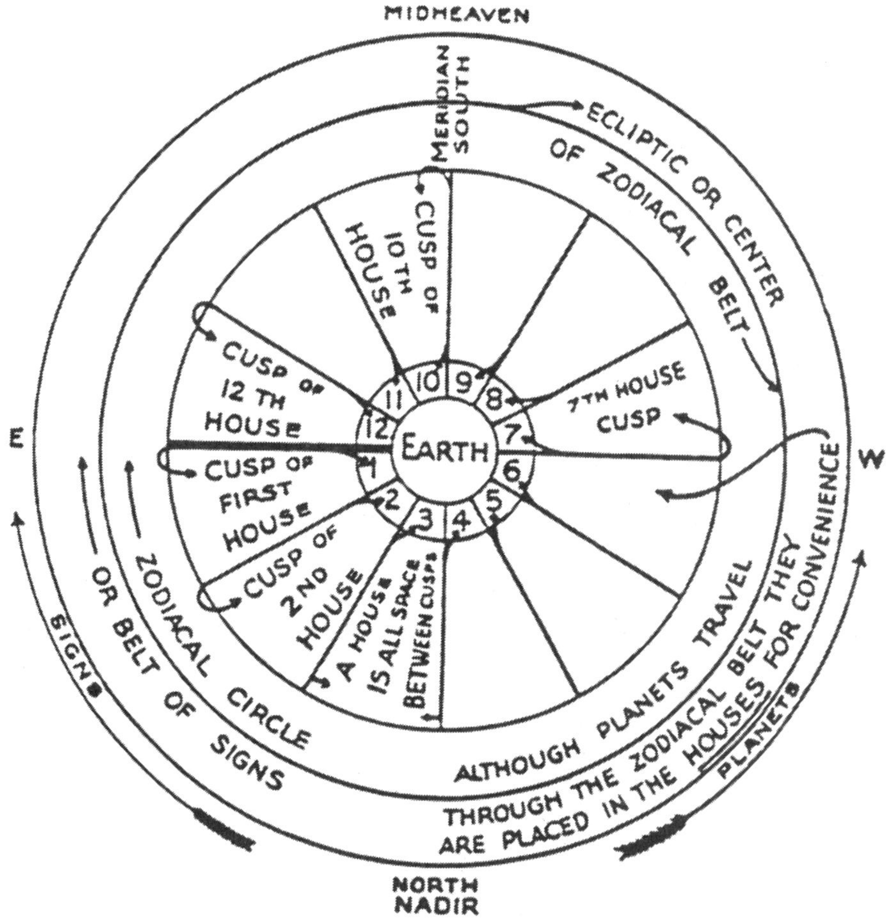

EXPLAINING DISTINCTION BETWEEN A "HOUSE " AND A "SIGN"

Signs are the twelve divisions of the Zodiac. Houses are twelve segments of space between the Earth and the Zodiac. (Consider the earth as in the center for the sake of convenience.)

S&P 500 INDEX

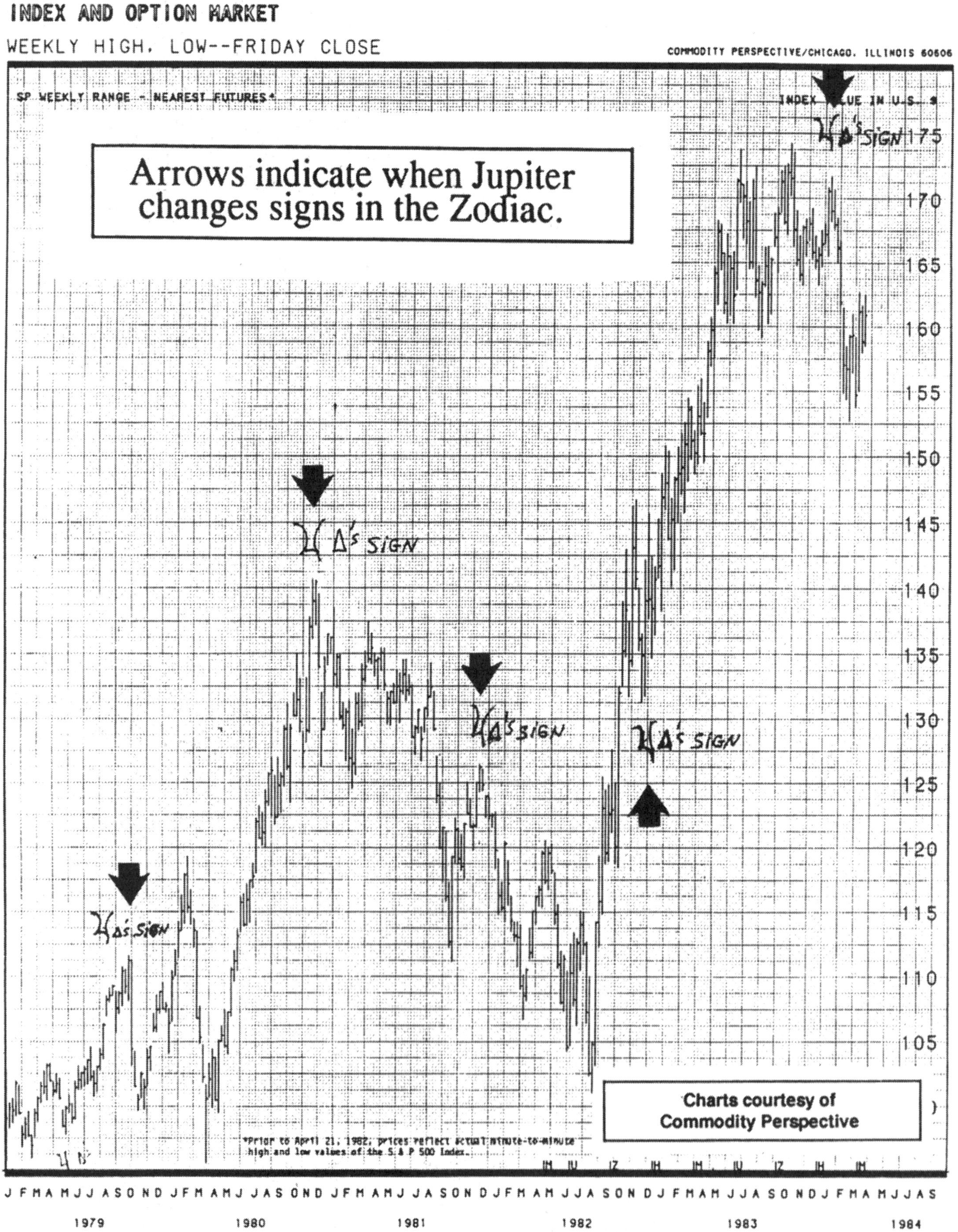
INDEX AND OPTION MARKET
WEEKLY HIGH, LOW--FRIDAY CLOSE
COMMODITY PERSPECTIVE/CHICAGO, ILLINOIS 60606
SP WEEKLY RANGE - NEAREST FUTURES*
INDEX VALUE IN U.S. $
Arrows indicate when Jupiter changes signs in the Zodiac.
♃Δ's SIGN
175
170
165
160
155
150
145
140
135
130
125
120
115
110
105
Charts courtesy of Commodity Perspective
*Prior to April 21, 1982, prices reflect actual minute-to-minute high and low values of the S & P 500 Index.
J F M A M J J A S O N D J F M A M J J A S O N D J F M A M J J A S O N D J F M A M J J A S O N D J F M A M J J A S O N D J F M A M J J A S
1979
1980
1981
1982
1983
1984

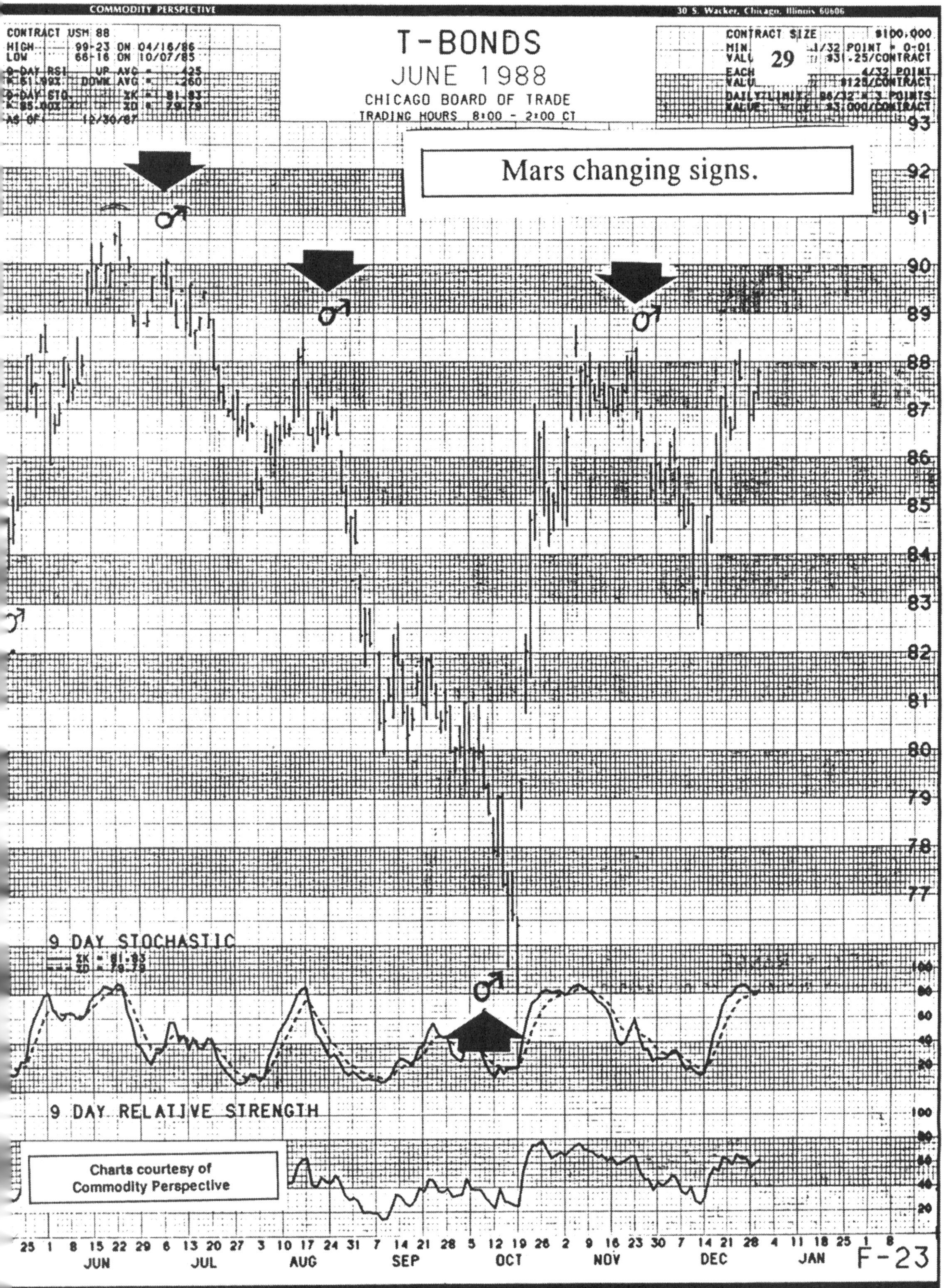
COMMODITY PERSPECTIVE
30 S. Wacker, Chicago, Illinois 60606
T-BONDS
JUNE 1988
CHICAGO BOARD OF TRADE
TRADING HOURS 8:00 - 2:00 CT
CONTRACT USM 88
HIGH 99-23 ON 04/16/86
LOW 66-16 ON 10/07/85
CONTRACT SIZE $100,000
Mars changing signs.
9 DAY STOCHASTIC
9 DAY RELATIVE STRENGTH
Charts courtesy of
Commodity Perspective
25 1 8 15 22 29 6 13 20 27 3 10 17 24 31 7 14 21 28 5 12 19 26 2 9 16 23 30 7 14 21 28 4 11 18 25 1 8
JUN JUL AUG SEP OCT NOV DEC JAN

Charts courtesy of
Commodity Perspective

T-BONDS

SEPTEMBER 1983

COMMODITY PERSPECTIVE/CHICAGO, ILLINOIS 60606

CHICAGO BOARD OF TRADE

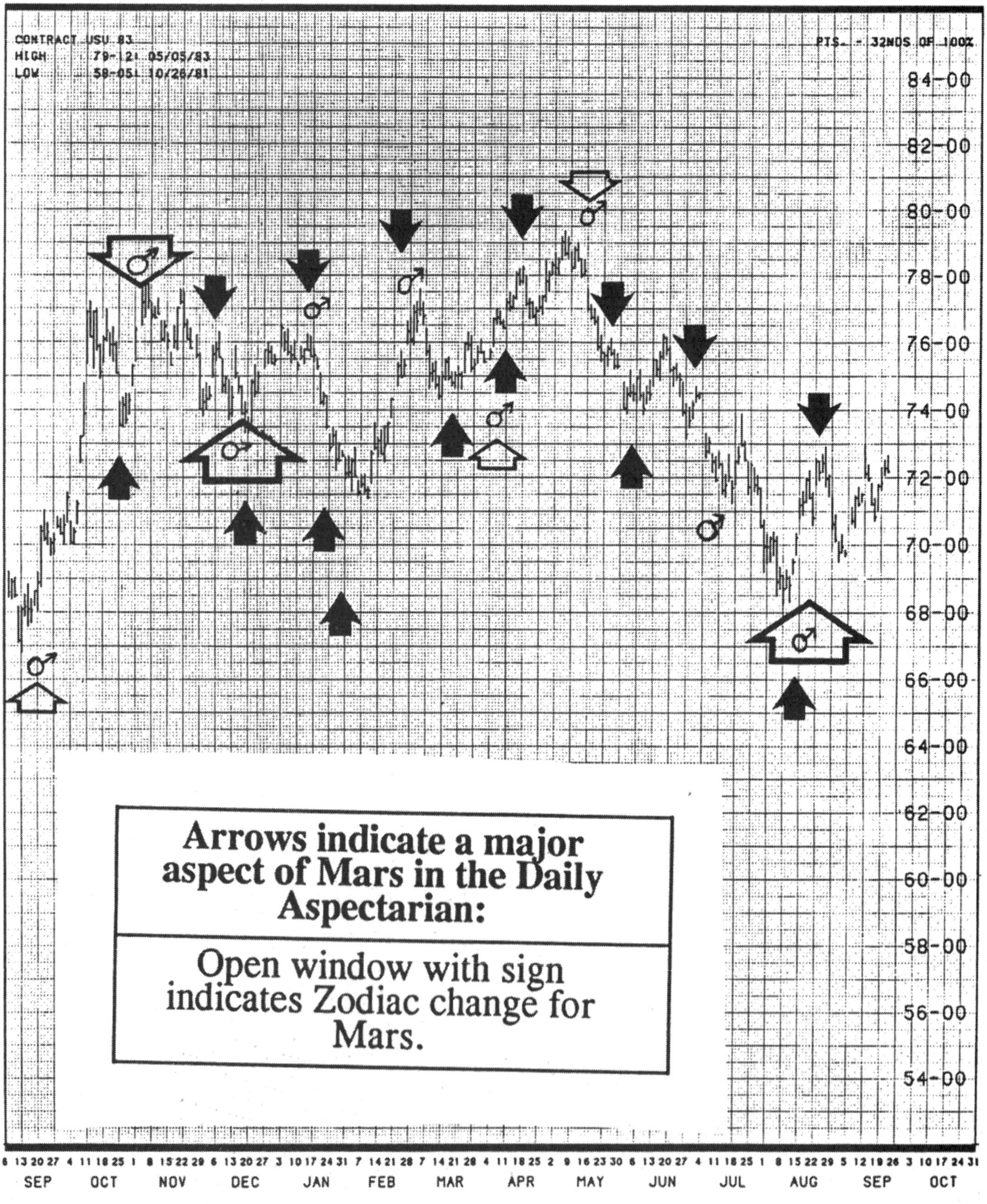

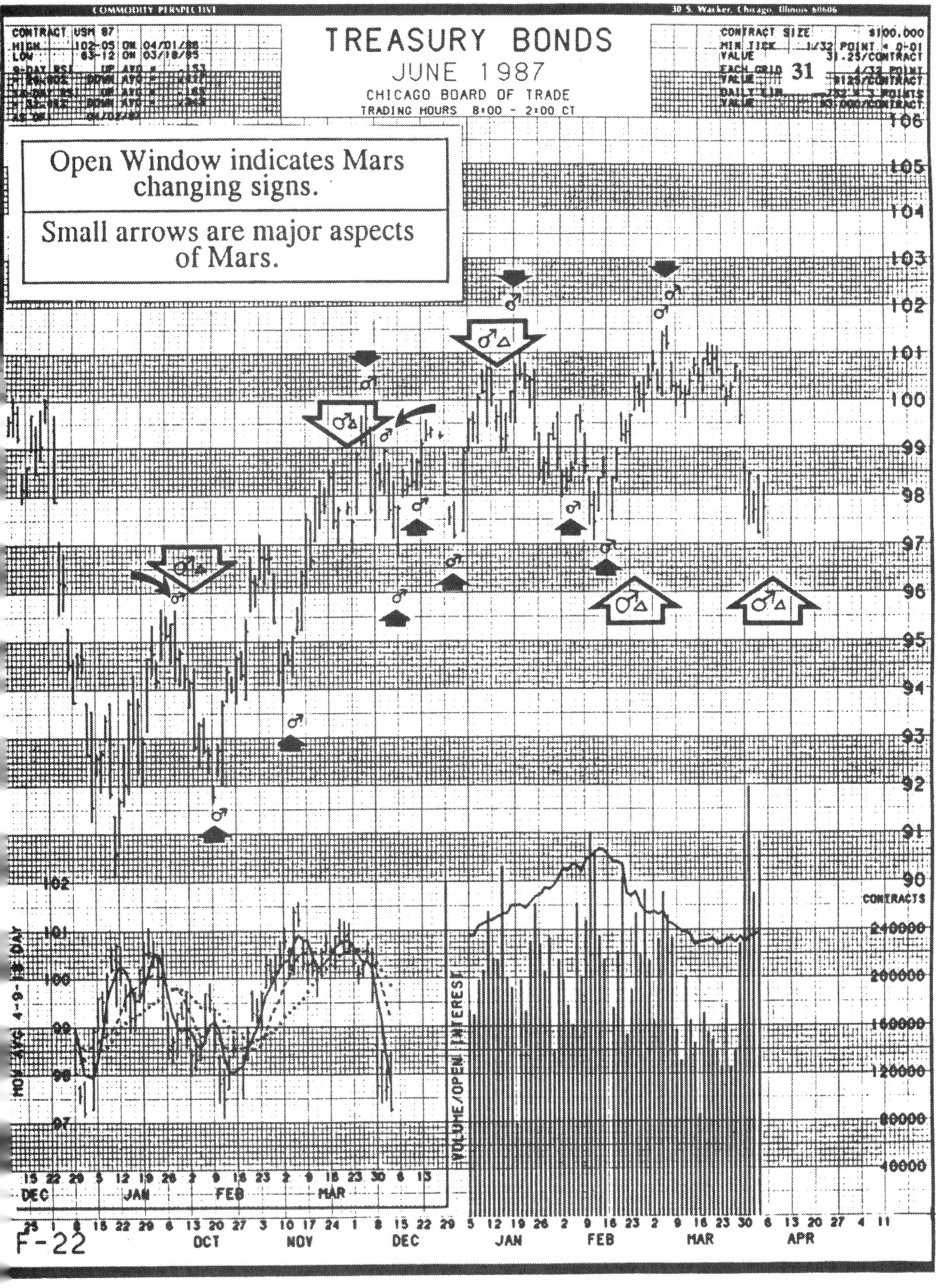
COMMODITY PERSPECTIVE
30 S. Wacker, Chicago, Illinois 60606
TREASURY BONDS
JUNE 1987
CHICAGO BOARD OF TRADE
TRADING HOURS 8:00 - 2:00 CT
CONTRACT USM 87
CONTRACT SIZE $100,000
31
Open Window indicates Mars changing signs.
Small arrows are major aspects of Mars.
106
105
104
103
102
101
100
99
98
97
96
95
94
93
92
91
90
CONTRACTS
240000
200000
160000
120000
80000
40000
MOV AVG 4-9-18 DAY
VOLUME/OPEN INTEREST
DEC
JAN
FEB
MAR
OCT
NOV
DEC
JAN
FEB
MAR
APR

F-22

T-BONDS

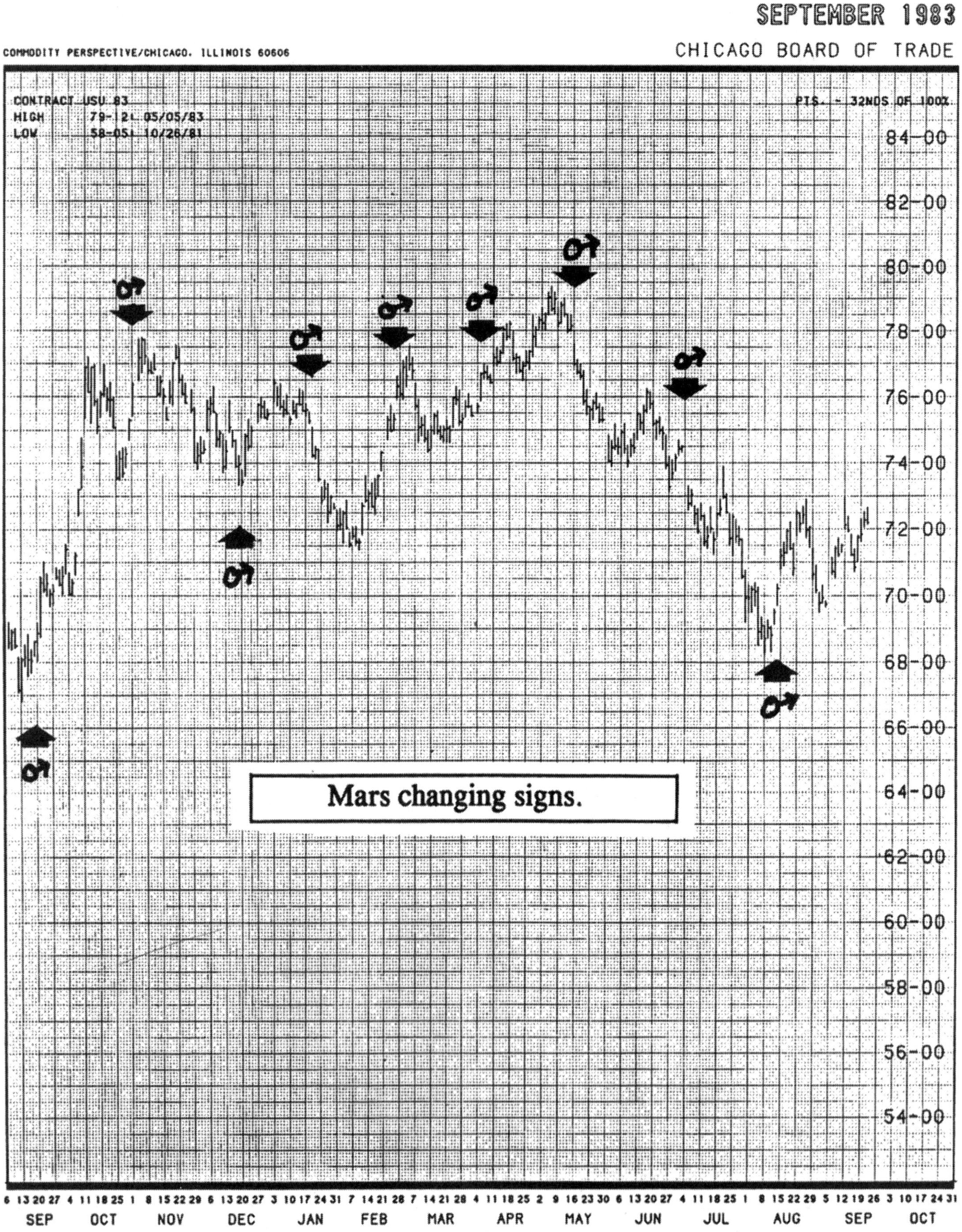

Mars changing signs.

CHANGING STRENGTH BY HOUSE

The Strength of the Houses (in order of the strongest to the weakest) is: 1st, 10th, 7th, 4th, 11th, 8th, 9th, 12th, 2nd, 3rd, 5th, and 6th.

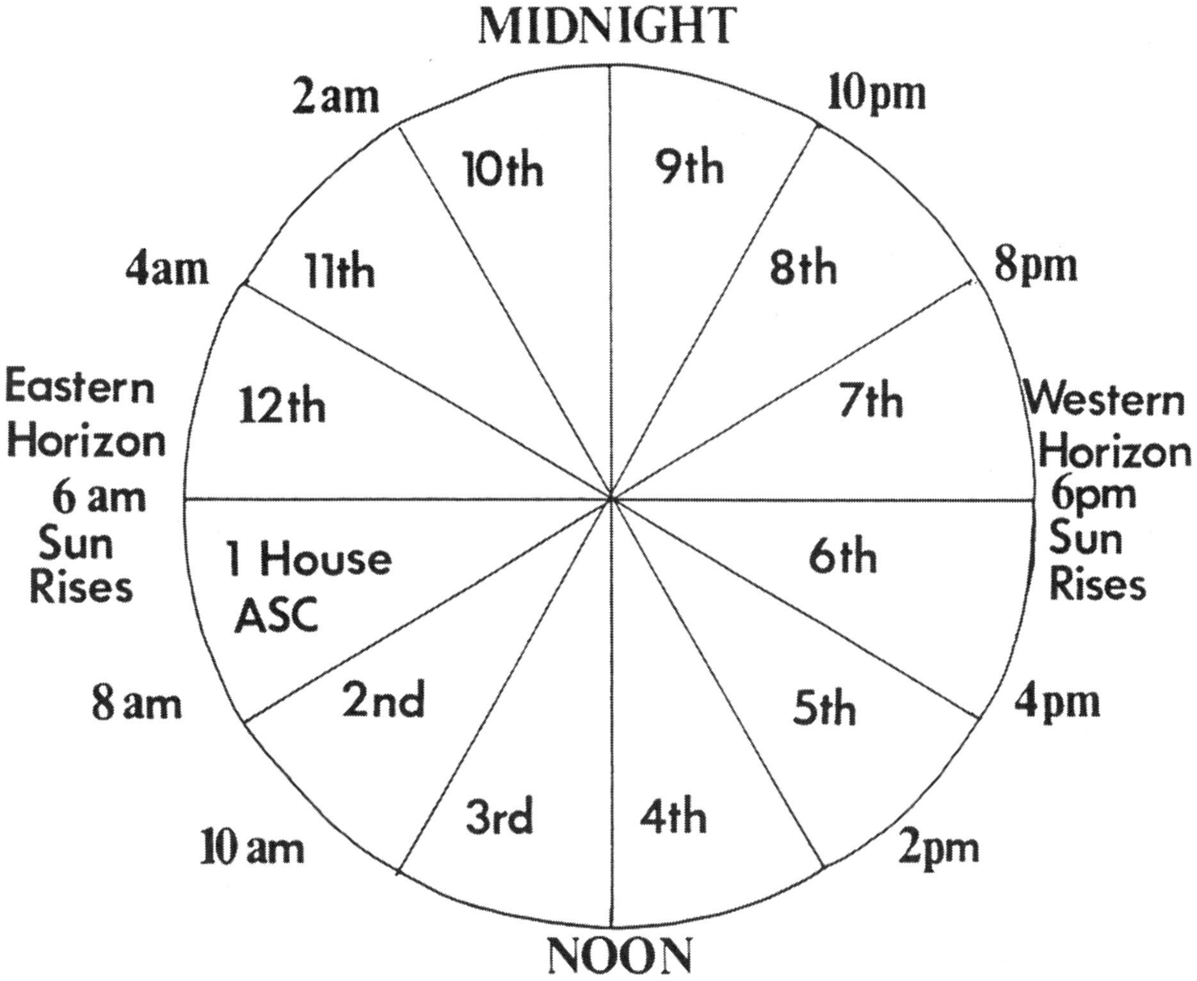

THE KEY TO THE ENTIRE PLANETARY HOUSE PATTERN

	♂	♀	☿	☽	☉	☿	♀	♂	♃	♄	♅	♆
♈	1	12	11	10	9	8	7	6	5	4	3	2
♉	2	1	12	11	10	9	8	7	6	5	4	3
♊	3	2	1	12	11	10	9	8	7	6	5	4
♋	4	3	2	1	12	11	10	9	8	7	6	5
♌	5	4	3	2	1	12	11	10	9	8	7	6
♍	6	5	4	3	2	1	12	11	10	9	8	7
♎	7	6	5	4	3	2	1	12	11	10	9	8
♏	8	7	6	5	4	3	2	1	12	11	10	9
♐	9	8	7	6	5	4	3	2	1	12	11	10
♑	10	9	8	7	6	5	4	3	2	1	12	11
♒	11	10	9	8	7	6	5	4	3	2	1	12
♓	12	11	10	9	8	7	6	5	4	3	2	1

THE ZODIACAL SIGNS

Symbol	Sign	Symbol	Sign
♈	Aries	♎	Libra
♉	Taurus	♏	Scorpio
♊	Gemini	♐	Sagittarius
♋	Cancer	♑	Capricorn
♌	Leo	♒	Aquarius
♍	Virgo	♓	Pisces

This table lists the planet, house and the zodiac sign that rules each planet as interpreted by Luther Jensen in *Astro Cycles and Speculative Markets* published by Lambert-Gann Publishing of Pomeroy, Washington. **It has withstood the test of time.**

Eclipses

Solar and lunar eclipses usually receive extensive press coverage, probably because these events can be seen with the naked eye in different parts of the world. As a trader, eclipses present "special" opportunitites. The neophyte financial astrologer will get very excited about the appearance of an eclipse because it is such an important astrological event. One must study market action at the time of an eclipse in order to determine strategy. It was necessary to go back 50 years of the stock market to ascertain what effect the solar or lunar eclipse would have on mass psychology (i.e. stock prices).

The following observations will be helpful in implementing trading strategies for the stock market and grains:

1. Eclipses are excellent short term change in trend indicators. The effect will take hold within 2 days of the actual event.

2. Solar eclipses usually have more effect than lunar eclipses.

3. If the stock market does not appear to be affected by the eclipse it is a <u>very</u> strong indication that the trend of the market before the eclipse will continue for some time.

SOLAR ECLIPSES & PLANETARY POSITION

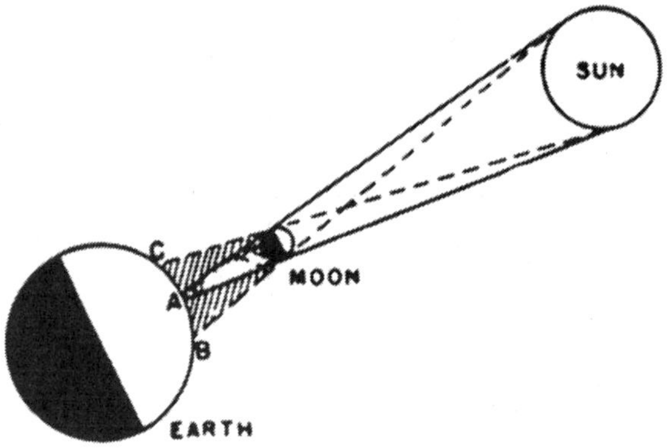

A total eclipse at *A*. A partial within *B*-*C*.

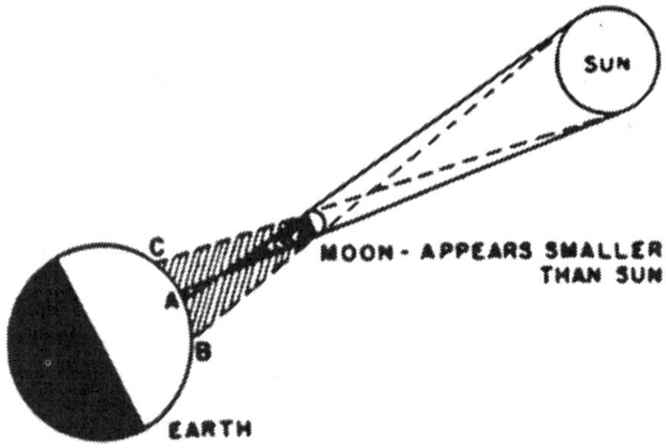

Annular eclipse at *A*. A partial within *B*-*C*.

This illustrates a planet's position during an eclipse of the Sun. Remember that the diameter of the Sun is 400 times that of the Moon. It is easier to see how the Sun's rays are affected by an eclipse using this model.

SOYBEANS

37 NOVEMBER 1976

Chicago Board of Trade

COMMODITY PERSPECTIVE/CHICAGO, ILLINOIS 60604

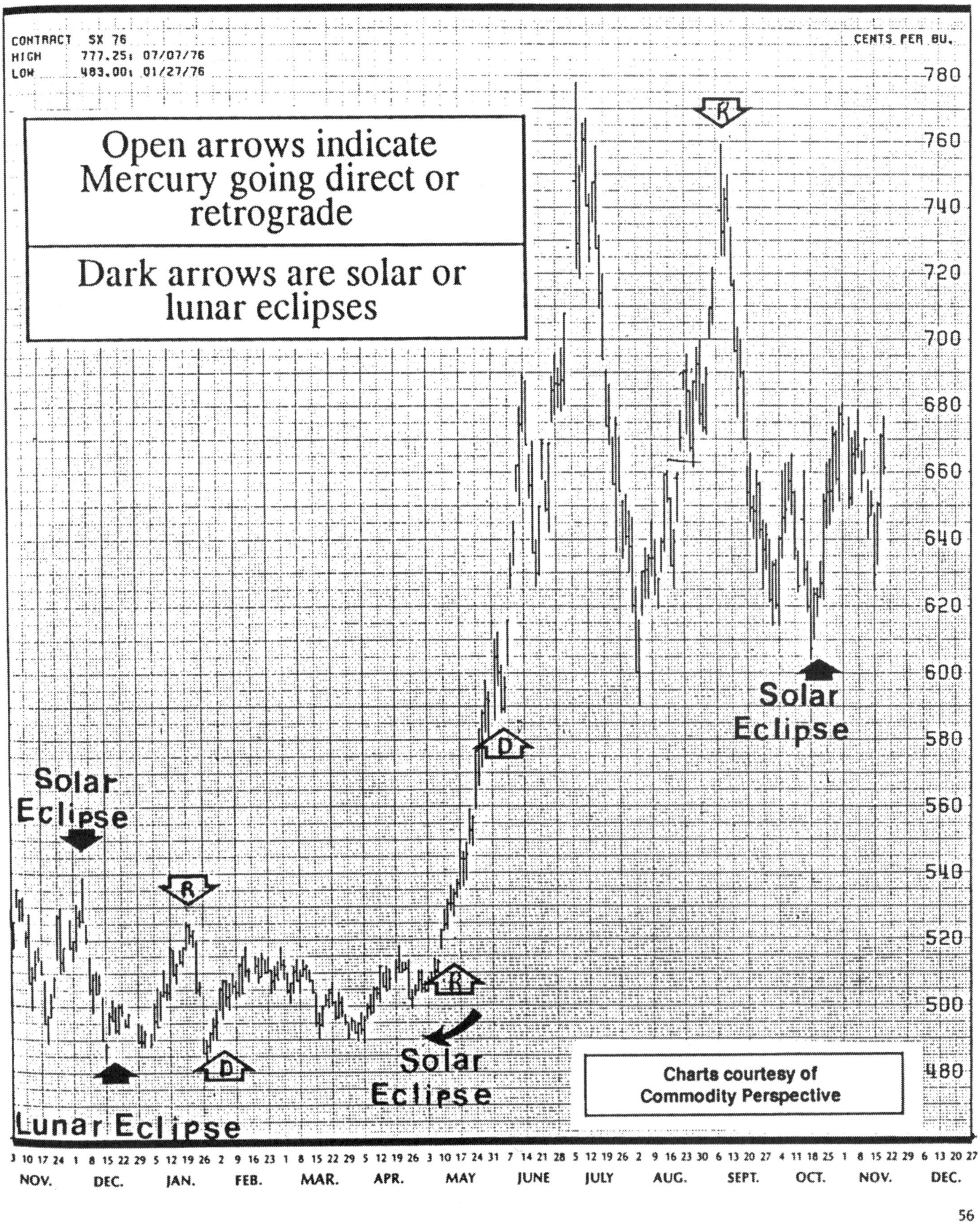

THE EQUINOXES AND SOLSTICES

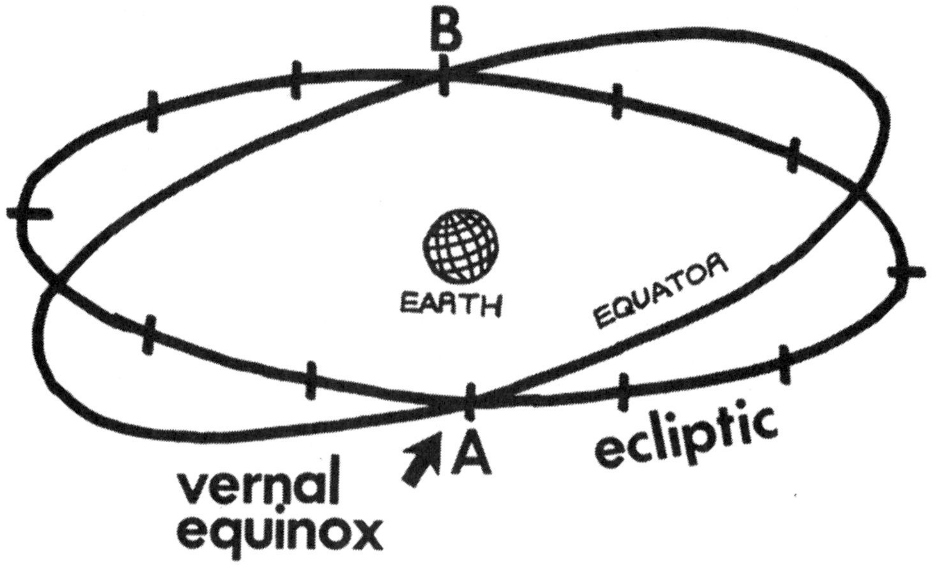

The plane of the Zodiac intersects the celestial equator at an angle of approximately 23°28'. The two points of intersection (A+B) are called the equinoxes.

Retrograde Motion

Retrograde motion of a planet occurs when a planet moves faster than another planet in its orbit. It appears that the planet is moving backwards but, in fact, it is not. Major price changes may occur in commodity and stock prices very near these time periods. Mercury retrograde conditions affect the grains and livestock, and Jupiter and Uranus in retrograde, affect stock prices. Pluto retrograde has an effect on gold prices.

- The Sun and Moon are never retrograde or stationary.
- Mercury is retrograde 24 days and is stationary about one day before and after.
- Venus is retrograde 42 days and is stationary two or three days before and after.
- Mars is retrograde for 80 days and is stationary two or three days before or after.
- Jupiter is retrograde 120 days and is stationary about five days before and after.
- Mercury, Venus, Mars, and Jupiter in retrograde motion have an effect on price action. Why this occurs is unknown but the astute trader should be aware of those times.

GOLD

International Monetary Market

Weekly High, Low—Friday Close

COMMODITY PERSPECTIVE/CHICAGO, ILLINOIS 60604

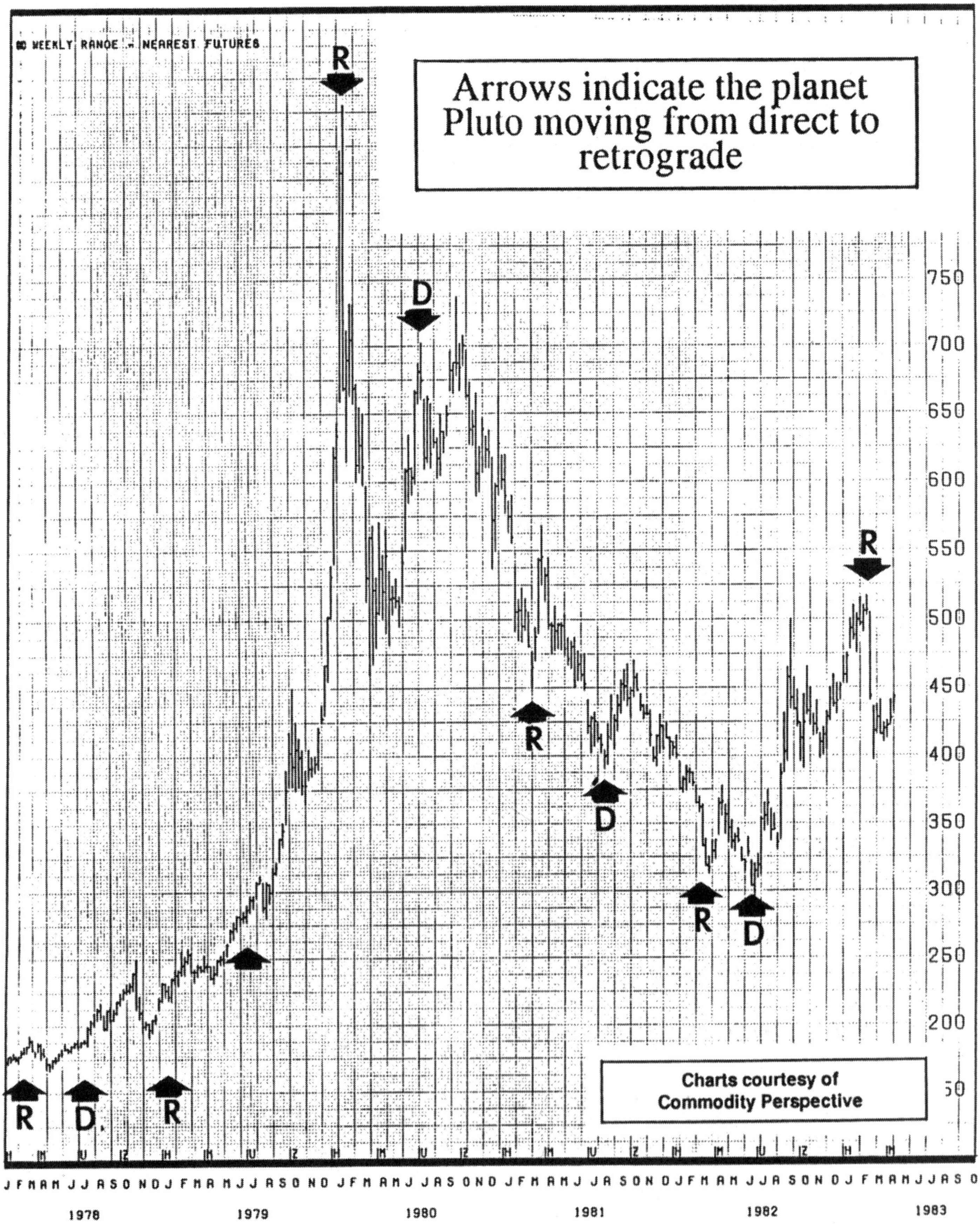

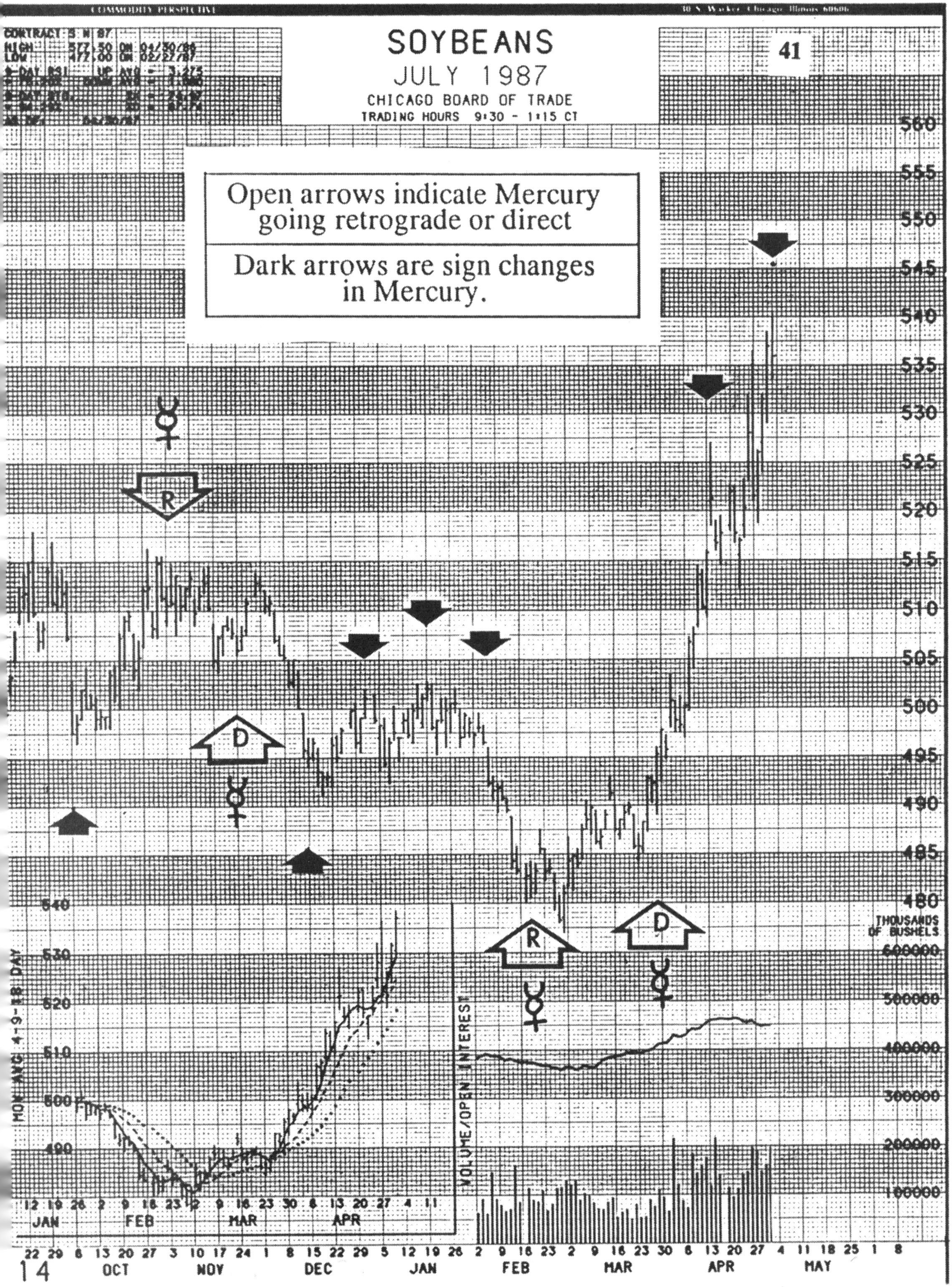
SOYBEANS
JULY 1987
CHICAGO BOARD OF TRADE
TRADING HOURS 9:30 - 1:15 CT
41
Open arrows indicate Mercury going retrograde or direct
Dark arrows are sign changes in Mercury.
R
D
R
D
560
555
550
545
540
535
530
525
520
515
510
505
500
495
490
485
480
THOUSANDS OF BUSHELS
600000
500000
400000
300000
200000
100000
MOV AVG 4-9-18 DAY
VOLUME/OPEN INTEREST
JAN
FEB
MAR
APR
OCT
NOV
DEC
JAN
FEB
MAR
APR
MAY

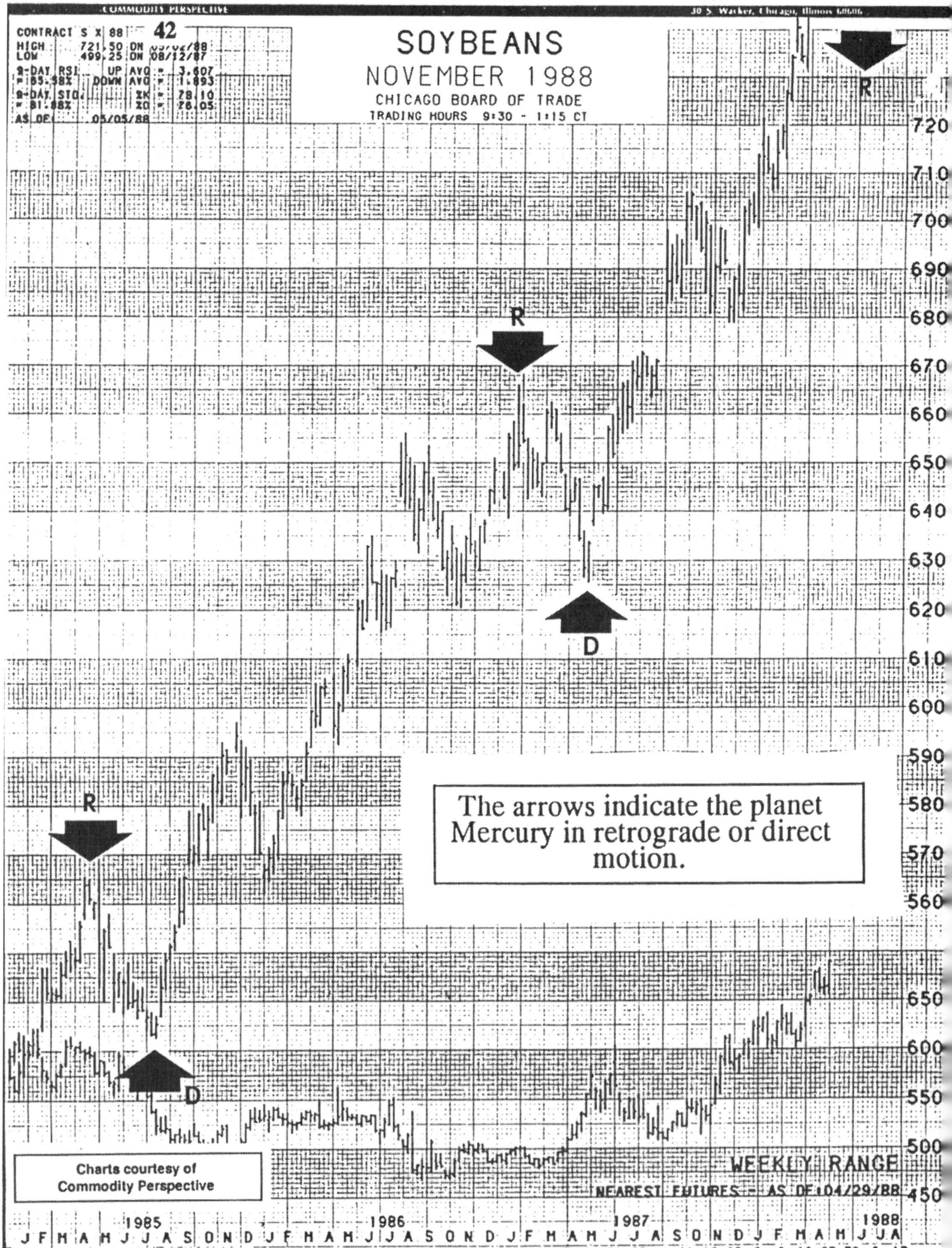

The arrows indicate the planet Mercury in retrograde or direct motion.

Charts courtesy of Commodity Perspective

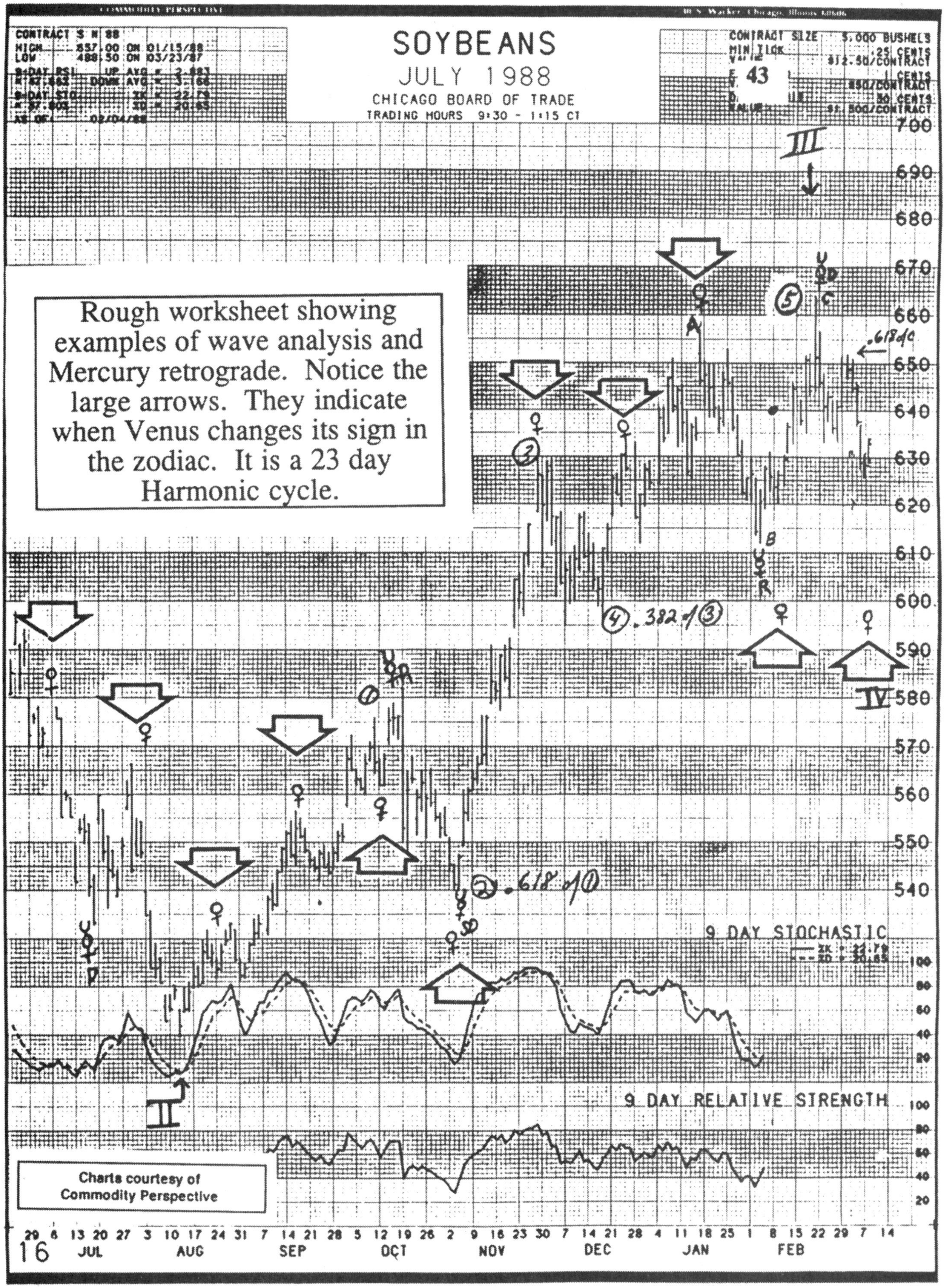
SOYBEANS
JULY 1988
CHICAGO BOARD OF TRADE
TRADING HOURS 9:30 - 1:15 CT
Rough worksheet showing examples of wave analysis and Mercury retrograde. Notice the large arrows. They indicate when Venus changes its sign in the zodiac. It is a 23 day Harmonic cycle.
9 DAY STOCHASTIC
9 DAY RELATIVE STRENGTH
Charts courtesy of Commodity Perspective
JUL
AUG
SEP
OCT
NOV
DEC
JAN
FEB

Lunar Phases

The moon revolves around the earth every 28 days. It moves from a new moon to the first quarter moon, then to a full moon, then on to the third quarter moon and returns to a new moon.

I have listed the lunar phases in order of importance to the short term timing of stocks and commodities:

1. Maximum or "0" Declination
   The moon is either at its further distance from the equator or at the equator "0."

2. True node of the Moon
   The true node of the moon is the only part of our solar system that turns counterclockwise. When it moves from retrograde or direct or vice-versa, it will affect prices.

3. Full moon--New Moon--Quarter Moon

4. Apogee and Perigee.
   Apogee is where the moon is farthest from the earth and spinning the slowest.
   Perigee is where the moon is closest to the earth and spinning the fastest.

5. Moon Void of Course
   The moon is going from one sign of the zodiac to another sign. It is a short period of time and usually lasts a few hours. During this time markets are unstable and may experience many wild price swings.

How to Use the Lunar Phenomena in Timing

A. Look for several lunar events occurring on the same day (i.e. true node change, full moon, and maximum declination.) Use any combinations of the five events. Usually you will find two events at a critical timing day.

B. It is of great significance when these lunar events happen on the same day as significant planetary aspects (angles). As an example, examine the top in Gold on December 14th 1987:

1. Venus square Jupiter
2. Moon on equator "0"
3. Quarter moon

The same phenomenon occurred on the high in the stock market on August 24th-26th 1987.

1. Three major conjunctions
2. Moon on equator "0"
3. True moon node going direct

The rally high of October 5th, 1987 just preceding the "panic."

1. Venus sextile Uranus
2. Moon on equator "0"
3. Full moon
4. Lunar eclipse--Oct. 7th

Lunar cycles exhibit an unusual characteristic that bears watching. Once the market has shown a tendency to turn on a certain phenomenon (i.e. apogee or maximum declination) it remains that way for at least one or two lunar cycles.

If you will take some time to familiarize yourself with these ideas, I think you will find that you will be amply rewarded. "Defy human nature--Do the work! The most important tool a technician uses is---an eraser." (Jim Twentyman)

THE PHASES OF THE MOON

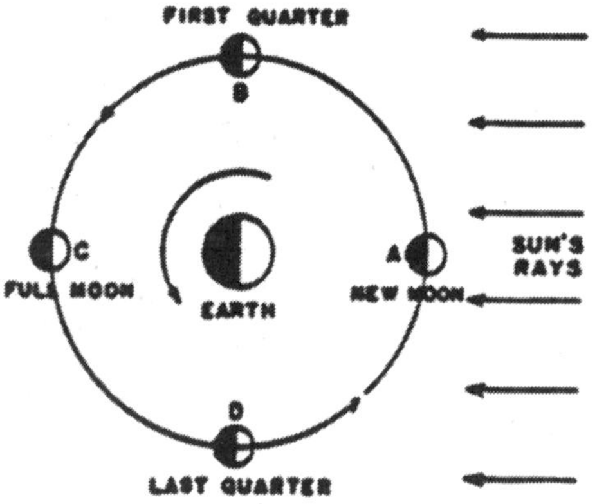

This illustration shows the movement of the Moon around Earth. The Moon's movement towards a Full Moon is referred to as a "waxing" Moon and its movement toward a New Moon is called a "waning" Moon. The "Farmer's Almanac" mentions the New Moon & Full Moon aspects to its readers as an aid in planting and harvesting. Twenty eight days are needed to complete this cycle.

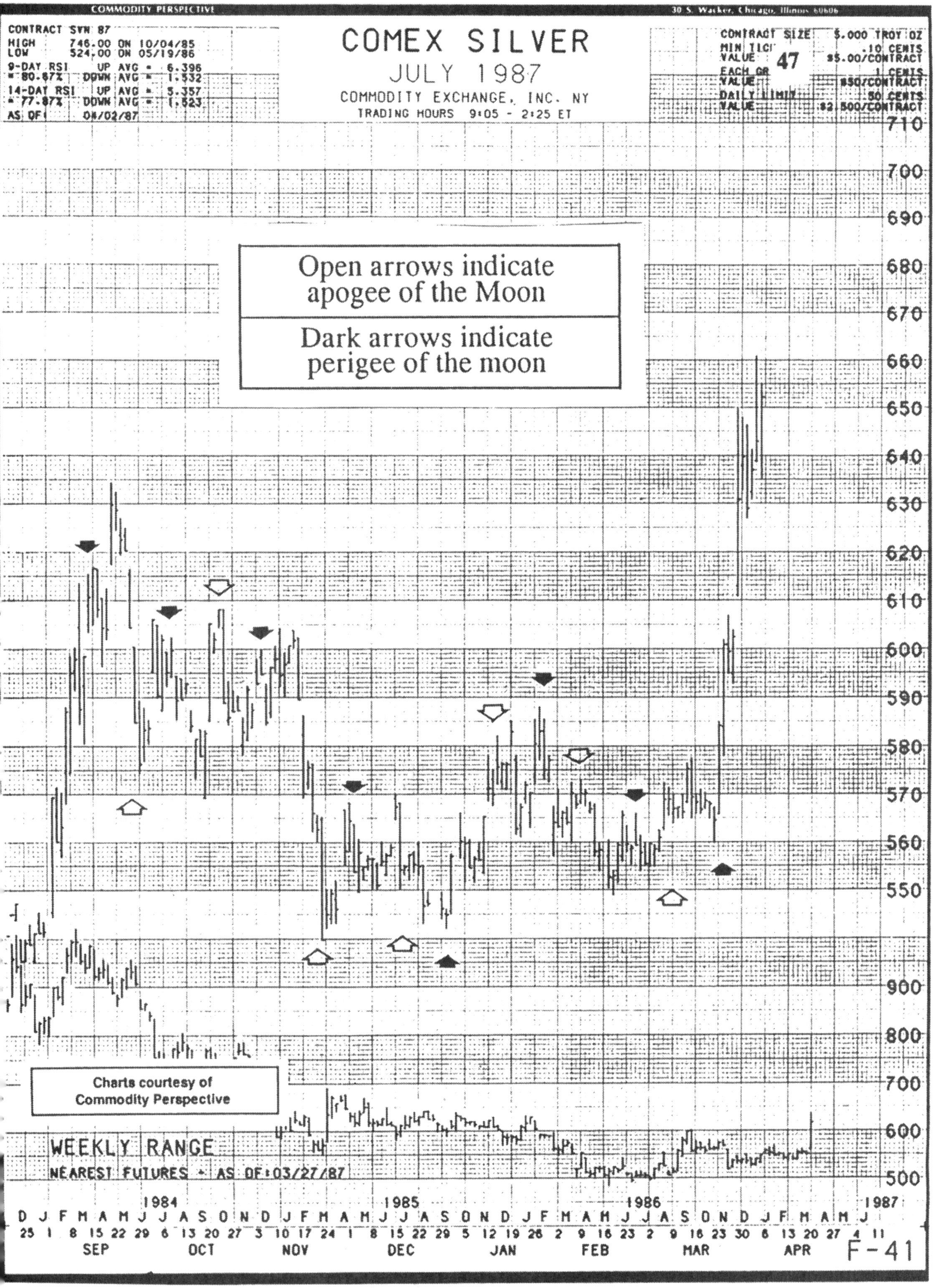
COMMODITY PERSPECTIVE
30 S. Wacker, Chicago, Illinois 60606
CONTRACT SVN 87
HIGH 746.00 ON 10/04/85
LOW 524.00 ON 05/19/86
9-DAY RSI UP AVG = 6.396
= 80.67% DOWN AVG = 1.532
14-DAY RSI UP AVG = 5.357
= 77.87% DOWN AVG = 1.523
AS OF: 04/02/87
COMEX SILVER
JULY 1987
COMMODITY EXCHANGE, INC. NY
TRADING HOURS 9:05 - 2:25 ET
CONTRACT SIZE 5,000 TROY OZ
MIN TICK VALUE .10 CENTS $5.00/CONTRACT
EACH GR VALUE 1 CENTS $50/CONTRACT
DAILY LIMIT VALUE 50 CENTS $2,500/CONTRACT
47
Open arrows indicate apogee of the Moon
Dark arrows indicate perigee of the moon
Charts courtesy of Commodity Perspective
WEEKLY RANGE
NEAREST FUTURES - AS OF: 03/27/87
710
700
690
680
670
660
650
640
630
620
610
600
590
580
570
560
550
900
800
700
600
500
1984
1985
1986
1987
D J F M A M J J A S O N D J F M A M J J A S O N D J F M A M J J A S O N D J F M A M J
25 1 8 15 22 29 6 13 20 27 3 10 17 24 1 8 15 22 29 5 12 19 26 2 9 16 23 2 9 16 23 30 6 13 20 27 4 11
SEP
OCT
NOV
DEC
JAN
FEB
MAR
APR
F-41

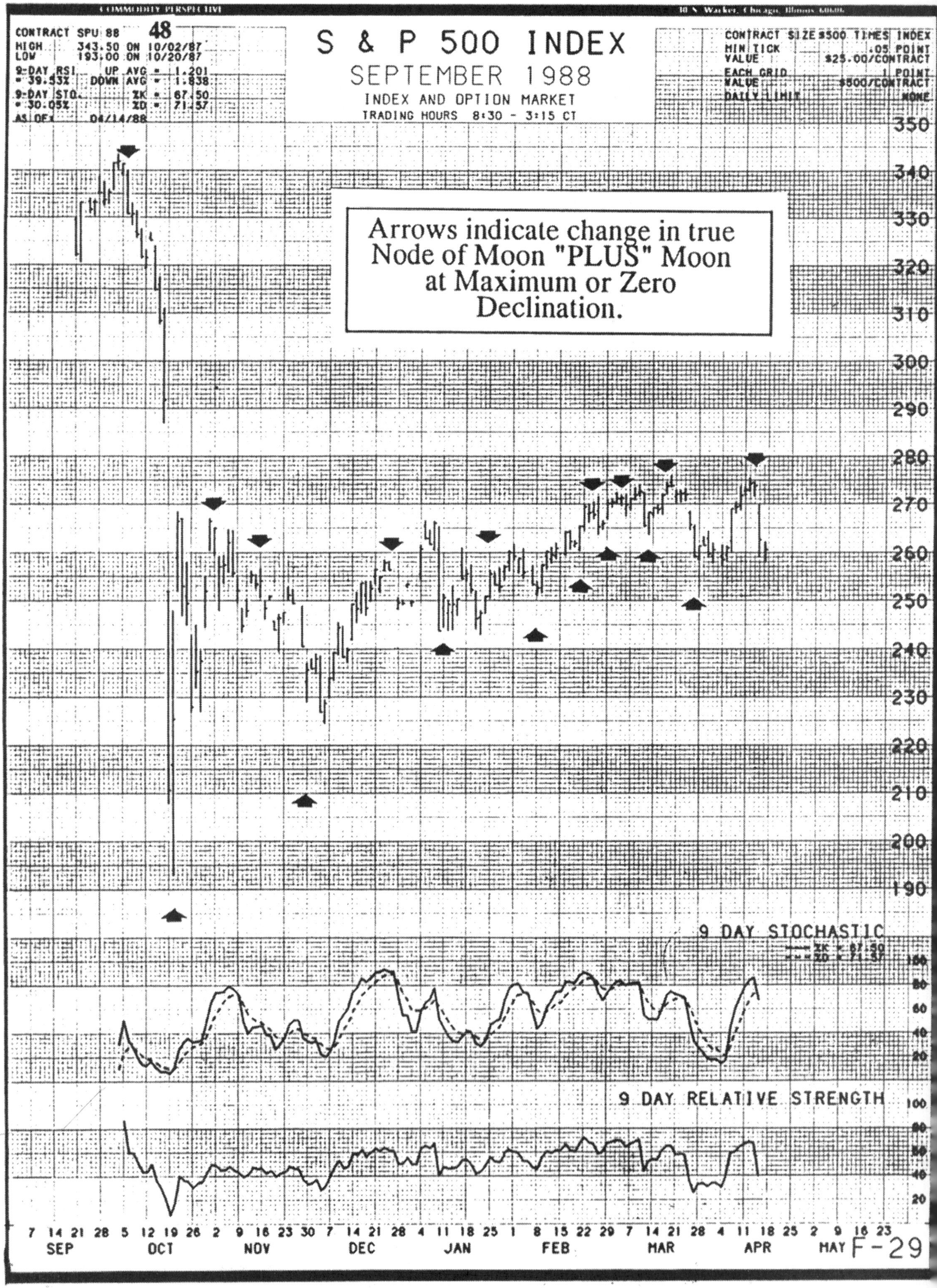
COMMODITY PERSPECTIVE
CONTRACT SPU 88 48
HIGH 343.50 ON 10/02/87
LOW 193.00 ON 10/20/87
9-DAY RSI UP AVG = 1.201
= 39.53% DOWN AVG = 1.838
9-DAY STO. %K = 67.50
= 30.05% %D = 71.57
AS OF: 04/14/88
S & P 500 INDEX
SEPTEMBER 1988
INDEX AND OPTION MARKET
TRADING HOURS 8:30 - 3:15 CT
CONTRACT SIZE $500 TIMES INDEX
MIN TICK .05 POINT
VALUE $25.00/CONTRACT
EACH GRID 1 POINT
VALUE $500/CONTRACT
DAILY LIMIT NONE
Arrows indicate change in true Node of Moon "PLUS" Moon at Maximum or Zero Declination.
9 DAY STOCHASTIC
%K = 67.50
%D = 71.57
9 DAY RELATIVE STRENGTH
SEP OCT NOV DEC JAN FEB MAR APR MAY

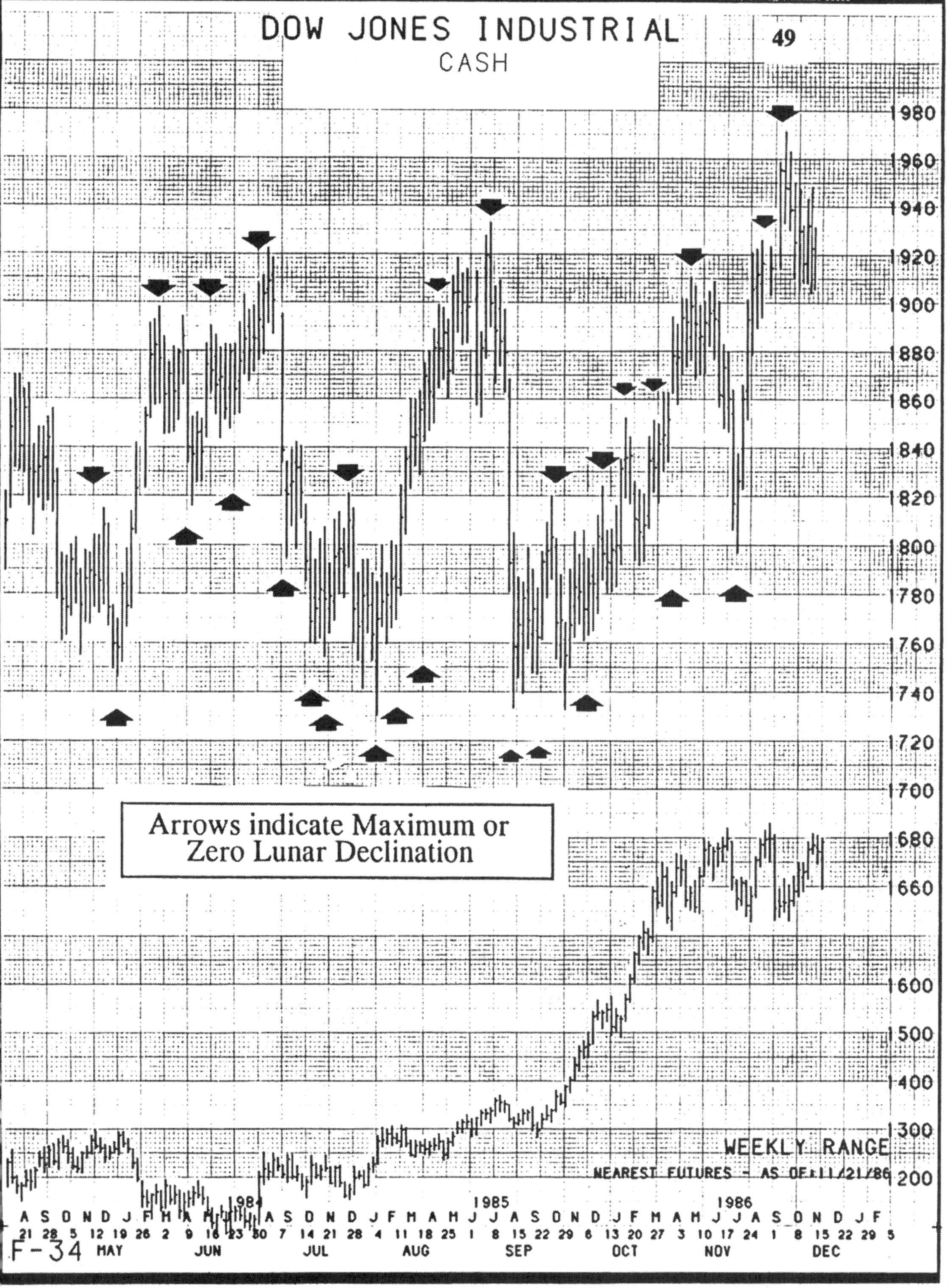
DOW JONES INDUSTRIAL
CASH
49
Arrows indicate Maximum or Zero Lunar Declination
980
960
940
920
900
880
860
840
820
800
780
760
740
720
700
680
660
600
500
400
300
200
WEEKLY RANGE
NEAREST FUTURES - AS OF:11/21/86
1984
1985
1986
A S O N D J F M A M J J A S O N D J F M A M J J A S O N D J F M A M J J A S O N D J F
21 28 5 12 19 26 2 9 16 23 30 7 14 21 28 4 11 18 25 1 8 15 22 29 6 13 20 27 3 10 17 24 1 8 15 22 29 5
MAY JUN JUL AUG SEP OCT NOV DEC

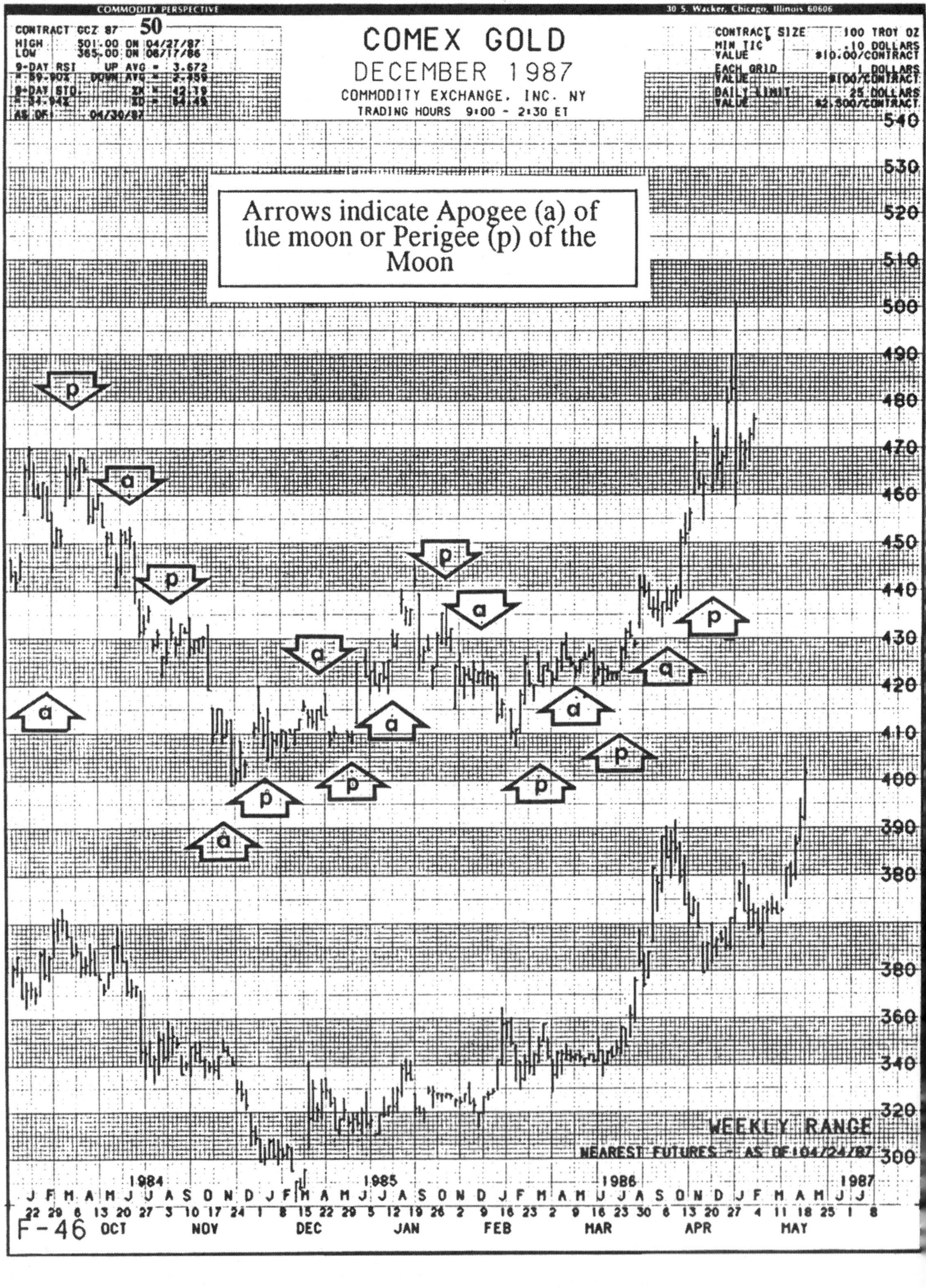
COMMODITY PERSPECTIVE
30 S. Wacker, Chicago, Illinois 60606
CONTRACT GCZ 87
50
HIGH 501.00 ON 04/27/87
LOW 365.00 ON 06/17/86
COMEX GOLD
DECEMBER 1987
COMMODITY EXCHANGE, INC. NY
TRADING HOURS 9:00 - 2:30 ET
CONTRACT SIZE 100 TROY OZ
Arrows indicate Apogee (a) of the moon or Perigee (p) of the Moon
WEEKLY RANGE
NEAREST FUTURES - AS OF 04/24/87
1984
1985
1986
1987
F-46

SOYBEANS

51 NOVEMBER 1982

Chicago Board of Trade

COMMODITY PERSPECTIVE/CHICAGO, ILLINOIS 60604

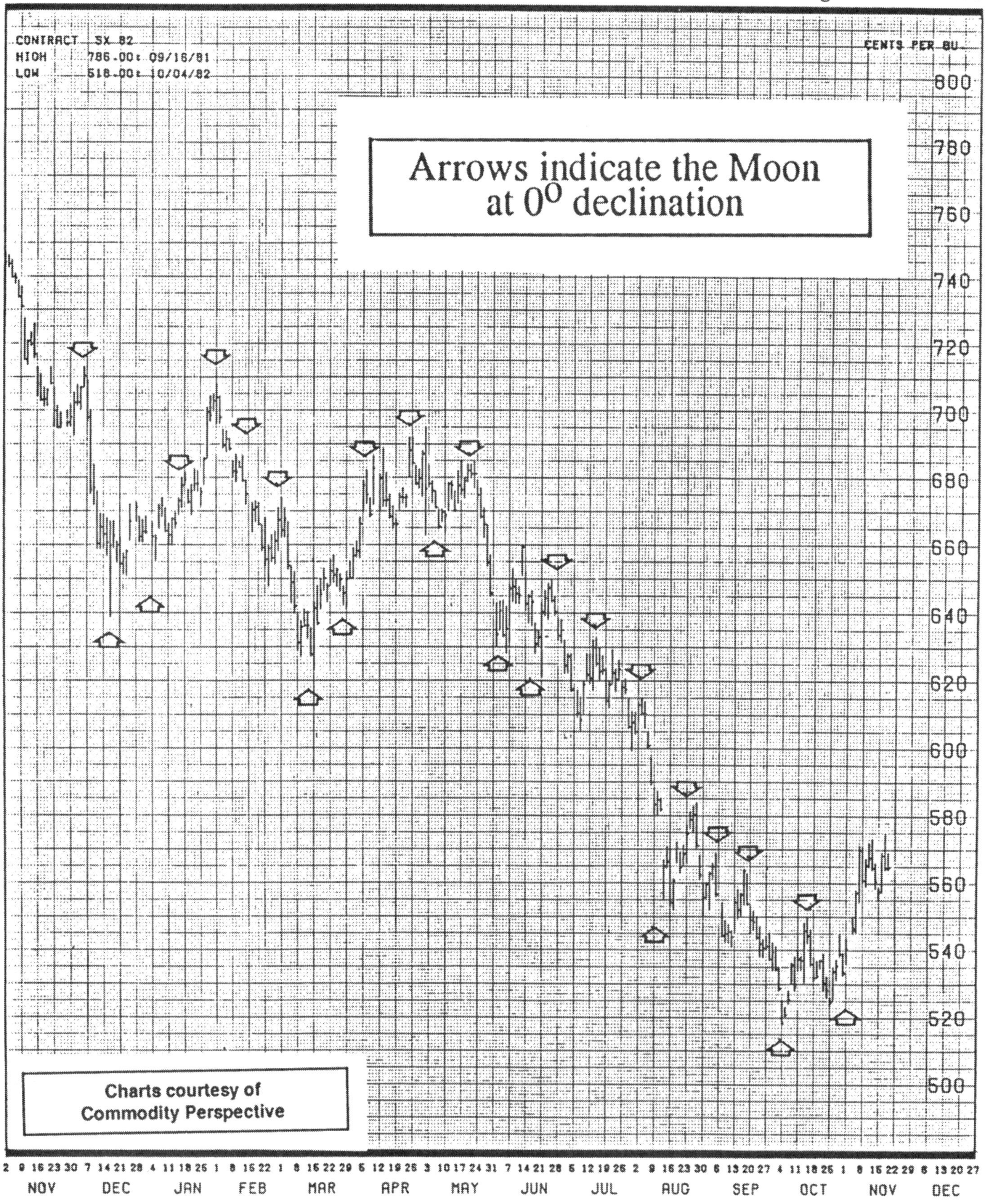

SILVER (N.Y.)

MAY 1978

Commodity Exchange, Inc. N.Y.

COMMODITY PERSPECTIVE/CHICAGO, ILLINOIS 60604

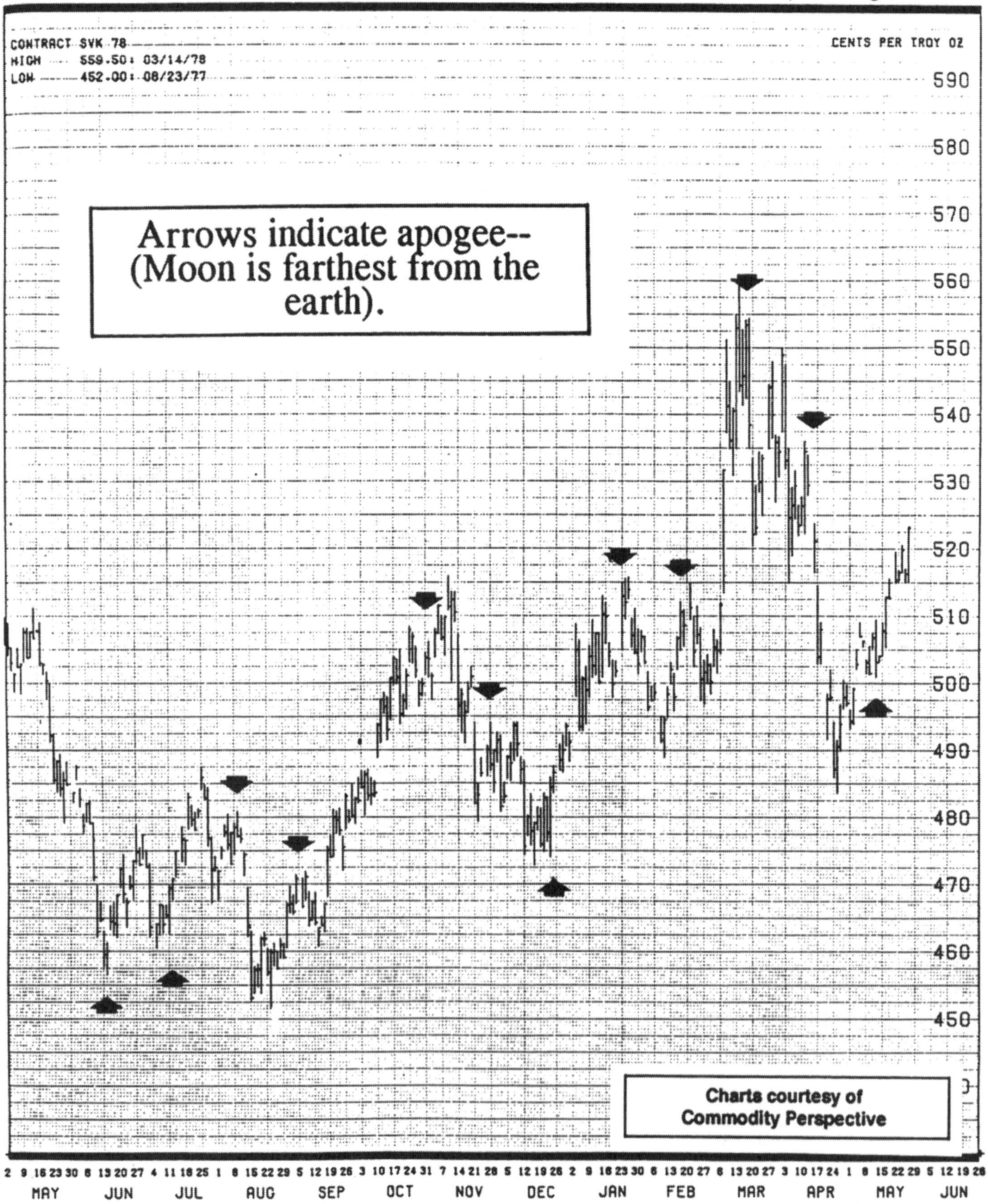

S&P 500 INDEX

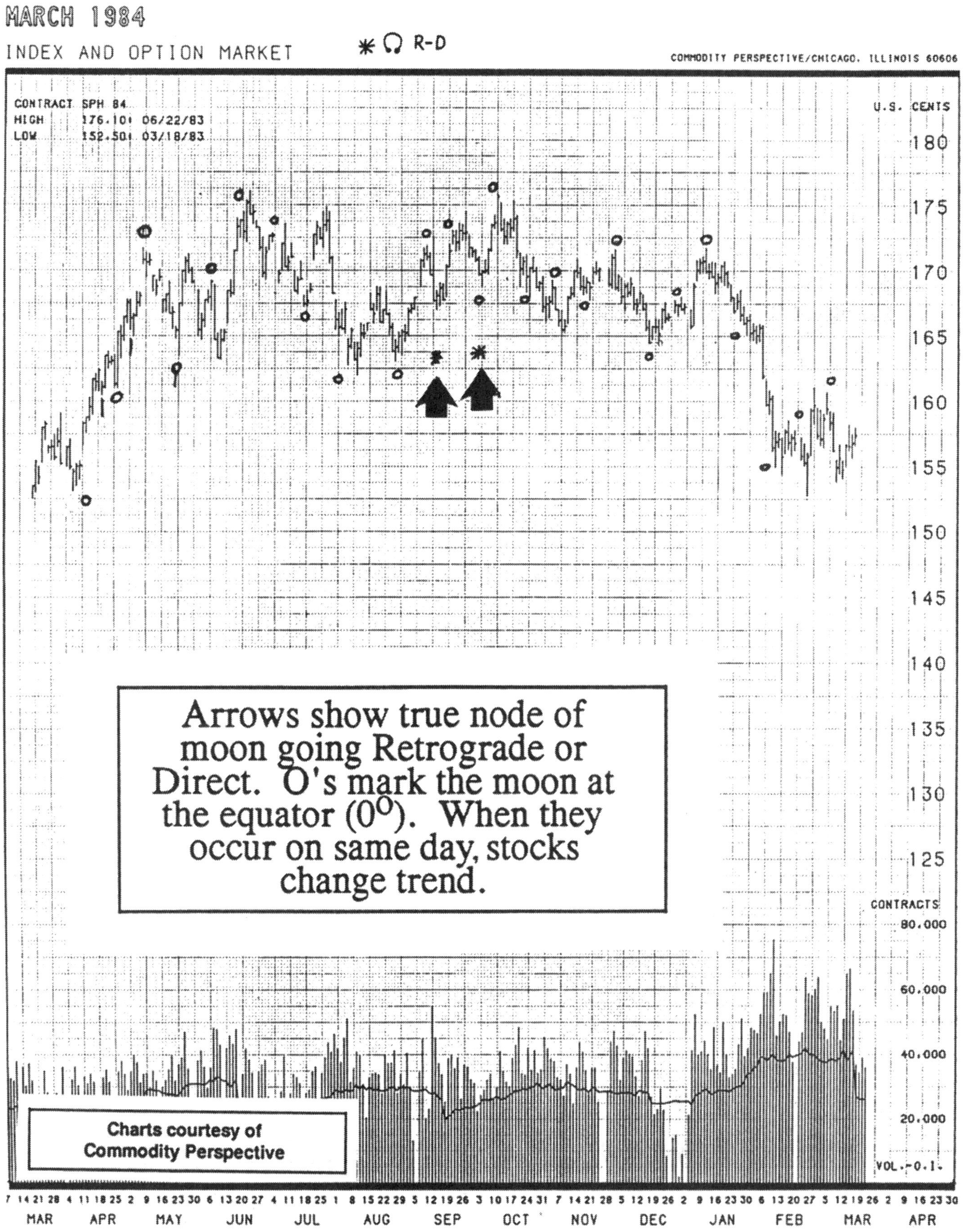

Arrows show true node of moon going Retrograde or Direct. O's mark the moon at the equator (0°). When they occur on same day, stocks change trend.

Charts courtesy of Commodity Perspective

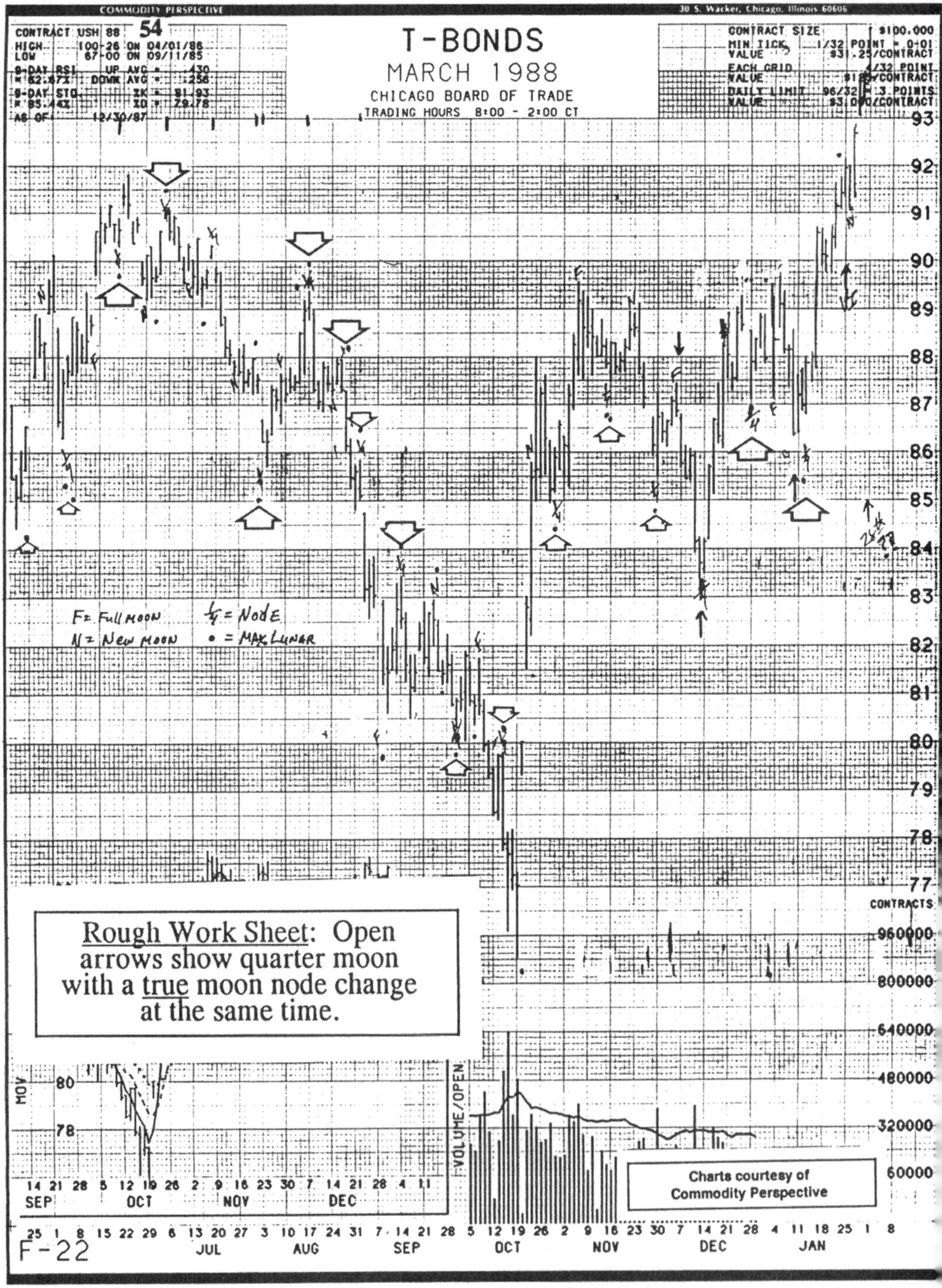

Rough Work Sheet: Open arrows show quarter moon with a true moon node change at the same time.

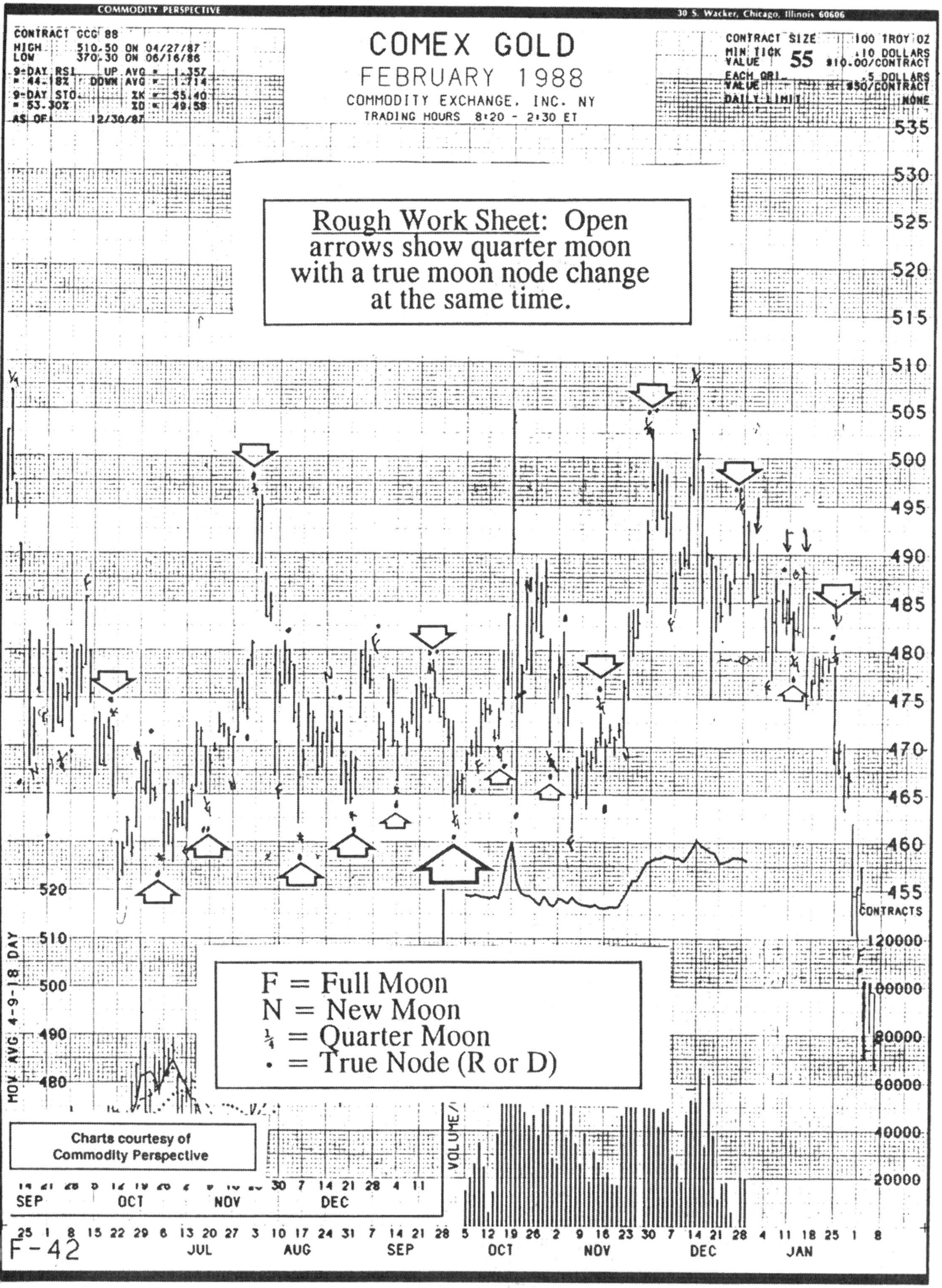
COMMODITY PERSPECTIVE
30 S. Wacker, Chicago, Illinois 60606
COMEX GOLD
FEBRUARY 1988
COMMODITY EXCHANGE, INC. NY
TRADING HOURS 8:20 - 2:30 ET
Rough Work Sheet: Open arrows show quarter moon with a true moon node change at the same time.
F = Full Moon
N = New Moon
¼ = Quarter Moon
• = True Node (R or D)
Charts courtesy of Commodity Perspective
JUL
AUG
SEP
OCT
NOV
DEC
JAN

Charts courtesy of
Commodity Perspective

T-BONDS

SEPTEMBER 1983

CHICAGO BOARD OF TRADE

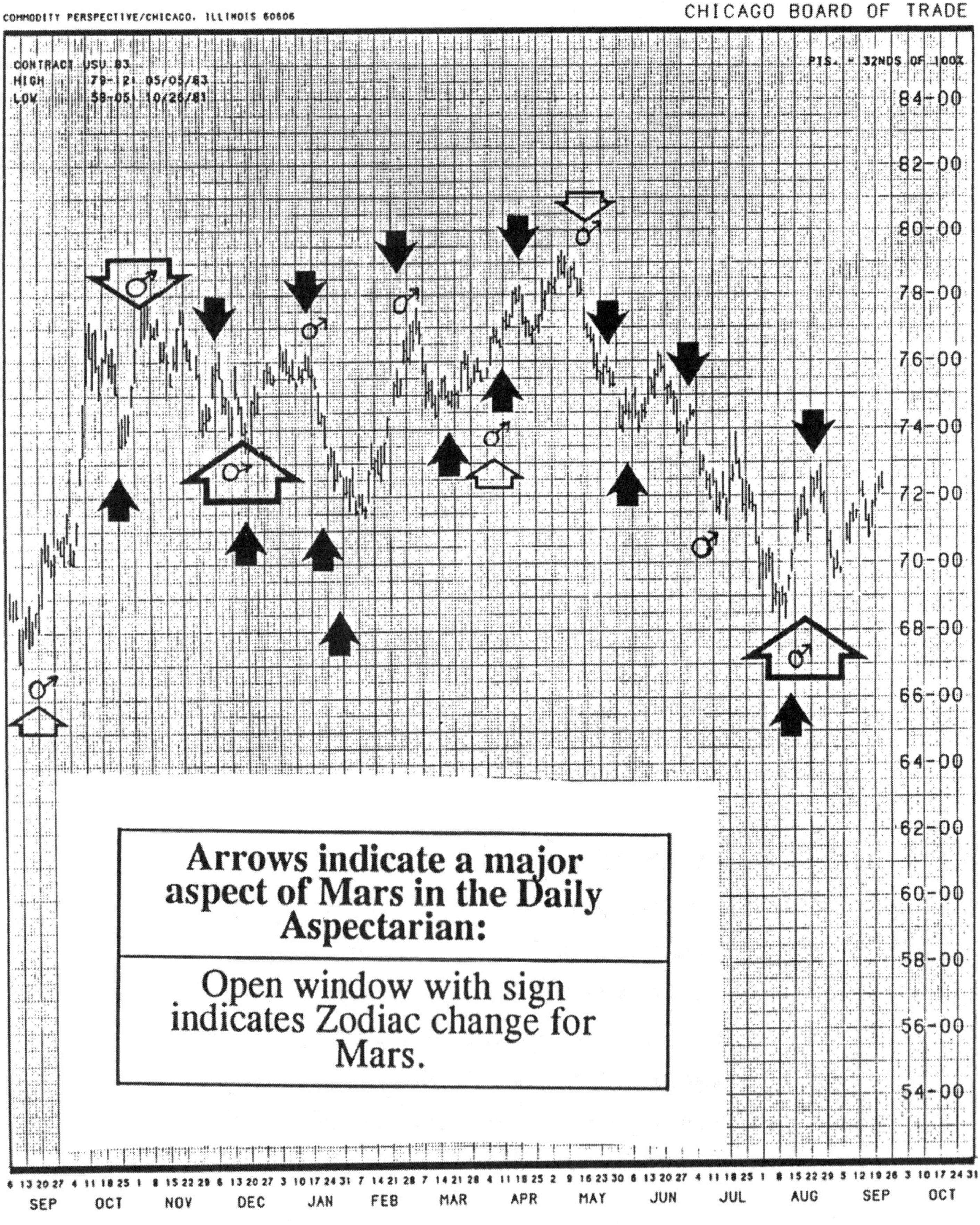

Arrows indicate a major aspect of Mars in the Daily Aspectarian:

Open window with sign indicates Zodiac change for Mars.

History of Astro-economics

Luther J. Jensen

Luther J. Jensen wrote *Astro Cycles and Speculative Markets* in 1935. He was able to accomplish something that very few astrologers have been able to do. He was widely quoted in financial circles and in the press. His book is still the starting point for almost everyone interested in learning Financial Astrology. It takes the reader from natural laws of vibration through sun spots, and planetary cycles.

Jensen spent considerable time with the Zodiac and mentions the various houses and signs. The book is easy to understand but **not** in the first reading because the subject matter is foreign to most students. If Luther Jensen had access to our present day computer systems, he would have been able to accomplish a considerable quantity of research on astrology. Jensen's handling of the Signs, Rulerships and Houses was presented like the expert he had become. The book is a must in any library of financial astrology.

Lt.Cmdr. David Williams

Financial Astrology by Lt.Cmdr. David Williams is the best book on the subject in over 50 years. Cmdr. Williams compiled significant economic cycles and how they related to business cycles. He explains how the ancients were aware of the Zodiac and their signs as early as 6000 B.C. His concise historical journey through ages of transformation in astrology is very

interesting. Sun spots are explained in several areas of the text. One realizes the power of our solar activity as it relates to weather, tele-communications, health problems, climatology, and agriculture. The book is packed with scientific proof of the effect on business and other economic activity by the Sun and planets.

Cmdr. Williams, was a tireless researcher and because of his knowledge in this subject was able to research several of the most important business cycle theories based on planetary phenomena. I will list a few of the ones that, in my opinion, were most important to understanding financial astrology.

Notable Works from "Financial Astrology"

1. *Benner's Prophesies of Future Ups and Downs in Prices* by Samuel Benner. Sam Benner studied cycles in pigiron, corn, hogs, and in general business conditions. He compared Jupiter's Major Equinox of 11.86 years with his 11 year cycle and found them to be similar.
2. *The Origin of the Eight Year Generating Cycle*, a paper published by H.L. Moore of Columbia University dealt with the Venus, Earth and Sun in inferior conjunction. This was also correlated to Sun spots.
3. Louise McWhirters, *McWhiter Theory of Stock market Forecasting* (1938) is based on the 19 year cycle of the Moon's north Node as it passes through the Zodiac. If her research proves to be correct, our current economy has peaked and we are already in a severe recessionary period.

4. The Jupiter cycles with Saturn and Uranus are covered extensively over long periods of time. This section was a real eye opener for me because I began to look at these planetary aspects from a trader's viewpoint. Some of the examples that appeared to be incorrect were in actuality wonderful trading opportunities from a technical standpoint. The stock market was doing the opposite of what was to be expected but **that** fact was telling me to expect the opposite to occur. Cmdr. Williams compared these aspects to times associated with financial panics.
5. Edward Dewey and Edward Daiken collaborated on *Cycles The Science of Prediction* in 1947. This book is paraphrased by Williams into the 9.2 year market cycle and the 38 to 41 month market cycle. All I did was correlate the planetary cycles within this time frame and discover the certain time periods of each of these cycles. Dewey, Daiken and Cmdr. Williams have done more towards **legitimizing** astro-economics than anyone in recent times.
6. The Mars-Jupiter aspects of conjunctions and opposition were discussed as they related to times of fear and panic. Again Williams was warning this "aspect" due in the fall of 1987, where prices would fall precipitously. **Five years before it happened!**

There is so much important material covered in "Financial Astrology" that it is an injustice to highlight minute parts. It is the true **treasure chest** of astrology.

James Mars Langham

James Mars Langham wrote several books on the subject of planetary causes of price trends. They have long since been out of print. He was another tireless researcher and concentrated on the aspects of several combinations of planets (i.e. Mars opposition Uranus, Venus opposition Uranus, and many others). It is an excellent book of reference to the early 1900's price behavior. All of Langham's assumptions were tested using the *Blue Star* software program in order to determine the highest probability trades. They work the same way now as they did in the 1930's.

W.D. Gann

W.D. Gann has received more fame in the last ten years than he did when he was alive. In all my years of study no one has as much mystery surrounding him. He left few clues to his approach to astrology. *The Tunnel Through the Air* is reported to be an autobiographical sketch of Gann's early years. This book mentions the Bible and natural laws of harmony, cause and effect. He made reference to the solar and lunar cycles of various years and their relationship to prices. If a non-astrologer were to read the book it would most probably mean very little as a timing tool. On a few of his old charts were comments such as "the faster moving planets are the key," and "the retrograde motion of Mercury will affect the trend in grain prices." Both of these comments prove that Gann was an astute financial astrologer. It is mind-boggling to think what he might have accomplished with the

use of modern day computers. Many students of Gann have twisted and massaged many of his ideas, but the quality of his basic geometric approach to price and time cannot be denied. The bottom line is this--W.D. Gann left very few clues to his "astrological" approach to the markets.

Gann published *The Magic Word* in 1950 just four years before his death. This work, in my opinion, was the culmination of Gann's study in Pythagorian mathematics, the Bible, the Kabala, and Freemasonry. It was his most important work!

George Bayer

The original research of the Mercury-Jupiter aspects and Mercury-Saturn aspects was done by George Bayer. (This is covered in greater detail in the "Wheat" division of this book.) He also published under several pseudonyms. Should you ever come across one of his books, it would be wise to buy it--they are worth hundreds of dollars to collectors. George Bayer studied the Wheat market from the 1400's until his death in 1949.

He lived in Monterey, California, and would go east when the time to trade Wheat was near. Evidently, he was a member of the exchange and liked to visit his comrades.

Norman Winski

Norm Winski is a member of the Chicago Board Options Exchange (C.B.O.E.). As I understand, he only trades stocks and bonds using financial astrology. Reports of his successful trading have appeared in the press because of his unique approach. He has made astrology appear to be the <u>useful tool</u> it is. Winski is

well respected by his collegues. Although I have never personally met the man, our phone conversations have always been pleasant and informative. He has the most extensive financial astrological library that is in existence. He purchased the Evangeline Adams collection. Evangline Adams was the personal astrologer of J. Pierpont Morgan. When asked by reporters about financial astrology, J.P. Morgan replied "Millionaires don't use astrology, but billionaires do!" Norman Winski can be reached at CBOE #802 400 So. LaSalle, Chicago, IL 60605.

Jack Gillien

Jack Gillien wrote *Key to Speculation on the New York Stock Exchange*. He is a syndicated columnist and has received more recent publicity than anyone in financial astrology. He is extremely busy and quite successful. He operates a telephone update for the stock market. He can be reached at P.O. Box 555179 Orlando, FL 32855.

Bill Foster

Bill Foster is the editor of the *Rocky Mountain Forecaster*. This newsletter is specifically geared to the commodity markets. I personally know that he is well versed and extremely competent in all areas of financial astrology. He has several research papers that are available and a teaching course that is quite comprehensive. He can be reached at Box 1093 Reseda, CA 91335.

Larry Berg

Larry Berg is an astute financial astrologer who operates an advisory service called *Astro Stock Market Advisory*. He may be reached at 5816 Webster St. Omaha, NE 68132.

Raymond A. Merriman

Ray operates *MMA Cycles*. His service consists of a newsletter and hotline service. Ray is an adept technician, knowledgeable financial astrologer and notable author. He may be reached at P.O. Box 1074 Birmingham, MI 48012.

Carol Mull

Carol Mull is a financial astrologer and publishes *The Wall Street Astrologer* She is well known in the astrological community and lectures extensively. She can be reached at Mull Publications P.O. Box 11133 Indianapolis, IN 46201.

Arch Crawford

Arch Crawford publishes *Crawford Perspectives*. He is one of the most highly publicized financial astrologers on Wall Street. He is seen on the Financial News Network each week. Arch can be contacted via Crawford Perspectives 205 E. 78th St. NY, NY 10021.

Mason Sexton

Mason Sexton publishes "Harmonic Research" one of the best available technical outlook publications for the stock market. His

combination of financial astrology and expert technical analysis leaves the reader with little doubt on the correct course of action. Mason can be reached at Harmonic Research 650 Fifth Ave. New York, NY 10019.

Fibonacci and Planetary Cycles

Many of the planetary (synodic) cycles conform to the Fibonacci Summation Series. A brief discussion of the Fibonacci number sequence follows, however those of you wanting to expand your knowledge in the subject to improve your trading should contact Ed Dobson at Traders Press P.O. Box 10344 Greenville S.C. 29603. He provides an excellent reference source of the use of Fibonacci numbers and their application to price action.

Leonardo Fibonacci de Pisa was a 12th century Italian mathematician. He spent several years in Egypt studying the pyramids, to arrive at his Fibonacci number sequence. The sequence of Fibonacci numbers is as follows:

0,1,1,2,3,5,8,13,21,34,55,89,144 ⟶ infinity

(0+1=1)...(1+1=2)...(1+2=3)...(2+3=5)...etc

5 ÷ 8 = .625	2.618 - 1.618= 1
8 ÷ 13= .615	1.618 -.618 = 1
13 ÷ 21 = .619	1 - .618 = .382
21 ÷ 34 = .618	2.618 x .382 = 1
34 ÷ 55 = .617	2.618 x .618= 1.618
55 ÷ 89 = .617	1.618 x .618 = 1
89 ÷ 144 = .618	.618 x .618 = .382
144 ÷ 233 = .618	1.618 x 1.618 = 2.618

Robert Prechter's newsletter, *The Elliott Wave Theorist* has popularized the use of these Fibonacci ratios in market analysis.

Mr. Prechter's book the *Elliott Wave Principle* will give the interested student a good start in studying the mathematics of the market place. It is an absolute must in any market technicians library. (New Classics Library Box 1618 Gainsville, GA. 30305).

Joe DiNapoli of Coast Investment Software has an excellent "Applications Manual" on the use of Fibonacci numbers in trading using a proportional divider. (8851 Albatross Dr. Huntington Beach, CA 92646).

The trading signals that are discussed in a later section of this book are based on the Fibonacci number sequence. After researching hundreds of price patterns over a twenty year period these two were the most consistent.

The importance of Fibonacci numbers cannot be over-emphasized! It's relationship to natural harmonic vibration is not by chance. It was the Venus-Uranus synodic period of 225 days (365 days X .618) that awakened me to the market timing potential of astrology. As you look at each of the planetary combinations discussed in this book you will see this Fibonacci relationship reappear time and time again.

Those of you who are interested in learning more about pattern recognition techniques should consider John R. Hill's classic *Stock and Commodity Market Trend Trading by Advanced Technical Analysis*. He can be reached at Commodity Research Institute P.O. Box 1866 Hendersonville, N. Carolina 28739

SECTION TWO:

THE EPHEMERIS

Section Two:

The Ephemeris

The Ephemeris Explained

The Ephemeris is the book that gives the exact location of the planets of our Solar System. The various astrological ephemerides are compiled from the *National Almanac* issued by the U.S. Government. It will be necessary for you to purchase an ephemeris. There are several vendors that make this data available. I strongly recommend that you purchase *The American Ephemeris 1981 to 1990* from A.C.S. Publications P.O. Box 16430 San Diego, California 92116-0430 ($6.00). This book is constantly by my side and I usually wear one or more out each year.

When you finish reading and studying this section of the book, you will be able to go to an ephemeris and understand what you are reading. My thanks to Neil Michelsen of A.C.S. for his permission to use his ephemeris in our examples. I chose to go through each important segment of the ephemeris on one page. This keeps you from leafing through pages trying to find something. The chart examples also have indications of where to look in the ephemeris. You will become accustomed to using this book daily. Major research projects that include years of data are

best accomplished by the use of "Blue Star," which is a computerized ephemeris.

The ephemeris is separated into four parts:

1. Longitude--Measurement along the ecliptic in terms of signs and degrees from the first point of the zodiac.

2. Declination and Latitude--The degree of distance of any place north or south of the earth's equator.

3. Daily Aspectarian--Indicates aspects (angles) of all planets and the time it occurs in G.M.T. (Greenwich Mean Time)

4. Lunar phenomena--Apogee, Perigee, Full and New Moon, Maximum Declination

Let's take a close look at what this ephemeris is telling us. The word cycle is derived from the Greek word for "circle." We know that the book measures the distance between planets "exactly." What we must determine is whether these planets have an effect on prices of certain stocks and commodities. This task will not be easy because you must learn the terminology--**THEN** you examine the price and time of each market.

At times you will get frustrated and confused. Put the ephemeris aside for awhile and return to it at a later date.

"Knowledge of astrology makes man aware of the time and character of the operations of nature and so provides him the **OPPORTUNITY** to think and plan, **BEFORE** it is time to **ACT**; and to use discrimination in his reactions to planetary aspects, in accordance with the extent of his awareness and ability to control and determine his actions."

Llewellyn George

KEY TO THE EPHEMERIS

Planets
- ☉ Sun
- ☽ Moon
- ☊ Moon's node
- ☿ Mercury
- ♀ Venus
- ♂ Mars
- ♃ Jupiter
- ♄ Saturn
- ♅ Uranus
- ♆ Neptune
- ♇ Pluto

D Direct
R Retrograde

Signs
- ♈ Aries
- ♉ Taurus
- ♊ Gemini
- ♋ Cancer
- ♌ Leo
- ♍ Virgo
- ♎ Libra
- ♏ Scorpio
- ♐ Sagittarius
- ♑ Capricorn
- ♒ Aquarius
- ♓ Pisces

Sidereal Times given for midnight (0h) Universal Time at 0° longitude (Greenwich). All planetary positions are given for midnight (0h) Ephemeris Time except ☽ 12 Hour positions which are given for 12h Ephemeris Time.

Aspect and Moon phenomena times are given in Ephemeris Time.

☽ PHENOMENA	VOID OF COURSE ☽ Last Aspect	☽ Ingress
● new Moon ☽ first quarter ○ full ☾ third quarter Sun eclipse Moon eclipse	Last major aspect before Moon enters new sign	Moon enters new sign
Maximum and 0° declination		
Maximum and 0° latitude	Apogee Perigee	

Major Aspects
- ☌ conjunction (0°)
- ⚹ sextile (60°)
- □ square (90°)
- △ trine (120°)
- ☍ opposition (180°)

Minor Aspects
- ⚼ sesquare (135°)
- ⚻ quincunx (150°)
- ⚺ semisextile (30°)
- ∠ semisquare (45°)

Aspects in Declination
- ∥ parallel
- ⋕ contraparallel

SD Stationary going direct
SR Stationary going retrograde

☉ ♒ Sun enters Aquarius

LONGITUDE

DAY	SID. TIME	☉	☽	☽ 12 Hour	MEAN ☊	TRUE ☊	☿	♀	♂	♃	♄	♅	♆	♇
	h m s	° ′ ″	° ′ ″	° ′ ″	° ′	° ′	° ′	° ′	° ′	° ′	° ′	° ′	° ′	° ′
1 Tu	18 35 1	8♋ 32 46	1♉ 2 33	7♉ 1 43	26♈ 14.3	27♈R20.8	3♌ 27.3	17♍ 44.8	20♑R12.8	22♓ 38.1	4♐R 7.3	19♐R36.2	4♑R18.5	4♏R33.9
2 W	18 38 57	9 49 59	12 58 46	18 54 18	26 11.1	27 19.8	4 4.3	18 54.1	19 57.7	22 40.2	4 4.1	19 34.0	4 16.9	4 35.5
3 Th	18 42 54	10 47 12	24 48 30	0♊ 42 53	26 7.9	27 16.7	4 37.2	20 3.3	19 42.2	22 42.2	4 1.0	19 31.7	4 15.3	4 35.1
4 F	18 46 50	11 44 25	6♊ 36 33	12 31 14	26 4.8	27 11.0	3 6.0	21 12.4	19 26.3	22 44.0	3 57.9	19 29.5	4 13.7	4 34.7
5 Sa	18 50 47	12 41 38	18 26 19	24 22 25	26 1.6	27 2.6	5 30.5	22 21.3	19 10.0	22 45.6	3 54.9	19 27.3	4 12.1	4 34.3
6 Su	18 54 43	13 38 52	0♋ 19 47	6♋ 18 40	25 58.4	26 51.8	5 50.6	23 30.4	18 53.4	22 47.0	3 52.0	19 25.1	4 10.3	4 34.0
7 M	18 58 40	14 36 5	12 19 13	18 21 37	25 55.2	26 39.2	6 6.2	24 39.2	18 36.6	22 48.2	3 49.2	19 23.0	4 8.9	4 33.7
8 Tu	19 2 37	15 33 19	24 25 58	0♌ 32 24	25 52.1	26 25.8	6 17.3	25 47.9	18 19.5	22 49.3	3 46.4	19 20.8	4 7.4	4 33.4
9 W	19 6 33	16 30 32	6♌ 41 2	12 51 58	25 48.9	26 12.9	6♌R 23.7	26 36.5	18 2.2	22 50.1	3 43.7	19 18.7	4 5.8	4 33.2
10 Th	19 10 30	17 27 46	19 5 19	25 21 15	25 45.7	26 1.4	6 23.4	28 5.0	17 44.8	22 50.7	3 41.1	19 16.7	4 4.2	4 33.0
11 F	19 14 26	18 25 0	1♍ 39 34	8♍ 1 29	25 42.3	25 52.3	6 22.3	29 13.3	17 27.3	22 51.1	3 38.6	19 14.6	4 2.6	4 32.8
12 Sa	19 18 23	19 22 13	14 26 12	20 54 19	25 39.3	25 46.1	6 14.5	0♎ 21.6	17 9.8	22♓R 51.4	3 36.1	19 12.6	4 1.1	4 32.7
13 Su	19 22 19	20 19 27	27 26 3	4♎ 1 49	25 36.2	25 42.8	6 2.0	1 29.7	16 52.3	22 51.4	3 33.8	19 10.6	3 59.5	4 32.6
14 M	19 26 16	21 16 41	10♎ 41 47	17 26 18	25 33.0	25D 41.6	5 45.0	2 37.8	16 34.8	22 51.3	3 31.5	19 8.6	3 58.0	4 32.5
15 Tu	19 30 12	22 13 54	24 13 37	1♏ 9 56	25 29.8	25R 41.6	5 23.6	3 45.6	16 17.3	22 50.9	3 29.3	19 6.7	3 56.5	4D 32.5
16 W	19 34 9	23 11 7	8♏ 9 24	15 14 4	25 26.6	25 41.3	4 58.0	4 53.4	16 0.3	22 50.4	3 27.2	19 4.8	3 55.0	4 32.5
17 Th	19 38 6	24 8 21	22 23 52	29 38 33	25 23.5	25 40.0	4 28.6	6 1.0	15 43.3	22 49.6	3 25.2	19 2.9	3 53.5	4 32.6
18 F	19 42 2	25 5 35	6♐ 57 43	14♐ 20 54	25 20.3	25 36.2	3 55.7	7 8.5	15 26.6	22 48.7	3 23.2	19 1.1	3 52.0	4 32.6
19 Sa	19 45 59	26 2 49	21 47 15	29 13 55	25 17.1	25 29.8	3 19.9	8 15.9	15 10.1	22 47.6	3 21.4	18 59.3	3 50.5	4 32.8
20 Su	19 49 55	27 0 4	6♑ 43 52	14♑ 13 53	25 13.9	25 20.9	2 41.3	9 23.1	14 54.0	22 46.3	3 19.6	18 57.5	3 49.1	4 32.9
21 M	19 53 52	27 57 19	21 44 54	29 11 36	25 10.8	25 10.3	2 1.3	10 30.1	14 38.2	22 44.8	3 17.9	18 55.8	3 47.6	4 33.1
22 Tu	19 57 48	28 54 34	6♒ 34 52	13♒ 53 41	25 7.6	24 59.2	1 19.9	11 37.0	14 22.8	22 43.1	3 16.4	18 54.1	3 46.2	4 33.3
23 W	20 1 45	29 51 30	21 7 7	28 14 28	25 4.4	24 48.8	0 38.0	12 43.8	14 7.9	22 41.2	3 14.9	18 52.4	3 44.8	4 33.6
24 Th	20 5 42	0♌ 49 6	5♓ 13 13	12♓ 9 3	25 1.2	24 40.2	29♋ 56.3	13 50.4	13 53.4	22 39.1	3 13.5	18 50.8	3 43.4	4 33.8
25 F	20 9 38	1 46 23	18 55 49	25 35 35	24 58.0	24 34.1	29 13.6	14 56.8	13 39.4	22 36.8	3 12.2	18 49.2	3 42.0	4 34.1
26 Sa	20 13 35	2 43 41	2♈ 8 34	8♈ 35 6	24 54.9	24 30.5	28 36.6	16 3.1	13 26.0	22 34.3	3 11.0	18 47.7	3 40.6	4 34.5
27 Su	20 17 31	3 41 0	14 55 38	21 10 43	24 51.7	24D 29.0	28 0.1	17 9.2	13 13.1	22 31.7	3 9.8	18 46.2	3 39.2	4 34.9
28 M	20 21 28	4 38 20	27 20 56	3♉ 26 37	24 48.5	24R 28.8	27 26.7	18 15.2	13 0.9	22 28.8	3 8.8	18 44.7	3 37.9	4 35.3
29 Tu	20 25 24	5 35 41	9♉ 29 24	15 28 59	24 45.3	24 28.8	26 37.0	19 21.0	12 49.3	22 25.8	3 7.9	18 43.3	3 36.6	4 35.7
30 W	20 29 21	6 33 3	21 26 22	27 22 12	24 42.2	24 27.9	26 31.8	20 26.6	12 38.3	22 22.6	3 7.0	18 41.9	3 35.3	4 36.2
31 Th	20 33 17	7♌ 30 26	3♊ 17 6	9♊ 11 40	24♈ 39.0	24♈ 23.3	26♋ 11.4	21♎ 32.0	12♑ 28.0	22♓ 19.1	3♐ 6.3	18♐ 40.3	3♑ 34.0	4♏ 36.8

DECLINATION and LATITUDE

DAY	☉ DECL	☽ DECL	☽ LAT	☽ 12hr DECL	☿ DECL	☿ LAT	♀ DECL	♀ LAT	♂ DECL	♂ LAT	♃ DECL	♃ LAT	♄ DECL	♄ LAT
1	23N 9	12N 9	0N20	14N40	18N47	0S37	17N14	1N49	26S32	3S 0	4S 4	1S14	19S 3	1N58
2	23 5	17 2	1 22	19 14	18 25	0 30	16 52	1 47	26 38	3 4	4 3	1 14	19 3	1 57
3	23 0	21 15	2 20	23 2	18 4	1 3	16 28	1 46	27 4	3 8	4 2	1 13	19 2	1 57
4	22 55	24 34	3 12	25 31	17 43	1 19	16 3	1 44	27 10	3 11	4 2	1 13	19 2	1 57
5	22 50	26 51	3 56	27 33	17 23	1 34	15 41	1 43	27 16	3 15	4 2	1 13	19 1	1 57
6	22 45	27 56	4 29	27 39	17 3	1 49	15 17	1 41	27 21	3 18	4 1	1 16	19 1	1 57
7	22 39	27 42	4 51	27 5	16 45	2 4	14 52	1 39	27 27	3 21	4 1	1 16	19 1	1 56
8	22 32	26 9	4 60	24 54	16 28	2 19	14 27	1 37	27 32	3 24	4 1	1 16	19 0	1 56
9	22 25	23 22	4 55	21 33	16 12	2 34	14 1	1 35	27 38	3 27	4 1	1 17	19 0	1 56
10	22 18	19 29	4 37	17 11	15 57	2 49	13 36	1 33	27 43	3 30	4 1	1 17	18 60	1 56
11	22 11	14 41	4 4	12 1	15 43	3 4	13 10	1 31	27 48	3 33	4 1	1 17	18 60	1 56
12	22 3	9 12	3 19	6 15	15 31	3 18	12 43	1 28	27 53	3 35	4 1	1 17	18 59	1 55
13	21 54	3 13	2 23	0 6	15 20	3 32	12 17	1 26	27 57	3 37	4 2	1 18	18 59	1 55
14	21 46	3S 2	1 18	6S11	15 11	3 46	11 50	1 23	28 2	3 40	4 2	1 18	18 59	1 55
15	21 37	9 17	0 8	12 20	15 4	3 58	11 23	1 21	28 6	3 42	4 2	1 18	18 59	1 55
16	21 27	15 16	1S 3	18 1	14 59	4 10	10 56	1 18	28 10	3 44	4 3	1 19	18 58	1 55
17	21 17	20 34	2											
18	21 7	24 45	3											
19	20 57	27 21	4											
20	20 46	28 1	4											
21	20 34	26 37	4											
22	20 23	23 22	4											
23	20 11	18 43	4											
24	19 59	13 8	3											
25	19 46	7 5	2											
26	19 33	0 55	1											
27	19 20	5N 6	0											
28	19 6	10 46	0											
29	18 53	13 54	1 19	18 13	16 17	4 33	[illegible]	[illegible]	[illegible]	[illegible]	[illegible]	[illegible]	[illegible]	[illegible]
30	18 38	20 20	2 18	22 13	16 31	4 23	4 14	0 29	28 42	3 53	4 18	1 23	18 58	1 31
31	18N24	23N56	3N10	23N21	16N[illegible]	[illegible]	[illegible]	0N24	28S42	3S53	4S19	1S23	18S58	[illegible]

DAY	♅ DECL	♅ LAT	♆ DECL	♆ LAT	♇ DECL	♇ LAT
1	23S 8	0S 6	22S16	1N 6	2N45	16N45
5	23 7	0 6	22 16	1 6	2 43	16 42
9	23 6	0 6	22 16	1 6	2 42	16 40
13	23 6	0 6	22 17	1 6	2 40	16 38
17	23 5	0 6	22 17	1 6	2 37	16 36
21	23 5	0 6	22 17	1 6	2 35	16 33
25	23 4	0 6	22 18	1 6	2 33	16 31
29	23S 4	0S 6	22S18	1N 6	2N30	16N28

☽ PHENOMENA dy	hr	
4	8	APOGE
19	20	PERIC
31	21	APOGE
27	18	0

VOID OF COURSE ☽ LAST ASPT	☽ INGRESS
2 7pm42	3 ♊ 10am33
5 8am47	5 ♋ 11pm20
7 8pm49	8 ♌ 10am57
10 6pm54	10 ♍ 8pm51
12 3pm36	13 ♎ 4am41
14 8pm11	15 ♏ 9am59
17 3am 6	17 ♐ 12pm35
19 1am37	19 ♑ 1pm11
21 10am41	21 ♒ 1pm18
22 8pm16	23 ♓ 2pm39
25 5pm48	25 ♈ 8pm 3
28 0am11	28 ♉ 5am12
30 9am59	30 ♊ 5pm20

dy	hr	mn	PHASE	
7	4	36	14♋48	●
14	20	11	22♎ 5	☽
21	10	41	28♑23	○
28	15	35	5♉16	☾

The Daily Aspectarian gives the "aspects" (angles) of each planet.

DAILY ASPECTARIAN

Day	Aspect	Time
1 T	♅∠♇	4am 6
	☽□♆	3 6
	☽⊼♄	6 8
	☉☍♅	6 20
	☽△♆	6 31
	☽☍♅	7 6
	☽⊼♇	7 7
	☽∠♃	1pm16
	☉☍☽	3 6
	☽∥♀	11 8
	☿△♄	11 54
2 W	☽∥♆	6am32
	♀☍♆	7 44
	☿⊼♆	8 29
	☽∥♄	10 32
	☽☍♆	12pm44
	☽□♀	1 17
	☽⊼♅	1 18
	♀△♅	1 23
	☽△♂	1 51
	♀⊼♂	6 1
	☽☍♃	7 42
	☿☍♅	8 6
	☿□♇	10 23
3 Th	☉∠☽	2am 9
	☽∥♆	6 43
	☉∥☽	11 34
	☽∥♅	12pm41
	☿⚹♆	6 23
	☽⊼♄	6 38
	☽⚹♆	7 10
	☽☍♂	7 40
	☽⊼♇	7 32
	☽⚹♆	8 48
4	☉⚹☽	11am20
5 S	☽⚹♂	1am26
	☽⊼♅	2 3
	☽☍♇	2 18
	☽∠♆	4 19
	☽∥♂	6 34
	♀⊼♃	8 36
	☽□♃	8 46
	☽☍♀	8 47
6 Su	♂∠♄	2am26
	☽⊼♄	7 4
	☽⊼♆	7 42
	☽△♇	8 30
	☽⚹♆	11 20
	☽∠♀	6pm 7
7 M	☉☍☽	4am56
	☽∥♂	3 17
	☽⊼♂	12pm12
	☽☍♄	12 32
	☽⊼♅	1 39
	☽△♃	8 49
8 T	☽⚹♀	2am58
	☽△♄	6pm13
	☽⊼♆	6 58
	☽☍♅	7 23
	☽□♇	7 31
	☽☍♆	11 26
9 W	☽∥♅	1am48
	☽☍♃	2 13
	☉∥☽	6 38
	☽∥♆	7 24
	♆SR	8pm28
	☉☍☽	8 37
	☽⊼♂	9 29
	☽☍♆	11 58
10 Th	☽△♅	0am22
	☽∥♄	2 37
	☉∥♆	3 14
	☉☍♂	3 29
	☽⊼♃	7 13
	☽⊼♀	6pm34
	☽∥♆	6 56
11 F	☽☍♂	1am28
	☉∠☽	3 33
	☽⊼♄	3 44
	☽△♆	4 29
	☽☍♇	5 27
	☉☍♄	5 28
	☽∥♀	7 32
	☽⚹♆	8 49
	♀ ♎	4pm24
	☉☍♅	8 6
12 S	☽△♂	4am58
	☽□♅	8 31
	☽∠♇	9 29
	☉☍☽	9 53
	☽∠♆	12pm26
	☽⊼♃	3 36
	♃SR	5 6
	☽∥♃	8 49
13 Su	☽∥♇	2am 9
	♀☍♂	6 20
	☽⚹♀	8 6
	☽⊼♄	11 7
	☽☍♆	11 53
	☽0S	12pm24
	☽⚹♇	12 36
	☽☍♆	3 19
	☽∥♇	10 53
14 M	☽∥♃	3am48
	☽☍♂	10 16
	☽∠♀	1pm28
	☽⊼♄	1 53
	☽☍♅	2 59
	♀□♄	6 24
	☉☍☽	8 11
	☽⊼♃	9 32
15 T	♀△♆	3am45
	♅SD	6 34
	☽∥♀	7 38
	☉△♃	3pm24
	☽⊼♄	3 38
	☽☍♇	4 36
	☽⊼♆	4 43
	☽∠♅	5 2
	☽⚹♇	5 49
	☽☍♀	5 55
	☽□♆	6 43
	☽∥♆	10 30
	☽☍♃	11 28
16 W	♆⚹♀	1am10
	☽☍♂	1pm 2
	☽∥♄	4 20
	☽∠♆	6 9
	☽☍♅	6 25
	♆□♇	8 36
17 Th	☽△♃	0am43
	☉△☽	3 6
	☉∥☽	3 32
	☽∥♆	8 58
	☽∥♅	1pm30
	☽∠♂	1 31
	☽⊼♄	6 10
	☽⚹♆	6 57
	☽△♆	7 14
	☿☍♅	8 2
	☽⚹♇	8 3
18 F	☽□♀	0am19
	☿⊼♆	2 42
	☉☍☽	5 27
	☽⚹♂	1pm31
	☽☍♆	6 39
	☽⊼♅	7 30
	☽∠♇	8 23
	☿△♄	10 59
19 S	☽□♃	1am37
	☉☍☽	7 18
	☽⊼♆	3pm45
	☽⚹♄	6 31
	☽☍♆	7 18
	☽☍♇	8 27
20 Su	☽△♀	4am32
	☽☍♂	12pm47
	☽∠♄	6 28
	☽☍♅	7 29
21 M	☽☍♃	1am36
	☽☍♀	6 32
	☉☍☽	10 41
	☽⊼♆	3pm51
	☽☍♄	6 37
	☽⚹♆	7 26
	☽∠♅	7 39
	☽□♇	8 42
22 T	☽∥♅	1am45
	☽△♃	1 51
	☽∥♆	6 11
	☽⊼♀	8 56
	☽☍♂	12pm35
	☉☍☽	4 45
	☽∠♆	8 3
	☽☍♅	8 16
	☽∥♄	10 52
23 W	☽⊼♃	2am37
	☉ ♌	3 23
	☉☍♆	11 11
	☽∠♂	1pm17
	☽∥♆	3 13
	☽⊼♆	3 19
	☉☍☽	3 50
	☽⊼♄	8 31
	☽☍♆	9 22
	☿ ♋	9 54
	☽△♇	10 49
24 Th	♀△♂	0am54
	☿∠♀	2pm44
	☽☍♂	2 48
	☽☍♆	4 6
	☽⊼♀	4 18
	☉☍☽	7 52
	☽☍♅	11 48
25 F	☽☍♇	1am 9
	☽∥♀	1 43
	☽☍♃	6 35
	☽∥♃	11 15
	☽∥♇	3pm40
	☽△♆	3 48
26 S	☉△☽	1am10
	☽△♄	1 35
	☽□♆	2 50
	☽0N	3 34
	☽⊼♇	4 31
	☉△♄	11 12
	☽∥♇	1pm34
	☽∥♃	8 22
	☽☍♂	8 48
	☉⊼♆	11 17
27 Su	☉☍♅	2am 6
	☽∥♀	2 15
	☽⊼♀	4 40
	☽☍♄	6 11
	☽△♅	7 20
	☽☍♃	2pm33
	☉□♇	10 43
28 M	☽☍♆	0am11
	♀☍♅	10 32
	☽⊼♄	11 23
	☽△♆	12pm20
	☽☍♅	12 34
	☽☍♀	12 46
	☽⊼♇	2 16
	☉∥♄	3 17
	☉□☽	3 35
	☽∠♃	7 53
29 T	☽∥♆	2am 0
	♀∠♇	5 27
	☽△♂	6 33
	☉∥☽	2pm48
	☽∥♄	4 5
	☽☍♆	6 15
	☽⊼♅	6 29
	♀∥♃	8 53
	☽△♀	9 47
30 W	☽☍♃	1am53
	☽☍♆	9 59
	☽∥♆	12pm19
	☽☍♂	12 22
	☽∥♅	5 34
	☉☍♃	7 33
	☽⊼♄	11 38
31 Th	☽⊼♆	0am34
	☽⊼♇	2 42
	☉☍☽	9 20
	☽∠♆	3pm42
	♀⊼♃	4 26
	☽☍♂	6 24

LONGITUDE

DAY	SID. TIME	☉	☽	☽ 12 Hour	MEAN ☊	TRUE ☊	☿	♀	♂	♃	♄	♅	♆	♇
	h m s	° ' "	° ' "	° ' "	° '	° '	° '	° '	° '	° '	° '	° '	° '	° '
1 Th	10 33	10♓ 35 41	21♒ 20 28	27♒ 16 43	11♊ 21.3	11♊R32.1	3♓ 38.6	13♒ 18.7	21♏ 32.2	7♑ 50.4	16♏R21.5	13♐ 25.8	1♑ 7.9	1♏R56.8
2 F	10 39	11 35 54	3♓ 12 44	9♓ 8 41	11 18.1	11 18.0	5 46.6	14 32.7	22 11.6	7 59.8	16 20.9	13 26.7	1 9.0	1 55.9
3 Sa	10 43	12 36 6	15 4 43	21 0 59	11 14.9	11 3.0	7 33.7	15 46.8	22 30.7	8 9.2	16 20.2	13 27.6	1 10.0	1 55.0
4 Su	10 47 45	13 36 15	26 57 38	2♈ 34 52	11 11.8	10 48.3	9 25.8	17 0.8	22 49.4	8 18.4	16 19.4	13 28.4	1 11.0	1 54.1
5 M	10 51 41	14 36 23	8♈ 32 51	14 31 48	11 8.6	10 35.1	11 16.9	18 14.8	23 7.4	8 27.4				53.1
6 Tu	10 55 38	15 36 29	20											32.1
7 W	10 59 34	16 36 33	2											31.1
8 Th	11 3 31	17 36 34	13											30.0
9 F	11 7 27	18 36 34	27											48.9
10 Sa	11 11 24	19 36 32	10											47.8
11 Su	11 15 21	20 36 27	23											46.7
12 M	11 19 17	21 36 20	6											45.5
13 Tu	11 23 14	22 36 12	20											44.3
14 W	11 27 10	23 36 0	3											43.1
15 Th	11 31 7	24 35 47	20											41.9
16 F	11 35 3	25 35 31	3											40.6
17 Sa	11 39 0	26 35 13	20											39.3
18 Su	11 42	27 34 53	3											8.0
19 M	11 46	28 34 31	20											6.7
20 Tu	11 50	29 34 7	3											5.4
21 W	11 54	0♈ 33 42	19											4.0
22 Th	11 58	1 33 15	3											2.6
23 F	12	2 32 46	16											1.2
24 Sa	12 6	3 32 15	29											9.8
25 Su	12 10 32	4 31 42	12♑									13 32.6	1 24.3	1 28.3
26 M	12 14 29	5 31 8	24 23 13	0♒ 25 14	10 1.9	9 0.1	21 28.2	14 9.5	27 41.8	11 7.6	15 37.2	13 32.3	1 24.6	1 26.9
27 Tu	12 18 25	6 30 32	6♒ 24 57	12 22 53	9 58.7	8 56.0	23 7.2	15 23.5	27 48.7	11 13.7	15 34.2	13 31.8	1 24.8	1 25.4
28 W	12 22 22	7 29 54	18 19 36	24 15 27	9 55.5	8 49.4	24 41.8	16 37.6	27 55.0	11 19.6	15 31.2	13 31.3	1 25.1	1 23.9
29 Th	12 26 19	8 29 14	0♓ 10 53	6♓ 6 15	9 52.3	8 40.4	26 11.9	17 51.6	28 0.6	11 25.3	15 28.2	13 30.8	1 25.2	1 22.4
30 F	12 30 15	9 28 33	12 1 51	17 57 38	9 49.2	8 29.7	27 36.9	19 5.6	28 5.6	11 30.9	15 25.0	13 30.2	1 25.4	1 20.9
31 Sa	12 34 12	10♈ 27 49	23♓ 54 50	29♓ 52 39	9♊ 46.0	8♊ 18.2	28♈ 56.6	20♓ 19.6	28♏ 9.9	11♑ 36.3	15♏ 21.8	13♐ 29.6	1♑ 25.5	1♏ 19.5

The arrows indicate a change of sign in the Zodiac. The example is the Sun moving from Pisces into Aries.

DECLINATION and LATITUDE

DAY	☉ DECL	☽ DECL	☽ LAT	☽ 12hr DECL	☿ DECL	☿ LAT	♀ DECL	♀ LAT	♂ DECL	♂ LAT	♃ DECL	♃ LAT	♄ DECL	♄ LAT
1	7S36	18S49	4S41	16S37	11S60	2S 5	17S20	0S32	16S40	1N37	22S57	0N15	14S21	2N29
2	7 13	14 35	4 56	12 45	11 19	2 4	17 1	0 34	16 46	1 37	22 57	0 15	14 21	2 29
3	6 50	10 25	4 58	8 4	10 36	2 1	16 42	0 37	16 51	1 36	22 56	0 15	14 20	2 29
4	6 27	5 36	4 47	3 5	9 52	1 59	16 22	0 39	16 56	1 36	22 56	0 15	14 20	2 30
5	6 4	0 31	4 24	2N 3	9 7	1 55	16 2	0 42	17 1	1 36	22 55	0 15	14 19	2 30
6	5 40	4N37	3 49	7 9	8 20	1 52	15 41	0 44	17 6	1 35	22 55	0 15	14 19	2 30
7	5 17	9 38	3 3	12 3	7 33	1 47	15 19	0 47	17 10	1 35	22 54	0 15	14 18	2 30
8	4 54	14 21	2 8	16 32	6 44	1 42	14 58	0 49	17 15	1 34	22 54	0 15	14 18	2 30
9	4 30	18 34	1 6	20 24	5 54	1 37	14 36	0 51	17 20	1 34	22 53	0 15	14 17	2 31
10	4 7	22 1	0N 1	23 23	5 3	1 31	14 13	0 53	17 24	1 33	22 53	0 15	14 17	2 31
11	3 43	24 26	1 10	25 10	4 11	1 25	13 50	0 55	17 28	1 33	22 52	0 15	14 16	2 31
12	3 20	25 32	2 16	25 31	3 18	1 17	13 27	0 57	17 32	1 32	22 52	0 15	14 15	2 31
13	2 56	25 5	3 17	24 14	2 24	1 10	13 4	0 59	17 36	1 32	22 51	0 15	14 15	2 31
14	2 32	22 58	4 8	21 19	1 29	1 2	12 40	1 1	17 40	1 31	22 51	0 15	14 14	2 32
15	2 9	19 17	4 44	16 55	0 34	0 53	12 15	1 3	17 44	1 31	22 50	0 14	14 13	2 32
16	1 45	14 15	5 0	11 22	0N22	0 44	11 51	1 5	17 48	1 30	22 50	0 14	14 13	2 32
17	1 21	8 17	4 56	5 5	1 18	0 34	11 26	1 7	17 51	1 29	22 49	0 14	14 12	2 32
18	0 58	1 50	4 30	1S26	2 15	0 23	11 0	1 9	17 55	1 29	22 49	0 14	14 11	2 32
19	0 34	4S39	3 46	7 46	3 11	0 13	10 35	1 10	17 58	1 28	22 48	0 14	14 10	2 33
20	0 10	10 45	2 48	13 32	4 8	0 2	10 9	1 12	18 2	1 27	22 48	0 14	14 9	2 33
21	0N13	16 5	1 40	18 25	5 3	0N10	9 43	1 14	18 5	1 27	22 47	0 14	14 9	2 33
22	0 37	20 24	0 29	22 6	5 58	0 22	9 16	1 15	18 8	1 26	22 47	0 14	14 8	2 33
23	1 1	23 29	0S41	24 32	6 53	0 34	8 50	1 16	18 11	1 25	22 46	0 14	14 7	2 33
24	1 24	25 14	1 48	25 37	7 46	0 46	8 23	1 18	18 13	1 24	22 46	0 14	14 6	2 33
25	1 48	25 39	2 47	25 23	8 38	0 58	7 56	1 19	18 16	1 23	22 45	0 14	14 5	2 34
26	2 12	24 48	3 37	23 56	9 28	1 10	7 28	1 20	18 19	1 22	22 45	0 14	14 4	2 34
27	2 35	22 48	4 17	21 26	10 16	1 22	7 1	1 22	18 21	1 21	22 44	0 14	14 3	2 34
28	2 59	19 51	4 45	18 3	11 2	1 34	6 33	1 23	18 24	1 20	22 44	0 14	14 2	2 34
29	3 22	16 5	5 0	13 58	11 46	1 46	6 5	1 24	18 26	1 19	22 44	0 14	14 1	2 34
30	3 45	11 43	5 3	9 21	12 27	1 57	5 37	1 25	18 28	1 18	22 43	0 13	13 60	2 34
31	4N 9	6S53	4S52	4S22	13N 6	2N 8	5S 9	1S25	18S30	1N17	22S43	0N13	13S59	2N35

DAY	♅ DECL	♅ LAT	♆ DECL	♆ LAT	♇ DECL	♇ LAT
1	22S22	0N 3	22S16	1N11	4N 3	17N14
5	22 22	0 3	22 15	1 11	4 6	17 16
9	22 23	0 3	22 15	1 11	4 9	17 17
13	22 23	0 3	22 15	1 11	4 12	17 19
17	22 23	0 3	22 15	1 11	4 15	17 20
21	22 23	0 3	22 15	1 11	4 18	17 22
25	22 23	0 3	22 15	1 11	4 21	17 23
29	22S23	0N 3	22S15	1N12	4N24	17N24

☽ PHENOMENA

dy	hr	
2	11	APOGE
16	21	PERIG
29	16	APOGE

MAX/0 DECL dy	hr	° '
5	2	0
12	5	25N34
18	7	0
24	20	25S40

MAX/0 LAT dy	hr	° '
2	16	4S59
10	0	0
16	7	5N 1
22	10	0
29	17	5S 3

VOID OF COURSE ☽

LAST ASPT	☽ INGRESS
1 1am 6	1 ♓ 5pm30
3 5pm26	4 ♈ 6am 5
5 8pm55	6 ♉ 6pm10
8 5pm25	9 ♊ 4am30
11 4am26	11 ♋ 11am49
13 11am22	13 ♌ 3pm22
15 9am14	15 ♍ 3pm48
17 10am11	17 ♎ 2pm52
18 12pm19	19 ♏ 2pm49
21 12pm32	21 ♐ 5pm42
22 10pm35	24 ♑ 0am37
26 6am38	26 ♒ 11am10
28 7pm34	28 ♓ 11pm38
31 8am36	31 ♈ 12pm15

dy	hr	mn	PHASE
2	18	32	12♓22 ●
10	18	28	20♊23 ☽
17	10	11	27♍ 1 ○
24	7	59	3♑52 ☾

DAILY ASPECTARIAN

Day	Aspect	Time
1 Th	☽□♂	1am 6
	☿⚹♅	2 21
	☽∠♃	3 4
	☽☍♀	10 30
	☽☍♂	1pm25
	☽⚹♆	7 49
	☽△♇	9 25
2 F	☽☍♄	3am16
	☽⚹♆	6 7
	☽⚹♃	9 48
	☿☍♂	3pm 7
	☉⚹☽	6 32
	☽□♅	8 43
	☽☍♆	11 9
3 Sa	☽⚹♀	1am35
	☽△♄	2 32
	☽⊼♇	3 43
	☿∠♆	7 38
	☿⚹♃	8 0
	☿□♄	10 44
	☽△♂	3pm26
	☉☍☽	7 35
	☉□♅	8 49
4 Su	☽☍♇	7am11
	☽□♆	8 31
	☽⊼♄	8 47
	☽⚹♇	9 57
	☽∠♀	11 22
	☽⊼♂	10pm27
	☽□♃	11 8
5 M	☽0N	2am27
	☽⚹♆	5 43
	☽△♅	9 15
	☉⚹☽	12pm32
	☽⚹♄	2 52
	☽⚹♀	8 55
	☽☍♇	9 40
6 T	☿□♅	4am26
	☉☍☽	4 39
	☽⚹♂	5 14
	☽⊼♅	3pm12
	☽☍♆	3 17
	☉△♄	4 4
	☽∠♆	5 10
	☽△♆	8 35
	☉⚹☽	9 6
	☽⚹♇	9 50
7 W	☉⊼♇	5am42
	♂∠♃	6 30
	☽△♃	11 33
	☿△♄	3pm26
	☽⚹♅	8 44
	☿⊼♇	10 41
	☽☍♄	11 41
8 Th	☽⊼♆	2am 3
	☽⚹♄	2 4
	☽☍♀	3 1
	☽⚹♆	4 1
	☉⚹☽	5 7
	♀∠♆	5 27
	☽□♀	2pm32
	☽☍♂	4 23
	☽⊼♃	5 2
	☽⚹♂	5 23
	☉⚹♆	5 33
9 F	☽⚹♆	6am34
	☽⚹♇	7 36
	♀∠♃	6pm32
	♀☍♄	8 17
	☉☍♇	8 55
	☽⚹♃	9 47
10 Sa	☽☍♆	1am54
	☽☍♅	2 57
	♀□♂	3 9
	☽⚹♅	5 54
	☽△♃	7 16
	☽⚹♄	10 49
	☽⊼♇	11 34
	☉□☽	6pm28
	☽□♆	10 33
	♆☍♇	11 58
11 Su	☽⚹♂	2am33
	☽△♀	4 26
	☽⊼♄	1pm53
	☽⚹♆	2 6
	☽△♇	2 57
	☉☍♆	10 15
12 M	☽⚹♃	4am31
	♀△♂	5 4
	☽⊼♂	5 37
	☽⊼♀	9 31
	☽⚹♅	11 33
	☽△♄	4pm 0
13 T	☉△☽	3am13
	☽△♂	7 39
	☽△♆	11 22
	☽⊼♅	12pm57
	☽⚹♀	1 23
	☽⚹♆	5 33
	☽□♇	6 13
14 W	☽☍♃	1am 0
	☽☍♅	4 32
	☽☍♆	5 31
	☉☍☽	5 54
	☽⚹♃	7 24
	♀ ♓	12pm36
	☽△♅	1 33
	☽⊼♆	3 47
	☿ ♈	4 28
	☽□♄	5 36
	☽⊼♆	6 1
	♆⚹♀	10 50
15 Th	☿⊼♄	5am15
	☽⊼♃	7 43
	☉⚹☽	7 43
	☽☍♂	7 53
	☿□♆	8 36
	☽□♂	9 14
	☿⚹♇	12pm52
	☿0N	2 29
	♀⚹♆	2 35
	☽△♆	5 54
	☽⚹♀	6 12
	☽⚹♇	6 27
	☽⚹♆	7 18
	♀△♇	9 16
16 F	☽☍♄	0am11
	☽△♃	7 34
	☽☍♀	10 49
	☉△♂	12pm16
	☽□♅	1 7
	☽⚹♄	4 57
	☽∠♇	5 58
17 Sa	☉☍♆	0am54
	☽⚹♂	9 2
	☉⚹☽	10 1
	☽☍♇	3p
	☽∠♄	4
	☽□♆	5
	☽⚹♇	5
	☽⚹♀	9
	☽☍♆	10 4
18 Su	☽⚹♆	1am24
	☉☍☽	3 24
	♅SR	6 21
	☽0S	6 43
	☽□♃	7 4
	☽∠♂	9 0
	☉☍☽	9 40
	☽⚹♅	12pm19
	☽⚹♄	4 6
	☽☍♆	5 34
	☽☍♇	10 34
	☽⊼♀	11 24
19 M	☽⚹♂	9am24
	☽∠♅	12pm29
	☉⚹☽	1 24
	☽⚹♆	5 5
	☽⊼♇	5 27
	☽☍♀	9 42
	♆⊼♃	11 52
20 T	☽△♀	2am 9
	♆☍♇	4 16
	☽⚹♃	8 14
	☽⚹♆	9 28
	☉ ♈	10 26
	☽⚹♅	1pm22
	☽☍♄	2 48
	☉☍☽	4 12
	☽∠♄	5 15
	☿⊼♂	5 54
	☽∠♆	6 8
21 W	☉⚹♄	6am33
	☽∠♃	10 3
	☽☍♂	10 27
	☽⚹♂	12pm32
	♆△♅	2 31
	☽⊼♆	3 16
	☉□♆	7 58
	☽⚹♆	8 9
	☉△☽	8 10
	☽⚹♇	8 26
	☉⚹♇	11 45
22 Th	☽□♀	11am11
	☽⚹♃	12pm55
	☽☍♆	1 11
	☽☍♅	2 18
	☽☍♃	5 32
	☽⚹♅	6 0
	♆⚹♄	6 48
	☽⚹♄	10 2
	☽△♆	10 35
	☽∠♇	11 26
23 F	♀⚹♃	7am31
	☽⚹♂	7pm43
24 Sa	☽∠♄	1am55
	☽⚹♆	3 17
	☽⚹♇	3 27
	☉□☽	7 59
	♆☍♀	11 10
	☽∠♃	9pm46
25 Su	☽∠♂	0am46
	☽⚹♀	1 38
	☽⚹♅	2 41
	☽⚹♄	6 48
	♀□♅	11 59
	☽□♆	5pm16
26 M	☽⚹♂	6am38
	☽∠♅	8 14
	☽∠♀	10 34
	☽⚹♆	1pm59
	☽□♇	2 1
27 T	☉⚹☽	0am12
	☽☍♃	0 38
	♀△♄	3 20
	☽☍♅	5 57
	☽☍♆	5 11
	♆⊼♇	7 52
	☽⚹♃	9 45
	☽⚹♅	2pm18
	☽□♄	6 21
	♀⊼♇	7 39
	☽∠♆	8 8
	☽⚹♀	8 10
28 W	☉∠☽	9am12
	☽☍♂	9 42
	☽⚹♆	2pm47
	☽∠♃	4 19
	☽□♂	7 34
29 Th	☽△♇	2am25
	☽⚹♆	2 31
	☽☍♄	11 46
	☉⚹☽	6pm21
	☽☍♆	8 38
	☽⚹♃	10 57
30 F	☽∠♆	1am20
	☽□♅	2 59
	☽△♄	6 49
	☽⊼♇	8 43
	♆⊼♂	8 57
	♆⊼♅	3pm45
	☽⚹♀	3 56
31 Sa	☽△♂	8am36
	☽☍♀	9 12
	☽⚹♆	11 19
	☽☍♇	11 43
	☉☍☽	12pm 7
	☽⊼♄	12 55
	☽⚹♇	2 52
	☽□♆	3 6
	☉☍♇	5 44
	☿ ♉	8 27

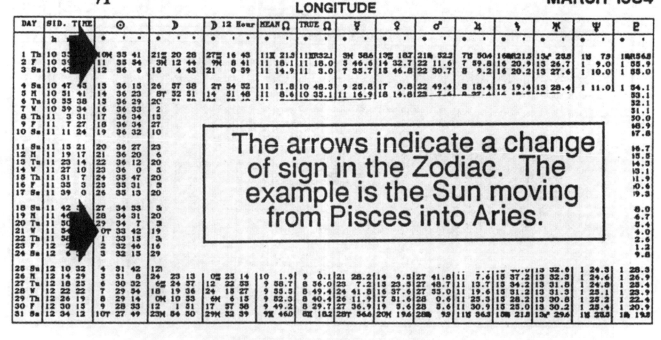

LONGITUDE

DAY	SID. TIME	☉	☽	☽ 12 Hour	MEAN ☊	TRUE ☊	☿	♀	♂	♃	♄	♅	♆	♇
	h m s	° ' "	° ' "	° ' "	° '	° '	° '	° '	° '	° '	° '	° '	° '	° '
1 Tu	12 36 14	10♈ 58 8	0♑ 20 2	7♑ 23 9	1♉ 3.4	0♉R 6.7	18♓ 3.2	28♈ 20.2	1♑ 53.6	9♓ 11.9	9♐R34.3	22♐R21.9	5♑ 48.0	6♏R40.1
2 W	12 40 11	11 57 20	14 22 43	21 18 36	1 0.2	0 7.0	18 14.8	29 34.3	2 25.2	9 25.2	9 33.0	22 21.7	5 48.2	6 38.7
3 Th	12 44 7	12 56 31	28 10 45	4♒ 59 9	0 57.1	0 6.5	18 31.6	0♉ 48.3	2 54.7	9 38.4	9 31.6	22 21.4	5 48.4	6 37.2
4 F	12 48 4	13 55 40	11♒ 43 49	18 24 46	0 53.9	0 5.1	18 53.3	2 2.3	3 24.0	9 51.6	9 30.1	22 21.0	5 48.6	6 35.6
5 Sa	12 52 0	14 54 47	25 2 3	1♓ 33 44	0 50.7	0 3.2	19 19.6	3 16.3	3 53.1	10 4.8	9 28.6	22 20.6	5 48.7	6 34.1
6 Su	12 55 57	15 53 52	8♓ 3 53	14 32 34	0 47.5	0 1.1	19 50.4	4 30.2	4 22.0	10 17.8	9 26.9	22 20.1	5 48.7	6 32.6
7 M	12 59 53	16 52 53	20 55 51	27 15 51	0 44.4	29♈ 59.1	20 25.3	5 44.1	4 50.7	10 30.8	9 25.1	22 19.6	5R 48.8	6 31.0
8 Tu	13 3 50	17 51 37	3♈ 32 39	9♈ 46 22	0 41.2	29 57.5	21 4.3	6 58.0	5 19.2	10 43.8	9 23.3	22 19.1	5 48.8	6 29.4
9 W	13 7 46	18 50 56	15 57 7	22 3 4	0 38.0	29 56.5	21 47.0	8 11.8	5 47.5	10 56.6	9 21.3	22 18.4	5 48.7	6 27.8
10 Th	13 11 43	19 49 53	28 10 23	4♉ 13 17	0 34.8	29D 56.2	22 33.3	9 25.6	6 15.6	11 9.5	9 19.3	22 17.8	5 48.7	6 26.2
11 F	13 15 40	20 48 49	10♉ 13 59	16 12 45	0 31.7	29 56.5	23 23.0	10 39.4	6 43.4	11 22.2	9 17.1	22 17.1	5 48.6	6 24.6
12 Sa	13 19 36	21 47 42	22 9 54	28 5 45	0 28.5	29 57.1	24 16.0	11 53.1	7 11.1	11 34.9	9 14.9	22 16.3	5 48.4	6 23.0
13 Su	13 23 33	22 46 33	4♊ 0 42	9♊ 53 7	0 25.3	29 58.0	25 12.0	13 6.8	7 38.4	11 47.5	9 12.6	22 15.5	5 48.3	6 21.4
14 M	13 27 29	23 45 22	15 49 29	21 44 15	0 22.1	29 58.8	26 10.9	14 20.5	8 5.6	12 0.1	9 10.2	22 14.6	5 48.1	6 19.7
15 Tu	13 31 26	24 44 9	27 39 35	3♋ 37 1	0 18.9	29 59.5	27 12.7	15 34.1	8 32.5	12 12.5	9 7.8	22 13.7	5 47.9	6 18.1
16 W	13 35 22	25 42 54	9♋ 36 6	15 37 43	0 15.8	29 59.9	28 17.0	16 47.7	8 59.1	12 24.9	9 5.2	22 12.8	5 47.6	6 16.5
17 Th	13 39 19	26 41 36	21 42 27	27 50 51	0 12.6	0♉R 0.1	29 24.0	18 1.3	9 25.5	12 37.2	9 2.6	22 11.8	5 47.3	6 14.8
18 F	13 43 15	27 40 16	4♌ 3 29	10♌ 20 32	0 9.4	0 0.0	0♈ 33.4	19 14.8	9 51.7	12 49.5	8 59.9	22 10.7	5 47.0	6 13.1
19 Sa	13 47 12	28 38 54	16 43 31	23 11 51	0 6.2	29♈ 59.9	1 45.1	20 28.3	10 17.6	13 1.7	8 57.1	22 9.7	5 46.6	6 11.3
20 Su	13 51 9	29 37 30	29 46 15	6♍ 26 39	0 3.1	29 59.7	2 59.1	21 41.7	10 43.2	13 13.7	8 54.2	22 8.5	5 46.3	6 9.8
21 M	13 55 5	0♉ 36 4	13♍ 14 14	20 8 3	29♈ 59.3	29 59.7	4 15.4	22 55.1	11 8.3	13 25.8	8 51.3	22 7.3	5 45.8	6 8.1
22 Tu	13 59 2	1 34 35	27 8 21	4♎ 14 54	29 56.7	29 59.7	5 33.7	24 8.5	11 33.6	13 37.7	8 48.2	22 6.1	5 45.4	6 6.4
23 W	14 2 58	2 33 4	11♎ 27 17	18 44 58	29 53.5	29 59.9	6 54.2	25 21.8	11 58.3	13 49.5	8 45.1	22 4.8	5 44.9	6 4.7
24 Th	14 6 55	3 31 31	26 7 15	3♏ 33 16	29 50.3	0♉R 0.0	8 16.7	26 35.1	12 22.8	14 1.3	8 42.0	22 3.5	5 44.4	6 3.0
25 F	14 10 51	4 29 57	11♏ 2 4	18 32 37	29 47.2	0 0.0	9 41.2	27 48.3	12 47.0	14 13.0	8 38.7	22 2.2	5 43.8	6 1.3
26 Sa	14 14 48	5 28 20	26 3 51	3♐ 34 38	29 44.0	29♈ 59.8	11 7.7	29 1.5	13 10.9	14 24.5	8 35.4	22 0.8	5 43.3	5 59.6
27 Su	14 18 44	6 26 42	11♐ 3 57	18 30 48	29 40.8	29 59.3	12 36.1	0♊ 14.7	13 34.4	14 36.1	8 32.1	21 59.3	5 42.7	5 57.9
28 M	14 22 41	7 25 3	25 54 18	3♑ 13 42	29 37.6	29 58.6	14 6.4	1 27.8	13 57.7	14 47.5	8 28.6	21 57.9	5 42.1	5 56.2
29 Tu	14 26 38	8 23 22	10♑ 28 23	17 37 54	29 34.5	29 57.9	15 38.6	2 40.9	14 20.6	14 58.8	8 25.1	21 56.3	5 41.4	5 54.3
30 W	14 30 34	9♉ 21 39	24♑ 41 55	1♒ 40 16	29♈ 31.3	29♈ 57.2	17♈ 12.6	3♊ 53.9	14♑ 43.1	15♓ 10.0	8♐ 21.6	21♐ 54.8	5♑ 40.7	5♏ 52.9

DECLINATION and LATITUDE

DAY	☉ DECL	☽ DECL	☽ LAT	☽ 12hr DECL	☿ DECL	☿ LAT	♀ DECL	♀ LAT	♂ DECL	♂ LAT	♃ DECL	♃ LAT	♄ DECL	♄ LAT
1	4N20	28S 1	4S34	28S 3	4S41	0N 3	10N19	0S37	23S34	0S 8	8S57	0S54	19S56	1N59
2	4 44	27 42	5 4	26 53	4 49	0S11	10 47	0 35	23 35	0 10	8 52	0 54	19 55	1 59
3	5 7	25 41	5 16	24 6	4 55	0 24	11 15	0 32	23 36	0 11	8 47	0 54	19 55	1 59
4	5 30	22 13	5 9	20 4	4 58	0 37	11 43	0 30	23 37	0 13	8 42	0 54	19 55	1 59
5	5 53	17 40	4 46	15 6	4 59	0 49	12 11	0 28	23 38	0 14	8 38	0 54	19 54	1 60
6	6 15	12 23	4 9	9 33	4 58	1 1	12 38	0 25	23 38	0 16	8 33	0 54	19 54	1 60
7	6 38	6 39	3 19	3 42	4 54	1 12	13 5	0 23	23 39	0 18	8 28	0 54	19 54	1 60
8	7 1	0 48	2 21	2N12	4 48	1 22	13 31	0 20	23 40	0 19	8 23	0 55	19 53	1 60
9	7 23	5N 6	1 17	7 56	4 40	1 32	13 58	0 18	23 40	0 21	8 18	0 55	19 53	1 60
10	7 45	10 40	0 10	13 16	4 30	1 41	14 24	0 15	23 41	0 23	8 14	0 55	19 52	2 0
11	8 8	15 47	0N57	18 7	4 18	1 50	14 49	0 13	23 41	0 25	8 9	0 55	19 52	2 0
12	8 30	20 15	2 0	22 11	4 5	1 58	15 15	0 10	23 42	0 27	8 4	0 55	19 52	2 0
13	8 52	23 52	2 58	25 18	3 49	2 5	15 40	0 7	23 42	0 29	7 60	0 55	19 51	2 0
14	9 13	26 28	3 48	27 20	3 32	2 12	16 4	0 5	23 42	0 30	7 55	0 56	19 51	2 1
15	9 35	27 54	4 29	28 8	3 13	2 18	16 28	0 2	23 42	0 32	7 50	0 56	19 50	2 1
16	9 56	28 3	4 58	27 37	2 52	2 23	16 52	0N 1	23 43	0 34	7 46	0 56	19 50	2 1
17	10 18	26 52	5 14	25 46	2 30	2 28	17 15	0 3	23 43	0 36	7 41	0 56	19 49	2 1
18	10 39	24 22	5 17	22 39	2 6	2 32	17 38	0 6	23 43	0 38	7 37	0 56	19 49	2 1
19	10 60	20 39	5 4	18 23	1 41	2 36	18 0	0 9	23 43	0 41	7 32	0 56	19 48	2 1
20	11 21	15 51	4 36	13 6	1 14	2 39	18 22	0 11	23 43	0 43	7 28	0 57	19 48	2 1
21	11 41	10 9	3 52	7 2	0 47	2 41	18 44	0 14	23 43	0 45	7 23	0 57	19 47	2 1
22	12 1	3 47	2 53	0 26	0 17	2 43	19 3	0 17	23 43	0 47	7 19	0 57	19 47	2 1
23	12 22	2S39	1 41	6S23	0N13	2 45	19 25	0 19	23 43	0 49	7 14	0 57	19 46	2 1
24	12 42	9 43	0 21	13 1	0 45	2 45	19 45	0 22	23 43	0 52	7 10	0 57	19 45	2 1
25	13 1	16 6	1S 1	18 58	1 18	2 46	20 4	0 25	23 43	0 54	7 6	0 57	19 43	2 1
26	13 21	21 32	2 20	23 45	1 52	2 45	20 23	0 27	23 43	0 56	7 1	0 58	19 44	2 2
27	13 40	25 33	3 29	26 54	2 27	2 44	20 42	0 30	23 43	0 59	6 57	0 58	19 44	2 2
28	13 59	27 46	4 23	28 8	3 4	2 43	20 59	0 33	23 43	1 1	6 53	0 58	19 43	2 2
29	14 18	27 60	4 59	27 24	3 41	2 41	21 17	0 35	23 43	1 4	6 49	0 58	19 43	2 2
30	14N37	26S22	5S16	24S56	4N19	2S38	21N33	0N38	23S43	1S 6	6S45	0S58	19S42	2N 2

DAY	♅ DECL	♅ LAT	♆ DECL	♆ LAT	♇ DECL	♇ LAT
1	23S18	0S 5	22S14	1N 5	2N24	17N 3
5	23 18	0 5	22 14	1 5	2 27	17 4
9	23 18	0 5	22 14	1 5	2 29	17 5
13	23 18	0 5	22 13	1 6	2 32	17 5
17	23 18	0 5	22 13	1 6	2 34	17 5
21	23 17	0 5	22 13	1 6	2 36	17 6
25	23 17	0 5	22 13	1 6	2 38	17 6
29	23S17	0S 5	22S13	1N 6	2N40	17N 6

☽ PHENOMENA

dy	hr	
13	12	APOGE
25	18	PERIG

MAX/0 DECL

dy	hr	° '
1	8	28S 7
8	3	0
15	15	28N 9
22	14	0
28	15	28S 8

MAX/0 LAT

dy	hr	° '
3	3	5S16
10	3	0
17	16	5N17
24	6	0
30	9	5S17

VOID OF COURSE ☽

LAST ASPT		☽ INGRESS		
2	6am48	3	♒	3am12
4	7pm 7	5	♓	9am 4
7	2am38	7	♈	5pm13
9	12pm26	10	♉	3am37
12	4am36	12	♊	3pm32
14	11pm 0	15	♋	4am43
17	10am36	17	♌	4pm11
19	11pm43	20	♍	0am28
21	6pm24	22	♎	4am31
23	5pm25	24	♏	6am16
26	5am 9	26	♐	6[illegible]
27	5pm36	28	♑	6[illegible]
29	9am43	30	♒	9[illegible]

dy	hr	mn	PHAS[illegible]
1	19	31	11♑46 ☾
9	6	9	19♈ 6 ● P
17	10	36	27♋ 8 ☽
24	12	47	4♏ 3 ○ T

DAILY ASPECTARIAN

1 Tu: ☽☌♂ 2am48; ☽☌♆ 9 18; ☽⚹♇ 10 45; ☽⚹♃ 3pm21; ☽⚻♄ 3 43; ☉□☽ 7 31
2 W: ☽⚹♆ 6am48; ☉∥☿ 7 56; ♀ ♉ 8 20; ♃□♄ 12pm48; ☽⚻♅ 1 49; ☽∠♄ 5 37; ☽∠♃ 5 42
3 Th: ☽□♀ 3am 5; ☽⚻♂ 8 39; ☽∠♆ 9 39; ☽⚻☿ 1pm27; ☽□♇ 2 32; ☽∥♂ 3 22; ☽∠♅ 4 12; ☽∥♅ 5 22; ☽⚹♄ 8 2; ☽⚻♃ 8 36; ☽∥♆ 11 37
4 F: ☉⚹☽ 4am15; ☽∠♂ 12pm26; ☽∥♄ 12 47; ☽⚻☿ 1 17; ☽∠☿ 4 20; ☽⚹♅ 7 7
5 S: ☉∠☽ 9am38; ☽⚹♀ 4pm39; ☽⚹♂ 4 30; ♀△♂ 7 40; ☽⚹♆ 7 46; ☽△♇ 9 8; ☽∥♀ 11 0
6 Su: ☽□♄ 2am30; ☽☌♃ 4 9; ☿∠♀ 12pm 7; ☉⚻☽ 3 43; ☽∥♃ 4 25; ☽☌☿ 11 0; ☽∠♀ 11 35
7 M: ☉∥☽ 0am 4; ☽⚼♇ 1 6; ♀△♆ 1 31; ☽□♅ 2 38; ☽∥☿ 7 15; ♆SR 1pm10; ♀☍♇ 2 53; ☽∥♇ 3 1
8 Tu: ☽0N 3am 2; ☽□♂ 3 33; ☽□♆ 4 22; ☽⚹♇ 5 39; ☿⚼♅ 6 48; ☽⚹♀ 7 18; ☽△♄ 11 14; ☽∥♇ 1pm10; ☿⚼♇ 1 32; ☽⚻♃ 2 6; ☽∥☿ 10 16
9 W: ♂☌♆ 1am 2; ☉☌☽ 6 9; ☉∥☽ 10 21; ☽⚻☿ 12pm10; ☽△♅ 12 26; ☽∥♃ 1 26; ☿□♅ 4 15; ☽⚼♄ 4 25; ☽∠♃ 7 57; ♀⚻♄ 10 0
10 Th: ♂⚹♇ 8am40; ☽△♆ 3pm10; ☽☍♇ 4 23; ☽△♂ 4 42; ☽⚼♅ 6 7; ☽∥♀ 6 49; ☽∠☿ 8 1; ☽⚻♄ 10 7
11 F: ☽☌♀ 0am37; ☉△♃ 1; ☽⚹♃ 2; ♀⚹♃ 4; ☽⚼♆ 9; ☽∥♄ 9; ☉⚻☽ 11
12 S: ☽⚼♂ 0; ☽⚻♅ 0; ☽⚹☿ 4; ☉△♅ 11; ☽∥♆ 12; ☽∥♅ 7 43; ☽∥♂ 10 42
13 Su: ☽⚹♆ 3am38; ☽⚹♇ 4 45; ☽⚻♂ 7 40; ☉∠☽ 8 20; ☽⚻♄ 10 32; ☽□♃ 4pm 3; ☽⚻♀ 8 38
14 M: ☉⚼♄ 9am43; ☽⚼♇ 11 9; ☽⚻♅ 1pm 1; ☉⚹☽ 5 32; ☽□☿ 11 0
15: ☽∠♀ 6am32
S: ☽△♄ 4 39
☽0S 1 30
F: ☽△♃ 5 9
28: ☽⚹♀ 9am56
☉□☽ 10 36; ☽⚼♃ 11 45; ☿ ♈ 12pm34; ☽△☿ 4 33
18 F: ☽⚻♆ 3am18; ☽□♇ 4 8; ☉∠♃ 4 46; ☽∥♂ 4 49; ☽⚼♅ 5 58; ☽∥♅ 7 47; ☽△♄ 9 24; ☽⚻♂ 11 28; ☽∥♆ 2pm44; ☽⚻♃ 4 37
19: ☽⚼☿ 0am 3
☽⚹♇ 11 28; ☽□♄ 4pm18; ☉∥☽ 6 11; ☽△♂ 8 12
21 M: ☽⚻♃ 0am20; ☉⚼☽ 4 27; ☽∥♃ 10 46; ☽∠♇ 1pm42; ☽□♅ 3 24; ☽△♀ 6 24
22 T: ♆□☿ 3am29; ☽∥♇ 4 11; ☉⚻☽ 8 4; ☿⚻♇ 9 37; ☽∥☿ 1pm29
☽⚹♅ 5 23; ☽∠♄ 8 3
24 Th: ♀☍♄ 0am30; ☽⚻♀ 0 49; ☽⚼♃ 4 43; ☿△♄ 6 58; ☉∥☽ 11 23; ☉☍☽ 12pm47; ☽⚹♆ 3 30; ☽☍♇ 3 59; ☽∠♅ 5 36; ☽⚻♄ 8 11; ☽⚻☿ 9 37; ♀⚼♂ 11 22
25: ☽⚹♂ 2am52
☉☍♇ 12pm30; ☽⚻♆ 3 25; ☽⚻♇ 3 30; ☉⚻☽ 4 5; ♀ ♊ 7 11; ☽☌♄ 7 37
27 Su: ☽△☿ 2am44; ☽⚻♂ 4 8; ☽□♃ 5 46; ☿∥♇ 8 10; ☉⚼♅ 1pm 6; ☽∠♇ 3 56; ☽☌♅ 5 36; ☉⚼☽ 5 56; ☿□♂ 8 36
☽∠♄ 9 43
30 W: ☽∠♃ 9am32; ☽△♀ 5pm25; ☽⚻♆ 6 57; ☽□♇ 7 17; ☽∥♂ 8 26; ☽∠♅ 9 6; ☽∥♅ 11 18; ☽⚹♄ 11 34

The arrows indicate a lunar and a solar eclipse.

LONGITUDE

DAY	SID. TIME	☉	☽	☽ 12 Hour	MEAN ☊	TRUE ☊	☿	♀	♂	♃	♄	♅	♆	♇
	h m s	° ' "	° ' "	° ' "	° '	° '	° '	° '	° '	° '	° '	° '	° '	° '
1 Th	10 35 55	10♓ 35 41	21♒ 20 28	27♒ 16 43	11♊ 21.3	11♊R32.1	3♓ 58.6	13♒ 18.7	21♏ 52.2	7♑ 50.4	16♏R21.5	13♐ 25.8	1♑ 7.9	1♏R56.8
2 F	10 39 52	11 35 54	3♓ 12 44	9♓ 8 41	11 18.1	11 18.0	5 46.6	14 32.7	22 11.6	7 59.8	16 20.9	13 26.7	1 9.0	1 55.9
3 Sa	10 43 48	12 36 6	15 4 43	21 0 39	11 14.9	11 3.0	7 35.7	15 46.8	22 30.7	8 9.2	16 20.2	13 27.6	1 10.0	1 55.0
4 Su	10 47 45	13 36 15	26 57 38	2♈ 54 52	11 11.8	10 48.3	9 25.8	17 0.8	22 49.4	8 18.4	16 19.4	13 28.4	1 11.0	1 54.1
5 M	10 51 41	14 36 23	8♈ 52 51	14 51 48	11 8.6	10 35.1	11 16.9	18 14.8	23 7.6	8 27.4	16 18.5	13 29.1	1 11.9	1 53.1
6 Tu	10 55 38	15 36 29	20 51 59	26 53 40	[illegible].4	10 24.5	13 9.1	19 28.9	23 25.3	8 36.4	16 17.4	13 29.8	1 12.9	1 52.1
7 W	10 59 34	16 36 33	2♉ 57 12	9♉ 2 38	[illegible]2	10 16.8	15 2.2	20 42.9	23 42.9	8 45.2	16 16.3	13 30.4	1 13.8	1 51.1
8 Th	11 3 31	17 36 34	15 11 23	21 22 3[illegible]	[illegible]	10 12.3	16 56.4	21 56.9	23 59.9	8 53.9	16 15.1	13 31.0	1 14.6	1 50.0
9 F	11 7 27	18 36 34	27 38 4	3♊ 37 2[illegible]	[illegible]	10D 10.3	18 51.5	23 11.0	24 16.5	9 2.5	16 13.8	13 31.5	1 15.4	1 48.9
10 Sa	11 11 24	19 36 32	10♊ 21 16	16 50 2[illegible]	[illegible]	10R 10.1	20 47.4	24 25.0	24 32.6	9 10.9	16 12.4	13 32.0	1 16.2	1 47.8
11 Su	11 15 21	20 36 27	23 25 17	0♋ 6 20	[illegible].5	10 10.2	22 44.2	25 39.0	24 48.3	9 19.3	16 10.9	13 32.4	1 17.0	1 46.7
12 M	11 19 17	21 36 20	6♋ 53 58	13 48 28	10 [illegible]6.3	10 9.3	24 41.7	26 53.1	25 3.5	9 27.5	16 9.2	13 32.8	1 17.8	1 45.5
13 Tu	11 23 14	22 36 12	20 50 2	27 58 37	10 43.2	10 6.8	26 39.8	28 7.1	25 18.2	9 35.5	16 7.5	13 33.1	1 18.5	1 44.3
14 W	11 27 10	23 36 0	3♌ 14 3	12♌ 33 34	10 40.0	10 1.6	28 38.5	29 21.1	25 32.5	9 43.5	16 5.8	13 33.3	1 19.1	1 43.1
15 Th	11 31 7	24 35 47	20 3 30	27 35 59	10 36.8	9 53.8	0♈ 37.4	0♓ 35.2	25 46.2	9 51.3	16 3.9	13 33.5	1 19.8	1 41.9
16 F	11 35 3	25 35 31	5♍ 12 15	12♍ 50 59	10 33.6	9 44.0	2 36.4	1 49.2	25 59.5	9 58.9	16 1.9	13 33.7	1 20.4	1 40.6
17 Sa	11 39 0	26 35 13	20 30 49	28 10 15	10 30.5	9 33.2	4 35.3	3 3.2	26 12.2	10 6.4	15 59.8	13 33.8	1 20.9	1 39.3
18 Su	11 42 56	27 34 53	5♎ 47 50	13♎ 22 10	10 27.3	9 22.7	6 33.9	4 17.3	26 24.4	10 13.8	15 57.6	13R 33.8	1 21.5	1 38.0
19 M	11 46 53	28 34 31	20 52 1	28 16 20	10 24.1	9 13.8	8 31.8	5 31.3	26 36.1	10 21.0	15 55.4	13 33.8	1 22.0	1 36.7
20 Tu	11 50 50	29 34 7	5♏ 34 16	12♏ 45 14	10 20.9	9 7.2	10 28.8	6 45.3	26 47.2	10 28.1	15 53.0	13 33.7	1 22.5	1 35.4
21 W	11 54 46	0♈ 33 42	19 48 52	26 45 2	10 17.8	9 3.2	12 24.4	7 59.3	26 57.8	10 35.1	15 50.6	13 33.6	1 22.9	1 34.0
22 Th	11 58 43	1 33 15	3♐ 33 45	10♐ 15 16	10 14.6	9D 1.6	14 18.3	9 13.4	27 7.8	10 41.9	15 48.1	13 33.4	1 23.3	1 32.6
23 F	12 2 39	2 32 46	16 49 33	23 18 10	10 11.4	9 1.6	16 10.1	10 27.4	27 17.2	10 48.6	15 45.5	13 33.2	1 23.7	1 31.2
24 Sa	12 6 36	3 32 15	29 40 32	5♑ 57 37	10 8.2	9R 2.1	17 59.2	11 41.4	27 26.0	10 55.1	15 42.8	13 33.0	1 24.0	1 29.8
25 Su	12 10 32	4 31 42	12♑ 10 1	18 18 20	10 5.0	9 1.9	19 45.5	12 55.5	27 34.2	11 1.4	15 40.0	13 32.6	1 24.3	1 28.3
26 M	12 14 29	5 31 8	24 23 13	0♒ 25 14	10 1.9	9 0.1	21 28.2	14 9.5	27 41.8	11 7.6	15 37.2	13 32.3	1 24.6	1 26.9
27 Tu	12 18 25	6 30 32	6♒ 24 57	12 22 53	9 58.7	8 56.0	23 7.2	15 23.5	27 48.7	11 13.7	15 34.2	13 31.8	1 24.8	1 25.4
28 W	12 22 22	7 29 54	18 19 36	24 15 27	9 55.5	8 49.4	24 41.8	16 37.6	27 55.0	11 19.6	15 31.2	13 31.3	1 25.1	1 23.9
29 Th	12 26 19	8 29 14	0♓ 10 33	6♓ 6 13	9 52.3	8 40.4	26 11.9	17 51.6	28 0.6	11 25.3	15 28.2	13 30.8	1 25.2	1 22.4
30 F	12 30 15	9 28 33	12 1 51	17 57 58	9 49.2	8 29.7	27 36.9	19 5.6	28 5.6	11 30.9	15 25.0	13 30.2	1 25.4	1 20.9
31 Sa	12 34 12	10♈ 27 49	23♓ 54 50	29♓ 52 39	9♊ 46.0	8♊ 18.2	28♈ 56.6	20♓ 19.6	28♏ 9.9	11♑ 36.3	15♏ 21.8	13♐ 29.6	1♑ 25.5	1♏ 19.3

DECLINATION and LATITUDE

DAY	☉ DECL	☽ DECL	☽ LAT	☽ 12hr DECL	☿ DECL	☿ LAT	♀ DECL	♀ LAT	♂ DECL	♂ LAT	♃ DECL	♃ LAT	♄ DECL	♄ LAT
1	7S36													
2	7 13													
3	6 50													
4	6 27													
5	6 4													
6	5 40													
7	5 17													
8	4 54													
9	4 30													
10	4 7													
11	3 43													
12	3 20													
13	2 56													
14	2 32													
15	2 9													
16	1 45													
17	1 21													
18	0 58	1 50	4 30	1S26	2 15	0 23	11 0	1 9	17 55	1 29	22 49	0 14	14 11	2 32
19	0 34	4S39	3 46	7 46	3 11	0 13	10 33	1 10	17 58	1 28	22 48	0 14	14 10	2 33
20	0 10	10 45	2 48	13 32	4 8	0 2	10 9	1 12	18 2	1 27	22 48	0 14	14 9	2 33
21	0N13	16 5	1 40	18 23	5 3	0N10	9 43	1 14	18 5	1 27	22 47	0 14	14 9	2 33
22	0 37	20 24	0 29	22 6	5 58	0 22	9 16	1 15	18 8	1 26	22 47	0 14	14 8	2 33
23	1 1	23 29	0S41	24 32	6 53	0 34	8 50	1 16	18 11	1 25	22 46	0 14	14 7	2 33
24	1 24	25 14	1 48	25 37	7 46	0 46	8 23	1 18	18 13	1 24	22 46	0 14	14 6	2 33
25	1 48	25 39	2 47	25 23	8 38	0 58	7 56	1 19	18 16	1 23	22 45	0 14	14 5	2 34
26	2 12	24 48	3 37	23 36	9 28	1 10	7 28	1 20	18 19	1 22	22 45	0 14	14 4	2 34
27	2 35	22 48	4 17	21 26	10 16	1 22	7 1	1 22	18 21	1 21	22 44	0 14	14 3	2 34
28	2 59	19 51	4 45	18 3	11 2	1 34	6 33	1 23	18 24	1 20	22 44	0 14	14 2	2 34
29	3 22	16 5	5 0	13 58	11 46	1 46	6 5	1 24	18 26	1 19	22 44	0 14	14 1	2 34
30	3 45	11 43	5 3	9 21	12 27	1 57	5 37	1 25	18 28	1 18	22 43	0 13	13 60	2 34
31	4N 9	6S33	4S52	4S22	13N 6	2N 8	5S 9	1S25	18S30	1N17	22S43	0N13	13S59	2N35

The arrows indicate a true Moon Node change (A) and Lunar phenomenon (B) near the same time. This is a very good indicator for a short term change in trend for stocks.

DAY	♅ DECL	♅ LAT	♆ DECL	♆ LAT	♇ DECL	♇ LAT
	22S22	0N 3	22S16	1N11	4N 3	17N14
	22 22	0 3	22 15	1 11	4 6	17 16
	22 23	0 3	22 15	1 11	4 9	17 17
	22 23	0 3	22 15	1 11	4 12	17 19
	22 23	0 3	22 15	1 11	4 15	17 20
	22 23	0 3	22 15	1 11	4 18	17 22
	22 23	0 3	22 15	1 11	4 21	17 23
	22S23	0N 3	22S15	1N12	4N24	17N24

☽ PHENOMENA dy	hr	
2	11	APOGE
16	21	PERIG
29	16	APOGE

MAX/0 DECL dy	hr	° '
5	2	0
12	5	25N34
18	7	0
24	20	25S40

MAX/[illegible] dy	hr	
2	16	[illegible]
10	0	[illegible]
16	7	[illegible]
22	10	[illegible]
29	17	[illegible]3

VOID OF COURSE ☽ LAST ASPT		☽ INGRESS		
1	1am 6	1	♓	5pm30
3	3pm26	4	♈	6am 8
5	8pm55	6	♉	6pm10
8	5pm25	9	♊	4am30
11	4am26	11	♋	11am49
13	11am22	13	♌	3pm22
15	9am14	15	♍	3pm48
17	10am11	17	♎	2pm52
18	12pm19	19	♏	2pm49
21	12pm32	21	♐	5pm42
22	10pm35	24	♑	0am37
26	6am38	26	♒	11am10
28	7pm34	28	♓	11pm38
31	8am36	31	♈	12pm15

dy	hr	mn	PHASE	
2	18	32	12♓22	●
10	18	28	20♊23	☽
17	10	11	27♍ 1	○
24	7	59	3♑52	☾

DAILY ASPECTARIAN

Day	Aspect	Time
1 Th	☽□♂	1am 6
	☿⚹♅	2 21
	☽∠♃	3 4
	☽∥♀	10 30
	☽∥♂	1pm25
	☽⚹♆	7 49
	☽△♇	9 25
2 F	☽∥♄	3am16
	☽⚺♆	6 7
	☽⚹♃	9 48
	☿∥♂	3pm 7
	☉⚺☽	6 32
	☽□♅	8 43
	☽∥♆	11 9
3 Sa	☽⚹♀	1am35
	☽△♄	2 32
	☽⚼♇	3 43
	☿∠♆	7 38
	☿⚹♃	8 0
	☿□♄	10 44
	☽△♂	3pm26
	☉∥☽	7 35
	☉□♅	8 49
4 Su	☽∥♇	7am11
	☽□♆	8 31
	☽⚼♄	8 47
	☽⚻♇	9 57
	☽∠♀	11 22
	☽⚼♂	10pm27
	☽□♃	11 8
5 M	☽0N	2am27
	☽⚻♆	3 43
	☽△♅	9 15
	☉⚻☽	12pm32
	☽⚻♄	2 52
	☽⚹♀	8 55
	☽∥♇	9 40
6 T	☿□♅	4am26
	☉∥☽	4 39
	☽⚻♂	5 14
	☽⚼♅	3pm12
	☽∥♆	3 17
	☉△♄	4 4
	☽∠♆	5 10
	☽△♆	8 35
	☉∠☽	9 6
	☽☍♇	9 50
7 W	☉⚼♇	5am42
	♂∠♃	6 30
	☽△♃	11 33
	☿△♄	3pm26
	☽⚻♅	8 44
	☿⚼♇	10 41
	☽∥♄	11 41
8 Th	☽⚼♆	2am 3
	☽☍♄	2 4
	☽∥♀	3 1
	☽⚹♆	4 1
	☉⚺☽	5 7
	♄∠♆	5 27
	☽□♀	2pm32
	☽∥♂	4 23
	☽⚼♃	5 2
	☽☍♂	5 25
	☉☍♆	5 33
9 F	☽⚻♆	6am34
	☽⚻♇	7 56
	♀∠♃	6pm32
	♀∥♄	8 17
	☉∥♇	8 55
	☽⚻♃	9 47
10 Sa	☽∥♆	1am34
	☽∥♅	2 57
	♀□♂	3 9
	☽☍♅	5 54
	☽∥♃	7 16
	☽⚻♄	10 49
	☽⚼♇	11 54
	☉□☽	6pm28
	☽□♆	10 33
	☿∥♇	11 58
11 Su	☽⚻♂	2am33
	☽△♀	4 26
	☽⚼♄	1pm33
	☽☍♆	2 6
	☽△♇	2 57
	☉∥♆	10 15
12 M	☽☍♃	4am31
	☿△♂	5 4
	☽⚼♂	5 37
	☽⚼♀	9 31
	☽⚻♅	11 33
	☽△♄	4pm 0
13 T	☉△☽	3am13
	☽△♂	7 39
	☽△♆	11 22
	☽⚼♅	12pm37
	☽⚻♀	1 23
	☽⚻♆	3 33
	☽□♇	6 13
14 W	☽∥♃	1am 0
	☽∥♅	4 32
	☽∥♆	5 31
	☉☍☽	5 54
	☽⚻♃	7 24
	♀ ♓	12pm36
	☽△♅	1 33
	☽⚼♆	3 47
	☿ ♈	4 28
	☽□♄	5 36
	☽⚼♆	6 1
	☿⚹♀	10 50
15 Th	☿⚼♄	3am15
	☽⚼♃	7 43
	☉⚻☽	7 45
	☽∥♂	7 53
	☿□♆	8 36
	☽□♂	9 14
	☿⚻♇	12pm32
	☿0N	2 29
	♀⚹♆	2 35
	☽△♆	5 54
	☽☍♆	6 12
	☽⚹♇	6 27
	☽⚻♆	7 18
	☿△♇	9 16
16 F	☽∥♄	0am11
	☽△♃	7 34
	☽∥♀	10 49
	☉△♂	12pm16
	☽□♅	1 7
	☽⚹♄	4 57
	☽∠♇	5 58
17 Sa	☉∥♆	0am34
	☽⚹♂	9 2
	☉☍☽	10 11
	☽∥♇	3pm 4
	☽∠♄	4 24
	☽□♆	5 0
	☽⚻♇	5 27
	☽⚻♀	9 25
	☽∥♆	10 40
18 Su	☽☍♆	1am24
	☉∥☽	3 24
	♅SR	6 21
	☽0S	6 43
	☽□♃	7 4
	☽∠♂	9 0
	☉∥☽	9 40
	☽⚹♅	12pm19
	☽⚻♄	4 6
	☽∥♆	5 34
	☽∥♇	10 34
	☽⚼♆	11 24
19 M	☽⚻♂	9am24
	☽∠♅	12pm29
	☉⚻☽	1 24
	☽⚹♆	5 5
	☽⚺♇	5 27
	☽∥♀	9 42
	☿□♃	11 52
20 T	☽△♀	2am 9
	☿∥♇	4 16
	☽⚹♃	8 14
	☽⚻♆	9 28
	☉ ♈	10 26
	☽⚻♅	1pm22
	☽∥♄	2 48
	☉☍☽	4 12
	☽⚺♄	5 15
	☿⚼♂	5 54
	☽∠♆	6 8
21 W	☉⚼♄	6am33
	☽∠♃	10 3
	☽∥♂	10 27
	☽⚺♂	12pm32
	☿△♅	2 31
	☽⚼♆	3 16
	☉□♆	7 58
	☽⚻♆	8 9
	☉△☽	8 10
	☽⚹♇	8 26
	☉⚻♇	11 45
22 Th	☽□♀	11am11
	☽⚻♃	12pm35
	☽∥♆	1 11
	☽∥♅	2 18
	☽∥♃	5 32
	☽⚺♅	6 0
	☿⚻♄	6 48
	☽⚻♄	10 2
	☽△♆	10 35
	☽∠♇	11 26
23 F	♀⚹♃	7am31
	☽⚻♂	7pm43
24 Sa	☽∠♄	1am58
	☽⚺♆	3 17
	☽⚹♇	3 27
	☉□☽	7 59
	☿∥♀	11 10
	☽⚺♃	9pm46
25 Su	☽∠♂	0am48
	☽⚹♀	1 38
	☽⚻♅	2 41
	☽⚹♄	6 48
	♀□♅	11 59
	☽□♆	5pm18
26 M	☽⚹♂	6am38
	☽∠♅	8 14
	☽∠♀	10 34
	☽⚻♆	1pm59
	☽□♇	2 1
27 T	☉⚹☽	0am12
	☽∥♃	0 38
	♀△♄	3 20
	☽∥♅	3 57
	☽∥♆	5 11
	♆⚹♇	7 52
	☽⚻♃	9 45
	☽⚹♅	2pm18
	☽□♄	6 21
	☿⚼♇	7 39
	☽∠♆	8 8
	☽⚻♀	8 10
28 W	☉∠☽	9am12
	☽∥♂	9 42
	☽⚹♆	2pm47
	☽∠♃	4 19
	☽□♂	7 34
29 Th	☽△♇	2am23
	☽⚹♆	2 31
	☽∥♄	11 46
	☉⚺☽	6pm21
	☽∥♆	8 38
	☽⚹♃	10 57
30 F	☽∠♆	1am20
	☽□♅	2 59
	☽△♄	6 49
	☽⚼♇	8 43
	☿⚻♂	8 57
	☿⚼♅	3pm45
	☽⚺♀	3 56
31 Sa	☽△♂	8am36
	☽∥♀	9 12
	☽⚻♆	11 19
	☽∥♇	11 43
	☉∥☽	12pm 7
	☽⚼♄	12 55
	☽⚻♇	2 52
	☽□♆	3 6
	☉∥♇	5 44
	☿ ♉	8 27

LONGITUDE

DAY	SID. TIME	☉	☽	☽ 12 Hour	MEAN ☊	TRUE ☊	☿	♀	♂	♃	♄	♅	♆	♇
	h m s	° ' "	° ' "	° ' "	° '	° '	° '	° '	° '	° '	° '	° '	° '	° '
1 Th	10 35 55	10♓ 35 41	21♒ 20 28	27♒ 16 43	11♊ 21.3	11♊R32.1	3♓ 58.6	13♒ 18.7	21♏ 52.2	7♑ 50.4	16♏R21.5	13♐ 25.8	1♑ 7.9	1♏R56.8
2 F	10 39 52	11 35 54	3♓ 12 44	9♓ 8 41	11 18.1	11 18.0	5 46.6	14 32.7	22 11.6	7 59.8	16 20.9	13 26.7	1 9.0	1 55.9
3 Sa	10 43 48	12 36 6	15 4 43	21 0 59	11 14.9	11 3.0	7 35.7	15 46.8	22 30.7	8 9.2	16 20.2	13 27.6	1 10.0	1 55.0
4 Su	10 47 45	13 36 15	26 57 38	2♈ 54 52	11 11.8	10 48.3	9 25.8	17 0.8	22 49.4	8 18.4	16 19.4	13 28.4	1 11.0	1 54.1
5 M	10 51 41	14 36 23	8♈ 52 31	14 51 48	11 8.6	10 35.1	11 16.9	18 14.8	23 7.6	8 27.4	16 18.5	13 29.1	1 11.9	1 53.1
6 Tu	10 55 38	15 36 29	20 51 59	26 53 40	11 5.4	10 24.3	13 9.1	19 28.9	23 25.3	8 36.4	16 17.4	13 29.8	1 12.9	1 52.1
7 W	10 59 34	16 36 33	2♉ 57 12	9♉ 2 58	11 2.2	10 16.8	15 2.2	20 42.9	23 42.9	8 45.2	16 16.3	13 30.4	1 13.8	1 51.1
8 Th	11 3 31	17 36 34	15 11 23	21 22 55	10 59.1	10 12.3	16 56.4	21 56.9	23 59.9	8 53.9	16 15.1	13 31.0	1 14.6	1 50.0
9 F	11 7 27	18 36 34	27 38 4	3♊ 57 20	10 55.9	10D 10.3	18 51.3	23 11.0	24 16.3	9 2.5	16 13.8	13 31.5	1 15.4	1 48.9
10 Sa	11 11 24	19 36 32	10♊ 21 16	16 50 25	10 52.7	10R 10.1	20 47.4	24 25.0	24 32.6	9 10.9	16 12.4	13 32.0	1 16.2	1 47.8
11 Su	11 15 21	20 36 27	23 25 17	0♋ 6 20	10 49.5	10 10.2	22 44.2	25 39.0	24 48.3	9 19.3	16 10.9	13 32.4	1 17.0	1 46.7
12 M	11 19 17	21 36 20	6♋ 53 58	13 48 28	10 46.3	10 9.5	24 41.7	26 53.1	25 3.5	9 27.5	16 9.2	13 32.8	1 17.8	1 45.5
13 Tu	11 23 14	22 36 12	20 30 2	27 58 37	10 43.2	10 6.8	26 39.8	28 7.1	25 18.2	9 35.5	16 7.5	13 33.1	1 18.5	1 44.3
14 W	11 27 10	23 36 0	3♌ 14 3	12♌ 35 54	10 40.0	10 1.6	28 38.5	29 21.1	25 32.5	9 43.5	16 5.8	13 33.3	1 19.1	1 43.1
15 Th	11 31 7	24 35 47	20 3 30	27 35 39	10 36.8	9 53.8	0♈ 37.4	0♓ 35.2	25 46.2	9 51.3	16 3.9	13 33.5	1 19.8	1 41.9
16 F	11 35 3	25 35 31	3♍ 12 15	12♍ 30 39	10 33.6	9 44.0	2 36.4	1 49.2	25 59.3	9 58.9	16 1.9	13 33.7	1 20.4	1 40.6
17 Sa	11 39 0	26 35 13	20 30 49	28 10 15	10 30.5	9 33.2	4 35.3	3 3.2	26 12.2	10 6.4	15 59.8	13 33.8	1 20.9	1 39.3
18 Su	11 42 36	27 34 53	5♎ 47 50	13♎ 22 10	10 27.3	9 22.7	6 33.9	4 17.3	26 24.4	10 13.8	15 57.6	13R 33.8	1 21.5	1 38.0
19 M	11 46 53	28 34 31	20 32 1	28 16 20	10 24.1	9 13.8	8 31.8	5 31.3	26 36.1	10 21.0	15 55.4	13 33.8	1 22.0	1 36.7
20 Tu	11 50 50	29 34 7	5♏ 34 16	12♏ 45 14	10 20.9	9 7.2	10 28.8	6 45.3	26 47.2	10 28.1	15 53.0	13 33.7	1 22.5	1 35.4
21 W	11 54 46	0♈ 33 42	19 48 32	26 45 2	10 17.8	9 3.2	12 24.4	7 39.3	26 57.8	10 35.1	15 50.6	13 33.6	1 22.9	1 34.0
22 Th	11 58 43	1 33 13	3♐ 33 45	10♐ 15 16	10 14.6	9D 1.6	14 18.3	9 13.4	27 7.8	10 41.9	15 48.1	13 33.4	1 23.3	1 32.6
23 F	12 2 39	2 32 46	16 49 53	23 18 10	10 11.4	9 1.6	16 10.1	10 27.4	27 17.2	10 48.6	15 45.5	13 33.2	1 23.7	1 31.2
24 Sa	12 6 36	3 32 15	29 40 32	5♑ 37 37	10 8.2	9R 2.1	17 59.2	11 41.4	27 26.0	10 55.1	15 42.8	13 33.0	1 24.0	1 29.8
25 Su	12 10 32	4 31 42	12♑ 10 1	18 18 20	10 5.0	9 1.9	19 43.5	12 55.5	27 34.2	11 1.4	15 40.0	13 32.6	1 24.3	1 28.3
26 M	12 14 29	5 31 8	24 23 13	0♒ 25 14	10 1.9	9 0.1	21 28.2	14 9.5	27 41.8	11 7.6	15 37.2	13 32.3	1 24.6	1 26.9
27 Tu	12 18 25	6 30 32	6♒ 24 57	12 22 53	9 58.7	8 56.0	23 7.2	15 23.5	27 48.7	11 13.7	15 34.2	13 31.8	1 24.8	1 25.4
28 W	12 22 22	7 29 54	18 19 36	24 15 27	9 55.5	8 49.4	24 41.8	16 37.6	27 55.0	11 19.6	15 31.2	13 31.3	1 25.1	1 23.9
29 Th	12 26 19	8 29 14	0♓ 10 33	6♓ 6 15	9 52.3	8 40.4	26 11.9	17 51.6	28 0.6	11 25.3	15 28.2	13 30.8	1 25.2	1 22.4
30 F	12 30 15	9 28 33	12 1 51	17 57 58	9 49.2	8 29.7	27 36.9	19 5.6	28 5.6	11 30.9	15 25.0	13 30.2	1 25.4	1 20.9
31 Sa	12 34 12	10♈ 27 49	23♓ 54 50	29♓ 52 39	9♊ 46.0	8♊ 18.2	28♈ 36.6	20♓ 19.6	28♏ 9.9	11♑ 36.3	15♏ 21.8	13♐ 29.6	1♑ 28.5	1♏ 19.3

DECLINATION and LATITUDE

DAY	☉ DECL	☽ DECL	☽ LAT	☽ 12hr DECL	☿ DECL	☿ LAT	♀ DECL	♀ LAT	♂ DECL	♂ LAT	♃ DECL	♃ LAT	♄ DECL	♄ LAT
1	7S36	18S49	4S41	16S37	11S60	2S 5	17S20	0S32	16S40	1N37	22S37	0N13	14S21	2N29
2	7 13	14 35	4 56	12 45	11 19	2 4	17 1	0 34	16 46	1 37	22 37	0 13	14 21	2 29
3	6 50	10 28	4 58	8 4	10 36	2 1	16 42	0 37	16 51	1 36	22 36	0 13	14 20	2 29
4	6 27	5 36	4 47	3 5	9 52	1 59	16 22	0 39	16 56	1 36	22 56	0 13	14 20	2 30
5	6 4	0 31	4 24	2N 3	9 7	1 55	16 2	0 42	17 1	1 36	22 35	0 13	14 19	2 30
6	5 40	4N37	3 49	7 9	8 20	1 52	15 41	0 44	17 6	1 35	22 35	0 13	14 19	2 30
7	5 17	9 38	3 3	12 3	7 33	1 47	15 19	0 47	17 10	1 35	22 54	0 13	14 18	2 30
8	4 54	14 21	2 8	16 32	6 44	1 42	14 58	0 49	17 15	1 34	22 54	0 15	14 18	2 30
9	4 30	18 34	1 6	20 24	5 54	1 37	14 36	0 51	17 20	1 34	22 33	0 15	14 17	2 31
10	4 7	22 1	0N 1	23 23	5 3	1 31	14 13	0 53	17 24	1 33	22 53	0 15	14 17	2 31
11	3 43	24 26	1 10	25 10	4 11	1 25	13 50	0 55	17 28	1 33	22 52	0 15	14 16	2 31
12	3 20	25 32	2 16	25 31	3 18	1 17	13 27	0 57	17 32	1 32	22 52	0 15	14 15	2 31
13	2 56	25 5	3 17	24 14	2 24	1 10	13 4	0 59	17 36	1 32	22 51	0 15	14 15	2 31
14	2 32	22 58	4 8	21 19	1 29	1 2	12 40	1 1	17 40	1 31	22 51	0 15	14 14	2 32
15	2 9	19 17	4 44	16 33	0 34	0 53	12 15	1 3	17 44	1 31	22 50	0 14	14 13	2 32
16	1 45	14 15	5 0	11 22	0N22	0 44	11 51	1 5	17 48	1 30	22 50	0 14	14 13	2 32
17	1 21	8 17	4 56	5 5	1 18	0 34	11 26	1 7	17 51	1 29	22 49	0 14	14 12	2 32
													11	2 32
													10	2 33
													9	2 33
													9	2 33
													8	2 33
													7	2 33
													6	2 33
													5	2 34
													4	2 34
27	[illegible]	[illegible]	[illegible]	[illegible]	[illegible]	[illegible]	[illegible]	[illegible]	[illegible]	[illegible]	[illegible]	[illegible]	3	2 34
28	2 59	19 51	4 45	18 3	11 2	1 34	6 33	1 23	18 24	1 20	22 44	0 14	14 2	2 34
29	3 22	16 5	5 0	13 58	11 46	1 46	6 5	1 24	18 26	1 19	22 44	0 14	14 1	2 34
30	3 45	11 43	5 3	9 21	12 27	1 57	5 37	1 25	18 28	1 18	22 43	0 13	13 60	2 34
31	4N 9	6S53	4S52	4S22	13N 6	2N 8	5S 9	1S25	18S30	1N17	22S43	0N13	13S59	2N35

The arrows indicate when the moon is exactly on the Equator.

DAY	♅ DECL	♅ LAT	♆ DECL	♆ LAT	♇ DECL	♇ LAT
1	22S22	0N 3	22S16	1N11	4N 3	17N14
5	22 22	0 3	22 15	1 11	4 6	17 16
9	22 23	0 3	22 15	1 11	4 9	17 17
13	22 23	0 3	22 15	1 11	4 12	17 19
17	22 23	0 3	22 15	1 11	4 15	17 20
21	22 23	0 3	22 15	1 11	4 18	17 22
25	22 23	0 3	22 15	1 11	4 21	17 23
29	22S23	0N 3	22S15	1N12	4N24	17N24

☽ PHENOMENA

dy	hr	
2	11	APOGE
16	21	PERIG
29	16	APOGE

MAX/0 DECL.

dy	hr	° '
5	2	0
12	5	25N34
18	7	0
24	20	25S40

MAX/0 LAT

dy	hr	° '
2	16	4S59
10	0	0
16	7	5N 1
22	10	0
29	17	5S 3

VOID OF COURSE ☽

LAST ASPT		☽ INGRESS		
1	1am 6	1	♓	5pm30
3	3pm26	4	♈	6am 8
6	8pm55	6	♉	4pm10
8	5pm25	9	♊	4am30
11	4am26	11	♋	11am49
13	11am22	13	♌	5pm22
15	9am14	15	♍	5pm48
17	10am11	17	♎	2pm52
18	12pm19	19	♏	2pm49
21	12pm52	21	♐	5pm42
22	10pm35	24	♑	0am37
26	6am38	26	♒	11am10
28	7pm34	28	♓	11pm38
31	5am36	31	♈	12pm15

dy	hr	mn	PHASE
2	18	32	12♓22 ●
10	18	28	20♊23 ☽
17	10	11	27♍ 1 ○
24	7	59	3♑52 ☾

DAILY ASPECTARIAN

Day	Aspect	Time
1 Th	☽□♂	1am 6
	☿⚹♆	2 21
	☽∠♃	3 [illegible]
	☽∥♀	10 [illegible]
	☽∥♂	1pm [illegible]
	☽⚹♆	7 [illegible]
	☽△♇	9 [illegible]
2 F	☽∥♄	3am16
	☽⊼♆	6 7
	☽⚹♃	9 48
	☿∥♂	3pm 7
	☉⊼☽	6 32
	☽□♅	8 43
	☽∥☿	11 9
3 Sa	☽×♀	1am35
	☽△♄	2 32
	☽Q♇	3 43
	♀∠♆	7 38
	☿⚹♃	8 0
	☿□♄	10 44
	☽△♂	3pm26
	☉∥☽	7 35
	☉□♅	8 49
4 Su	☽∥♇	7am11
	☽□♆	8 31
	☽Q♄	8 47
	☽⚹♇	9 57
	☽∠♀	11 22
	☽Q♂	10pm27
	☽□♃	11 8
5 M	☽0N	2am27
	☽×♆	5 43
	☽△♅	9 15
	☉×☽	12pm32
	☽⊼♄	2 52
	☽⚹♀	8 58
	☽∥♇	9 40
6 T	☿□♅	4am26
	☉∥☽	4 39
	☽⊼♂	5 14
	☽Q♅	3pm12
	☽∥☿	3 17
	☉△♄	4 4
	☽∠☿	5 10
	☽△☿	8 33
	☉∠☽	9 6
	☽⊼♇	9 50
7 W	☉⚹♇	8am42
	♂∠♃	6 30
	☽△♃	11 33
	☿△♄	3pm26
	☽⊼♅	8 44
	☿Q♇	10 41
	☽∥♄	11 41
8 Th	☽Q☿	2am 3
	☽⊼♄	2 4
	☽∥♀	3 1
	☽⚹☿	4 1
	☉⚹☽	5 7
	♄∠☿	5 27
	☽□♀	2pm32
	☽∥♂	4 23
	☽Q♃	5 2
	☽⊼♂	5 25
	☉⊼☿	5 33
9 F	☽×☿	6am34
	☽×♇	7 56
	♀∠♃	6pm52
	♀∥♄	8 17
	☉∥♇	8 53
	☽⊼♃	9 47
10 Sa	☽∥☿	1am54
	☽∥♅	2 57
	♀□♂	3 9
	☽⊼♅	5 54
	☽∥♃	7 16
	☽⊼♄	10 49
	☽Q♇	11 54
	☉□☽	6pm28
	☽□☿	10 33
	☿∥♇	11 58
11 Su	☽×♂	2am33
	☽△♀	4 26
	☽Q♄	1pm33
	☽⊼☿	2 6
	☽△♇	2 57
	☉∥☿	10 15
12 M	☽⊼♃	4am31
	☿△♂	5 4
	☽Q♂	5 37
	☽Q♀	9 31
	☽⊼♅	11 33
	☽△♄	4pm 0
13 T	☉△☽	3am13
	☽△♂	7 39
	☽△☿	11 22
	☽Q♅	12pm57
	☽×♀	1 23
	☽⊼☿	5 33
	☽□♇	6 13
14 W	☽∥♃	1am 0
	☽∥♅	4 32
	☽∥☿	5 31
	☉⊼☽	5 54
	☽⊼♃	7 24
	♀ ♓	12pm36
	☽△♅	1 33
	☽Q☿	3 47
	☿ ♈	4 28
	☽□♄	5 36
	☽Q☿	6 1
	☿×♀	10 50
15 Th	☿Q♄	5am15
	☽Q♃	7 43
	☉×☽	7 45
	☽∥♂	7 53
	☿□♆	8 36
	☽□♂	9 14
	☿×♇	12pm32
	☿0N	2 29
	♀⚹♆	2 33
	☽△☿	5 54
	☽⊼♀	6 12
	☽⚹♇	6 27
	☽⊼☿	7 18
	♀△♇	9 16
16 F	☽∥♄	0am11
	☽△♃	7 34
	☽∥♀	10 49
	☉△♂	12pm16
	☽□♅	1 7
	☽⚹♄	4 57
	☽∠♇	5 58
17 Sa	☉∥☿	0am34
	☽⚹♂	9 2
	☉☍☽	10 11
	☽∥♇	3pm 4
	☽⊼♄	4 24
	☽□☿	5 0
	☽×♇	5 27
	☽⊼♀	9 25
	☽∥☿	10 40
18 Su	☽⊼☿	1am24
	☉∥☽	3 24
	♅SR	6 21
	☽0S	6 43
	☽□♃	7 4
	☽∠♂	9 0
	☉∥☽	9 40
	☽⚹♆	12pm19
	☽×♄	4 6
	☽∥☿	5 34
	☽∥♇	10 34
	☽Q♀	11 24
19 M	☽×♂	9am24
	☽∠♆	12pm29
	☉×☽	1 24
	☽⚹☿	3 5
	☽⚹♇	5 27
	☽∥♀	9 42
	☿□♃	11 52
20 T	☽△♀	2am 9
	☿∥♇	4 16
	☽⚹♃	8 14
	☽⊼☿	9 28
	☉ ♈	10 26
	☽⊼♅	1pm22
	☽∥♄	2 48
	☉Q☽	4 12
	☽⊼♄	5 15
	☿Q♂	5 54
	☽∠☿	6 8
21 W	☉Q♄	6am33
	☽∠♃	10 3
	☽∥♂	10 27
	☽Q♂	12pm32
	☿△♅	2 31
	☽Q☿	3 16
	☉□☿	7 58
	☽×☿	8 9
	☉△☽	8 10
	☽×♇	8 26
	☉⊼♇	11 45
22 Th	☽□♀	11am11
	☽×♃	12pm55
	☽∥☿	1 11
	☽∥♅	2 18
	☽∥♃	5 32
	☽Q♅	6 0
	☿⊼♄	6 48
	☽×♄	10 2
	☽△☿	10 35
	☽∠♇	11 26
23 F	♀⚹♃	7am31
	☽×♂	7pm43
24 Sa	☽⊼♄	1am58
	☽⊼☿	3 17
	☽⚹♇	3 27
	☉□☽	7 59
	☿∥♀	11 10
	☽⊼♃	9pm46
25 Su	☽∠♂	0am48
	☽⚹♀	1 38
	☽⊼♅	2 41
	☽⚹♄	6 48
	♀□♅	11 59
	☽□☿	5pm18
26 M	☽Q♂	6am38
	☽∠♅	8 14
	☽∠♀	10 34
	☽×☿	1pm59
	☽□♇	2 1
27 T	☉⚹☽	0am12
	☽∥♃	0 38
	♀△♄	3 20
	☽∥♅	3 57
	☽∥☿	5 11
	☿⊼♇	7 52
	☽×♃	9 48
	☽⚹♅	2pm18
	☽□♄	6 21
	♀Q♇	7 39
	☽∠☿	8 8
	☽×♀	8 10
28 W	☉∠☽	9am12
	☽∥♂	9 42
	☽⚹☿	2pm47
	☽△♃	4 19
	☽□♂	7 34
29 Th	☽△♇	2am25
	☽⚹☿	2 31
	☽∥♄	11 46
	☉×☽	6pm21
	☽∥☿	8 58
	☽⚹♃	10 57
30 F	☽∠☿	1am20
	☽□♅	2 59
	☽△♄	6 49
	☽Q♇	8 43
	☿⊼♂	8 57
	☿Q♅	5pm45
	☽⊼♀	8 56
31 Sa	☽△♂	8am36
	☽∥♀	9 12
	☽×☿	11 19
	☽∥♇	11 43
	☉∥☽	12pm 7
	☽Q♄	12 55
	☽⊼♇	2 52
	☽□☿	3 6
	☉∥♇	5 44
	☿ ♉	8 27

LONGITUDE

DAY	SID. TIME	☉	☽	☽ 12 Hour	MEAN ☊	TRUE ☊	☿	♀	♂	♃	♄	♅	♆	♇
	h m s	° ' "	° ' "	° ' "	° '	° '	° '	° '	° '	° '	° '	° '	° '	° '
1 Th	10 35 55	10♓ 35 41	21♒ 20 28	27♒ 16 43	11♊ 21.3	11♊R32.1	3♓ 58.6	13♒ 18.7	21♏ 52.2	7♑ 50.4	16♏R21.5	13♐ 25.8	1♑ 7.9	1♏R56.8
2 F	10 39 52	11 35 54	3♓ 12 44	9♓ 8 41	11 18.1	11 18.0	5 46.6	14 32.7	22 11.6	7 59.8	16 20.9	13 26.7	1 9.0	1 55.9
3 Sa	10 43 48	12 36 6	15 4 43	21 0 39	11 14.9	11 3.0	7 35.7	15 46.8	22 30.7	8 9.2	16 20.2	13 27.6	1 10.0	1 55.0
4 Su	10 47 43	13 36 15	26 57 38	2♈ 54 52	11 11.8	10 48.3	9 25.8	17 0.8	22 49.4	8 18.4	16 19.4	13 28.4	1 11.0	1 54.1
5 M	10 51 41	14 36 23	8♈ 52 51	14 51 48	11 8.6	10 35.1	11 16.9	18 14.8	23 7.6	8 27.4	16 18.5	13 29.1	1 11.9	1 53.1
6 Tu	10 55 38	15 36 29	20 51 59	26 53 40	11 5.4	10 24.5	13 9.1	19 28.9	23 25.3	8 36.4	16 17.4	13 29.8	1 12.9	1 52.1
7 W	10 59 34	16 36 33	2♉ 57 12	9♉ 2 38	11 2.2	10 16.8	15 2.2	20 42.9	23 42.9	8 45.2	16 16.3	13 30.4	1 13.8	1 51.1
8 Th	11 3 31	17 36 34	15 11 23	21 22 55	10 59.1	10 12.3	16 56.4	21 56.9	23 59.9	8 53.9	16 15.1	13 31.0	1 14.6	1 50.0
9 F	11 7 27	18 36 34	27 38 4	3♊ 57 20	10 55.9	10D 10.3	18 51.5	23 11.0	24 16.5	9 2.5	16 13.8	13 31.5	1 15.4	1 48.9
10 Sa	11 11 24	19 36 32	10♊ 21 16	16 50 25	10 52.7	10R 10.1	20 47.4	24 25.0	24 32.6	9 10.9	16 12.4	13 32.0	1 16.2	1 47.8
11 Su	11 15 21	20 36 27	23 25 17	0♋ 6 20	10 49.5	10 10.2	22 44.2	25 39.0	24 48.3	9 19.3	16 10.9	13 32.4	1 17.0	1 46.7
12 M	11 19 17	21 36 20	6♋ 33 58	13 48 28	10 46.3	10 9.3	24 41.7	26 53.1	25 3.5	9 27.5	16 9.2	13 32.8	1 17.8	1 45.5
13 Tu	11 23 14	22 36 12	20 30 2	27 38 37	10 43.2	10 6.8	26 39.8	28 7.1	25 18.2	9 35.5	16 7.3	13 33.1	1 18.5	1 44.3
14 W	11 27 10	23 36 0	5♌ 14 3	12♌ 33 34	10 40.0	10 1.6	28 38.3	29 21.1	25 32.5	9 43.5	16 5.8	13 33.3	1 19.1	1 43.1
15 Th	11 31 7	24 35 47	20 3 30	27 35 39	10 36.8	9 53.8	0♈ 37.4	0♓ 35.2	25 46.2	9 51.3	16 3.9	13 33.5	1 19.8	1 41.9
16 F	11 35 3	25 35 31	5♍ 12 15	12♍ 50 39	10 33.6	9 44.0	2 36.4	1 49.2	25 59.5	9 58.9	16 1.9	13 33.7	1 20.4	1 40.6
17 Sa	11 39 0	26 35 13	20 30 49	28 10 15	10 30.5	9 33.2	4 35.3	3 3.2	26 12.2	10 6.4	15 59.8	13 33.8	1 20.9	1 39.3
18 Su	11 42 56	27 34 33	5♎ 47 50	13♎ 22 10	10 27.3	9 22.7	6 33.9	4 17.3	26 24.4	10 13.8	15 57.6	13R 33.8	1 21.5	1 38.0
19 M	11 46 53	28 34 31	20 52 1	28 16 20	10 24.1	9 13.8	8 31.8	5 31.3	26 36.1	10 21.0	15 55.4	13 33.8	1 22.0	1 36.7
20 Tu	11 50 50	29 34 7	5♏ 34 16	12♏ 45 14	10 20.9	9 7.2	10 26.8	6 45.3	26 47.2	10 28.1	15 53.0	13 33.7	1 22.5	1 35.4
21 W	11 54 46	0♈ 33 42	19 48 52	26 45 2	10 17.8	9 3.2	12 24.4	7 59.3	26 57.8	10 35.1	15 50.6	13 33.6	1 22.9	1 34.0
22 Th	11 58 43	1 33 15	3♐ 33 43	10♐ 15 16	10 14.6	9D 1.6	14 18.3	9 13.4	27 7.8	10 41.9	15 48.1	13 33.4	1 23.3	1 32.6
23 F	12 2 39	2 32 46	16 49 53	23 18 10	10 11.4	9 1.6	16 10.1	10 27.4	27 17.2	10 48.6	15 45.5	13 33.2	1 23.7	1 31.2
24 Sa	12 6 36	3 32 15	29 40 32	5♑ 57 37	10 8.2	9R 2.1	17 59.2	11 41.4	27 26.0	10 55.1	15 42.8	13 33.0	1 24.0	1 29.8
25 Su	12 10 32	4 31 42	12♑ 10 1	18 18 20	10 5.0	9 1.9	19 45.5	12 55.5	27 34.2	11 1.4	15 40.0	13 32.6	1 24.3	1 28.3
26 M	12 14 29	5 31 8	24 23 13	0♒ 25 14	10 1.9	9 0.1	21 28.2	14 9.5	27 41.8	11 7.6	15 37.2	13 32.3	1 24.6	1 26.9
27 Tu	12 18 25	6 30 32	6♒ 24 57	12 22 33	9 58.7	8 56.0	23 7.2	15 23.5	27 48.7	11 13.7	15 34.2	13 31.8	1 24.8	1 25.4
28 W	12 22 22	7 29 54	18 19 36	24 15 27	9 55.5	8 49.4	24 41.8	16 37.6	27 55.0	11 19.6	15 31.2	13 31.3	1 25.1	1 23.9
29 Th	12 26 19	8 29 14	0♓ 10 33	6♓ 6 15	9 52.3	8 40.4	26 11.9	17 51.6	28 0.6	11 25.3	15 28.2	13 30.8	1 25.2	1 22.4
30 F	12 30 15	9 28 33	12 1 51	17 57 58	9 49.2	8 29.7	27 36.9	19 5.6	28 5.6	11 30.9	15 25.0	13 30.2	1 25.4	1 20.9
31 Sa	12 34 12	10♈ 27 49	23♓ 54 30	29♓ 52 39	9♊ 46.0	8♊ 18.2	28♈ 56.6	20♓ 19.6	28♏ 9.9	11♑ 36.3	15♏ 21.8	13♐ 29.6	1♑ 25.5	1♏ 19.5

DECLINATION and LATITUDE

DAY	☉ DECL	☽ DECL	☽ LAT	☽ 12hr DECL	☿ DECL	☿ LAT	♀ DECL	♀ LAT	♂ DECL	♂ LAT	♃ DECL	♃ LAT	♄ DECL	♄ LAT
1	7S36	18S49	4S41	16S37	11S60	2S 5	17S20	0S32	16S40	1N37	22S37	0N15	14S21	2N29
2	7 13	14 55	4 36	12 45	11 19	2 4	17 1	0 34	16 46	1 37	22 57	0 15	14 21	2 29
3	6 50	10 28	4 58	8 4	10 36	2 1	16 42	0 37	16 51	1 36	22 56	0 15	14 20	2 29
4	6 27	5 36	4 47	3 5	9 52	1 39	16 22	0 39	16 56	1 36	22 56	0 15	14 20	2 30
5	6 4	0 31	4 24	2N 3	9 7	1 35	16 2	0 42	17 1	1 36	22 55	0 15	14 19	2 30
6	5 40	4N37	3 49	7 9	8 20	1 52	15 41	0 44	17 6	1 35	22 55	0 15	14 19	2 30
7	5 17	9 38	3 3	12 3	7 33	1 47	15 19	0 47	17 10	1 35	22 54	0 15	14 18	2 30
8	4 54	14 21	2 8	16 32	6 44	1 42	14 58	0 49	17 15	1 34	22 54	0 15	14 18	2 30
9	4 30	18 34	1 6	20 24	5 54	1 37	14 36	0 51	17 20	1 34	22 53	0 15	14 17	2 31
10	4 7	22 1	0N 1	23 23	5 3	1 31	14 13	0 53	17 24	1 33	22 53	0 15	14 17	2 31
11	3 43	24 26	1 10	25 10	4 11	1 25	13 50	0 55	17 28	1 33	22 52	0 15	14 16	2 31
12	3 20	25 32	2 16	25 31	3 18	1 17	13 27	0 57	17 32	1 32	22 52	0 15	14 15	2 31
13														31
14														32
15														32
16														32
17														32
18														32
19														33
20														33
21														33
22														33
23														33
24														33
25														34
26														34
27														34
28														34
29	3 22	16 5	5 0	13 38	[illegible]	[illegible]	[illegible]	[illegible]	[illegible]	[illegible]	[illegible]	[illegible]	[illegible]	2 34
30	3 45	11 43	5 3	9 21	12 27	1 37	5 37	1 25	18 28	1 18	22 43	0 13	13 60	2 34
31	4N 9	6S33	4S52	4S22	13N 6	2N 8	3S 9	1S25	18S30	1N17	22S43	0N13	13S59	2N35

DAY	♅ DECL	♅ LAT	♆ DECL	♆ LAT	♇ DECL	♇ LAT
1	22S22	0N 3	22S16	1N11	4N 3	17N14
5	22 22	0 3	22 15	1 11	4 6	17 16
9	22 23	0 3	22 15	1 11	4 9	17 17
13	22 23	0 3	22 15	1 11	4 12	17 19
17	22 23	0 3	22 15	1 11	4 15	17 20
21	22 23	0 3	22 15	1 11	4 18	17 22
25	22 23	0 3	22 15	1 11	4 21	17 23
29	22S23	0N 3	22S15	1N12	4N24	17N24

The arrows indicate when the Moon is at Maximum Declination North (or South) of the Equator.

☽ PHENOMENA

dy	hr	
2	11	APOGE
16	21	PERIC
29	16	APOGE

MAX/0 DECL.

dy	hr	° '
5	2	0
12	5	25N34
18	7	0
24	20	25S40

MAX/0 LAT.

dy	hr	° '
2	16	4S59
10	0	0
16	7	5N 1
22	10	0
29	17	5S 3

VOID OF COURSE ☽

LAST ASPT		☽ INGRESS		
1	1am 6	1	♓	5pm30
3	3pm26	4	♈	6am 8
5	8pm55	6	♉	6pm10
8	5pm25	9	♊	4am30
11	4am26	11	♋	11am49
13	11am22	13	♌	5pm22
15	9am14	15	♍	3pm46
17	10am11	17	♎	2pm52
[illegible]	12pm19	19	♏	2pm49
[illegible]	2pm32	21	♐	8pm42
[illegible]	[illegible]pm35	24	♑	0am37
[illegible]	[illegible]am38	26	♒	11am10
[illegible]	7pm34	28	♓	11pm38
31	8am36	31	♈	12pm15

dy	hr	mn	PHASE	
2	18	32	12♓22	●
10	18	28	20♊23	☽
17	10	11	27♍ 1	○
24	7	59	3♑52	☾

DAILY ASPECTARIAN

Day	Aspect	Time
1 Th	☽□♂	1am 6
	♀✶♅	2 21
	☽∠♃	3 4
	☽∥♀	10 30
	☽∥♂	1pm25
	☽✶☿	7 49
	☽△♇	9 23
2 F	☽∥♄	3am16
	☽✶☿	6 7
	☽✶♃	9 48
	♀∥♂	3pm 7
	☉⚺☽	6 32
	☽□♅	8 43
	☽∥♆	11 9
3 Sa	☽⊼☿	1am33
	☽△♄	2 32
	☽⚼♇	3 43
	☿∠♆	7 38
	♆✶♃	8 0
	♀□♄	10 44
	☽△♂	3pm26
	☉∥☽	7 33
	☉□♅	8 49
4 Su	☽∥♇	7am11
	☽□♆	8 31
	☽⚼♄	8 47
	☽⊼♇	9 57
	☽∠♀	11 22
	☽⊼♂	10pm27
	☽□♃	11 8
5 M	☽0N	2am27
	☽✶☿	5 43
	☽△♅	9 13
	☉✶☽	12pm32
	☽⊼♄	2 32
	☽✶♀	8 55
	☽∥♇	9 40
6 T	☿□♅	4am26
	☉∥☽	4 39
	☽⊼♂	5 14
	☽⚼♅	3pm12
	☽∥☿	3 17
	☉△♄	4 4
	☽∠♆	5 10
	☽△♆	8 35
	☉∠☽	9 6
	☽⊼♇	9 50
7 W	☉⚼♇	5am42
	♂∠♃	6 30
	☽△♃	11 33
	☿△♄	3pm26
	☽⊼♅	8 44
	☿⚼♇	10 41
	☽∥♄	11 41
8 Th	☽⚼♆	2am 3
	☽⊼♄	2 4
	☽∥♀	3 1
	☽✶♆	4 1
	☉✶☽	5 7
	♄∠♆	5 27
	☽□☿	2pm32
	☽∥♂	4 23
	☽⚼♃	5 2
	☽⊼♂	5 23
	☉⚺☿	5 33
9 F	☽⊼♆	6am34
	☽⊼♇	7 36
	♀∠♃	6pm32
	♀∥♄	8 17
	☉∥♇	8 33
	☽⊼♃	9 47
10 Sa	☽∥♆	1am34
	☽∥♅	2 37
	♀□♂	3 9
	☽⊼♅	5 54
	☽∥♃	7 16
	☽⊼♄	10 49
	☽⚼♇	11 54
	☉□☽	6pm28
	☽□♆	10 33
	☿∥♇	11 58
11 Su	☽⊼♂	2am33
	☽△♀	4 26
	☽⚼♄	1pm33
	☽⊼♆	2 6
	☽△♇	2 57
	☉∥♆	10 15
12 M	☽⊼♃	4am31
	☿△♂	5 4
	☽⚼♂	5 37
	☽⚼♀	9 31
	☽⊼♅	11 33
	☽△♄	4pm 0
13 T	☉△☽	3am13
	☽△♂	7 39
	☽△☿	11 22
	☽⚼♅	12pm57
	☽⊼♀	1 23
	☽⊼♆	5 33
	☽□♇	6 13
14 W	☽∥♃	1am 0
	☽∥♅	4 32
	☽∥♆	5 31
	☉⚼☽	5 54
	☽⊼♃	7 24
	♀ ♓	12pm36
	☽△♅	1 33
	☽⚼♆	3 47
	☿ ♈	4 28
	☽□♄	5 36
	☽⚼☿	6 1
	☿✶♀	10 50
15 Th	☿⚼♄	5am15
	☽⚼♃	7 43
	☉⊼☽	7 43
	☽∥♂	7 53
	☿□♆	8 36
	☽□♂	9 14
	☿✶♇	12pm32
	☿0N	2 29
	♀✶♆	2 35
	☽△♆	5 54
	☽⊼♀	6 12
	☽✶♇	6 27
	☽⊼☿	7 18
	♀△♇	9 16
16 F	☽∥♄	0am11
	☽△♃	7 34
	☽∥♀	10 49
	☉△♂	12pm16
	☽□♅	1 7
	☽✶♄	4 57
	☽∠♇	5 58
17 S	☉∥☿	0am54
	☽✶♂	9 2
	☉☍☽	10 11
	☽∥♇	3pm 4
	☽∠♄	4 24
	☽□♆	5 0
	☽✶♇	5 27
	☽⊼♀	9 25
	☽∥☿	10 40
18 Su	☽⊼♆	1am24
	☉∥☽	3 24
	♅SR	6 21
	☽0S	6 43
	☽□♃	7 4
	☽∠♂	9 0
	☉∥☽	9 40
	☽✶♅	12pm19
	☽⊼♄	4 6
	☽∥♆	5 34
	☽∥♇	10 34
	☽⚼♀	11 24
19 M	☽⊼♂	9am24
	☽∠♅	12pm29
	☉⊼☽	1 24
	☽✶♆	5 5
	☽⚼♇	5 27
	☽∥♀	9 42
	☿□♃	11 52
20 T	☽△♀	2am 9
	☿∥♇	4 16
	☽✶♃	8 14
	☽⊼♆	9 28
	☉ ♈	10 26
	☽⊼♅	1pm22
	☽∥♄	2 48
	☉⚼☽	4 12
	☽⊼♄	5 15
	☿⚼♂	5 54
	☽∠♆	6 8
21 W	☉⚼♄	6am33
	☽∠♃	10 3
	☽∥♂	10 27
	☽⚼♂	12pm32
	☿△♅	2 31
	☽⚼♅	3 16
	☉□♆	7 58
	☽⊼♆	8 9
	☉△☽	8 10
	☽⊼♇	8 26
	☉⊼♇	11 45
22 Th	☽□♀	11am11
	☽⊼♃	12pm58
	☽∥♆	1 11
	☽∥♅	2 18
	☽∥♃	5 32
	☽⚼♅	6 0
	♆⊼♄	6 46
	☽⊼♄	10 2
	☽△♆	10 35
	☽∠♇	11 26
23 F	♀✶♃	7am31
	☽⊼♂	7pm43
24 S	☽∠♄	1am58
	☽⚼♆	3 17
	☽✶♇	3 27
	☉□☽	7 59
	☿∥♀	11 10
	☽⚼♃	9pm46
25 Su	☽∠♂	0am48
	☽✶♀	1 38
	☽⊼♅	2 41
	☽✶♄	6 48
	♀□♅	11 59
	☽□☿	5pm18
26 M	☽✶♂	6am38
	☽∠♅	8 14
	☽∠♀	10 34
	☽⊼♆	1pm59
	☽□♇	2 1
27 T	☉✶☽	0am12
	☽∥♃	0 38
	♀△♄	3 20
	☽∥♅	3 57
	☽∥♆	5 11
	♆✶♇	7 52
	☽⊼♃	9 45
	☽✶♅	2pm18
	☽□♄	6 21
	♀⚼♇	7 39
	☽∠♆	8 8
	☽⊼♀	8 10
28 W	☉∠☽	9am12
	☽∥♂	9 42
	☽✶☿	2pm47
	☽∠♃	4 19
	☽□♂	7 34
29 Th	☽△♇	2am23
	☽✶♆	2 31
	☽∥♄	11 46
	☉⊼☽	6pm21
	☽∥♆	8 38
	☽✶♃	10 57
30 F	☽∠♆	1am20
	☽□♅	2 59
	☽△♄	6 49
	☽⚼♇	8 43
	☿⊼♂	8 57
	☿⚼♆	3pm45
	☽⚼♀	3 56
31 S	☽△♂	8am36
	☽∥♀	9 12
	☽⊼☿	11 19
	☽∥♇	11 43
	☉∥☽	12pm 7
	☽⚼♄	12 55
	☽⊼♇	2 52
	☽□♆	3 6
	☉∥♇	5 44
	☿ ♉	8 27

LONGITUDE

DAY	SID. TIME	☉	☽	☽ 12 Hour	MEAN ☊	TRUE ☊	☿	♀	♂	♃	♄	♅	♆	♇
	h m s	° ' "	° ' "	° ' "	° '	° '	° '	° '	° '	° '	° '	° '	° '	° '
1 Th	10 35 35	10♓ 35 41	21♒ 20 28	27♒ 16 43	11♊ 21.3	11♊R32.1	3♓ 58.6	13♒ 18.7	21♏ 52.2	7♑ 50.4	16♏R21.5	13♐ 25.8	1♑ 7.9	1♏R56.8
2 F	10 39 32	11 35 54	3♓ 12 44	9♓ 8 41	11 18.1	11 18.0	5 46.6	14 32.7	22 11.6	7 59.8	16 20.9	13 26.7	1 9.0	1 55.9
3 Sa	10 43 48	12 36 6	15 4 43	21 0 59	11 14.9	11 3.0	7 35.7	15 46.8	22 30.7	8 9.2	16 20.2	13 27.6	1 10.0	1 55.0
4 Su	10 47 45	13 36 15	26 57 38	2♈ 54 52	11 11.8	10 48.3	9 25.8	17 0.8	22 49.4	8 18.4	16 19.4	13 28.4	1 11.0	1 54.1
5 M	10 51 41	14 36 23	8♈ 52 51	14 51 48	11 8.6	10 35.1	11 16.9	18 14.8	23 7.6	8 27.4	16 18.5	13 29.1	1 11.9	1 53.1
6 Tu	10 55 38	15 36 29	20 51 59	26 53 40	11 5.4	10 24.3	13 9.1	19 28.9	23 25.3	8 36.4	16 17.4	13 29.8	1 12.9	1 52.1
7 W	10 59 34	16 36 33	2♉ 57 12	9♉ 2 38	11 2.2	10 16.8	15 2.2	20 42.9	23 42.9	8 45.2	16 16.3	13 30.4	1 13.8	1 51.1
8 Th	11 3 31	17 36 34	15 11 23	21 22 35	10 59.1	10 12.3	16 56.4	21 56.9	23 59.9	8 53.9	16 15.1	13 31.0	1 14.6	1 50.0
9 F	11 7 27	18 36 34	27 38 4	3♊ 57 20	10 55.9	10D 10.3	18 51.5	23 11.0	24 16.5	9 2.5	16 13.8	13 31.5	1 15.4	1 48.9
10 Sa	11 11 24	19 36 32	10♊ 21 16	16 50 25	10 52.7	10R 10.1	20 47.4	24 25.0	24 32.6	9 10.9	16 12.4	13 32.0	1 16.2	1 47.8
11 Su	11 15 21	20 36 27	23 25 17	0♋ 6 20	10 49.5	10 10.2	22 44.2	25 39.0	24 48.3	9 19.3	16 10.9	13 32.4	1 17.0	1 46.7
12 M	11 19 17	21 36 20	6♋ 53 58	13 48 28	10 46.3	10 9.5	24 41.7	26 53.1	25 3.5	9 27.5	16 9.2	13 32.8	1 17.8	1 45.5
13 Tu	11 23 14	22 36 12	20 50 2	27 58 37	10 43.2	10 6.8	26 39.8	28 7.1	25 18.2	9 35.5	16 7.5	13 33.1	1 18.5	1 44.3
14 W	11 27 10	23 36 0	3♌ 14 3	12♌ 35 54	10 40.0	10 1.6	28 38.5	29 21.1	25 32.5	9 43.5	16 5.8	13 33.3	1 19.1	1 43.1
15 Th	11 31 7	24 35 47	20 3 30	27 35 59	10 36.8	9 53.8	0♈ 37.4	0♓ 35.2	25 46.2	9 51.3	16 3.9	13 33.5	1 19.8	1 41.9
16 F	11 35 3	25 35 31	3♍ 12 15	12♍ 50 59	10 33.6	9 44.0	2 36.4	1 49.2	25 59.5	9 58.9	16 1.9	13 33.7	1 20.4	1 40.6
17 Sa	11 39 0	26 35 13	20 30 49	28 10 15	10 30.3	9 33.2	4 35.3	3 3.2	26 12.2	10 6.4	15 59.8	13 33.8	1 20.9	1 39.3
18 Su	11 42 56	27 34 53	3♎ 47 50	13♎ 22 10	10 27.3	9 22.7	6 33.9	4 17.3	26 24.4	10 13.8	15 57.6	13R 33.8	1 21.5	1 38.0
19 M	11 46 53	28 34 31	20 52 1	28 16 20	10 24.1	9 13.8	8 31.8	5 31.3	26 36.1	10 21.0	15 55.4	13 33.8	1 22.0	1 36.7
20 Tu	11 50 50	29 34 7	3♏ 34 16	12♏ 45 14	10 20.9	9 7.2	10 28.8	6 45.3	26 47.2	10 28.1	15 53.0	13 33.7	1 22.5	1 35.4
21 W	11 54 46	0♈ 33 42	19 48 52	26 45 2	10 17.8	9 5.2	12 24.4	7 59.3	26 57.8	10 35.1	15 50.6	13 33.6	1 22.9	1 34.0
22 Th	11 58 43	1 33 15	3♐ 33 45	10♐ 15 16	10 14.6	9D 1.6	14 18.3	9 13.4	27 7.8	10 41.9	15 48.1	13 33.4	1 23.3	1 32.6
23 F	12 2 39	2 32 46	16 49 55	23 18 10	10 11.4	9 1.6	16 10.1	10 27.4	27 17.2	10 48.6	15 45.5	13 33.2	1 23.7	1 31.2
24 Sa	12 6 36	3 32 15	29 40 32	5♑ 57 37	10 8.2	9R 2.1	17 59.2	11 41.4	27 26.0	10 55.1	15 42.8	13 33.0	1 24.0	1 29.8
25 Su	12 10 32	4 31 42	12♑ 10 1	18 18 20	10 5.0	9 1.9	19 45.5	12 55.5	27 34.2	11 1.4	15 40.0	13 32.6	1 24.3	1 28.3
26 M	12 14 29	5 31 8	24 23 13	0♒ 25 14	10 1.9	9 0.1	21 28.2	14 9.5	27 41.8	11 7.6	15 37.2	13 32.3	1 24.6	1 26.9
27 Tu	12 18 25	6 30 32	6♒ 24 57	12 22 53	9 58.7	8 56.0	23 7.2	15 23.5	27 48.7	11 13.7	15 34.2	13 31.8	1 24.8	1 25.4
28 W	12 22 22	7 29 54	18 19 36	24 15 27	9 55.5	8 49.4	24 41.8	16 37.6	27 55.0	11 19.6	15 31.2	13 31.3	1 25.1	1 23.9
29 Th	12 26 19	8 29 14	0♓ 10 33	6♓ 6 15	9 52.3	8 40.4	26 11.9	17 51.6	28 0.6	11 25.3	15 28.2	13 30.8	1 25.2	1 22.4
30 F	12 30 15	9 28 33	12 1 51	17 57 58	9 49.2	8 29.7	27 36.9	19 5.6	28 5.6	11 30.9	15 25.0	13 30.2	1 25.4	1 20.9
31 Sa	12 34 12	10♈ 27 49	23♓ 54 50	29♓ 32 39	9♊ 46.0	8♊ 18.2	28♈ 56.6	20♓ 19.6	28♏ 9.9	11♑ 36.3	15♏ 21.8	13♐ 29.6	1♑ 25.5	1♏ 19.3

DECLINATION and LATITUDE

DAY	☉ DECL	☽ DECL	☽ LAT	☽ 12hr DECL	☿ DECL	☿ LAT	♀ DECL	♀ LAT	♂ DECL	♂ LAT	♃ DECL	♃ LAT	♄ DECL	♄ LAT
1	7S36	18S49	4S41	16S37	11S60	2S 3	17S20	0S32	16S40	1N37	22S57	0N13	14S21	2N29
2	7 13	14 55	4 36	12 45	11 19	2 4	17 1	0 34	16 46	1 37	22 57	0 13	14 21	2 29
3	6 50	10 28	4 58	8 4	10 36	2 1	16 42	0 37	16 51	1 36	22 56	0 13	14 20	2 29
4	6 27	5 36	4 47	3 5	9 52	1 59	16 22	0 39	16 56	1 36	22 56	0 13	14 20	2 30
5	6 4	0 31	4 24	2N 3	9 7	1 55	16 2	0 42	17 1	1 36	22 55	0 13	14 19	2 30
6	5 40	4N37	3 49	7 9	8 20	1 52	15 41	0 44	17 6	1 35	22 55	0 13	14 19	2 30
7	5 17	9 38	3 3	12 3	7 33	1 47	15 19	0 47	17 10	1 35	22 54	0 13	14 18	2 30
8	4 54	14 21	2 8	16 32	6 44	1 42	14 58	0 49	17 15	1 34	22 54	0 13	14 18	2 30
9	4 30	18 34	1 6	20 24	5 54	1 37	14 36	0 51	17 20	1 34	22 53	0 13	14 17	2 31
10	4 7	22 1	0N 1	23 23	5 3	1 31	14 13	0 53	17 24	1 33	22 53	0 13	14 17	2 31
11	3 43	24 26	1 10	25 10	4 11	1 25	13 50	0 55	17 28	1 33	22 52	0 13	14 16	2 31
12	3 20	25 32	2 16	25 31	3 18	1 17	13 27	0 57	17 32	1 32	22 52	0 13	14 15	2 31
13	2 56	25 3	3 17	24 14	2 24	1 10	13 4	0 59	17 36	1 32	22 51	0 13	14 15	2 31
14	2 32	[illegible]	[illegible]	[illegible]	[illegible]	[illegible]	[illegible]	[illegible]	[illegible]	[illegible]	[illegible]	[illegible]	[illegible]	[illegible]
15	2 9													
16	1 45													
17	1 21													
18	0 58													
19	0 34													
20	0 10													
21	0N13													
22	0 37													
23	1 1													
24	1 24													
25	1 48													
26	2 12													
27	2 35	[illegible]	[illegible]	[illegible]	[illegible]	[illegible]	[illegible]	[illegible]	[illegible]	[illegible]	[illegible]	[illegible]	[illegible]	[illegible]
28	2 59	19 31	4 45	18 3	11 2	1 34	6 33	1 23	18 24	1 20	22 44	0 14	14 2	2 34
29	3 22	16 5	5 0	13 58	11 46	1 46	6 3	1 24	18 26	1 19	22 44	0 14	14 1	2 34
30	3 45	11 43	5 3	9 21	12 27	1 37	5 37	1 25	18 28	1 18	22 43	0 13	13 60	2 34
31	4N 9	6S33	4S52	4S22	13N 6	2N 8	3S 9	1S23	18S30	1N17	22S43	0N13	13S59	2N35

The arrows indicate a Full Moon and New Moon as well as waxing and waning Moon.

DAY	♅ DECL	♅ LAT	♆ DECL	♆ LAT	♇ DECL	♇ LAT
1	22S22	0N 3	22S16	1N11	4N 3	17N14
5	22 22	0 3	22 15	1 11	4 6	17 16
9	22 23	0 3	22 15	1 11	4 9	17 17
13	22 23	0 3	22 15	1 11	4 12	17 19
17	22 23	0 3	22 15	1 11	4 15	17 20
21	22 23	0 3	22 15	1 11	4 18	17 22
25	22 23	0 3	22 15	1 11	4 21	17 23
29	22S23	0N 3	22S15	1N12	4N24	17N24

☽ PHENOMENA		
dy	hr	
2	11	APOGE
16	21	PERIG
29	16	APOGE
MAX/0 DECL.		
dy	hr	° '
5	2	0
12	5	25N34
18	7	0
24	20	25S40
MAX/0 LAT		
dy	hr	° '
2	16	4S59
10	0	0
16	7	5N[illegible]
22	10	0
29	17	5S 3

VOID OF COURSE ☽ LAST ASPT		☽ INGRESS		
1	1am 6	1	♓	5pm30
3	5pm26	4	♈	6am 8
6	8pm55	6	♉	6pm10
8	5pm23	9	♊	4am30
11	4am26	11	♋	11am49
13	11am22	13	♌	3pm22
15	9am14	15	♍	3pm48
17	10am11	17	♎	2pm32
18	12pm19	19	♏	2pm49
21	12pm32	21	♐	5pm42
22	10pm35	24	♑	0am37
26	6am38	26	♒	11am10
28	7pm34	28	♓	11pm38
31	8am36	31	♈	12pm15

dy	hr	mn		PHASE
2	18	32	12♓22	●
10	18	28	20♊23	☽
17	10	11	27♍ 1	○
24	7	59	3♑52	☾

DAILY ASPECTARIAN

Day	Aspect	Time
1 Th	☽☌♂	1am 6
	♀✶♅	2 21
	☽⚼♃	3 4
	☽∥♀	10 30
	☽∥♂	1pm25
	☽✶☿	7 49
	☽△♇	9 25
2 F	☽∥♄	3am16
	☽⚺☿	6 7
	☽✶♃	9 48
	☿∥♂	3pm 7
	☉☌☽	6 32
	☽□♅	8 43
	☽∥☿	11 9
3 Sa	☽✶♀	1am35
	☽△♄	2 32
	☽⚻♇	3 43
	♀∠☿	7 38
	☿✶♃	8 0
	♀□♄	10 44
	☽△♂	3pm26
	☉∥☽	7 33
	☉□♅	8 49
4 Su	☽∥♇	7am11
	☽□☿	8 31
	☽⚻♄	8 47
	☽✶♇	9 57
	☽∠♀	11 22
	☽⚻♂	10pm27
	☽□♃	11 8
5 M	☽0N	2am27
	☽✶☿	5 43
	☽△♅	9 15
	☉✶☽	12pm32
	☽⚻♄	2 32
	☽✶♀	8 35
	☽∥♇	9 40
6 T	☿□♅	4am26
	☉∥☽	4 39
	☽⚻♂	5 14
	☽⚻♅	3pm12
	☽∥☿	3 17
	☉△♄	4 4
	☽∠☿	5 10
	☽△☿	8 35
	☉∠☽	9 6
	☽⚻♇	9 50
7 W	☉⚻♇	5am42
	♂⚼♃	6 30
	☽△♃	11 33
	☿△♄	3pm26
	☽⚻♅	8 44
	☿⚻♇	10 41
	☽∥♄	11 41
8 Th	☽⚻☿	2am 3
	☽⚻♄	2 4
	☽∥♀	3 1
	☽✶☿	4 1
	☉✶☽	5 7
	♄∠☿	5 27
	☽□♀	2pm32
	☽∥♂	4 23
	☽⚻♃	5 2
	☽⚻♂	5 25
	☉⚺☿	8 33
9 F	☽⚺☿	6am34
	☽✶♇	7 36
	♀∠♃	6pm32
	♀∥♄	8 17
	☉∥♇	8 55
	☽⚼♃	9 47
10 Sa	☽∥☿	1am34
	☽∥♅	2 57
	♀□♂	3 9
	☽⚻♅	5 34
	☽∥♃	7 16
	☽⚻♄	10 49
	☽⚻♇	11 34
	☉□☽	6pm28
	☽□☿	10 33
	☿∥♇	11 58
11 Su	☽✶♂	2am33
	☽△♀	4 26
	☽⚻♄	1pm33
	☽⚻☿	2 6
	☽△♇	2 57
	☉∥☿	10 15
12 M	☽⚻♃	4am31
	☿△♂	5 4
	☽⚻♂	5 37
	☽⚻♀	9 31
	☽✶♅	11 33
	☽△♄	4pm 0
13 T	☉△☽	3am13
	☽△♂	7 39
	☽△☿	11 22
	☽⚻♅	12pm57
	☽✶♀	1 23
	☽✶☿	5 33
	☽☍♇	6 13
14 W	☽∥♃	1am 0
	☽∥♅	4 32
	☽∥☿	5 31
	☉⚻☽	5 54
	☽⚼♃	7 24
	♀ ♓	12pm36
	☽△♅	1 33
	☽⚻☿	3 47
	☿ ♈	4 28
	☽□♄	5 36
	☽⚻☿	6 1
	☿✶♀	10 50
15 Th	☿⚻♄	5am15
	☽⚻♃	7 43
	☉✶☽	7 45
	☽∥♂	7 53
	☿□☿	8 36
	☽☍♂	9 14
	☿✶♇	12pm32
	☿0N	2 29
	♀✶☿	2 35
	☽△☿	5 54
	☽⚻♀	6 12
	☽✶♇	6 27
	☽✶☿	7 18
	♀△♇	9 16
16 F	☽∥♄	0am11
	☽△♃	7 34
	☽∥♀	10 49
	☉△♂	12pm16
	☽□♅	1 7
	☽✶♄	4 57
	☽∠♇	5 58
17 Sa	☉∥☿	0am34
	☽✶♂	9 2
	☉☍☽	10 11
	☽∥♇	3pm 4
	☽∠♄	4 24
	☽□☿	5 0
	☽✶♇	8 27
	☽✶♀	9 25
	☽∥☿	10 40
18 Su	☽⚻☿	1am24
	☉∥☽	3 24
	♅SR	6 21
	☽0S	6 43
	☽□♃	7 4
	☽∠♂	9 0
	☉∥☽	9 40
	☽✶♅	12pm19
	☽✶♄	4 6
	☽∥☿	8 34
	☽∥♇	10 34
	☽⚻♀	11 24
19 M	☽✶♂	9am24
	☽∠♅	12pm29
	☉⚻☽	1 24
	☽✶☿	3 5
	☽⚻♇	5 27
	☽∥♀	9 42
	☿□♃	11 52
20 T	☽△♀	2am 9
	☿∥♇	4 16
	☽✶♃	8 14
	☽⚻☿	9 28
	☉ ♈	10 26
	☽✶♅	1pm22
	☽∥♄	2 48
	☉⚻☽	4 12
	☽⚻♄	5 15
	☿⚻♂	5 54
	☽∠☿	6 8
21 W	☉⚻♄	6am33
	☽⚼♃	10 3
	☽∥♂	10 27
	☽⚻♂	12pm32
	☿△♅	2 31
	☽⚻☿	3 16
	☉□☿	7 58
	☽✶☿	8 9
	☉△☽	8 10
	☽✶♇	8 26
	☉✶♇	11 45
22 Th	☽□♀	11am11
	☽⚼♃	12pm55
	☽∥☿	1 11
	☽∥♅	2 18
	☽∥♃	5 32
	☽⚻♅	6 0
	☿✶♄	6 48
	☽✶♄	10 2
	☽△☿	10 35
	☽∠♇	11 26
23 F	♀✶♃	7am31
	☽⚻♂	7pm43
24 Sa	☽⚻♄	1am58
	☽⚻☿	3 17
	☽✶♇	3 27
	☉□☽	7 59
	☿∥♀	11 10
	☽⚼♃	9pm46
25 Su	☽⚼♂	0am48
	☽✶♀	1 38
	☽⚻♅	2 41
	☽✶♄	6 48
	♀□♅	11 59
	☽□☿	5pm18
26 M	☽⚻♂	6am38
	☽⚼♅	8 14
	☽∠♀	10 34
	☽⚻☿	1pm59
	☽□♇	2 1
27 T	☉✶☽	0am12
	☽∥♃	0 38
	♀△♄	3 20
	☽∥♅	3 57
	☽∥☿	5 11
	☿☍♇	7 52
	☽⚼♃	9 45
	☽✶♅	2pm18
	☽□♄	6 21
	♀⚻♇	7 39
	☽∠☿	8 8
	☽✶♀	8 10
28 W	☉∠☽	9am12
	☽∥♂	9 42
	☽✶☿	2pm47
	☽⚼♃	4 19
	☽□♂	7 34
29 Th	☽△♇	2am25
	☽✶☿	2 31
	☽∥♄	11 46
	☉✶☽	6pm21
	☽∥☿	8 38
	☽✶♃	10 57
30 F	☽∠☿	1am20
	☽□♅	2 59
	☽△♄	6 49
	☽⚻♇	8 43
	☿⚻♂	8 57
	☿⚻♅	3pm45
	☽⚺♀	3 56
31 Sa	☽△♂	8am36
	☽∥♀	9 12
	☽✶☿	11 19
	☽∥♇	11 43
	☉∥☽	12pm 7
	☽⚻♄	12 55
	☽✶♇	2 52
	☽□☿	3 6
	☉∥♇	5 44
	☿ ♉	8 27

LONGITUDE

DAY	SID. TIME	☉	☽	☽ 12 Hour	MEAN ☊	TRUE ☊	☿	♀	♂	♃	♄	♅	♆	♇
	h m s	° ' "	° ' "	° ' "	° '	° '	° '	° '	° '	° '	° '	° '	° '	° '
1 Th	10 33 35	10♓ 33 41	21♒ 20 28	27♒ 16 43	11♊ 21.3	11♊R32.1	3♓ 58.6	13♒ 18.7	21♏ 52.2	7♑ 50.4	16♏R21.5	13♐ 25.8	1♑ 7.9	1♏R56.8
2 F	10 39 32	11 35 34	3♓ 12 44	9♓ 8 41	11 18.1	11 18.0	5 46.6	14 32.7	22 11.6	7 59.8	16 20.9	13 26.7	1 9.0	1 55.9
3 Sa	10 43 48	12 36 6	15 4 43	21 0 59	11 14.9	11 3.0	7 35.7	15 46.8	22 30.7	8 9.2	16 20.2	13 27.6	1 10.0	1 55.0
4 Su	10 47 45	13 36 15	26 37 38	2♈ 54 32	11 11.8	10 48.3	9 25.8	17 0.8	22 49.4	8 18.4	16 19.4	13 28.4	1 11.0	1 54.1
5 M	10 51 41	14 36 23	8♈ 32 31	14 51 48	11 8.6	10 35.1	11 16.9	18 14.8	23 7.6	8 27.4	16 18.5	13 29.1	1 11.9	1 53.1
6 Tu	10 55 38	15 36 29	20 51 59	26 53 40	11 5.4	10 24.5	13 9.1	19 28.9	23 25.5	8 36.4	16 17.4	13 29.8	1 12.9	1 52.1
7 W	10 59 34	16 36 33	2♉ 57 12	9♉ 2 58	11 2.2	10 16.8	15 2.2	20 42.9	23 42.9	8 45.2	16 16.3	13 30.4	1 13.8	1 51.1
8 Th	11 3 31	17 36 34	15 11 23	21 22 35	10 59.1	10 12.3	16 56.4	21 56.9	23 59.9	8 53.9	16 15.1	13 31.0	1 14.6	1 50.0
9 F	1								.3	9 2.5	16 13.8	13 31.5	1 15.4	1 48.9
10 Sa	1								.6	9 10.9	16 12.4	13 32.0	1 16.2	1 47.8
11 Su	1								.3	9 19.3	16 10.9	13 32.4	1 17.0	1 46.7
12 M	1								.5	9 27.5	16 9.2	13 32.8	1 17.8	1 45.5
13 Tu	1								.2	9 35.5	16 7.5	13 33.1	1 18.3	1 44.3
14 W	1								.5	9 43.5	16 5.8	13 33.3	1 19.1	1 43.1
15 Th	1								.2	9 51.3	16 3.9	13 33.5	1 19.8	1 41.9
16 F	1								.5	9 58.9	16 [illegible].9	13 33.7	1 20.4	1 40.6
17 Sa	1								.2	10 6.4	1[illegible].8	13 33.8	1 20.9	1 39.3
18 Su	1								.4	10 13.8	1[illegible]	13R 33.8	1 21.5	1 38.0
19 M	1								.1	10 21.0	1[illegible]	13 33.8	1 22.0	1 36.7
20 Tu	1								.2	10 28.1	1[illegible]0	13 33.7	1 22.5	1 35.4
21 W	1								.8	10 35.1	1[illegible].6	13 33.6	1 22.9	1 34.0
22 Th	1								.8	10 41.9	15 [illegible].1	13 33.4	1 23.3	1 32.6
23 F	1								.2	10 48.6	15 45.5	13 33.2	1 23.7	1 31.2
24 Sa	1								.0	10 55.1	15 42.8	13 33.0	1 24.0	1 29.8
25 Su	1								.2	11 1.4	15 40.0	13 32.6	1 24.3	1 28.3
26 M	1								.8	11 7.6	15 37.2	13 32.3	1 24.6	1 26.9
27 Tu	1								.7	11 13.7	15 34.2	13 31.8	1 24.8	1 25.4
28 W	1								.0	11 19.6	15 31.2	13 31.3	1 25.1	1 23.9
29 Th	[illegible]								.6	11 25.3	15 28.2	13 30.8	1 25.2	1 22.4
30 F	12 30 15	9 28 33	12 1 51	17 37 38	9 49.2	8 29.7	27 36.9	19 5.6	28 5.6	11 30.9	15 25.0	13 30.2	1 25.4	1 20.9
31 Sa	12 34 12	10♈ 27 49	23♓ 54 50	29♓ 32 39	9♊ 46.0	8♊ 18.2	28♈ 36.6	20♓ 19.6	28♏ 9.9	11♑ 36.3	15♏ 21.8	13♐ 29.6	1♑ 25.5	1♏ 19.3

The arrows indicate when a planet moves into retrograde motion. At this time it appears from earth that the planet is moving slower (backward) but in fact it is not.

DECLINATION and LATITUDE

DAY	☉ DECL	☽ DECL	☽ LAT	☽ 12hr DECL	☿ DECL	☿ LAT	♀ DECL	♀ LAT	♂ DECL	♂ LAT	♃ DECL	♃ LAT	♄ DECL	♄ LAT
1	7S36	18S49	4S41	16S37	11S60	2S 5	17S20	0S32	16S40	1N37	22S37	0N13	14S21	2N29
2	7 13	14 33	4 36	12 45	11 19	2 4	17 1	0 34	16 46	1 37	22 57	0 15	14 21	2 29
3	6 50	10 28	4 58	8 4	10 36	2 1	16 42	0 37	16 51	1 36	22 56	0 15	14 20	2 29
4	6 27	5 36	4 47	3 5	9 52	1 59	16 22	0 39	16 56	1 36	22 56	0 15	14 20	2 30
5	6 4	0 31	4 24	2N 3	9 7	1 55	16 2	0 42	17 1	1 36	22 55	0 15	14 19	2 30
6	5 40	4N37	3 49	7 9	8 20	1 52	15 41	0 44	17 6	1 35	22 55	0 15	14 19	2 30
7	5 17	9 38	3 3	12 3	7 33	1 47	15 19	0 47	17 10	1 35	22 54	0 15	14 18	2 30
8	4 54	14 21	2 8	16 32	6 44	1 42	14 58	0 49	17 15	1 34	22 54	0 15	14 18	2 30
9	4 30	18 34	1 6	20 24	5 54	1 37	14 36	0 51	17 20	1 34	22 53	0 15	14 17	2 31
10	4 7	22 1	0N 1	23 23	5 3	1 31	14 13	0 53	17 24	1 33	22 53	0 15	14 17	2 31
11	3 43	24 26	1 10	25 10	4 11	1 25	13 50	0 55	17 28	1 33	22 52	0 15	14 16	2 31
12	3 20	25 32	2 16	25 31	3 18	1 17	13 27	0 57	17 32	1 32	22 52	0 15	14 15	2 31
13	2 56	25 5	3 17	24 14	2 24	1 10	13 4	0 59	17 36	1 32	22 51	0 15	14 15	2 31
14	2 32	22 58	4 8	21 19	1 29	1 2	12 40	1 1	17 40	1 31	22 51	0 15	14 14	2 32
15	2 9	19 17	4 44	16 55	0 34	0 53	12 15	1 3	17 44	1 31	22 50	0 14	14 13	2 32
16	1 45	14 15	5 0	11 22	0N22	0 44	11 51	1 5	17 48	1 30	22 50	0 14	14 13	2 32
17	1 21	8 17	4 56	5 5	1 18	0 34	11 26	1 7	17 51	1 29	22 49	0 14	14 12	2 32
18	0 58	1 30	4 30	1S26	2 15	0 23	11 0	1 9	17 55	1 29	22 49	0 14	14 11	2 32
19	0 34	4S39	3 46	7 46	3 11	0 13	10 35	1 10	17 58	1 28	22 48	0 14	14 10	2 33
20	0 10	10 45	2 48	13 32	4 8	0 2	10 9	1 12	18 2	1 27	22 48	0 14	14 9	2 33
21	0N13	16 5	1 40	18 23	5 3	0N10	9 43	1 14	18 5	1 27	22 47	0 14	14 9	2 33
22	0 37	20 24	0 29	22 6	5 58	0 22	9 16	1 15	18 8	1 26	22 47	0 14	14 8	2 33
23	1 1	23 29	0S41	24 32	6 53	0 34	8 50	1 16	18 11	1 25	22 46	0 14	14 7	2 33
24	1 24	25 14	1 48	25 37	7 46	0 46	8 23	1 18	18 13	1 24	22 46	0 14	14 6	2 33
25	1 48	25 39	2 47	25 25	8 38	0 58	7 56	1 19	18 16	1 23	22 45	0 14	14 5	2 34
26	2 12	24 48	3 37	23 56	9 28	1 10	7 28	1 20	18 19	1 22	22 45	0 14	14 4	2 34
27	2 35	22 48	4 17	21 26	10 16	1 22	7 1	1 22	18 21	1 21	22 44	0 14	14 3	2 34
28	2 59	19 51	4 45	18 3	11 2	1 34	6 33	1 23	18 24	1 20	22 44	0 14	14 2	2 34
29	3 22	16 5	5 0	13 58	11 46	1 46	6 5	1 24	18 26	1 19	22 44	0 14	14 1	2 34
30	3 45	11 43	5 3	9 21	12 27	1 37	5 37	1 25	18 28	1 18	22 43	0 13	13 60	2 34
31	4N 9	6S53	4S52	4S22	13N 6	2N 8	5S 9	1S25	18S30	1N17	22S43	0N13	13S59	2N35

DAY	♅ DECL	♅ LAT	♆ DECL	♆ LAT	♇ DECL	♇ LAT
1	22S22	0N 3	22S16	1N11	4N 3	17N14
5	22 22	0 3	22 15	1 11	4 6	17 16
9	22 23	0 3	22 15	1 11	4 9	17 17
13	22 23	0 3	22 15	1 11	4 12	17 19
17	22 23	0 3	22 15	1 11	4 15	17 20
21	22 23	0 3	22 15	1 11	4 18	17 22
25	22 23	0 3	22 15	1 11	4 21	17 23
29	22S23	0N 3	22S15	1N12	4N24	17N24

☽ PHENOMENA			VOID OF COURSE ☽ LAST ASPT		☽ INGRESS		
dy	hr		dy	time	dy	sign	time
2	11	APOGE	1	1am 6	1	♓	5pm30
16	21	PERIG	3	3pm26	4	♈	6am 8
29	16	APOGE	6	8pm55	6	♉	6pm10
MAX/0 DECL			8	5pm25	9	♊	4am30
dy	hr	° '	11	4am26	11	♋	11am49
5	2	0	13	11am22	13	♌	3pm22
12	5	25N34	15	9am14	15	♍	3pm46
18	7	0	17	10am11	17	♎	2pm52
24	20	25S40	18	12pm19	19	♏	2pm49
			21	12pm32	21	♐	5pm42
			22	10pm35	24	♑	0am37
			26	6am36	26	♒	11am10
			28	7pm34	28	♓	11pm38
			31	8am36	31	♈	12pm15

MAX/0 LAT		
dy	hr	° '
2	16	4S59
10	0	0
16	7	5N 1
22	10	0
29	17	5S 3

dy	hr	mn		PHASE
2	18	32	12♓22	●
10	18	28	20♊23	☽
17	10	11	27♍ 1	○
24	7	59	3♑52	☾

DAILY ASPECTARIAN

Day	Aspect	Time
1 Th	☽□♂	1am 6
	♀⚹♅	2 21
	☽∠♃	3 4
	☽∥♀	10 30
	☽∥♂	1pm25
	☽⚹☿	7 49
	☽△♇	9 25
2 F	☽∥♄	3am16
	☽⚻☿	6 7
	☽⚹♃	9 48
	♀∥♂	3pm 7
	☉⚻☽	6 32
	☽□♅	8 43
	☽∥☿	11 9
3 Sa	☽⚹♀	1am35
	☽△♄	2 32
	☽⚼♇	3 43
	♀∠☿	7 38
	☿⚹♃	8 0
	♀□♄	10 44
	☽△♂	3pm26
	☉∥☽	7 33
	☉□♅	8 49
4 Su	☽∥♇	7am11
	☽□☿	8 31
	☽⚼♄	8 47
	☽⚹♇	9 57
	☽∠♀	11 22
	☽⚼♂	10pm27
	☽□♃	11 8
5 M	☽0N	2am27
	☽⚹☿	3 43
	☽△♅	9 15
	☉⚹☽	12pm32
	☽⚻♄	2 32
	☽⚹♀	8 55
	☽∥♇	9 40
6 T	☿□♅	4am26
	☉∥☽	4 39
	☽⚻♂	5 14
	☽⚼♅	3pm12
	☽∥☿	3 17
	☉△♄	4 4
	☽∠☿	5 10
	☽△☿	8 35
	☉∠☽	9 6
	☽⚻♇	9 50
7 W	☉⚼♇	3am42
	♂∠♃	6 30
	☽△♃	11 33
	☿△♄	3pm26
	☽⚻♅	8 44
	☿⚼♇	10 41
	☽∥♄	11 41
8 Th	☽⚼☿	2am 3
	☽⚻♄	2 4
	☽∥♀	3 1
	☽⚹☿	4 1
	☉⚹☽	5 7
	♄∠☿	5 27
	☽□♀	2pm32
	☽∥♂	4 23
	☽⚼♃	5 2
	☽⚻♂	5 25
	☉⚻☿	8 33
9 F	☽⚹☿	6am34
	☽⚹♇	7 36
	♀∠♃	6pm52
	☿∥♄	8 17
	☉∥♇	8 55
	☽⚻♃	9 47
10 Sa	☽∥☿	1am54
	☽∥♅	2 57
	♀□♂	3 9
	☽⚻♅	5 54
	☽∥♃	7 16
	☽⚻♄	10 49
	☽⚼♇	11 34
	☉□☽	6pm28
	☽□☿	10 33
	☿∥♇	11 58
11 Su	☽⚹♂	2am33
	☽△♀	4 26
	☽⚼♄	1pm53
	☽⚻☿	2 6
	☽△♇	2 57
	☉∥☿	10 15
12 M	☽⚻♃	4am31
	☿△♂	3 4
	☽⚼♂	5 37
	☽⚼♀	9 31
	☽⚹♅	11 33
	☽△♄	4pm 0
13 T	☉△☽	3am13
	☽△♂	7 39
	☽△☿	11 22
	☽⚼♅	12pm37
	☽⚹♀	1 23
	☽⚹☿	5 33
	☽□♇	6 13
14 W	☽∥♃	1am 0
	☽∥♅	4 32
	☽∥☿	5 31
	☉⚼☽	5 54
	☽⚹♃	7 24
	♀ ♓	12pm36
	☽△♅	1 33
	☽⚼☿	3 47
	☿ ♈	4 28
	☽□♄	5 36
	☽⚼☿	6 1
	☿⚹♀	10 50
15 Th	☿⚼♄	3am13
	☽⚼♃	7 4[illegible]
	☉⚹☽	7 4[illegible]
	☽∥♂	7 [illegible]
	☿□☿	8 [illegible]
	☽□♂	9 [illegible]
	☿⚹♇	12p[illegible]
	☿0N	2 [illegible]
	♀⚹☿	2 3[illegible]
	☽△☿	5 54
	☽⚻♀	6 12
	☽⚹♇	6 27
	☽⚹☿	7 18
	♀△♇	9 16
16 F	☽∥♄	0am11
	☽△♃	7 34
	☽∥♀	10 49
	☉△♂	12pm16
	☽□♅	1 7
	☽⚹♄	4 57
	☽∠♇	5 58
17 Sa	☉∥☿	0am54
	☽⚹♂	9 2
	☉⚻☽	10 11
	☽∥♇	3pm 4
	☽∠♄	4 24
	☽□☿	5 0
	☽⚹♇	8 27
	☽⚹♀	9 25
	☽∥☿	10 40
18	☽⚻☿	1am24
	☉∥☽	3 24
	♅SR	6 21
	☽0S	6 43
	☽□♃	7 4
	☽∠♂	9 0
	☉∥☽	9 40
	☽⚹♅	12pm19
	☽⚹♄	4 6
	☽∥☿	5 34
	☽∥♇	10 34
	☽⚼♀	11 24
19 M	☽⚹♂	9am24
	☽∠♅	12pm29
	☉⚹☽	1 24
	☽⚹☿	3 3
	☽⚼♇	5 27
	☽∥♀	9 42
	☿□♃	11 52
20 T	☽△♀	2am 9
	☿∥♇	4 16
	☽⚹♃	8 14
	☽⚻☿	9 28
	☉ ♈	10 26
	☽⚹♅	1pm22
	☽∥♄	2 48
	☉⚼☽	4 12
	☽⚻♄	5 15
	☿⚼♂	5 54
	☽∠☿	6 8
21 W	☉⚼♄	6am33
	☽∠♃	10 3
	☽∥♂	10 27
	☽⚼♂	12pm32
	☿△♅	2 31
	☽⚼☿	3 16
	☉□☿	7 58
	☽⚻☿	8 9
	☉△☽	8 10
	☽⚹♇	8 26
	☉⚻♇	11 45
22 Th	☽□♀	11am11
	☽⚹♃	12pm55
	☽∥☿	1 11
	☽∥♅	2 18
	☽∥♃	5 32
	☽⚼♅	6 0
	☿⚻♄	6 48
	☽⚻♄	10 2
	☽△☿	10 35
	☽∠♇	11 26
23 F	♀⚹♃	7am31
	☽⚹♂	7pm43
24 Sa	☽∠♄	1am55
	☽⚻☿	3 17
	☽⚹♇	3 27
	☉□☽	7 59
	☿∥♀	11 10
	☽∠♃	9pm46
25 Su	☽∠♂	0am46
	☽⚹♀	1 38
	☽⚹♅	2 41
	☽⚹♄	4 48
	♀□♅	11 59
	☽□☿	5pm18
26 M	☽⚼♂	6am38
	☽∠♅	8 14
	☽∠♀	10 34
	☽⚹☿	1pm59
	☽□♇	2 1
27 T	☉⚹☽	0am12
	☽∥♃	0 38
	♀△♄	3 20
	☽∥♅	3 57
	☽∥☿	5 11
	☿⚹♇	7 52
	☽⚹♃	9 45
	☽⚹♅	2pm18
	☽□♄	6 21
	♀⚼♇	7 39
	☽∠☿	8 8
	☽⚹♀	8 10
28 W	☉∠☽	9am12
	☽∥♂	9 42
	☽⚹☿	2pm47
	☽∠♃	4 19
	☽□♂	7 34
29 Th	☽△♇	2am25
	☽⚹☿	2 31
	☽∥♄	11 46
	☉⚹☽	6pm21
	☽∥☿	8 38
	☽⚹♃	10 57
30 F	☽∠☿	1am20
	☽□♅	2 59
	☽△♄	6 49
	☽⚼♇	8 43
	☿⚹♂	8 57
	☿⚼♅	3pm45
	☽⚹♀	3 56
31 Sa	☽△♂	8am36
	☽∥♀	9 12
	☽⚹☿	11 19
	☽∥♇	11 43
	☉∥☽	12pm 7
	☽⚼♄	12 55
	☽⚹♇	2 52
	☽□☿	3 6
	☉∥♇	5 44
	☿ ♉	8 27

LONGITUDE

DAY	SID. TIME	☉	☽	☽ 12 Hour	MEAN ☊	TRUE ☊	☿	♀	♂	♃	♄	♅	♆	♇
	h m s	° ' "	° ' "	° ' "	° '	° '	° '	° '	° '	° '	° '	° '	° '	° '
1 Th	10 35 35	10♓ 35 41	21♒ 20 28	27♒ 16 43	11♊ 21.3	11♊R32.1	3♓ 38.6	13♒ 18.7	21♏ 52.2	7♑ 50.4	16♏R21.5	13♐ 25.8	1♑ 7.9	1♏R56.8
2 F	10 39 32	11 35 54	3♓ 12 44	9♓ 8 41	11 18.1	11 18.0	5 46.6	14 32.7	22 11.6	7 59.8	16 20.9	13 26.7	1 9.0	1 55.9
3 Sa	10 43 48	12 36 6	15 4 43	21 0 59	11 14.9	11 3.0	7 35.7	15 46.8	22 30.7	8 9.2	16 20.2	13 27.6	1 10.0	1 55.0
4 Su	10 47 45	13 36 15	26 57 38	2♈ 34 52	11 11.8	10 48.3	9 25.8	17 0.8	22 49.4	8 18.4	16 19.4	13 28.4	1 11.0	1 54.1
5 M	10 51 41	14 36 23	8♈ 32 51	14 31 48	11 8.6	10 35.1	11 16.9	18 14.8	23 7.6	8 27.4	16 18.5	13 29.1	1 11.9	1 53.1
6 Tu	10 55 38	15 36 29	20 31 39	26 33 40	11 5.4	10 24.5	13 9.1	19 28.9	23 25.5	8 36.4	16 17.4	13 29.8	1 12.9	1 32.1
7 W	10 59 34	16 36 33	2♉ 57 12	9♉ 2 38	11 2.2	10 16.8	15 2.2	20 42.9	23 42.9	8 45.2	16 16.3	13 30.4	1 13.8	1 31.1
8 Th	11 3 31	17 36 34	15 11 23	21 22 35	10 59.1	10 12.3	16 56.4	21 56.9	23 59.9	8 53.9	16 15.1	13 31.0	1 14.6	1 50.0
9 F	11 7 27	18 36 34	27 38 4	3♊ 57 20	10 55.9	10D 10.3	18 51.5	23 11.0	24 16.5	9 2.5	16 13.8	13 31.5	1 15.4	1 48.9
10 Sa	11 11 24	19 36 32	10♊ 21 16	16 50 25	10 52.7	10R 10.1	20 47.4	24 25.0	24 32.6	9 10.9	16 12.4	13 32.0	1 16.2	1 47.8
11 Su	11 15 21	20 36 27	23 25 17	0♋ 6 20	10 49.5	10 10.2	22 44.2	25 39.0	24 48.3	9 19.3	16 10.9	13 32.4	1 17.0	1 46.7
12 M	11 19 17	21 36 20	6♋ 33 38	13 48 28	10 46.3	10 9.5	24 41.7	26 53.1	25 3.5	9 27.5	16 9.2	13 32.8	1 17.8	1 45.5
13 Tu	11 23 14	22 36 12	20 30 2	27 38 37	10 43.2	10 6.8	26 39.8	28 7.1	25 18.2	9 35.5	16 7.5	13 33.1	1 18.5	1 44.3
14 W	11 27 10	23 36 0	3♌ 14 3	12♌ 35 34	10 40.0	10 1.6	28 38.5	29 21.1	25 32.5	9 43.5	16 5.8	13 33.3	1 19.1	1 43.1
15 Th	11 31 7	24 35 47	20 3 30	27 35 39	10 36.8	9 53.8	0♈ 37.4	0♓ 35.2	25 46.2	9 51.3	16 3.9	13 33.5	1 19.8	1 41.9
16 F	11 35 3	25 35 31	5♍ 12 15	12♍ 30 59	10 33.6	9 44.0	2 36.4	1 49.2	25 59.5	9 58.9	16 1.9	13 33.7	1 20.4	1 40.6
17 Sa	11 39 0	26 35 13	20 30 49	28 10 13	10 30.5	9 33.2	4 35.3	3 3.2	26 12.2	10 6.4	15 59.8	13 33.8	1 20.9	1 39.3
18 Su	11 42 56	27 34 53	3♎ 47 50	13♎ 22 10	10 27.3	9 22.7	6 33.9	4 17.3	26 24.4	10 13.8	15 57.6	13R 33.8	1 21.5	1 38.0
19 M	11 46 53	28 34 31	20 52 1	28 16 20	10 24.1	9 13.8	8 31.8	5 31.3	26 36.1	10 21.0	15 55.4	13 33.8	1 22.0	1 36.7
20 Tu	11 50 50	29 34 7	3♏ 34 16	12♏ 45 14	10 20.9	9 7.2	10 28.8	6 45.3	26 47.2	10 28.1	15 53.0	13 33.7	1 22.5	1 35.4
21 W	11 54 46	0♈ 33 42	19 48 52	26 45 2	10 17.8	9 3.2	12 24.4	7 59.3	26 57.8	10 35.1	15 50.6	13 33.6	1 22.9	1 34.0
22 Th	11 58 43	1 33 13	3♐ 33 45	10♐ 13 16	10 14.6	9D 1.6	14 18.3	9 13.4	27 7.8	10 41.9	15 48.1	13 33.4	1 23.3	1 32.6
23 F	12 2 39	2 32 46	16 49 55	23 18 10	10 11.4	9 1.6	16 10.1	10 27.4	27 17.2	10 48.6	15 45.5	13 33.2	1 23.7	1 31.2
24 Sa	12 6 36	3 32 15	29 40 32	5♑ 57 37	10 8.2	9R 2.1	17 59.2	11 41.4	27 26.0	10 55.1	15 42.8	13 33.0	1 24.0	1 29.8
25 Su	12 10 32	4 31 42	12♑ 10 1	18 18 20	10 5.0	9 1.9	19 45.5	12 55.3	27 34.2	11 1.4	15 40.0	13 32.6	1 24.3	1 28.3
26 M	12 14 29	5 31 8	24 23 13	0♒ 25 14	10 1.9	9 0.1	21 28.2	14 9.5	27 41.8	11 7.6	15 37.2	13 32.3	1 24.6	1 26.9
27 Tu	12 18 25	6 30 32	6♒ 24 37	12 22 55	9 58.7	8 56.0	23 7.2	15 23.5	27 48.7	11 13.7	15 34.2	13 31.8	1 24.8	1 25.4
28 W	12 22 22	7 29 34	18 19 36	24 15 27	9 55.5	8 49.4	24 41.8	16 37.6	27 55.0	11 19.6	15 31.2	13 31.3	1 25.1	1 23.9
29 Th	12 26 19	8 29 14	0♓ 10 53	6♓ 6 13	9 52.3	8 40.4	26 11.9	17 51.6	28 0.6	11 25.3	15 28.2	13 30.8	1 25.2	1 22.4
30 F	12 30 15	9 28 33	12 1 31	17 57 58	9 49.2	8 29.7	27 36.9	19 5.6	28 5.6	11 30.9	15 25.0	13 30.2	1 25.4	1 20.9
31 Sa	12 34 12	10♈ 27 49	23♓ 54 50	29♓ 52 39	9♊ 46.0	8♊ 18.2	28♈ 36.6	20♓ 19.6	28♏ 9.9	11♑ 36.3	15♏ 21.8	13♐ 29.6	1♑ 28.5	1♏ 19.3

DECLINATION and LATITUDE

DAY	☉ DECL	☽ DECL	☽ LAT	☽ 12hr DECL	☿ DECL	☿ LAT	♀ DECL	♀ LAT	♂ DECL	♂ LAT	♃ DECL	♃ LAT	♄ DECL	♄ LAT
1	7S36	18S49	4N41	16S37	11S60	2S 5	17S20	0S32	16S40	1N37	22S57	0N13	14S21	2N29
2	7 13	14 33	4 36	12 45	11 19	2 4	17 1	0 34	16 46	1 37	22 57	0 13	14 21	2 29
3	6 50	10 28	4 38	8 4	10 36	2 1	16 42	0 37	16 51	1 36	22 56	0 13	14 20	2 29
4	6 27	5 36	4 47	3 5	9 52	1 39	16 22	0 39	16 56	1 36	22 56	0 13	14 20	2 30
5														
6														
7														
8														
9														
10														
11														
12														
13														
14														
15														
16														
17														
18														
19														
20														
21														
22														
23														
24	1 24	25 14	1 48	25 37	7 46	0 46	8 23	1 18	18 13	1 24	22 46	0 14	14 6	2 33
25	1 48	25 39	2 47	25 25	8 38	0 58	7 56	1 19	18 16	1 23	22 45	0 14	14 5	2 34
26	2 12	24 48	3 37	23 56	9 28	1 10	7 28	1 20	18 19	1 22	22 45	0 14	14 4	2 34
27	2 35	22 48	4 17	21 26	10 16	1 22	7 1	1 22	18 21	1 21	22 44	0 14	14 3	2 34
28	2 59	19 51	4 45	18 3	11 2	1 34	6 33	1 23	18 24	1 20	22 44	0 14	14 2	2 34
29	3 22	16 5	5 0	13 58	11 46	1 46	6 3	1 24	18 26	1 19	22 44	0 14	14 1	2 34
30	3 45	11 43	5 3	9 21	12 27	1 57	5 37	1 25	18 28	1 18	22 43	0 13	13 60	2 34
31	4N 9	6S33	4S52	4S22	13N 6	2N 8	5S 9	1S23	18S30	1N17	22S43	0N13	13S59	2N35

The arrow indicates the apogee and perigee of the moon to earth. Apogee is the farthest point and Perigee the closest point.

DAY	♅ DECL	♅ LAT	♆ DECL	♆ LAT	♇ DECL	♇ LAT
1	22S22	0N 3	22S16	1N11	4N 3	17N14
5	22 22	0 3	22 15	1 11	4 6	17 16
9	22 23	0 3	22 15	1 11	4 9	17 17
13	22 23	0 3	22 15	1 11	4 12	17 19
17	22 23	0 3	22 15	1 11	4 15	17 20
21	22 23	0 3	22 15	1 11	4 18	17 22
25	22 23	0 3	22 15	1 11	4 21	17 23
29	22S23	0N 3	22S15	1N12	4N24	17N24

☽ PHENOMENA		
dy	hr	
2	11	APOGEE
16	21	PERIGEE
29	16	APOGEE

MAX/0 DECL. dy	hr	° '
3	2	0
12	5	25N34
18	7	0
24	20	25S40

MAX/0 LAT. dy	hr	° '
2	16	4N59
10	0	0
16	7	5N 1
22	10	0
29	17	5S 3

VOID OF COURSE ☽ LAST ASPT		☽ INGRESS		
1	1am 6	1	♓	5pm30
3	3pm26	4	♈	6am 8
5	8pm55	6	♉	6pm10
8	5pm25	9	♊	4am30
11	4am26	11	♋	11am49
13	11am22	13	♌	3pm22
15	9am14	15	♍	3pm48
17	10am11	17	♎	2pm52
18	12pm19	19	♏	2pm49
21	12pm32	21	♐	8pm42
22	10pm35	24	♑	0am37
26	6am38	26	♒	11am10
28	7pm34	28	♓	11pm38
31	8am36	31	♈	12pm15

dy	hr	mn	PHASE	
2	18	32	12♓22	●
10	18	28	20♊23	☽
17	10	11	27♍ 1	○
24	7	59	3♑52	☾

DAILY ASPECTARIAN

Day	Aspect	Time
1 Th	☽□♂	1am 6
	♀⚹♅	2 21
	☽∠♃	3 4
	☽∥♀	10 30
	☽∥♂	1pm25
	☽⚹☿	7 49
	☽△♇	9 25
2 F	☽∥♄	3am16
	☽⚺☿	6 7
	☽⚹♃	9 48
	☿∥♂	3pm 7
	☉⚺☽	6 32
	☽□♅	8 43
	☽∥☿	11 9
3 S	☽⚹♀	1am35
	☽△♄	2 32
	☽⚻♇	3 43
	☿∠♆	7 38
	☿⚹♃	8 0
	♀□♄	10 44
	☽△♂	3pm26
	☉∥☽	7 35
	☉□♅	8 49
4 Su	☽∥♇	7am11
	☽□☿	8 31
	☽⚻♄	8 47
	☽⚹♇	9 57
	☽∠♀	11 22
	☽⚻♂	10pm27
	☽□♃	11 8
5 M	☽0N	2am27
	☽⚹♆	3 43
	☽△♅	9 15
	☉⚹☽	12pm32
	☽⚹♄	2 32
	☽⚹♀	8 55
	☽∥♇	9 40
6 T	☿□♅	4am26
	☉∥☽	4 39
	☽⚹♂	5 14
	☽⚻♅	3pm12
	☽∥☿	3 17
	☉△♄	4 4
	☽∠♆	5 10
	☽△☿	8 38
	☉∠☽	9 6
	☽⚻♇	9 50
7 W	☉⚻♇	5am42
	♂∠♃	6 30
	☽△♃	11 33
	☿△♄	3pm26
	☽⚹♅	8 44
	☿⚻♇	10 41
	☽∥♄	11 41
8 Th	☽⚻☿	2am 3
	☽⚻♄	2 4
	☽∥♀	3 1
	☽⚹☿	4 1
	☉⚹☽	5 7
	♄∠♆	5 27
	☽□♀	2pm32
	☽∥♂	4 23
	☽⚻♃	5 2
	☽⚻♂	5 25
	☉⚻☿	5 33
9 F	☽⚹☿	6am34
	☽⚹♇	7 36
	♀∠♃	6pm32
	♀∥♄	8 17
	☉∥♇	8 35
	☽⚻♃	9 47
10 S	☽∥☿	1am34
	☽∥♅	2 57
	♀□♂	3 9
	☽⚻♅	5 54
	☽∥♃	7 16
	☽⚹♄	10 49
	☽⚻♇	11 34
	☉□☽	6pm28
	☽□☿	10 33
	☿∥♇	11 58
11 Su	☽⚹♂	2am33
	☽△♀	4 26
	☽⚻♄	1pm33
	☽⚻☿	2 6
	☽△♇	2 57
	☉∥☿	10 15
12 M	☽⚻♃	4am31
	☿△♂	5 4
	☽⚻♂	5 37
	☽⚻☿	9 31
	☽⚹♅	11 33
	☽△♄	4pm 0
13 T	☉△☽	3am13
	☽△♂	7 39
	☽△☿	11 22
	☽⚻♅	12pm57
	☽⚹♀	1 23
	☽⚹☿	5 33
	☽□♇	6 13
14 W	☽∥♃	1am 0
	☽∥♅	4 32
	☽∥☿	5 31
	☉⚻☽	5 54
	☽⚹♃	7 24
	♀ ♓	12pm36
	☽△♅	1 33
	☽⚻♆	3 47
	☿ ♈	4 28
	☽□♄	5 36
	☽⚻♆	6 1
	☿⚹♇	10 50
15 Th	♀⚻♄	3am13
	☽⚻♃	7 43
	☉⚹☽	7 45
	☽∥♂	7 53
	☿□♆	8 36
	☽□♂	9 14
	☿⚹♇	12pm32
	☿0N	2 29
	♀⚹♆	2 35
	☽△♆	5 54
	☽⚻♀	6 12
	☽⚹♇	6 27
	☽⚹☿	7 18
	♀△♇	9 16
16 F	☽∥♄	0am11
	☽△♃	7 34
	☽∥♀	10 49
	☉△♂	12pm16
	☽□♅	1 7
	☽⚹♄	4 57
	☽∠♇	5 58
17 S	☉∥☿	0am54
	☽⚹♂	9 2
	☉☍☽	10 11
	☽∥♇	3pm 4
	☽∠♄	4 24
	☽□☿	5 0
	☽⚹♇	8 27
	☽⚹♀	9 25
	☽∥☿	10 40
18 Su	☽⚻☿	1am24
	☉∥☽	3 24
	♅SR	6 21
	☽0S	6 43
	☽□♃	7 4
	☽∠♂	9 0
	☉∥☽	9 40
	☽⚹♅	12pm19
	☽⚹♄	4 6
	☽∥☿	5 34
	☽∥♇	10 34
	☽⚻♀	11 24
19 M	☽⚹♂	9am24
	☽∠♅	12pm29
	☉⚹☽	1 24
	☽⚹☿	5 5
	☽⚺♇	5 27
	☽∥♀	9 42
	☿□♃	11 52
20 T	☽△♀	2am 9
	☿∥♇	4 16
	☽⚹♃	8 14
	☽⚹☿	9 28
	☉ ♈	10 26
	☽⚹♅	1pm22
	☽∥♄	2 48
	☉☍☽	4 12
	☽⚻♄	5 15
	☿⚻♂	5 54
	☽∠☿	6 8
21 W	☉☍♄	6am33
	☽∠♃	10 3
	☽∥♂	10 27
	☽⚻♂	12pm32
	☿△♅	2 31
	☽⚻☿	3 16
	☉☍☿	7 58
	☽⚹☿	8 9
	☉△☽	8 10
	☽⚹♇	8 26
	☉☍♇	11 45
22 Th	☽□♀	11am11
	☽⚹♃	12pm55
	☽∥☿	1 11
	☽∥♅	2 18
	☽∥♃	5 32
	☽⚻♅	6 0
	☿⚻♄	6 48
	☽⚹♄	10 2
	☽△☿	10 35
	☽∠♇	11 26
23 F	♀⚹♃	7am31
	☽⚹♂	7pm43
24 S	☽∠♄	1am58
	☽⚺☿	3 17
	☽⚹♇	3 27
	☉□☽	7 59
	☿∥♀	11 10
	☽⚺♃	9pm46
25 Su	☽∠♂	0am48
	☽⚹♀	1 38
	☽⚹♅	2 41
	☽⚹♄	6 48
	♀□♅	11 59
	☽□☿	5pm18
26 M	☽⚹♂	6am38
	☽∠♅	8 14
	☽∠♀	10 34
	☽⚹☿	1pm59
	☽□♇	2 1
27 T	☉⚹☽	0am12
	☽∥♃	0 38
	♀△♄	3 20
	☽∥♅	3 57
	☽∥☿	5 11
	☿⚹♇	7 52
	☽⚹♃	9 45
	☽⚹♅	2pm18
	☽□♄	6 21
	♀⚻♇	7 39
	☽∠☿	8 8
	☽⚹♀	8 10
28 W	☉∠☽	9am12
	☽∥♂	9 42
	☽⚹☿	2pm47
	☽∠♃	4 19
	☽□♂	7 34
29 Th	☽△♇	2am25
	☽⚹☿	2 31
	☽∥♄	11 46
	☉⚹☽	6pm21
	☽∥☿	8 38
	☽⚹♃	10 57
30 F	☽∠☿	1am20
	☽□♅	2 59
	☽△♄	6 49
	☽⚻♇	8 43
	☿⚻♂	8 57
	☿⚻♅	3pm48
	☽⚺♀	3 56
31 S	☽△♂	8am36
	☽∥♀	9 12
	☽⚹☿	11 19
	☽∥♇	11 43
	☉∥☽	12pm 7
	☽⚻♄	12 58
	☽⚹♇	2 52
	☽□☿	3 6
	☉∥♇	5 44
	☿ ♉	8 27

LONGITUDE

DAY	SID. TIME	☉	☽	☽ 12 Hour	MEAN ☊	TRUE ☊	☿	♀	♂	♃	♄	♅	♆	♇
	h m s	° ' "	° ' "	° ' "	° '	° '	° '	° '	° '	° '	° '	° '	° '	° '
1 Tu	18 35 1	8♋ 32 46	1♉ 2 33	7♉ 1 43	26♈ 14.3	27♈R20.8	3♌ 27.3	17♌ 44.8	20♑R12.8	22♓ 38.1	4♐R 7.3	19♐R36.2	4♑R18.5	4♏R35.9
2 W	18 38 57	9 49 59	12 58 46	18 54 18	26 11.1	27 19.8	4 4.3	18 54.1	19 57.7	22 40.2	4 4.1	19 34.0	4 16.9	4 35.5
3 Th	18 42 54	10 47 12	24 48 50	0♊ 42 53	26 7.9	27 16.7	4 37.2	20 3.3	19 42.2	22 42.2	4 1.0	19 31.7	4 15.3	4 35.1
4 F	18 46 50	11 44 25	6♊ 36 53	12 31 14	26 4.8	27 11.0	5 6.0	21 12.4	19 26.3	22 44.0	3 57.9	19 29.5	4 13.7	4 34.7
5 Sa	18 50 47	12 41 38	18 26 19	24 22 25	26 1.6	27 2.6	5 30.3	22 21.5	19 10.0	22 45.6	3 54.9	19 27.3	4 12.1	4 34.3
6 Su	18 54 43	13 38 52	0♋ 19 47	6♋ 18 40	25 58.4	26 51.8	5 50.6	23 30.4	18 53.4	22 47.0	3 52.0	19 25.1	4 10.5	4 34.0
7 M	18 58 40	14 36 5	12 19 13	18 21 37	25 55.2	26 39.2	6 6.2	24 39.2	18 36.6	22 48.2	3 49.2	19 23.0	4 8.9	4 33.7
8 Tu	19 2 37	15 33 19	24 25 58	0♌ 32 24	25 52.1	26 25.8	6 17.3	25 47.9	18 19.5	22 49.3	3 46.4	19 20.8	4 7.4	4 33.4
9 W	19 6 33	16 30 32	6♌ 41 2	12 31 58	25 48.9	26 12.9	6R 23.7	26 56.5	18 2.2	22 50.1	3 43.7	19 18.7	4 5.8	4 33.2
10 Th	19 10 30	17 27 46	19 5 19	25 21 15	25 45.7	26 1.4	6 23.4	28 5.0	17 44.8	22 50.7	3 41.1	19 16.7	4 4.2	4 33.0
11 F	19 14 26	18 25 0	1♍ 39 34	8♍ 1 29	25 42.5	25 32.3	6 22.3	29 13.3	17 27.3	22 51.1	3 38.6	19 14.6	4 2.6	4 32.8
12 Sa	19 18 23	19 22 13	14 26 12	20 54 19	25 39.3	25 46.1	6 14.5	0♍ 21.6	17 9.8	22R 51.4	3 36.1	19 12.6	4 1.1	4 32.7
13 Su	19 22 19	20 19 27	27 26 5	4♎ 1 49	25 36.2	25 42.8	6 2.0	1 29.7	16 52.3	22 51.4	3 33.8	19 10.6	3 59.5	4 32.6
14 M	19 26 16	21 16 41	10♎ 41 47	17 26 18	25 33.0	25D 41.6	5 45.0	2 37.8	16 34.8	22 51.3	3 31.5	19 8.6	3 58.0	4 32.5
15 Tu	19 30 12	22 13 54	24 13 37	1♏ 9 56	25 29.8	25R 41.6	5 23.6	3 45.6	16 17.5	22 50.9	3 29.3	19 6.7	3 56.5	4D 32.5
16 W	19 34 9	23 11 7	8♏ 9 24	15 14 4	25 26.6	25 41.5	4 58.0	4 53.4	16 0.3	22 50.4	3 27.2	19 4.8	3 55.0	4 32.5
17 Th	19 38 6	24 8 21	22 23 52	29 38 33	25 23.5	25 40.0	4 28.6	6 1.0	15 43.3	22 49.6	3 25.2	19 2.9	3 53.5	4 32.6
18 F	19 42 2	25 5 33	6♐ 57 45	14♐ 20 54	25 20.3	25 36.2	3 55.7	7 8.5	15 26.6	22 48.7	3 23.2	19 1.1	3 52.0	4 32.6
19 Sa	19 45 59	26 2 49	21 47 15	29 15 55	25 17.1	25 29.8	3 19.9	8 15.9	15 10.1	22 47.6	3 21.4	18 59.3	3 50.5	4 32.8
20 Su	19 49 55	27 0 4	6♑ 43 52	14♑ 15 53	25 13.9	25 20.9	2 41.5	9 23.1	14 54.0	22 46.3	3 19.6	18 57.5	3 49.1	4 32.9
21 M	19 53 52	27 57 19	21 44 34	29 11 36	25 10.8	25 10.3	2 1.3	10 30.1	14 38.2	22 44.8	3 17.9	18 55.8	3 47.6	4 33.1
22 Tu	19 57 48	28 54 34	6♒ 34 32	13♒ 33 41	25 7.6	24 59.2	1 19.9	11 37.0	14 22.8	22 43.1	3 16.4	18 54.1	3 46.2	4 33.3
23 W	20 1 45	29 51 50	21 7 7	28 14 28	25 4.4	24 48.8	0 38.0	12 43.8	14 7.9	22 41.2	3 14.9	18 52.4	3 44.8	4 33.6
24 Th	20 5 42	0♌ 49 6	5♓ 13 13	12♓ 9 3	25 1.2	24 40.2	29♋ 36.3	13 50.4	13 53.4	22 39.1	3 13.5	18 50.8	3 43.4	4 33.8
25 F	20 9 38	1 46 23	18 55 49	25 33 35	24 58.0	24 34.1	29 13.6	14 56.8	13 39.4	22 36.8	3 12.2	18 49.2	3 42.0	4 34.1
26 Sa	20 13 35	2 43 41	2♈ 8 34	8♈ 35 6	24 54.9	24 30.3	28 36.6	16 3.1	13 26.0	22 34.3	3 11.0	18 47.7	3 40.6	4 34.5
27 Su	20 17 31	3 41 0	14 55 38	21 10 43	24 51.7	24D 29.0	28 0.1	17 9.2	13 13.1	22 31.7	3 9.8	18 46.2	3 39.2	4 34.9
28 M	20 21 28	4 38 20	27 20 56	3♉ 26 37	24 48.5	24R 28.8	27 26.7	18 15.2	13 0.9	22 28.8	3 8.8	18 44.7	3 37.9	4 35.3
29 Tu	20 25 24	5 35 41	9♉ 29 24	15 28 59	24 45.3	24 28.8	26 57.0	19 21.0	12 49.3	22 25.8	3 7.9	18 43.3	3 36.6	4 35.7
30 W	20 29 21	6 33 3	21 26 22	27 22 12	24 42.2	24 27.9	26 31.8	20 26.6	12 38.3	22 22.6	3 7.0	18 41.9	3 35.3	4 36.2
31 Th	20 33 17	7♌ 30 26	3♊ 17 6	9♊ 11 40	24♈ 39.0	24♈ 23.2	26♋ 11.4	21♍ 32.0	12♑ 28.0	22♓ 19.1	3♐ 6.3	18♐ 40.3	3♑ 34.0	4♏ 36.8

DECLINATION and LATITUDE

DAY	☉ DECL	☽ DECL	☽ LAT	☽ 12hr DECL	☿ DECL	☿ LAT	♀ DECL	♀ LAT	♂ DECL	♂ LAT	♃ DECL	♃ LAT	♄ DECL	♄ LAT
1	23N 9	12N 9	0N20	14N40	18N47	0S37	17N14	1N49	26S32	3S 0	4S 4	1S14	19S 3	1N58
2	23 5	17 2	1 22	19 14	18 25	0 50	16 52	1 47	26 58	3 4	4 3	1 14	19 3	1 57
3	23 0	21 15	2 20	23 2	18 4	1 5	16 28	1 46	27 4	3 8	4 2	1 15	19 2	1 57
4	22 55	24 34	3 12	25 51	17 43	1 19	16 3	1 44	27 10	3 11	4 2	1 15	19 2	1 57
5	22 50	26 31	3 56	27 33	17 23	1 34	15 41	1 43	27 16	3 15	4 2	1 15	19 1	1 57
6	22 45	27 56	4 29	27 59	17 3	1 49	15 17	1 41	27 21	3 18	4 1	1 16	19 1	1 57
7	22 39	27 42	4 51	27 5	16 45	2 4	14 52	1 39	27 27	3 21	4 1	1 16	19 1	1 56
8	22 32	26 9	4 60	24 54	16 28	2 19	14 27	1 37	27 32	3 24	4 1	1 16	19 0	1 56
9	22 25	23 22	4 55	21 33	16 12	2 34	14 1	1 35	27 38	3 27	4 1	1 17	19 0	1 56
10	22 18	19 29	4 37	17 11	15 57	2 49	13 36	1 33	27 43	3 30	4 1	1 17	18 60	1 56
11	22 11	14 41	4 4	12 1	15 43	3 4	13 10	1 31	27 48	3 33	4 1	1 17	18 60	1 56
12	22 3	9 12	3 19	6 15	15 31	3 18	12 43	1 28	27 53	3 35	4 1	1 17	18 59	1 55
13	21 54	3 13	2 23	0 6	15 20	3 32	12 17	1 26	27 57	3 37	4 2	1 18	18 59	1 55
14	21 46	3S 2	1 18	6S11	15 11	3 46	11 50	1 23	28 2	3 40	4 2	1 18	18 59	1 55
15	21 37	9 17	0 8	12 20	15 4	3 58	11 23	1 21	28 6	3 42	4 2	1 18	18 59	1 55
16	21 27	13 16	1S 5	18 1	14 59	4 10	10 56	1 18	28 10	3 44	4 3	1 19	18 58	1 55
17	21 17	20 34	2 16	22 30	14 55	4 21	10 28	1 15	28 14	3 45	4 3	1 19	18 58	1 54
18	21 7	24 45	3 19	26 17	14 53	4 31	10 0	1 12	28 17	3 47	4 4	1 19	18 58	1 54
19	20 57	27 21	4 10	27 36	14 53	4 39	9 32	1 9	28 21	3 48	4 5	1 20	18 58	1 54
20	20 4													
21	20 3													
22	20 2													
23	20 1													
24	19 5													
25	19 4													
26	19 3													
27	19 2													
28	19													
29	18 5													
30	18 3													
31	18N2													

DAY	♅ DECL	♅ LAT	♆ DECL	♆ LAT	♇ DECL	♇ LAT
1	23S 8	0S 6	22S16	1N 6	2N45	16N45
5	23 7	0 6	22 16	1 6	2 43	16 42
9	23 6	0 6	22 16	1 6	2 42	16 40
13	23 6	0 6	22 17	1 6	2 40	16 38
17	23 5	0 6	22 17	1 6	2 37	16 36
21	23 5	0 6	22 17	1 6	2 35	16 33
25	23 4	0 6	22 18	1 6	2 33	16 31
29	23S 4	0S 6	22S18	1N 6	2N30	16N28

The arrow indicates a very high number of aspects on this particular date.

☽ PHENOMENA

dy	hr	
4	8	APOGE
19	20	PERIG
31	21	APOGE

MAX/0 DECL

dy	hr	° '
6	8	28N 0
13	12	0
19	20	28S 3
26	4	0

MAX/0 LAT

dy	hr	° '
8	4	5N 0
15	2	0
21	5	5S 0
27	18	0

VOID OF COURSE ☽

LAST ASPT		☽ INGRESS		
2	7pm42	3	♊	10am33
5	8am47	5	♋	11pm20
7	8pm49	8	♌	10am37
10	6pm54	10	♍	8pm51
12	3pm36	13	♎	4am41
14	8pm11	15	♏	9am59
17	3am 6	17	♐	12pm35
19	1am37	19	♑	1pm11
21	10am41	21	♒	1pm18
22	8pm16	23	♓	2pm59
25	5pm48	25	♈	8pm 3
28	0am11	28	♉	5am12
30	9am59	30	♊	5pm20

dy	hr	mn	PHASE	
7	4	56	14♋48	●
14	20	11	22♎ 5	☽
21	10	41	28♑23	○
28	15	35	5♉16	☾

DAILY ASPECTARIAN

Day	Aspect	Time
1 T	♅∠♇	4am 6
	☽□☿	5 6
	☽⚻♄	6 8
	☉∥♅	6 20
	☽△☿	6 31
	☽⚼♅	7 6
	☽⚺♇	7 7
	☽∠♃	1pm16
	☉*☽	5 6
	☽∥♀	11 8
	☿△♄	11 54
2 W	☽∥☿	6am52
	♀⚼☿	7 44
	♀⚹☿	8 29
	☽∥♄	10 52
	☽⚼☿	12pm44
	☽□♀	1 17
	☽⚻♅	1 18
	♀△♅	1 23
	☽△♂	1 51
	♀⚻♂	6 1
	☽*♃	7 42
	☿⚼♅	8 6
	☿□♇	10 23
3 Th	☉∠☽	2am 9
	☽∥☿	6 43
	☉∥☽	11 34
	☽∥♅	12pm41
	♂⚹♅	6 28
	☽⚺♄	6 38
	☽⚹☿	7 10
	☽⚼♂	7 40
	☽⚹♇	7 52
	☽*☿	8 48
4	☉⚹☽	11am20
5 S	☽⚹♂	1am26
	☽⚺♅	2 3
	☽⚼♇	2 18
	☽∠☿	4 19
	☽∥♂	6 34
	♀⚹♃	8 36
	☽□♃	8 46
	☽*♀	8 47
6 Su	♂∠♄	2am26
	☽⚻♄	7 4
	☽⚺☿	7 42
	☽△♇	8 30
	☽⚹☿	11 20
	☽∠♀	6pm 7
7 M	☉⚺☽	4am56
	☽∥♂	3 17
	☽⚺♂	12pm12
	☽⚼♄	12 52
	☽⚻♅	1 59
	☽△♃	8 49
8 T	☽⚹♀	2am58
	☽△♄	6pm13
	☽⚻☿	6 38
	☽⚼♅	7 23
	☽□♇	7 31
	☽☍☿	11 26
9 W	☽∥♅	1am48
	☽⚼♃	2 13
	☉∥☽	6 38
	☽∥☿	7 24
	☿SR	8pm28
	☉⚹☽	8 37
	☽⚻♂	9 29
	☽☍☿	11 58
10 Th	☽△♅	0am22
	☽∥♄	2 37
	☉∥☿	5 14
	☉⚺♂	5 29
	☽⚹♃	7 13
	☽☍♀	6pm54
	☽∥☿	6 56
11 F	☽⚼♂	1am28
	☉∠☽	3 33
	☽□♄	3 44
	☽△☿	4 29
	☽*♇	[illegible] 27
	☉[illegible]	[illegible] 28
	☽∥[illegible]	[illegible] 32
	☽⚹[illegible]	[illegible]
	♀[illegible]	[illegible]
	☉[illegible]	[illegible]
12 S	☽△[illegible]	[illegible]
	☽□[illegible]	[illegible] 31
	☽∠[illegible]	[illegible] 29
	☉*☽	[illegible] 33
	☽∠☿	12pm26
	☽⚺♃	3 36
	♃SR	5 6
	☽∥♃	8 49
13 Su	☽∥♇	2am 9
	♀⚼♂	6 20
	☽⚹♀	8 6
	☽*♄	11 7
	☽□☿	11 55
	☽☌☊	12pm24
	☽⚹♇	12 56
	☽*☿	3 19
	☽∥♇	10 33
14 M	☽∥♃	3am48
	☽□♂	10 16
	☽∠♀	1pm28
	☽∠♄	1 53
	☽*♆	2 59
	♀□♄	6 24
	☉□☽	8 11
	☽⚻♃	9 32
15 T	♀△☿	3am43
	♇SD	6 34
	☽∥♀	7 38
	☉△♃	3pm24
	☽⚹♄	3 58
	♀*♇	4 36
	☽*☿	4 45
	☽∠♅	5 2
	☽☍♇	5 49
	☽*♀	5 53
	☽□☿	6 43
	☽∥☿	10 50
	☽☍♃	11 28
16 W	☿⚹♀	1am10
	☽*♂	1pm 2
	☽∥♄	4 20
	☽∠☿	6 9
	☽⚹♅	6 25
	☿□♇	8 56
17 Th	☽△♃	0am43
	☉△☽	3 6
	☉∥☽	3 32
	☽∥☿	8 58
	☽∥♅	1pm30
	☽∠♂	1 31
	☽⚺♄	6 10
	☽⚹☿	6 57
	☽△☿	7 14
	☿⚼♅	8 2
	☽⚹♇	8 3
18 F	☽□♀	0am19
	♀⚹☿	2 42
	☉⚼☽	5 27
	☽⚹♂	1pm31
	☽⚼☿	6 59
	☽☍♅	7 30
	☽∠♇	8 23
	☿△♄	10 59
19 S	☽□♃	1am37
	☉*☽	7 18
	☽⚻☿	5pm45
	☽⚹♄	6 31
	☽☍☿	7 18
	☽*♇	8 27
20 Su	☽△♀	4am32
	☽☍♂	12pm47
	☽∠♄	6 28
	☽⚹♅	7 29
21 M	☽*♃	1am36
	☽⚼♀	6 32
	☉⚺☽	10 41
	☽⚺☿	3pm51
	☽*♄	6 37
	☽⚹☿	7 26
	☽∠♅	7 39
	☽□♇	8 42
22 T	☽∥♅	1am43
	☽∠♃	1 51
	☽∥☿	6 11
	☽⚻♀	8 56
	☽⚹♂	12pm35
	☉∥☽	4 45
	☽∠☿	8 3
	☽*♅	8 16
	☽∥♄	10 52
23 W	☽⚹♃	2am37
	☉ ♌	3 25
	☉⚺☿	11 11
	☽∠♂	1pm17
	☽∥☿	3 13
	☽⚻☿	3 19
	☉⚻☽	3 50
	☽□♄	8 31
	☽*☿	9 22
	☿ ♋	9 54
	☽△♇	10 49
24 Th	♀△♂	0am54
	☿∠♀	2pm44
	☽*♂	2 48
	☽⚼☿	4 6
	☽⚺♀	4 18
	☉⚼☽	7 52
	☽□♅	11 48
25 F	☽⚼♇	1am 9
	☽∥♀	1 43
	☽⚺♃	6 35
	☽∥♃	11 15
	☽∥♇	3pm40
	☽△☿	5 46
26 S	☉△☽	1am10
	☽△♄	1 53
	☽□☿	2 50
	☽ON	3 34
	☽⚻♇	4 31
	☉△♄	11 12
	☽∥♇	1pm34
	☽∥♃	8 22
	☽□♂	8 48
	☉⚻☿	11 17
27 Su	☉⚼♅	2am 6
	☽∥♀	2 15
	☽⚻♀	4 40
	☽⚼♄	6 11
	☽△♅	7 20
	☽⚹♃	2pm33
	☉□♇	10 43
28 M	☽□☿	0am11
	♀□♅	10 32
	☽⚻♄	11 23
	☽△☿	12pm20
	☽⚼♅	12 34
	☽⚼♀	12 46
	☽⚺♇	2 16
	☉∥♄	3 17
	☉□☽	3 35
	☽∠♃	7 55
29 T	☽∥☿	2am 0
	♀∠♇	5 27
	☽△♂	6 33
	☉∥☽	2pm48
	☽∥♄	4 8
	☽⚼☿	6 15
	☽⚹♅	6 29
	♀∥♃	8 53
	☽△♀	9 47
30 W	☽*♃	1am53
	☽☍☿	9 59
	☽∥☿	12pm19
	☽⚼♂	12 22
	☽∥♅	5 34
	☉⚼♃	7 33
	☽⚺♄	11 38
31 Th	☽⚹☿	0am34
	☽*♇	2 42
	☉*☽	9 20
	☽∠☿	3pm42
	♀⚺♃	4 26
	☽⚹♂	6 24

LONGITUDE

DAY	SID. TIME	☉	☽	☽ 12 Hour	MEAN ☊	TRUE ☊	☿	♀	♂	♃	♄	♅	♆	♇
	h m s	° ' "	° ' "	° ' "	° '	° '	° '	° '	° '	° '	° '	° '	° '	° '
1 Tu	18 35 1	8♋ 52 46	1♉ 2 33	7♉ 1 43	26♈ 14.3	27♈R20.8	3♌ 27.3	17♌ 44.8	20♑R12.8	22♓ 38.1	4♐R 7.3	19♐R36.2	4♑R18.3	4♏R35.9
2 W	18 38 57	9 49 59	12 58 46	18 54 18	26 11.1	27 19.8	4 4.3	18 54.1	19 57.7	22 40.2	4 4.1	19 34.0	4 16.9	4 35.5
3 Th	18 42 54	10 47 12	24 48 50	0♊ 42 53	26 7.9	27 16.7	4 37.2	20 3.3	19 42.2	22 42.2	4 1.0	19 31.7	4 15.3	4 35.1
4 F	18 46 50	11 44 25	6♊ 36 33	12 31 14	26 4.8	27 11.0	5 6.0	21 12.4	19 26.3	22 44.0	3 57.9	19 29.5	4 13.7	4 34.7
5 Sa	18 50 47	12 41 38	18 26 19	24 22 25	26 1.6	27 2.6	5 30.5	22 21.5	19 10.0	22 45.6	3 54.9	19 27.3	4 12.1	4 34.3
6 Su	18 54 43	13 38 52	0♋ 19 47	6♋ 18 40	25 58.4	26 51.8	5 50.6	23 30.4	18 53.4	22 47.0	3 52.0	19 25.1	4 10.5	4 34.0
7 M	18 58 40	14 36 5	12 19 13	18 21 37	25 55.2	26 39.2	6 6.2	24 39.2	18 36.6	22 48.2	3 49.2	19 23.0	4 8.9	4 33.7
8 Tu	19 2 37	15 33 19	24 25 58	0♌ 32 24	25 52.1	26 25.8	6 17.3	25 47.9	18 19.5	22 49.3	3 46.4	19 20.8	4 7.4	4 33.4
9 W	19 6 33	16 30 32	6♌ 41 2	12 51 58	25 48.9	26 12.9	6R 23.7	26 56.5	18 2.2	22 50.1	3 43.7	19 18.7	4 5.8	4 33.2
10 Th	19 10 30	17 27 46	19 5 19	25 21 15	25 45.7	26 1.4	6 23.4	28 5.0	17 44.8	22 50.7	3 41.1	19 16.7	4 4.2	4 33.0
11 F	19 14 26	18 25 0	1♍ 39 34	8♍ 1 29	25 42.5	25 52.3	6 22.3	29 13.3	17 27.3	22 51.1	3 38.6	19 14.6	4 2.6	4 32.8
12 Sa	19 18 23	19 22 13	14 26 12	20 54 19	25 39.3	25 46.1	6 14.5	0♍ 21.6	17 9.8	22R 51.4	3 36.1	19 12.6	4 1.1	4 32.7
13 Su	19 22 19	20 19 27	27 26 3	4♎ 1 49	25 36.2	25 42.8	6 2.0	1 29.7	16 52.3	22 51.4	3 33.8	19 10.6	3 59.5	4 32.6
14 M	19 26 16	21 16 41	10♎ 41 47	17 26 18	25 33.0	25D 41.6	5 45.0	2 37.8	16 34.8	22 51.3	3 31.5	19 8.6	3 58.0	4 32.5
15 Tu	19 30 12	22 13 54	24 15 37	1♏ 9 56	25 29.8	25R 41.6	5 23.6	3 45.6	16 17.5	22 50.9	3 29.3	19 6.7	3 56.5	4D 32.5
16 W	19 34 9	23 11 7	8♏ 9 24	15 14 4	25 26.6	25 41.3	4 58.0	4 53.4	16 0.3	22 50.4	3 27.2	19 4.8	3 55.0	4 32.5
17 Th	19 38 6	24 8 21	22 23 32	29 38 33	25 23.5	25 40.0	4 28.6	6 1.0	15 43.3	22 49.6	3 25.2	19 2.9	3 53.5	4 32.6
18 F	19 42 2	25 5 35	6♐ 57 45	14♐ 20 54	25 20.3	25 36.2	3 55.7	7 8.5	15 26.6	22 48.7	3 23.2	19 1.1	3 52.0	4 32.6
19 Sa	19 45 59	26 2 49	21 47 15	29 15 55	25 17.1	25 29.8	3 19.9	8 15.9	15 10.1	22 47.6	3 21.4	18 59.3	3 50.5	4 32.8
20 Su	19 49 55	27 0 4	6♑ 45 52	14♑ 15 53	25 13.9	25 20.9	2 41.5	9 23.1	14 54.0	22 46.3	3 19.6	18 57.5	3 49.1	4 32.9
21 M	19 53 52	27 57 19	21 44 54	29 11 36	25 10.8	25 10.3	2 1.3	10 30.1	14 38.2	22 44.8	3 17.9	18 55.8	3 47.6	4 33.1
22 Tu	19 57 48	28 54 34	6♒ 34 52	13♒ 53 41	25 7.6	24 59.2	1 19.9	11 37.0	14 22.8	22 43.1	3 16.4	18 54.1	3 46.2	4 33.3
23 W	20 1 45	29 51 50	21 7 7	28 14 28	25 4.4	24 48.8	0 38.0	12 43.8	14 7.9	22 41.2	3 14.9	18 52.4	3 44.8	4 33.6
24 Th	20 5 42	0♌ 49 6	5♓ 13 13	12♓ 9 3	25 1.2	24 40.2	29♋ 56.3	13 50.4	13 53.4	22 39.1	3 13.5	18 50.8	3 43.4	4 33.8
25 F	20 9 38	1 46 23	18 55 49	25 35 35	24 58.0	24 34.1	29 15.6	14 56.8	13 39.4	22 36.8	3 12.2	18 49.2	3 42.0	4 34.1
26 Sa	20 13 35	2 43 41	2♈ 8 34	8♈ 35 6	24 54.9	24 30.5	28 36.6	16 3.1	13 26.0	22 34.3	3 11.0	18 47.7	3 40.6	4 34.5
27 Su	20 17 31	3 41 0	14 53 38	21 10 43	24 51.7	24D 29.0	28 0.1	17 9.2	13 13.1	22 31.7	3 9.8	18 46.2	3 39.2	4 34.9
28 M	20 21 28	4 38 20	27 20 56	3♉ 26 37	24 48.5	24R 28.8	27 26.7	18 15.2	13 0.9	22 28.8	3 8.8	18 44.7	3 37.9	4 35.3
29 Tu	20 25 24	5 35 41	9♉ 29 24	15 28 59	24 45.3	24 28.8	26 57.0	19 21.0	12 49.3	22 25.8	3 7.9	18 43.3	3 36.6	4 35.7
30 W	20 29 21	6 33 3	21 26 22	27 22 12	24 42.2	24 27.9	26 31.8	20 26.6	12 38.3	22 22.6	3 7.0	18 41.9	3 35.3	4 36.2
31 Th	20 33 17	7♌ 30 26	3♊ 17 6	9♊ 11 40	24♈ 39.0	24♈ 25.2	26♋ 11.4	21♍ 32.0	12♑ 28.0	22♓ 19.1	3♐ 6.3	18♐ 40.5	3♑ 34.0	4♏ 36.8

DECLINATION and LATITUDE

DAY	☉ DECL	☽ DECL	☽ LAT	☽ 12hr DECL	☿ DECL	☿ LAT	♀ DECL	♀ LAT	♂ DECL	♂ LAT	♃ DECL	♃ LAT	♄ DECL	♄ LAT
1	23N 9	12N 9	0N20	14N40	18N47	0S37	17N14	1N49	26S32	3S 0	4S 4	1S14	19S 3	1N58
2	23 5	17 2	1 22	19 14	18 25	0 50	16 32	1 47	26 38	3 4	4 3	1 14	19 3	1 57
3	23 0	21 15	2 20	23 2	18 4	1 5	16 28	1 46	27 4	3 8	4 2	1 15	19 2	1 57
4	22 55	24 34	3 12	25 51	17 43	1 19	16 3	1 44	27 10	3 11	4 2	1 15	19 2	1 57
5	22 50	26 31	3 56	27 33	17 23	1 34	15 41	1 43	27 16	3 15	4 2	1 15	19 1	1 57
6	22 45	27 36	4 29	27 59	17 3	1 49	15 17	1 41	27 21	3 18	4 1	1 16	19 1	1 57
7	22 39	27 42	4 51	27 5	16 45	2 4	14 52	1 39	27 27	3 21	4 1	1 16	19 1	1 56
8	22 32	26 9	4 60	24 54	16 28	2 19	14 27	1 37	27 32	3 24	4 1	1 16	19 0	1 56
9	22 25	23 22	4 55	21 33	16 12	2 34	14 1	1 35	27 38	3 27	4 1	1 17	19 0	1 56
10	22 18	19 29	4 37	17 11	15 57	2 49	13 36	1 33	27 43	3 30	4 1	1 17	18 60	1 56
11	22 11	14 41	4 4	12 1	15 43	3 4	13 10	1 31	27 48	3 33	4 1	1 17	18 60	1 56
12	22 3	9 12	3 19	6 15	15 31	3 18	12 43	1 28	27 53	3 35	4 1	1 17	18 59	1 55
13	21 54	3 13	2 23	0 6	15 20	3 32	12 17	1 26	27 57	3 37	4 2	1 18	18 59	1 55
14	21 46	3S 2	1 18	6S11	15 11	3 46	11 50	1 23	28 2	3 40	4 2	1 18	18 59	1 55
15	21 37	9 17	0 8	12 20	15 4	3 58	11 23	1 21	28 6	3 42	4 2	1 18	18 59	1 55
16	21 27	15 16	1S 5	18 1	14 59	4 10	10 56	1 18	28 10	3 44	4 3	1 19	18 58	1 55
17	21 17	20 34	2 16	22 50	14 55	4 21	10 28	1 15	28 14	3 45	4 3	1 19	18 58	1 54
18	21 7	24 45	3 19	26 17	14 53	4 31	10 0	1 12	28 17	3 47	4 4	1 19	18 58	1 54
19	20 57	27 21	4 10	27 36	14 53	4 39	9 32	1 9	28 21	3 48	4 5	1 20	18 58	1 54
												20	18 58	1 54
												20	18 58	1 53
												20	18 58	1 53
												21	18 58	1 53
												21	18 58	1 53
												21	18 58	1 53
												22	18 58	1 52
												22	18 58	1 52
												22	18 58	1 52
												23	18 58	1 52
												23	18 58	1 51
												S23	18S58	1N51

DAY	♅ DECL	♅ LAT	♆ DECL	♆ LAT	♇ DECL	♇ LAT
1	23S 8	0S 6	22S16	1N 6	2N45	16N45
5	23 7	0 6	22 16	1 6	2 43	16 42
9	23 6	0 6	22 16	1 6	2 42	16 40
13	23 6	0 6	22 17	1 6	2 40	16 38
17	23 5	0 6	22 17	1 6	2 37	16 36
21	23 5	0 6	22 17	1 6	2 35	16 33
25	23 4	0 6	22 18	1 6	2 33	16 31
29	23S 4	0S 6	22S18	1N 6	2N30	16N28

☽ PHENOMENA	VOID OF COURSE ☽ LAST ASPT	☽ INGRESS
dy hr	2 7pm42	3 ♊ 10am33
4 8 APOGE	5 8am47	5 ♋ 11pm20
19 20 PERIG	7 8pm49	8 ♌ 10am37
31 21 APOGE	10 6pm34	10 ♍ 8pm31
	12 3pm36	13 ♎ 4am41
MAX/0 DECL	14 8pm11	15 ♏ 9am59
dy hr ° '	17 3am 6	17 ♐ 12pm35
6 8 28N 0	19 1am37	19 ♑ 1pm11
13 12 0	21 10am41	21 ♒ 1pm18
19 20 28S 3	22 8pm16	23 ♓ 2pm39
26 4 0	25 5pm48	25 ♈ 8pm 3
	28 0am11	28 ♉ 5am12
	30 9am59	30 ♊ 5pm20

MAX/0 LAT dy hr ° '	dy hr mn	PHASE
8 4 5N 0	7 4 56	14♋48 ●
15 2 0	14 20 11	22♎ 5 ☽
21 5 5S 0	21 10 41	28♑23 ○
27 18 0	28 15 35	5♉16 ☾

Arrow indicates a low number of planetary aspects on that date

DAILY ASPECTARIAN

Day	Aspect	Time
1 T	♆∠♇	4am 6
	☽□☿	5 6
	☽⚹♄	6 8
	☉∥♅	20
	☽△☿	
	☽⚻♅	
	☽⚻♇	
	☽∠♃	
	☉☌☽	
	☽∥♀	
	☿△♄	
2 W	☽∥☿	6 52
	♀⚻☿	7 44
	☿⚹♆	8 29
	☽∥♄	10 52
	☽⚻☿	12pm44
	☽□♀	1 17
	☽⚻♅	1 18
	☿△♅	1 23
	☽△♂	1 51
	♀⚻♂	6 1
	☽⚹♃	7 42
	☿⚻♅	8 6
	☿□♇	10 23
3 Th	☉∠☽	2am 9
	☽∥☿	6 43
	☉∥☽	11 34
	☽∥♅	12pm41
	♂⚻♅	6 25
	☽⚻♄	6 38
	☽⚹☿	7 10
	☽⚻♂	7 40
	☽⚹♇	7 52
	☽⚹☿	8 48
4	☉⚹☽	11am20
5 S	☽⚹♂	1am26
	☽⚻♆	2 3
	☽⚻♇	2 18
	☽∠☿	4 19
	☽∥♂	6 34
	♀⚻♃	8 36
	☽□♃	8 46
	☽⚹♀	8 47
6 Su	♂∠♄	2am26
	☽⚻♄	7 4
	☽⚻☿	7 42
	☽△♇	8 30
	☽⚹☿	11 20
	☽∠♀	6pm 7
7 M	☉☌☽	4am56
	☽∥♂	5 17
	☽☍♂	12pm12
	☽∥♄	12 32
	☽⚻♅	1 59
	☽△♃	8 49
8 T	☽⚹♀	2am58
	☽△♄	6pm15
	☽⚻☿	6 38
	☽⚻♅	7 23
	☽□♇	7 31
	☽⚻☿	11 26
9 W	☽∥♅	1am48
	☽⚻♃	2 15
	☉∥☽	6 38
	☽∥☿	7 24
	☿SR	8pm28
	☉⚹☽	8 37
	☽⚻♂	9 29
	☽⚻☿	11 38
10 Th	☽△♅	0am22
	☽∥♄	2 37
	☉∥☿	5 14
	☉⚻♂	5 29
	☽⚻♃	7 13
	☽⚻♀	6pm34
	☽∥☿	6 36
11 F	☽⚻♂	1am28
	☉∠☽	3 35
	☽□♄	3 44
	☽△☿	4 29
	☽⚹♇	5 27
	☉⚻♄	5 28
	☽∥♀	7 32
	☽⚹☿	8 49
	♀ ♍	4pm24
	☉⚻♅	8 6
12 S	☽△♂	4am58
	☽□♅	8 51
	☽∠♇	9 29
	☉⚹☽	9 53
	☽∠☿	12pm26
	☽⚻♃	3 36
	♃SR	5 6
	☽∥♃	8 49
13 Su	☽∥♇	2am 9
	♀⚻♂	6 20
	☽⚹♀	8 6
	☽⚹♄	11 7
	☽□☿	11 53
	☽OS	12pm24
	☽⚹♇	12 56
	☽⚹☿	3 19
	☽∥♇	10 33
14 M	☽∥♃	3am48
	☽□♂	10 16
	☽∠♀	1pm28
	☽∠♄	1 53
	☽⚹♅	2 59
	♀□♄	6 24
	☉□☽	8 11
	☽⚻♃	9 32
15 T	☿△♆	3am45
	♇SD	6 34
	☽∥☿	7 38
	☉△♃	3pm24
	☽⚻♄	3 58
	♀⚹♇	4 36
	☽⚹☿	4 45
	☽∠♅	5 2
	☽⚻♇	5 49
	☽⚹♀	5 55
	☽□☿	6 43
	☽∥☿	10 50
	☽⚻♃	11 28
16 W	☿⚹♀	1am10
	☽⚹♂	1pm 2
	☽∥♄	4 20
	☽∠☿	6 9
	☽⚻♅	6 23
	☿□♇	8 56
17 Th	☽△♃	0am43
	☉△☽	3 6
	☉∥☽	3 32
	☽∥☿	8 58
	☽∥♅	1pm30
	☽∠♂	1 31
	☽☌♄	6 10
	☽⚹☿	6 57
	☽△☿	7 14
	☿⚻♅	8 2
	☽⚹♇	8 3
18 F	☽□♀	0am19
	☿⚹♆	2 42
	☉⚻☽	5 27
	☽⚹♂	1pm31
	☽⚻☿	6 39
	☽⚻♅	7 30
	☽∠♇	8 23
	☿△♄	10 59
19 S	☽□♃	1am37
	☉⚻☽	7 18
	☽⚹☿	5pm45
	☽⚻♄	6 31
	☽⚻☿	7 18
	☽⚹♇	8 27
20 Su	☽△♀	4am32
	☽⚻♂	12pm47
	☽∠♄	6 28
	☽⚻♅	7 29
21 M	☽⚹♃	1am36
	☽⚻♀	6 32
	☉☍☽	10 41
	☽⚻☿	3pm31
	☽⚹♄	6 37
	☽⚹☿	7 26
	☽∠♅	7 39
	☽□♇	8 42
22 T	☽∥♅	1am45
	☽∠♃	1 51
	☽∥☿	6 11
	☽⚻♀	8 56
	☽⚹♂	12pm35
	☉∥☽	4 45
	☽∠☿	8 3
	☽⚹♅	8 16
	☽∥♄	10 52
23 W	☽⚻♃	2am37
	☉ ♌	3 25
	☉⚻☿	11 11
	☽∠♂	1pm17
	☽∥☿	3 13
	☽⚻☿	3 19
	☉⚻☽	3 50
	☽□♄	8 31
	☽⚹☿	9 22
	☿ ♋	9 34
	☽△♇	10 49
24 Th	♀△♂	0am54
	☿∠♀	2pm44
	☽⚹♂	2 48
	☽⚻☿	4 6
	☽⚻☿	4 18
	☉⚻☽	7 52
	☽□♅	11 48
25 F	☽⚻♇	1am 9
	☽∥♀	1 43
	☽☌♃	6 35
	☽∥♃	11 15
	☽∥♇	5pm40
	☽△☿	5 48
26 S	☉△☽	1am10
	☽△♄	1 53
	☽□☿	2 50
	☽ON	3 34
	☽⚹♇	4 31
	☉△♄	11 12
	☽∥♇	1pm34
	☽∥♃	8 22
	☽□♂	8 48
	☉⚻☿	11 17
27 Su	☉⚻♅	2am 6
	☽∥♀	2 15
	☽⚹♀	4 40
	☽⚻♄	6 11
	☽△♅	7 20
	☽⚻♃	2pm33
	☉□♇	10 43
28 M	☽□☿	0am11
	♀□♅	10 32
	☽⚻♄	11 23
	☽△☿	12pm20
	☽⚻♅	12 34
	☽⚻♀	12 46
	☽⚻♇	2 16
	☉∥♄	3 17
	☉⚻☽	3 35
	☽∠♃	7 55
29 T	☽∥☿	2am 0
	♀∠♇	5 27
	☽△♂	6 33
	☉∥☽	2pm48
	☽∥♄	4 5
	☽⚻☿	6 15
	☽⚻♅	6 29
	♀∥♃	8 53
	☽△♀	9 47
30 W	☽⚹♃	1am33
	☽⚹☿	9 39
	☽∥☿	12pm19
	☽⚻♂	12 22
	☽∥♅	6 34
	☉⚻♃	7 33
	☽⚻♄	11 38
31 Th	☽⚻☿	0am34
	☽⚹♇	2 42
	☉⚹☽	9 20
	☽∠☿	3pm42
	♀⚻♃	4 26
	☽⚻♂	6 24

LONGITUDE

DAY	SID. TIME	☉	☽	☽ 12 Hour	MEAN ☊	TRUE ☊	☿	♀	♂	♃	♄	♅	♆	♇
	h m s	° ' "	° ' "	° ' "	° '	° '	° '	° '	° '	° '	° '	° '	° '	° '
1 Tu	18 35 1	8♋ 52 46	1♉ 2 33	7♉ 1 43	26♈ 14.3	27♈R 20.8	3♌ 27.3	17♌ 44.8	20♑R 12.8	22♓ 38.1	4♐R 7.3	19♐R 36.2	4♑R 18.5	4♏R 35.9
2 W	18 38 57	9 49 39	12 58 46	18 54 18	26 11.1	27 19.8	4 4.3	18 54.1	19 57.7	22 40.2	4 4.1	19 34.0	4 16.9	4 35.5
3 Th	18 42 54	10 47 12	24 48 50	0♊ 42 53	26 7.9	27 16.7	4 37.2	20 3.3	19 42.2	22 42.2	4 1.0	19 31.7	4 15.3	4 35.1
4 F	18 46 50	11 44 25	6♊ 36 53	12 31 14	26 4.8	27 11.0	5 6.0	21 12.4	19 26.3	22 44.0	3 57.9	19 29.5	4 13.7	4 34.7
5 Sa	18 50 47	12 41 38	18 26 19	24 22 25	26 1.6	27 2.6	5 30.3	22 21.3	19 10.0	22 45.6	3 54.9	19 27.3	4 12.1	4 34.3
6 Su	18 54 43	13 38 52	0♋ 19 47	6♋ 18 40	25 58.4	26 51.8	5 50.6	23 30.4	18 53.4	22 47.0	3 52.0	19 25.1	4 10.5	4 34.0
7 M	18 58 40	14 36 5	12 19 13	18 21 37	25 55.2	26 39.2	6 6.2	24 39.2	18 36.6	22 48.2	3 49.2	19 23.0	4 8.9	4 33.7
8 Tu	19 2 37	15 33 19	24 25 58	0♌ 32 24	25 52.1	26 25.8	6 17.3	25 47.9	18 19.5	22 49.3	3 46.4	19 20.8	4 7.4	4 33.4
9 W	19 6 33	16 30 32	6♌ 41 2	12 31 58	25 48.9	26 12.9	6R 23.7	26 56.5	18 2.2	22 50.1	3 43.7	19 18.7	4 5.8	4 33.2
10 Th	19 10 30	17 27 46	19 3 19	25 21 13	2[illegible] 45.7	26 1.4	6 23.4	28 5.0	17 44.8	22 50.7	3 41.1	19 16.7	4 4.2	4 33.0
11 F	19 14 26	18 25 0	1♍ 39 54	8♍ 1 29	2[illegible] 42.5	25 52.3	6 22.3	29 13.3	17 27.3	22 51.1	3 38.6	19 14.6	4 2.6	4 32.8
12 Sa	19 18 23	19 22 13	14 26 12	20 54 19	[illegible]9.3	25 46.1	6 14.5	0♍ 21.6	17 9.8	22R 51.4	3 36.1	19 12.6	4 1.1	4 32.7
13 Su	19 22 19	20 19 27	27 26 3	4♎ 1 49	[illegible]	25 42.8	6 2.0	1 29.7	16 52.3	22 51.4	3 33.8	19 10.6	3 59.5	4 32.6
14 M	19 26 16	21 16 41	10♎ 41 47	17 26 18	[illegible]	25D 41.6	5 45.0	2 37.8	16 34.8	22 51.3	3 31.5	19 8.6	3 58.0	4 32.5
15 Tu	19 30 12	22 13 54	24 13 37	1♏ 9 56	[illegible]	25R 41.6	5 23.6	3 45.6	16 17.5	22 50.9	3 29.3	19 6.7	3 56.5	4D 32.5
16 W	19 34 9	23 11 7	8♏ 9 24	15 14 4	[illegible]	25 41.5	4 58.0	4 53.4	16 0.3	22 50.4	3 27.2	19 4.8	3 55.0	4 32.3
17 Th	19 38 6	24 8 21	22 23 32	29 38 33	[illegible]	25 40.0	4 28.6	6 1.0	15 43.3	22 49.6	3 25.2	19 2.9	3 53.5	4 32.6
18 F	19 42 2	25 5 35	6♐ 37 43	14♐ 20 54	[illegible]	25 36.2	3 55.7	7 8.5	15 26.6	22 48.7	3 23.2	19 1.1	3 52.0	4 32.6
19 Sa	19 45 59	26 2 49	21 47 13	29 15 55	2[illegible]7.1	25 29.8	3 19.9	8 15.9	15 10.1	22 47.6	3 21.4	18 59.3	3 50.5	4 32.8
20 Su	19 49 55	27 0 4	6♑ 45 32	14♑ 13 55	25 13.9	25 20.9	2 41.5	9 23.1	14 54.0	22 46.3	3 19.6	18 57.5	3 49.1	4 32.9
21 M	19 53 52	27 57 19	21 44 54	29 11 36	25 10.8	25 10.3	2 1.3	10 30.1	14 38.2	22 44.8	3 17.9	18 55.8	3 47.6	4 33.1
22 Tu	19 57 48	28 54 34	6♒ 34 52	13♒ 33 41	25 7.6	24 59.2	1 19.9	11 37.0	14 22.8	22 43.1	3 16.4	18 54.1	3 46.2	4 33.3
23 W	20 1 45	29 51 50	21 7 7	28 14 28	2[illegible] 4.4	24 48.8	0 38.0	12 43.8	14 7.9	22 41.2	3 14.9	18 52.4	3 44.8	4 33.6
24 Th	20 5 42	0♌ 49 6	5♓ 13 13	12♓ 9 3	2[illegible] 1.2	24 40.2	29♋ 56.3	13 50.4	13 53.4	22 39.1	3 13.5	18 50.8	3 43.4	4 33.8
25 F	20 9 38	1 46 23	18 55 49	25 35 35	[illegible]8.0	24 34.1	29 15.6	14 56.8	13 39.4	22 36.8	3 12.2	18 49.2	3 42.0	4 34.1
26 Sa	20 13 35	2 43 41	2♈ 8 34	8♈ 35 6	[illegible].9	24 30.3	28 36.6	16 3.1	13 26.0	22 34.3	3 11.0	18 47.7	3 40.6	4 34.5
27 Su	20 17 31	3 41 0	14 55 38	21 10 43	[illegible]	24D 29.0	28 0.1	17 9.2	13 13.1	22 31.7	3 9.8	18 46.2	3 39.2	4 34.9
28 M	20 21 28	4 38 20	27 20 56	3♉ 26 57	[illegible]	24R 28.8	27 26.7	18 15.2	13 0.9	22 28.8	3 8.8	18 44.7	3 37.9	4 35.3
29 Tu	20 25 24	5 35 41	9♉ 29 24	15 28 59	[illegible]	24 28.8	26 57.0	19 21.0	12 49.3	22 25.8	3 7.9	18 43.3	3 36.6	4 35.7
30 W	20 29 21	6 33 3	21 26 22	27 22 12	[illegible].2	24 27.9	26 31.8	20 26.6	12 38.3	22 22.6	3 7.0	18 41.9	3 35.3	4 36.2
31 Th	20 33 17	7♌ 30 26	3♊ 17 6	9♊ 11 40	[illegible]39.0	24♈ 25.2	26♋ 11.4	21♍ 32.0	12♑ 28.0	22♓ 19.1	3♐ 6.3	18♐ 40.5	3♑ 34.0	4♏ 36.8

The arrows indicate the true node of the moon when it moves from Retrograde to Direct. This is a "very" important change of trend indicator in the stock market.

DAY	☉ DEC													
1	23N													
2	23													
3	23													
4	22 3													
5	22 5													
6	22 4													
7	22 3													
8	22 3													
9	22 2													
10	22 1													
11	22 1													
12	22													
13	21 5													
14	21 4[illegible]	[illegible]	[illegible]	[illegible]	[illegible]	[illegible]	[illegible]	[illegible]	[illegible]	[illegible]	[illegible]	[illegible]	[illegible]	[illegible]
15	21 37	9 17	0 8	12 20	15 4	3 58	11 23	1 21	28 6	5 42	4 2	1 18	18 59	1 35
16	21 27	13 16	1S 3	18 1	14 39	4 10	10 36	1 18	28 10	5 44	4 3	1 19	18 58	1 35
17	21 17	20 34	2 16	22 30	14 35	4 21	10 28	1 15	28 14	5 45	4 3	1 19	18 58	1 34
18	21 7	24 45	3 19	26 17	14 33	4 31	10 0	1 12	28 17	5 47	4 4	1 19	18 58	1 34
19	20 57	27 21	4 10	27 56	14 33	4 39	9 32	1 9	28 21	5 48	4 5	1 20	18 58	1 34
20	20 46	28 1	4 45	27 34	14 55	4 46	9 4	1 6	28 24	5 49	4 6	1 20	18 58	1 34
21	20 34	26 37	4 60	25 12	14 58	4 52	8 36	1 3	28 27	5 50	4 6	1 20	18 58	1 33
22	20 23	23 22	4 54	21 11	15 3	4 56	8 7	0 59	28 29	5 51	4 7	1 20	18 58	1 33
23	20 11	18 43	4 30	16 1	15 10	4 58	7 38	0 56	28 32	5 52	4 8	1 21	18 58	1 33
24	19 59	13 8	3 49	10 8	15 18	4 58	7 10	0 52	28 34	5 53	4 9	1 21	18 58	1 33
25	19 46	7 3	2 36	3 59	15 28	4 57	6 40	0 48	28 36	5 53	4 11	1 21	18 58	1 33
26	19 33	0 55	1 55	2N 8	15 39	4 54	6 11	0 45	28 37	5 53	4 12	1 22	18 58	1 32
27	19 20	5N 6	0 30	7 60	15 51	4 49	5 42	0 41	28 39	5 54	4 13	1 22	18 58	1 32
28	19 6	10 46	0N15	13 25	16 3	4 43	5 13	0 37	28 40	5 53	4 13	1 22	18 58	1 32
29	18 53	15 54	1 19	18 13	16 17	4 35	4 43	0 33	28 41	5 53	4 16	1 23	18 58	1 32
30	18 38	20 20	2 18	22 15	16 31	4 25	4 14	0 29	28 42	5 53	4 18	1 23	18 58	1 31
31	18N24	23N36	3N10	25N21	16N45	4S14	3N44	0N24	28S42	5S53	4S19	1S23	18S58	1N51

♅ DECL	♅ LAT	♆ DECL	♆ LAT	♇ DECL	♇ LAT
23S 8	0S 6	22S16	1N 6	2N45	16N45
23 7	0 6	22 16	1 6	2 43	16 42
23 6	0 6	22 16	1 6	2 42	16 40
23 6	0 6	22 17	1 6	2 40	16 38
23 5	0 6	22 17	1 6	2 37	16 36
23 5	0 6	22 17	1 6	2 35	16 33
23 4	0 6	22 18	1 6	2 33	16 31
23S 4	0S 6	22S18	1N 6	2N30	16N28

☽ PHENOMENA			VOID OF COURSE ☽ LAST ASPT		☽ INGRESS	
dy	hr		2	7pm42	3 ♊	10am33
4	8	APOGE	5	8am47	5 ♋	11pm20
19	20	PERIG	7	8pm49	8 ♌	10am37
31	21	APOGE	10	6pm54	10 ♍	8pm51
MAX/0 DECL			12	3pm36	13 ♎	4am41
dy	hr	° '	14	8pm11	15 ♏	9am59
6	8	28N 0	17	3am 6	17 ♐	12pm35
13	12	0	19	1am37	19 ♑	1pm11
19	20	28S 3	21	10am41	21 ♒	1pm18
26	4	0	22	8pm16	23 ♓	2pm59
			25	5pm48	25 ♈	8pm 3
			28	0am11	28 ♉	3am12
			30	9am59	30 ♊	5pm20

MAX/0 LAT		
dy	hr	° '
8	4	5N 0
13	2	0
21	5	5S 0
27	18	0

dy	hr	mn	PHASE
7	4	56	14♋48 ●
14	20	11	22♎ 3 ☽
21	10	41	28♑23 ○
28	15	35	5♉16 ☾

DAILY ASPECTARIAN

Day	Aspect	Time
1 T	♅∠♇	4am 6
	☽□♆	5 6
	☽⚻♄	6 8
	☉∥♅	6 20
	☽△♆	6 31
	☽⚼♅	7 6
	☽⚻♇	7 7
	☽∠♃	1pm16
	☉⚹☽	5 6
	☽∥♀	11 8
	☿△♄	11 54
2 W	☽∥♆	6am52
	♀⚼♆	7 44
	☿⚺♆	8 29
	☽∥♄	10 52
	☽⚼♆	12pm44
	☽□☿	1 17
	☽⚺♅	1 18
	♀△♅	1 23
	☽△♂	1 51
	♀⚺♂	6 1
	☽⚹♃	7 42
	☿⚼♅	8 6
	☿□♇	10 23
3 Th	☉∠☽	2am 9
	☽∥♆	6 43
	☉∥☽	11 34
	☽∥♅	12pm41
	♂⚺♆	6 25
	☽⚻♄	6 38
	☽⚺♆	7 10
	☽⚼♂	7 40
	☽⚹♇	7 52
	☽⚹♆	8 48
4	☉⚺☽	11am20
5 S	☽⚺♂	1am26
	☽⚻♅	2 3
	☽⚼♇	2 18
	☽∠♆	4 19
	☽∥♂	6 54
	☿⚺♃	8 36
	☽□♃	8 46
	☽⚹☿	8 47
6 Su	♂∠♄	2am26
	☽⚺♄	7 4
	☽⚻♆	7 42
	☽△♇	8 30
	☽⚺♆	11 20
	☽∠☿	6pm 7
7 M	☉⚹☽	4am56
	☽∥♂	3 17
	☽⚻♂	12pm12
	☽⚼♄	12 52
	☽⚺♅	1 59
	☽△♃	8 49
8 T	☽⚺♀	2am58
	☽△♄	6pm15
	☽⚺♆	6 38
	☽⚼♅	7 23
	☽□♇	7 51
	☽⚹♆	11 26
9 W	☽∥♅	1am48
	☽⚼♃	2 15
	☉∥☽	6 38
	☽∥♆	7 24
	☿SR	8pm28
	☉⚺☽	8 37
	☽⚺♂	9 29
	☽⚹♆	11 58
10 Th	☽△♅	0am22
	☽∥♄	2 37
	☉∥♆	5 14
	☉⚻♂	5 29
	☽⚺♃	7 13
	☽⚹♆	6pm34
	☽∥♆	6 36
11 F	☽⚼♂	1am28
	☉∠☽	3 35
	☽□♄	3 44
	☽△♆	4 29
	☽⚹♇	5 27
	☉⚼♄	5 28
	☽∥☿	7 32
	☽⚺☿	8 49
	♀ ♍	4pm24
	☉⚼♆	8 6
12 S	☽△♂	4am58
	☽□♅	8 51
	☽∠♇	9 29
	☉⚹☽	9 53
	☽∠♆	12pm26
	☽⚻♃	3 36
	♃SR	5 6
	☽∥♃	8 49
13 Su	☽∥♇	2am 9
	♀⚼♂	6 20
	☽⚺☿	8 6
	☽⚹♄	11 7
	☽□♆	11 55
	☽0S	12pm24
	☽⚺♇	12 56
	☽⚹♆	3 19
	☽∥♇	10 33
14 M	☽∥♃	3am48
	☽□♂	10 16
	☽∠♀	1pm28
	☽∠♄	1 53
	☽⚹♅	2 59
	♀□♄	6 24
	☉□☽	8 11
	☽⚺♃	9 32
15 T	♀△♆	3am45
	♇SD	6 34
	☽∥☿	7 38
	☉△♃	3pm24
	☽⚻♄	3 58
	♀⚹♇	4 36
	☽⚹♆	4 45
	☽⚼♅	5 2
	☽⚹♇	5 49
	☽⚹♀	5 55
	☽□♆	6 43
	☽∥♆	10 50
	☽⚼♃	11 28
16 W	☿⚺♀	1am10
	☽⚹♂	1pm 2
	☽∥♄	4 20
	☽∠♆	6 9
	☽⚺♅	6 25
	☿□♇	8 56
17 Th	☽△♃	0am43
	☉△☽	3 6
	☉∥☽	3 32
	☽∥♆	8 58
	☽∥♅	1pm30
	☽∠♂	1 31
	☽⚹♄	6 10
	☽⚺♆	6 37
	☽△☿	7 14
	☿⚼♅	8 2
	☽⚹♇	8 3
18 F	☽□♀	0am19
	☿⚺♆	2 42
	☉⚻☽	5 27
	☽⚺♂	1pm31
	☽⚼♆	6 39
	☽⚻♅	7 30
	☽∠♇	8 23
	☿△♄	10 59
19 S	☽□♃	1am37
	☉⚻☽	7 18
	☽⚺♆	5pm45
	☽⚺♄	6 31
	☽⚹♆	7 18
	☽⚹♇	8 27
20 Su	☽△♀	4am32
	☽⚹♂	12pm47
	☽∠♄	6 28
	☽⚺♅	7 29
21 M	☽⚹♃	1am36
	☽⚼♀	6 32
	☉☍☽	10 41
	☽⚻♆	3pm51
	☽⚹♄	6 37
	☽⚺♆	7 26
	☽⚻♅	7 39
	☽□♇	8 42
22 T	☽∥♅	1am45
	☽∠♃	1 51
	☽∥♆	6 11
	☽⚺♀	8 56
	☽⚺♂	12pm35
	☉∥☽	4 45
	☽∠♆	8 3
	☽⚹♅	8 16
	☽∥♄	10 52
23 W	☽⚺♃	2am37
	☉ ♌	3 25
	☉⚹♆	11 11
	☽∠♂	1pm17
	☽∥♆	3 13
	☽⚺♆	3 19
	☉⚺☽	3 30
	☽□♄	8 31
	☽⚹♆	9 22
	☿ ♋	9 54
	☽△♇	10 49
24 Th	♀△♂	0am54
	☿∠♀	2pm44
	☽⚹♂	2 48
	☽⚼♆	4 6
	☽⚻♇	4 18
	☉⚼☽	7 52
	☽□♅	11 48
25 F	☽⚼♇	1am 9
	☽∥☿	1 43
	☽⚻♃	6 35
	☽∥♃	11 15
	☽∥♇	5pm40
	☽△♆	5 48
26 S	☉△☽	1am10
	☽△♄	1 55
	☽□♆	2 50
	☽0N	3 34
	☽⚺♇	4 31
	☉△♄	11 12
	☽∥♇	1pm34
	☽∥♃	8 22
	☽□♂	8 48
	☉⚺♆	11 17
27 Su	☉⚼♅	2am 6
	☽∥♀	2 13
	☽⚺♆	4 40
	☽⚼♄	6 11
	☽△♅	7 20
	☽⚺♃	2pm33
	☉□♇	10 43
28 M	☽□♆	0am11
	♀□♅	10 32
	☽⚺♄	11 23
	☽△♆	12pm20
	☽⚼♅	12 34
	☽⚼♀	12 46
	☽⚻♇	2 16
	☉∥♄	3 17
	☉□☽	3 35
	☽∠♃	7 58
29 T	☽∥♆	2am 0
	♀∠♇	5 27
	☽△♂	6 33
	☉∥☽	2pm48
	☽∥♄	4 5
	☽∥♆	6 15
	☽⚺♅	6 29
	♀∥♃	8 53
	☽△♀	9 47
30 W	☽⚹♃	1am53
	☽⚹♆	9 59
	☽∥♆	12pm19
	☽⚼♂	12 22
	☽∥♅	5 34
	☉⚼♃	7 33
	☽⚻♄	11 38
31 Th	☽⚺♆	0am34
	☽⚺♇	2 42
	☉⚹☽	9 20
	☽∠♆	3pm42
	♀⚻♃	4 26
	☽⚺♂	6 24

LONGITUDE

DAY	SID. TIME	☉	☽	☽ 12 Hour	MEAN ☊	TRUE ☊	☿	♀	♂	♃	♄	♅	♆	♇
	h m s	° ' "	° ' "	° ' "	° '	° '	° '	° '	° '	° '	° '	° '	° '	° '
1 Th	10 35 55	10♓ 35 41	21♒ 20 28	27♒ 16 43	11♊ 21.3	11♊R32.1	3♓ 58.6	13♒ 18.7	21♏ 52.2	7♑ 50.4	16♏R21.3	13♐ 25.8	1♑ 7.9	1♏R56.8
2 F	10 39 52	11 35 54	3♓ 12 44	9♓ 8 41	11 18.1	11 18.0	5 46.6	14 32.7	22 11.6	7 59.8	16 20.9	13 26.7	1 9.0	1 55.9
3 Sa	10 43 48	12 36 6	15 4 43	21 0 59	11 14.9	11 3.0	7 35.7	15 46.8	22 30.7	8 9.2	16 20.2	13 27.6	1 10.0	1 55.0
4 Su	10 47 45	13 36 15	26 57 38	2♈ 54 52	11 11.8	10 48.3	9 25.8	17 0.8	22 49.4	8 18.4	16 19.4	13 28.4	1 11.0	1 54.1
5 M	10 51 41	14 36 23	8♈ 52 51	14 51 48	11 8.6	10 35.1	11 16.9	18 14.8	23 7.6	8 27.4	16 18.5	13 29.1	1 11.9	1 53.1
6 Tu	10 55 38	15 36 29	20 51 59	26 53 40	11 5.4	10 24.5	13 9.1	19 28.9	23 25.5	8 36.4	16 17.4	13 29.8	1 12.9	1 52.1
7 W	10 59 34	16 36 33	2♉ 57 12	9♉ 2 58	11 2.2	10 16.8	15 2.2	20 42.9	23 42.9	8 45.2	16 16.3	13 30.4	1 13.8	1 51.1
8 Th	11 3 31	17 36 34	15 11 23	21 22 55	10 59.1	10 12.3	16 56.4	21 56.9	23 59.9	8 53.9	16 15.1	13 31.0	1 14.6	1 50.0
9 F	11 7 27	18 36 34	27 38 4	3♊ 57 20	10 55.9	10D 10.3	18 51.5	23 11.0	24 16.5	9 2.5	16 13.8	13 31.5	1 15.4	1 48.9
10 Sa	11 11 24	19 36 32	10♊ 21 16	16 50 25	10 52.7	10R 10.1	20 47.4	24 25.0	24 32.6	9 10.9	16 12.4	13 32.0	1 16.2	1 47.8
11 Su	11 15 21	20 36 27	23 25 17	0♋ 6 20	10 49.5	10 10.2	22 44.2	25 39.0	24 48.3	9 19.3	16 10.9	13 32.4	1 17.0	1 46.7
12 M	11 19 17	21 36 20	6♋ 53 58	13 48 28	10 46.3	10 9.5	24 41.7	26 53.1	25 3.5	9 27.5	16 9.2	13 32.8	1 17.8	1 45.5
13 Tu	11 23 14	22 36 12	20 50 2	27 58 37	10 43.2	10 6.8	26 39.8	28 7.1	25 18.2	9 35.5	16 7.5	13 33.1	1 18.5	1 44.3
14 W	11 27 10	23 36 0	5♌ 14 3	12♌ 35 34	10 40.0	10 1.6	28 38.5	29 21.1	25 32.5	9 43.5	16 5.8	13 33.3	1 19.1	1 43.1
15 Th	11 31 7	24 35 47	20 3 30	27 35 59	10 36.8	9 53.8	0♈ 37.4	0♓ 35.2	25 46.2	9 51.3	16 3.9	13 33.5	1 19.8	1 41.9
16 F	11 35 3	25 35 31	5♍ 12 15	12♍ 50 39	10 33.6	9 44.0	2 36.4	1 49.2	25 59.5	9 58.9	16 1.9	13 33.7	1 20.4	1 40.6
17 Sa	11 39 0	26 35 13	20 30 49	28 10 15	10 30.5	9 33.2	4 35.3	3 3.2	26 12.2	10 6.4	15 59.8	13 33.8	1 20.9	1 39.3
18 Su	11 42 56	27 34 53	5♎ 47 30	13♎ 22 10	10 27.3	9 22.7	6 33.9	4 17.3	26 24.4	10 13.8	15 57.6	13R 33.8	1 21.5	1 38.0
19 M	11 46 53	28 34 31	20 52 1	28 16 20	10 24.1	9 13.8	8 31.8	5 31.3	26 36.1	10 21.0	15 55.4	13 33.8	1 22.0	1 36.7
20 Tu	11 50 50	29 34 7	5♏ 34 16	12♏ 45 14	10 20.9	9 7.2	10 28.8	6 45.3	26 47.2	10 28.1	15 53.0	13 33.7	1 22.5	1 35.4
21 W	11 54 46	0♈ 33 42	19 48 32	26 43 2	10 17.8	9 3.2	12 24.4	7 59.3	26 57.8	10 35.1	15 50.6	13 33.6	1 22.9	1 34.0
22 Th	11 58 43	1 33 15	3♐ 33 45	10♐ 15 16	10 14.6	9D 1.6	14 18.3	9 13.4	27 7.8	10 41.9	15 48.1	13 33.4	1 23.3	1 32.6
23 F	12 2 39	2 32 46	16 49 53	23 18 10	10 11.4	9 1.6	16 10.1	10 27.4	27 17.2	10 48.6	15 45.5	13 33.2	1 23.7	1 31.2
24 Sa	12 6 36	3 32 15	29 40 32	5♑ 57 37	10 8.2	9R 2.1	17 59.2	11 41.4	27 26.0	10 55.1	15 42.8	13 33.0	1 24.0	1 29.8
25 Su	12 10 32	4 31 42	12♑ 10 1	18 18 20	10 5.0	9 1.9	19 45.5	12 55.5	27 34.2	11 1.4	15 40.0	13 32.6	1 24.3	1 28.3
26 M	12 14 29	5 31 8	24 23 13	0♒ 25 14	10 1.9	9 0.1	21 28.2	14 9.5	27 41.8	11 7.6	15 37.2	13 32.3	1 24.6	1 26.9
27 Tu	12 18 25	6 30 32	6♒ 24 57	12 22 55	9 58.7	8 56.0	23 7.2	15 23.5	27 48.7	11 13.7	15 34.2	13 31.8	1 24.8	1 25.4
28 W	12 22 22	7 29 54	18 19 36	24 15 27	9 55.5	8 49.4	24 41.8	16 37.6	27 55.0	11 19.6	15 31.2	13 31.3	1 25.1	1 23.9
29 Th	12 26 19	8 29 14	0♓ 10 53	6♓ 6 15	9 52.3	8 40.4	26 11.9	17 51.6	28 0.6	11 25.3	15 28.2	13 30.8	1 25.2	1 22.4
30 F	12 30 15	9 28 33	12 1 31	17 57 58	9 49.2	8 29.7	27 36.9	19 5.6	28 5.6	11 30.9	15 25.0	13 30.2	1 25.4	1 20.9
31 Sa	12 34 12	10♈ 27 49	23♓ 54 50	29♓ 52 39	9♊ 46.0	8♊ 18.2	28♈ 56.6	20♓ 19.6	28♏ 9.9	11♑ 36.3	15♏ 21.8	13♐ 29.6	1♑ 25.5	1♏ 19.3

DECLINATION and LATITUDE

DAY	☉ DECL	☽ DECL	☽ LAT	☽ 12hr DECL	☿ DECL	☿ LAT	♀ DECL	♀ LAT	♂ DECL	♂ LAT	♃ DECL	♃ LAT	♄ DECL	♄ LAT
1	7S36	11												
2	7 13	1												
3	6 50	1												
4	6 27													
5	6 4													
6	5 40													
7	5 17													
8	4 54	1												
9	4 30	1												
10	4 7	2												
11	3 43	2												
12	3 20	2												
13	2 56	2												
14	2 32	2												
15	2 9	1												
16	1 45	1												
17	1 21													
18	0 58													
19	0 34													
20	0 10	1												
21	0N13	1												
22	0 37	20 24	0 29	22 6	5 38	0 22	9 16	1 13	18 8	1 26	22 47	0 14	14 8	2 33
23	1 1	23 29	0S41	24 32	6 53	0 34	8 50	1 16	18 11	1 25	22 46	0 14	14 7	2 33
24	1 24	25 14	1 48	25 37	7 46	0 46	8 23	1 18	18 13	1 24	22 46	0 14	14 6	2 33
25	1 48	25 39	2 47	25 23	8 38	0 58	7 56	1 19	18 16	1 23	22 45	0 14	14 5	2 34
26	2 12	24 48	3 37	23 56	9 28	1 10	7 28	1 20	18 19	1 22	22 45	0 14	14 4	2 34
27	2 35	22 48	4 17	21 26	10 16	1 22	7 1	1 22	18 21	1 21	22 44	0 14	14 3	2 34
28	2 59	19 31	4 45	18 3	11 2	1 34	6 33	1 23	18 24	1 20	22 44	0 14	14 2	2 34
29	3 22	16 3	5 0	13 58	11 46	1 46	6 5	1 24	18 26	1 19	22 44	0 14	14 1	2 34
30	3 45	11 43	5 3	9 21	12 27	1 57	5 37	1 25	18 28	1 18	22 43	0 13	13 60	2 34
31	4N 9	6S33	4S52	4S22	13N 6	2N 8	5S 9	1S25	18S30	1N17	22S43	0N13	13S59	2N35

DAY	♅ DECL	♅ LAT	♆ DECL	♆ LAT	♇ DECL	♇ LAT
	22S22	0N 3	22S16	1N11	4N 3	17N14
	2 22	0 3	22 16	1 11	4 6	17 16
	2 23	0 3	22 15	1 11	4 9	17 17
	2 23	0 3	22 15	1 11	4 12	17 19
	2 23	0 3	22 15	[illegible]	[illegible]	17 20
	2 23	0 3	22 15	[illegible]	[illegible]	17 22
	2 23	0 3	22 [illegible]	[illegible]	[illegible]	17 23
	22S23	0N 3	22S15	[illegible]	[illegible]	17N24

The Moon is Void of Course between 1 am on March 1st until 5 pm March 1st (GMT) It is during this time that the Moon is moving from the last aspect to the next sign of the Zodiac.

☽ PHENOMENA		
dy	hr	
2	11	APOGE
16	21	PERIG
29	16	APOGE

MAX/0 DECL		
dy	hr	° '
5	2	0
12	3	25N34
18	7	0
24	20	25S40

MAX/0 LAT		
dy	hr	° '
2	16	4S59
10	0	0
16	7	5N 1
22	10	0
29	17	5S 3

VOID OF COURSE ☽ LAST ASPT		☽ INGRESS		
1	1am 6	1	♓	5pm30
3	3pm26	4	♈	6am 8
5	8pm55	6	♉	6pm10
8	5pm25	9	♊	4am30
11	4am26	11	♋	11am49
13	11am22	13	♌	3pm22
15	9am14	15	♍	3pm48
17	10am11	17	♎	2pm52
18	12pm19	19	♏	2pm49
21	12pm32	21	♐	5pm42
22	10pm35	24	♑	0am37
26	6am38	26	♒	11am10
28	7pm34	28	♓	11pm38
31	8am36	31	♈	12pm15

dy	hr	mn		PHASE
2	18	32	12♓22	●
10	18	28	20♊23	☽
17	10	11	27♍ 1	○
24	7	59	3♑52	☾

DAILY ASPECTARIAN

Day	Aspect	Time
1 Th	☽□♂	1am 6
	♀⚹♅	2 21
	☽∠♃	3 4
	☽∥♀	10 30
	☽∥♂	1pm25
	☽⚹☿	7 49
	☽△♇	9 25
2 F	☽∥♄	3am16
	☽⚹☿	6 7
	☽⚹♃	9 48
	♀∥♂	3pm 7
	☉⚹☽	6 32
	☽□♅	8 43
	☽∥☿	11 9
3 Sa	☽⚹♀	1am35
	☽△♄	2 32
	☽⚻♇	3 43
	♀∠♆	7 38
	☿⚹♃	8 0
	♀□♄	10 44
	☽△♂	3pm26
	☉∥☽	7 33
	☉□♅	8 49
4 Su	☽∥♇	7am11
	☽□♆	8 31
	☽⚻♄	8 47
	☽⚹♇	9 57
	☽∠♀	11 22
	☽⚻♂	10pm27
	☽□♃	11 8
5 M	☽0N	2am27
	☽⚹☿	3 43
	☽△♅	9 15
	☉⚹☽	12pm32
	☽⚹♄	2 32
	☽⚹♀	8 55
	☽∥♇	9 40
6 T	☿□♅	4am26
	☉∥☽	4 39
	☽⚹♂	5 14
	☽⚻♅	3pm12
	☽∥☿	3 17
	☉△♄	4 4
	☽∠♆	5 10
	☽△♆	8 33
	☉∠☽	9 6
	☽☍♇	9 50
7 W	☉⚻♇	5am42
	♂∠♃	6 30
	☽△♃	11 33
	☿△♄	3pm26
	☽⚹♅	8 44
	☿⚻♇	10 41
	☽∥♄	11 41
8 Th	☽⚻♆	2am 3
	☽☍♄	2 4
	☽∥♀	3 1
	☽⚹☿	4 1
	☉⚹☽	5 7
	♄∠♆	5 27
	☽□♀	2pm32
	☽∥♂	4 23
	☽⚻♃	3 2
	☽☍♂	3 25
	☉⚹♆	5 33
9 F	☽⚹♆	6am34
	☽⚹♇	7 36
	♀∠♃	6pm32
	♀∥♄	8 17
	☉∥♇	8 33
	☽⚹♃	9 47
10 Sa	☽∥♆	1am34
	☽∥♅	2 37
	♀□♂	3 9
	☽☍♅	3 54
	☽∥♃	7 16
	☽⚹♄	10 49
	☽⚻♇	11 54
	☉☍☽	6pm28
	☽□☿	10 33
	☿∥♇	11 58
11 Su	☽⚹♂	2am33
	☽△♀	4 26
	☽⚻♄	1pm33
	☽☍☿	2 6
	☽△♇	2 57
	☉∥☿	10 15
12 M	☽☍♃	4am31
	☿△♂	5 4
	☽⚻♂	5 37
	☽⚻♀	9 31
	☽⚹♅	11 33
	☽△♄	4pm 0
13 T	☉△☽	3am13
	☽△♂	7 39
	☽△☿	11 22
	☽⚻♅	12pm37
	☽⚹♀	1 23
	☽⚹♆	5 33
	☽□♇	6 13
14 W	☽∥♃	1am 0
	☽∥♅	4 32
	☽∥♆	5 31
	☉⚻☽	5 34
	☽⚹♃	7 24
	☿ ♓	12pm36
	☽△♅	1 33
	☽⚻☿	3 47
	☿ ♈	4 28
	☽□♄	5 36
	☽⚻♆	6 1
	☿⚹♀	10 50
15 Th	☿⚻♄	5am15
	☽⚻♃	7 43
	☉☍☽	7 43
	☽∥♂	7 53
	☿□♆	8 36
	☽□♂	9 14
	☿⚹♇	12pm52
	☿0N	2 29
	♀⚹♆	2 33
	☽△♆	5 54
	☽☍♀	6 12
	☽⚹♇	6 27
	☽⚹♆	7 18
	☿△♇	9 16
16 F	☽∥♄	0am11
	☽△♃	7 34
	☽∥♀	10 49
	☉△♂	12pm16
	☽□♅	1 7
	☽⚹♄	4 57
	☽∠♇	5 38
17 S	☉∥☿	0am34
	☽⚹♂	9 2
	☉☍☽	10 11
	☽∥♇	3pm 4
	☽∠♄	4 24
	☽□♆	5 0
	☽⚹♇	5 27
	☽⚹♀	9 25
	☽∥♆	10 40
18 Su	☽☍♆	1am24
	☉∥☽	3 24
	♅SR	6 21
	☽0S	6 43
	☽□♃	7 4
	☽∠♂	9 0
	☉∥☽	9 40
	☽⚹♅	12pm19
	☽⚹♄	4 6
	☽∥☿	5 34
	☽∥♇	10 34
	☽⚻♀	11 24
19 M	☽⚹♂	9am24
	☽∠♅	12pm29
	☉⚹☽	1 24
	☽⚹♆	3 3
	☽⚹♇	5 27
	☽∥♀	9 42
	☿□♃	11 52
20 T	☽△♀	2am 9
	☿∥♇	4 16
	☽⚹♃	8 14
	☽⚹♆	9 28
	☉ ♈	10 26
	☽⚹♅	1pm22
	☽∥♄	2 46
	☉∥☽	4 12
	☽⚹♄	5 15
	☿⚻♂	5 34
	☽∠♆	6 8
21 W	☉⚻♄	6am33
	☽∠♃	10 3
	☽∥♂	10 27
	☽⚹♂	12pm32
	☿△♅	2 31
	☽⚻☿	3 16
	☉□☿	7 58
	☽⚹☿	8 9
	☉△☽	8 10
	☽⚹♇	8 26
	☉⚹♇	11 45
22 Th	☽□♀	11am11
	☽⚹♃	12pm35
	☽∥☿	1 11
	☽∥♅	2 18
	☽∥♃	5 32
	☽⚹♅	6 0
	☿⚹♄	6 48
	☽⚹♄	10 2
	☽△☿	10 35
	☽∠♇	11 26
23 F	♀⚹♃	7am31
	☽⚹♂	7pm43
24 S	☽∠♄	1am58
	☽⚹♆	3 17
	☽⚹♇	3 27
	☉☍☽	7 59
	☿∥♀	11 10
	☽⚹♃	9pm46
25 Su	☽∠♂	0am48
	☽⚹♀	1 38
	☽⚹♅	2 41
	☽⚹♄	6 48
	♀□♅	11 59
	☽□☿	5pm18
26 M	☽⚹♂	6am38
	☽∠♅	8 14
	☽∠♀	10 34
	☽⚹☿	1pm39
	☽□♇	2 1
27 T	☉⚹☽	0am12
	☽∥♃	0 38
	♀△♄	3 20
	☽∥♅	3 57
	☽∥☿	5 11
	☿⚹♇	7 52
	☽⚹♃	9 45
	☽⚹♅	2pm18
	☽□♄	6 21
	♀⚻♇	7 39
	☽∠☿	8 8
	☽⚹♀	8 10
28 W	☉∠☽	9am12
	☽∥♂	9 42
	☽⚹☿	2pm47
	☽∠♃	4 19
	☽□♂	7 34
29 Th	☽△♇	2am25
	☽⚹☿	2 31
	☽∥♄	11 46
	☉⚹☽	6pm21
	☽∥☿	8 38
	☽⚹♃	10 57
30 F	☽∠☿	1am20
	☽□♅	2 59
	☽△♄	6 49
	☽⚻♇	8 43
	☿⚹♂	8 57
	☿⚻♅	3pm45
	☽⚹♀	3 36
31 S	☽△♂	8am36
	☽∥♀	9 12
	☽⚹☿	11 19
	☽∥♇	11 43
	☉∥☽	12pm 7
	☽⚻♄	12 33
	☽⚹♇	2 32
	☽□☿	3 6
	☉∥♇	3 44
	☿ ♉	8 27

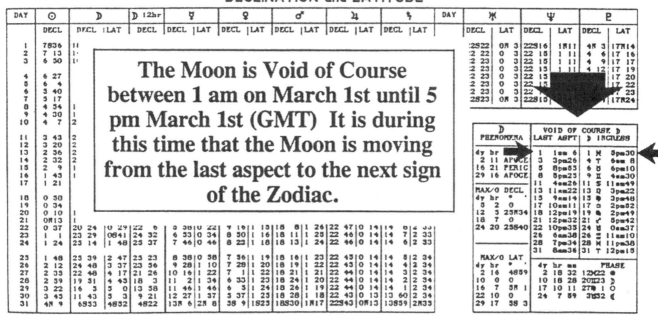

STANDARD DEVIATION OF DAILY ASPECTS

One of the primary reasons for the writing of this book was to alert traders of specific astrological and astronomical events. What I am going to discuss next is a situation that occurs infrequently in the daily search for clues to price-trend changes. This situation occurs when only 1 or 2 planetary aspects exist on a particular day; or just the opposite occurs--a large number of aspects are present.

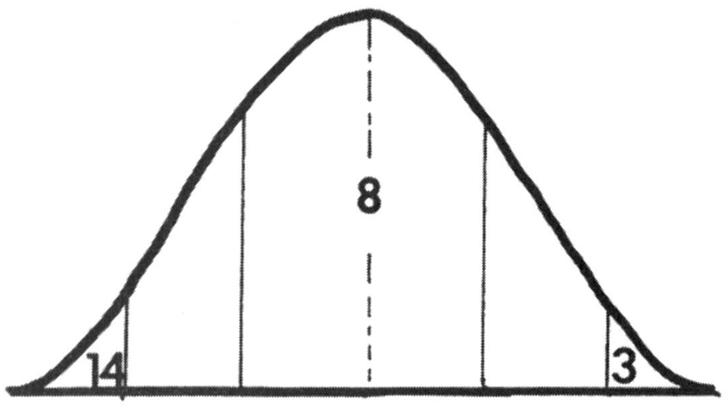

The average number of planetary aspects is approximately eight. Whenever you see a very small number of aspects (3 or less) or a large number of aspects (14 or more,) you can assume that something very dramatic is about to happen in the stock market. Why this affects the market I am not sure, but my opinion is that it works like a magnet. If there are very few aspects on one day, then the larger astro-cycle will take hold and pull the market either up or down.

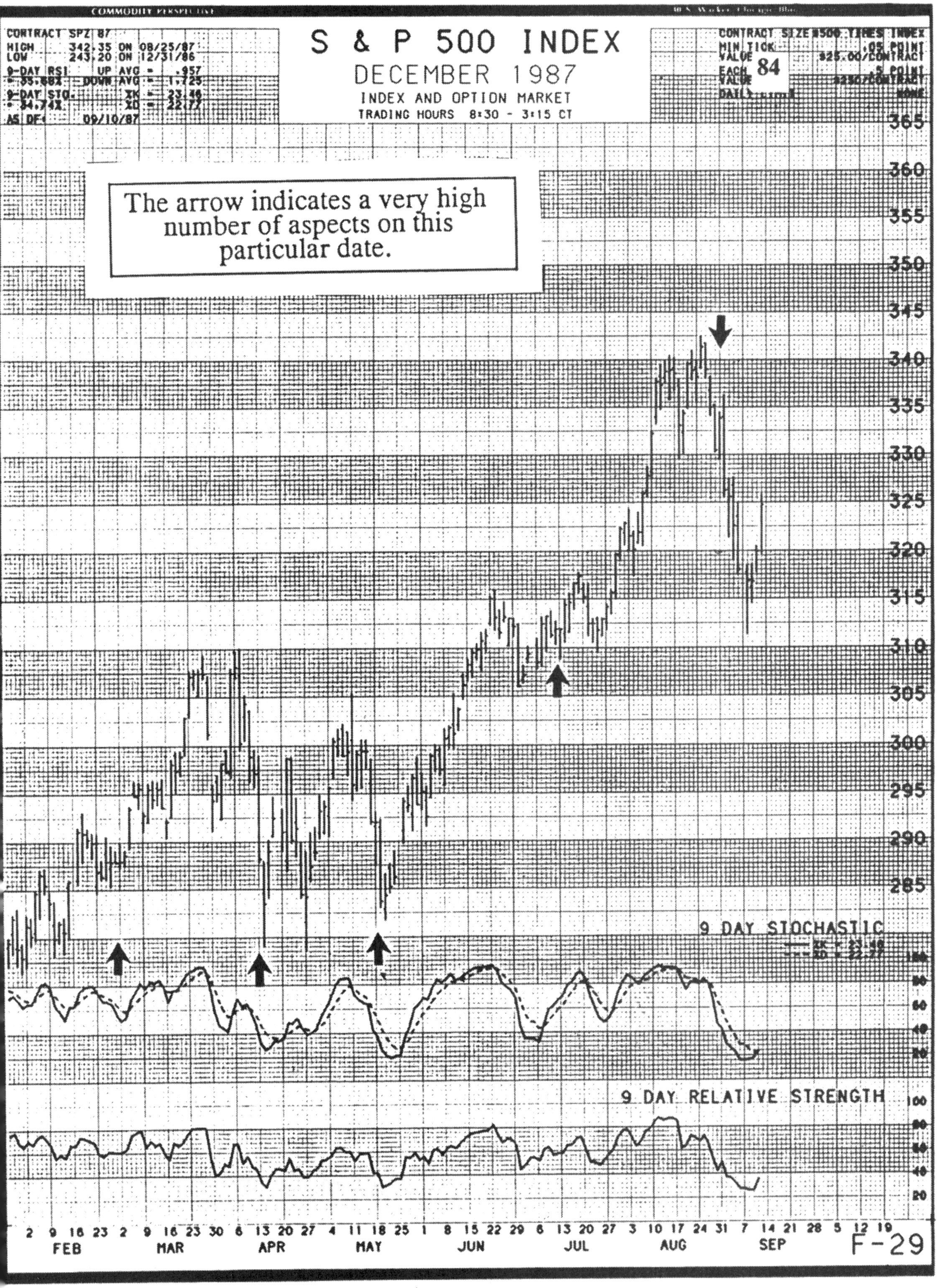

COMMODITY PERSPECTIVE
S & P 500 INDEX
DECEMBER 1987
INDEX AND OPTION MARKET
TRADING HOURS 8:30 - 3:15 CT
CONTRACT SPZ 87
HIGH 342.35 ON 08/25/87
LOW 243.20 ON 12/31/86
9-DAY RSI UP AVG = .957
= 35.68% DOWN AVG = 1.725
9-DAY STO. %K = 23.46
= 34.74% %D = 22.77
AS OF 09/10/87
CONTRACT SIZE $500 TIMES INDEX
MIN TICK .05 POINT
VALUE $25.00/CONTRACT
EACH .5 POINT
VALUE $250/CONTRACT
84
The arrow indicates a very high number of aspects on this particular date.
365
360
355
350
345
340
335
330
325
320
315
310
305
300
295
290
285
9 DAY STOCHASTIC
%K = 23.46
%D = 22.77
9 DAY RELATIVE STRENGTH
2 9 16 23 2 9 16 23 30 6 13 20 27 4 11 18 25 1 8 15 22 29 6 13 20 27 3 10 17 24 31 7 14 21 28 5 12 19
FEB MAR APR MAY JUN JUL AUG SEP
F-29

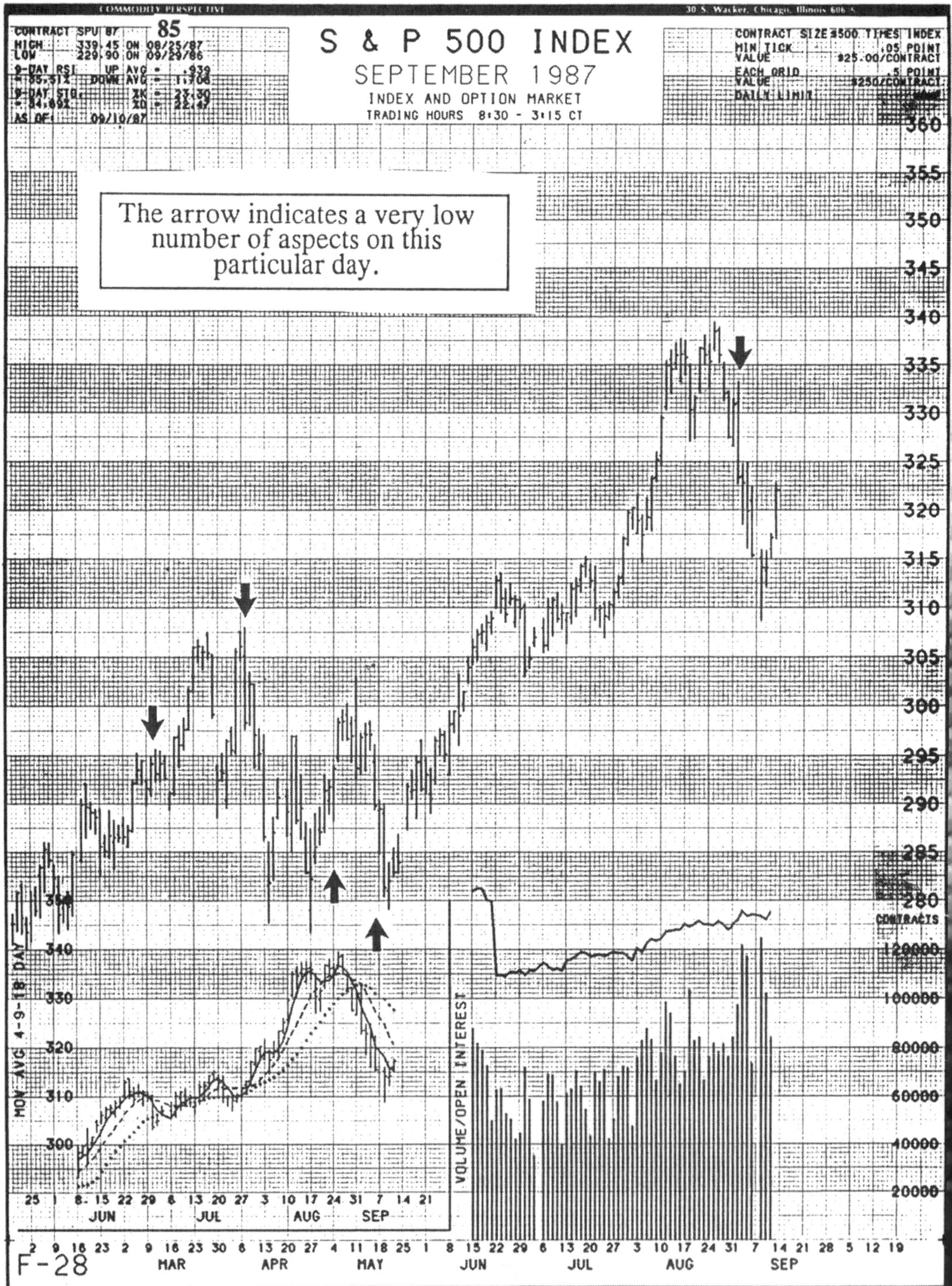
COMMODITY PERSPECTIVE
30 S. Wacker, Chicago, Illinois 606
85
S & P 500 INDEX
SEPTEMBER 1987
INDEX AND OPTION MARKET
TRADING HOURS 8:30 - 3:15 CT
CONTRACT SPU 87
HIGH 339.45 ON 08/25/87
LOW 229.90 ON 09/29/86
AS OF: 09/10/87
CONTRACT SIZE $500 TIMES INDEX
MIN TICK .05 POINT
VALUE $25.00/CONTRACT
EACH GRID .5 POINT
VALUE $250/CONTRACT
DAILY LIMIT
The arrow indicates a very low number of aspects on this particular day.
MON AVG 4-9-18 DAY
VOLUME/OPEN INTEREST
CONTRACTS
JUN
JUL
AUG
SEP
MAR
APR
MAY
F-28

SECTION THREE:

PLANETARY ASPECTS AND SYNODIC PERIODS

Section Three:

Planetary Aspects and Synodic Periods

Venus-Uranus

Venus revolves around the Sun in 61.8% of 1 year (365 days). Uranus revolves around the Sun in 84 years.

These two planets possess the unique Fibonacci relationship of .618! Figure I shows the relationship of Venus and Uranus when they are on opposite sides of the earth or in opposition (180° apart). This is how it would appear from the Earth looking up into the sky. It takes 225 days for Venus and Uranus to make a complete cycle from conjunction (0°) to conjunction (0°). If we take 365 days and multiply it by .618 the answer is 225 days. When I first witnessed this relationship it was apparent that the cyclical implications would be revealing because of the Fibonacci number sequence.

Donald Bradley in *Stock Market Prediction* by LLewellyn Publications mentioned this effect on stock prices when Venus and Uranus were at certain critical degrees (aspect). After studying this phenomenon for many months, certain applications became apparent from the **trader's viewpoint:**

1. The aspects were so accurate as a short-term trading and timing device that they could be used in trading stock index futures (636 aspects were tested, accurate to 92% +/- two days).

2. The sample size was excellent! Over 600 aspects in a 90-year period (1898-1987).

3. Some aspects were associated with bullish price action, and others with bearish price action. Conjunctions (0°), sextiles (60°) and trines (120°) are associated with strength in the stock market. Squares (90°) and oppositions (180°) are associated with weakness.

4. It was usually a short term (3 to 10 day) trend change, but more than 50% of the time the effect lasted several weeks.

The amount of research to verify this idea was frightening, but once I had seen the stock market reverse direction on these days, the question had to be answered. I have studied the technical implications of cycles in stocks and commodities for over twenty years, and I must admit that it is the single most accurate short-term timing mechanism I have researched. Figure II shows the last six months of the Standard & Poor's 500 futures index. Notice how the market abruptly changes trend on these days. How a trader may enter the market armed with this knowledge is a subject that deserves special attention. Trend changes occurred on October 5th, 1987, at Venus Trine Uranus (120°); November 24th, 1987, at Venus Conjunction Uranus (0°); January 14th, 1988, at Venus Sextile Uranus (60°); February 9th, 1988, at Venus Square Uranus (90°); and March 7th, 1988, at Venus Trine

Uranus (120°) Students of W.D. Gann have learned to respect these angular relationships.

Figure III shows that certain aspects have a positive effect and others have a negative effect.

For your convenience, I have listed the next six Venus-Uranus aspects in 1988. The serious market student owes it to himself to mark these days on his calendar:

May 19th Venus Opposition Uranus (180°)
May 27th Venus Opposition Uranus (180°)
Aug 3rd Venus Opposition Uranus (180°)
Oct 2nd Venus Trine Uranus (120°)
Oct 28th Venus Square Uranus (90°)
Nov 23rd Venus Sextile Uranus (60°)

The first three aspects are the same because of the retrograde motion of Venus or Uranus. My experience tells me that they will probably be more powerful than usual because of this retrograde motion. **Watch for changes in short-term trend on these dates!**

The S&P 500 chart on Figure II indicates the last two solar eclipses. Although eclipses bear no relationship to the Venus-Uranus aspects, eclipses are so astrologically significant that they were included in the chart.

Several other researchers have mentioned this Venus-Uranus correlation, such as James Mars Langham, *Cyclical Market Forecasting Stocks and Grain* and T.G. Butaney in *Forecasting Prices*.

THE MAJOR ASPECTS

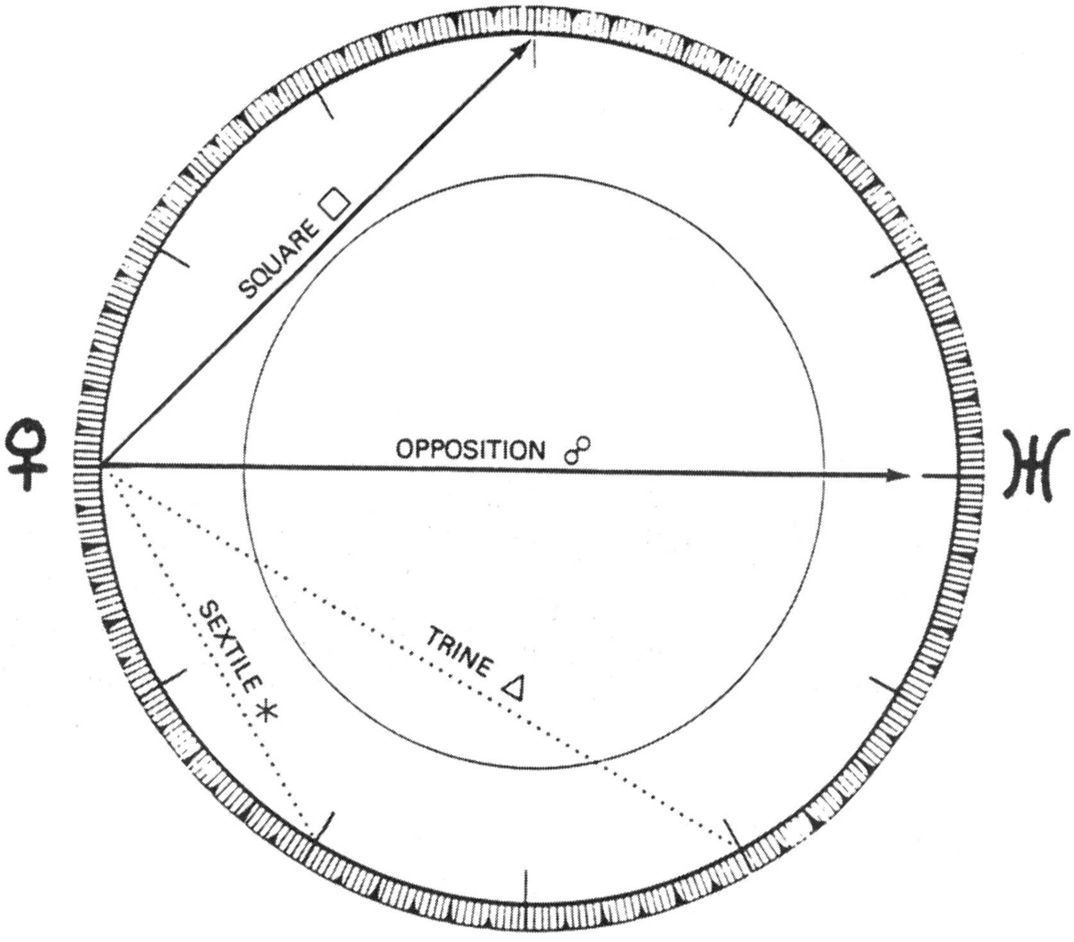

Figure I: This graph shows the relationship of Venus opposition Uranus. Planet Earth would be in the center. (Geocentric)

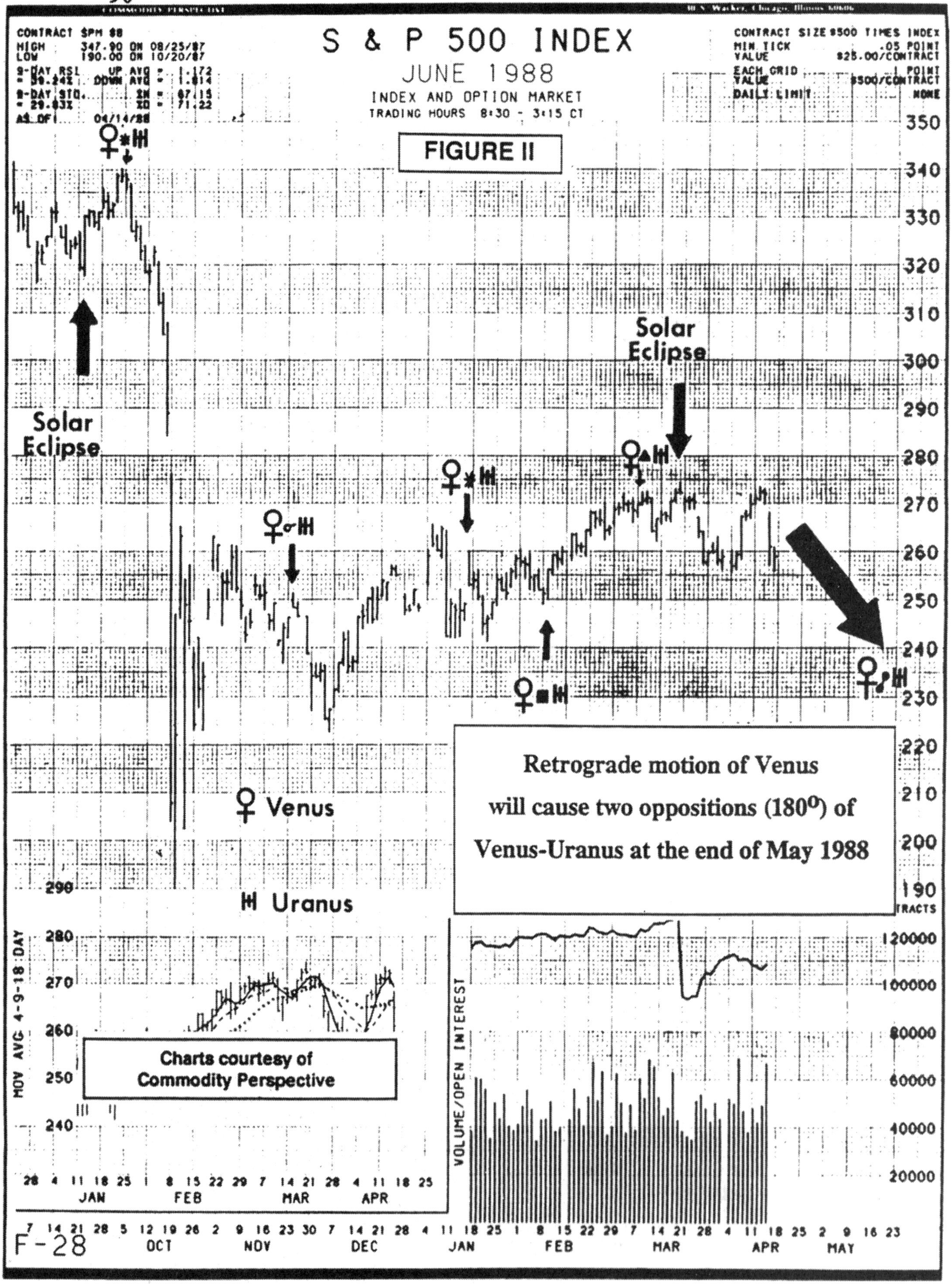

S & P 500 INDEX

JUNE 1988

INDEX AND OPTION MARKET

TRADING HOURS 8:30 - 3:15 CT

FIGURE II

Solar Eclipse

Solar Eclipse

♀ Venus

♅ Uranus

Retrograde motion of Venus will cause two oppositions (180°) of Venus-Uranus at the end of May 1988

Charts courtesy of Commodity Perspective

F-28

THE OBSERVED EFFECTS OF VENUS-URANUS ASPECTS (1898 - 1987)

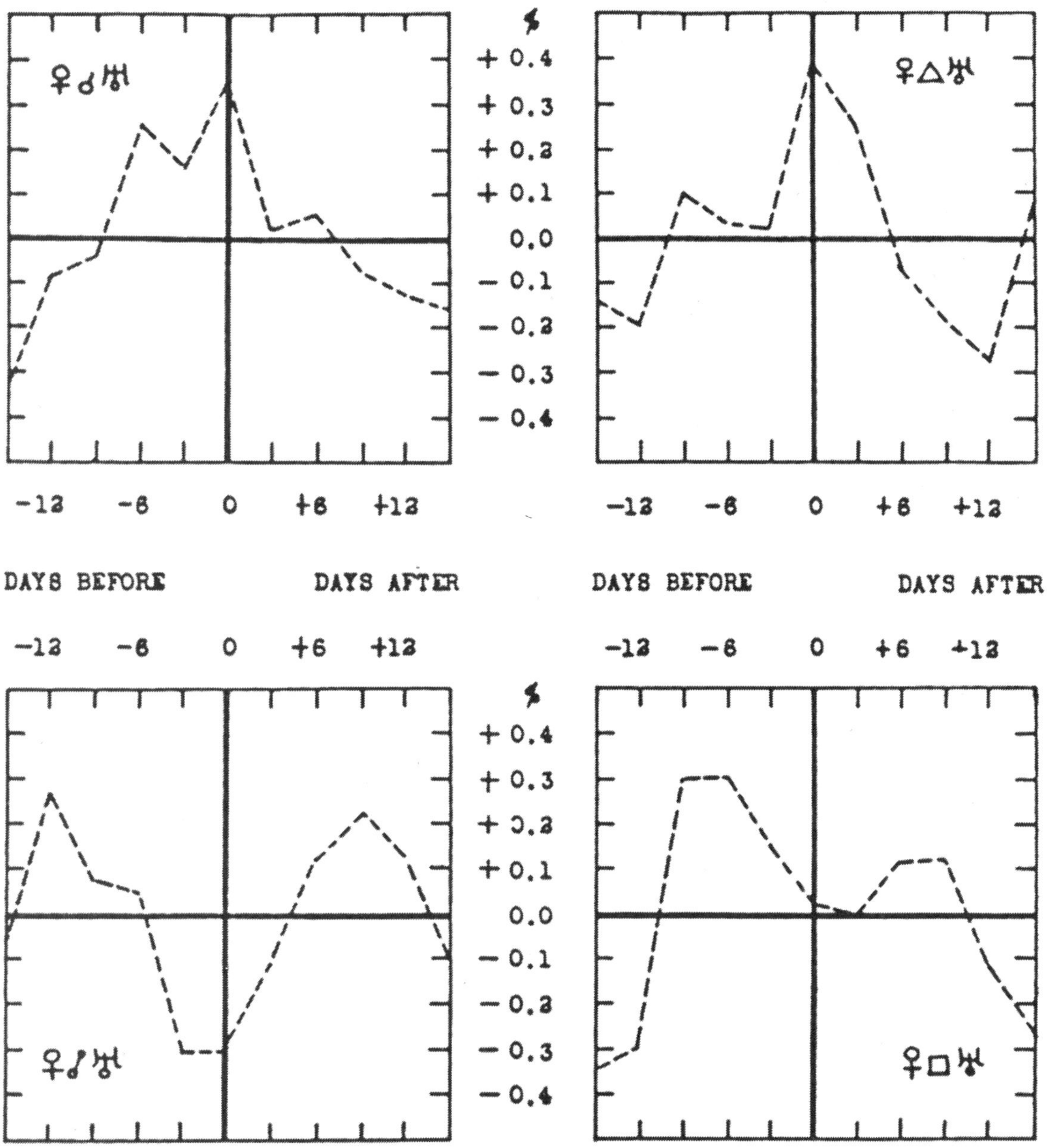

Figure III: Actual observed deviations due to the action of Venus-Uranus aspects. Broken line indicates course of Dow-Jones Industrials during 31-day periods centered on the dates when aspects were exact. Expressed as a percentage relatives of 15th day previous to aspect, taken as base, and corrected for trend by method of least squares. This experiment confirms astrological theory which claims that certain aspects are bullish, others bearish.

S&P 500 INDEX

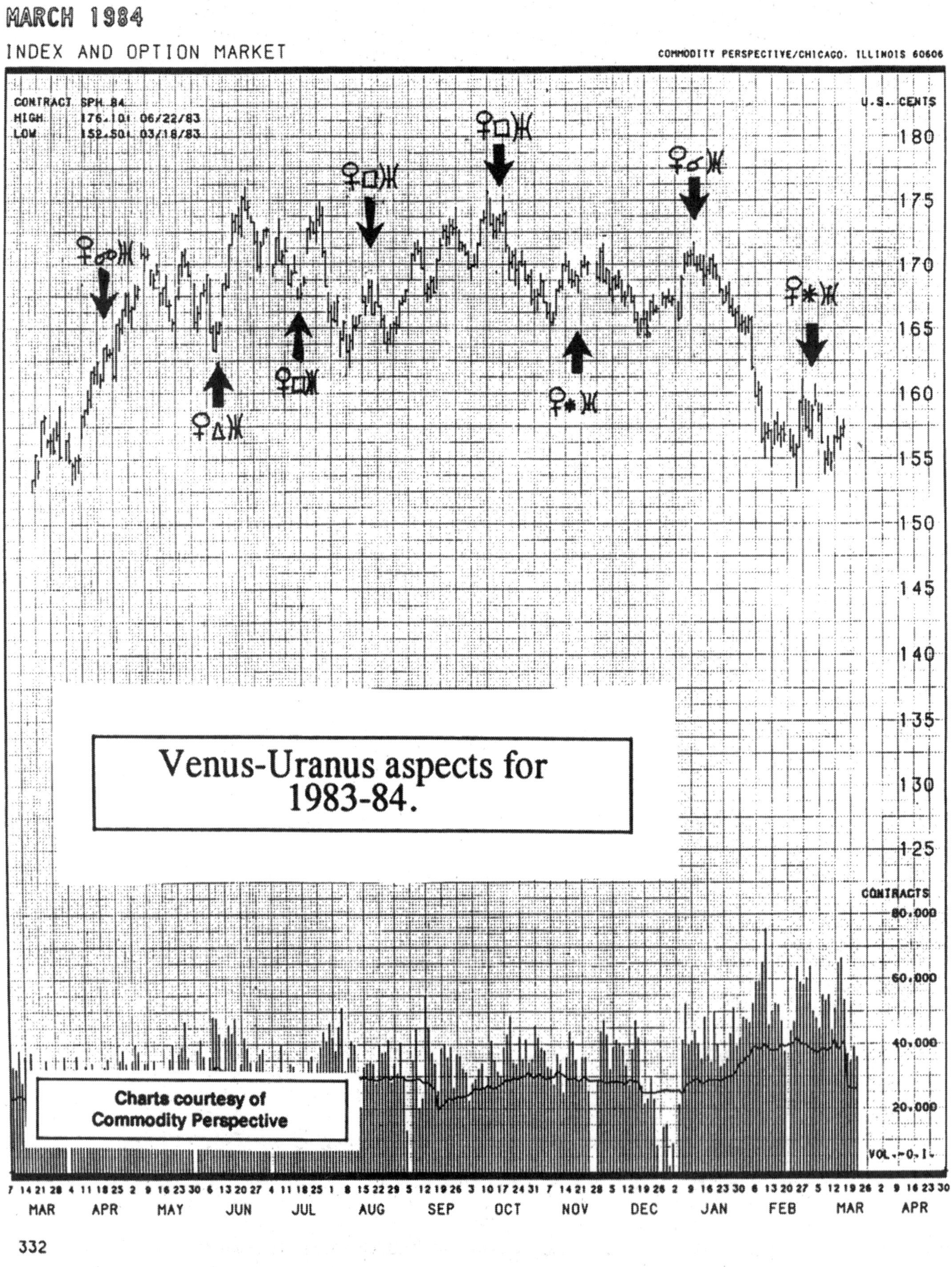

Venus-Uranus aspects for 1983-84.

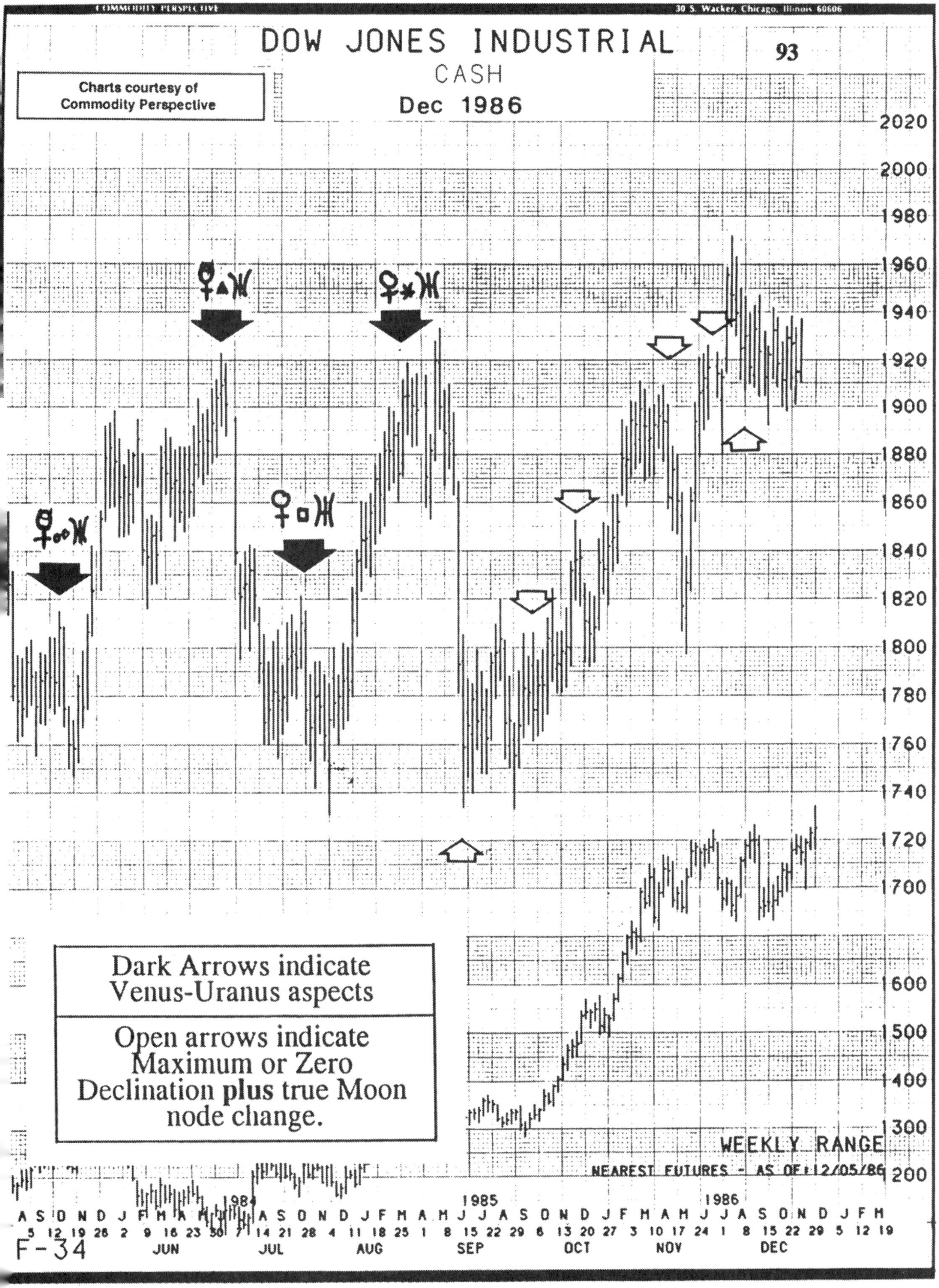
COMMODITY PERSPECTIVE
30 S. Wacker, Chicago, Illinois 60606
DOW JONES INDUSTRIAL
CASH
Dec 1986
93
Charts courtesy of
Commodity Perspective
Dark Arrows indicate
Venus-Uranus aspects
Open arrows indicate
Maximum or Zero
Declination plus true Moon
node change.
WEEKLY RANGE
NEAREST FUTURES - AS OF:12/05/86
1984
1985
1986
JUN
JUL
AUG
SEP
OCT
NOV
DEC
F-34

Jupiter-Saturn

The Jupiter-Saturn combination has been reported as one of the best indicators of long term economic activity. Lt.Cmdr. David Williams in *Financial Astrology* shows that the Jupiter-Saturn conjunction cycle was the most accurate of the astro-economic cycles he researched. From a trader's standpoint these are slower moving planets and their effect may take months to form.

Jupiter revolves around the Sun in 11.8 years. Saturn completes the revolution in 29.4 years. Their synodic period is 19.8 years. The Appendix lists the Jupiter-Saturn aspects for your convenience. It is my opinion that the Jupiter-Saturn aspects would be difficult to use in trading because of their long term implications. One should keep in mind when these aspects occur because of their significance to overall economic activity. Jupiter and Saturn are the largest planets in our solar system and Saturn is the only planet whose magnetic pull is touched by another planet, that planet being Jupiter.

Venus-Pluto

The planets Venus and Pluto have an average synodic period of 61.6% of one year! In other words it takes approximately 225 days for the two planets to meet at conjunction (0°) and travel through sextile (60°), square (90°), trine (120°) opposition (180°) and back to conjunction. These two aspects are excellent short term trend indicators in the stock market and gold market, especially the gold market. The high in gold in 1980 was associated with Pluto moving into "retrograde motion" and several major aspects of Venus. It is my opinion that the reason the Venus-Pluto aspects are so dependable is due to the Fibonacci relationship of the two planets. Whatever the reason may be, they still offer a powerful tool in timing gold and stock market transactions. The aspects usually work within two days of the exact aspect and the effect lasts for 5 to 10 trading days.

GOLD (N.Y.)

DECEMBER 1983

COMMODITY EXCHANGE, INC. NY

COMMODITY PERSPECTIVE/CHICAGO, ILLINOIS 60606

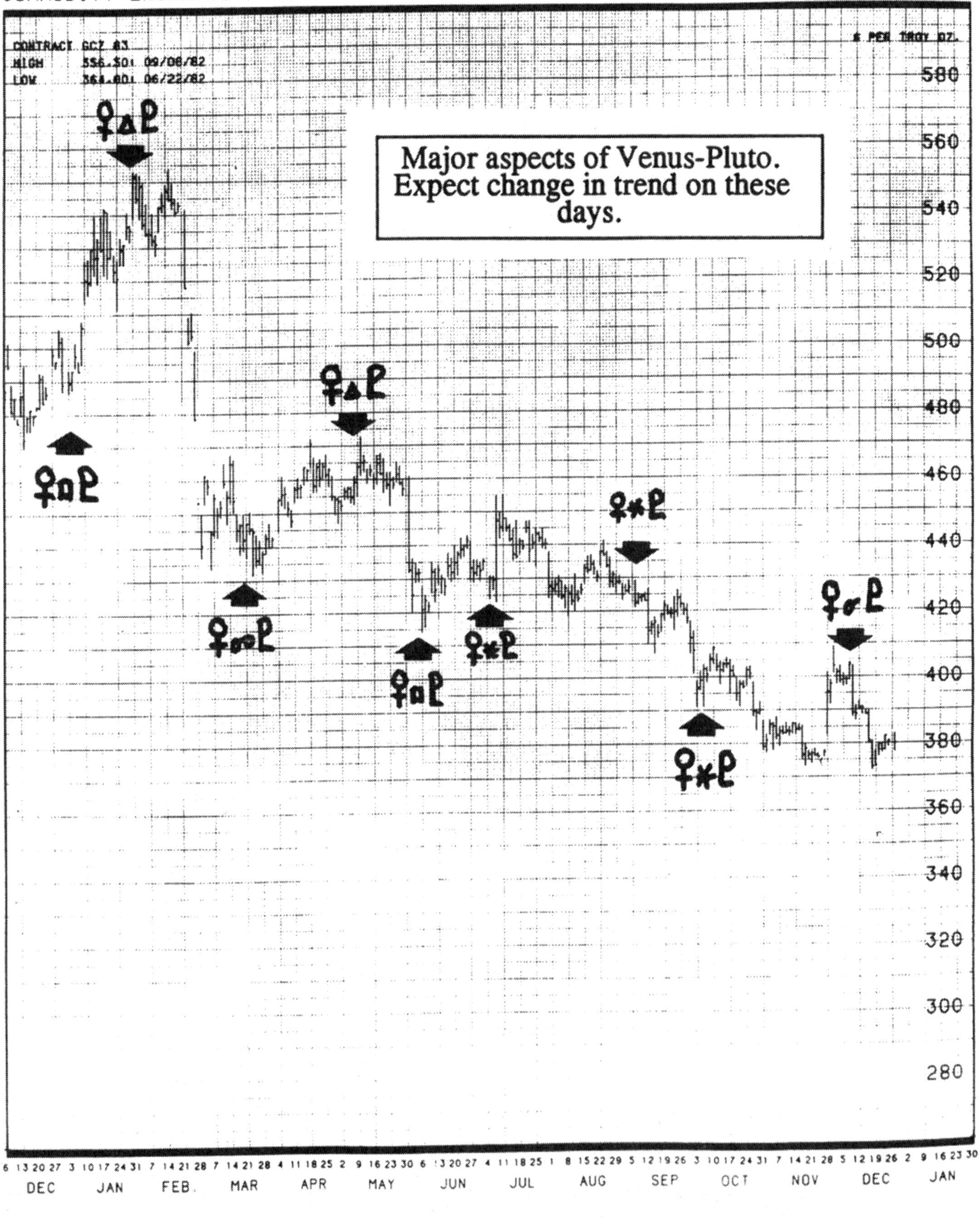

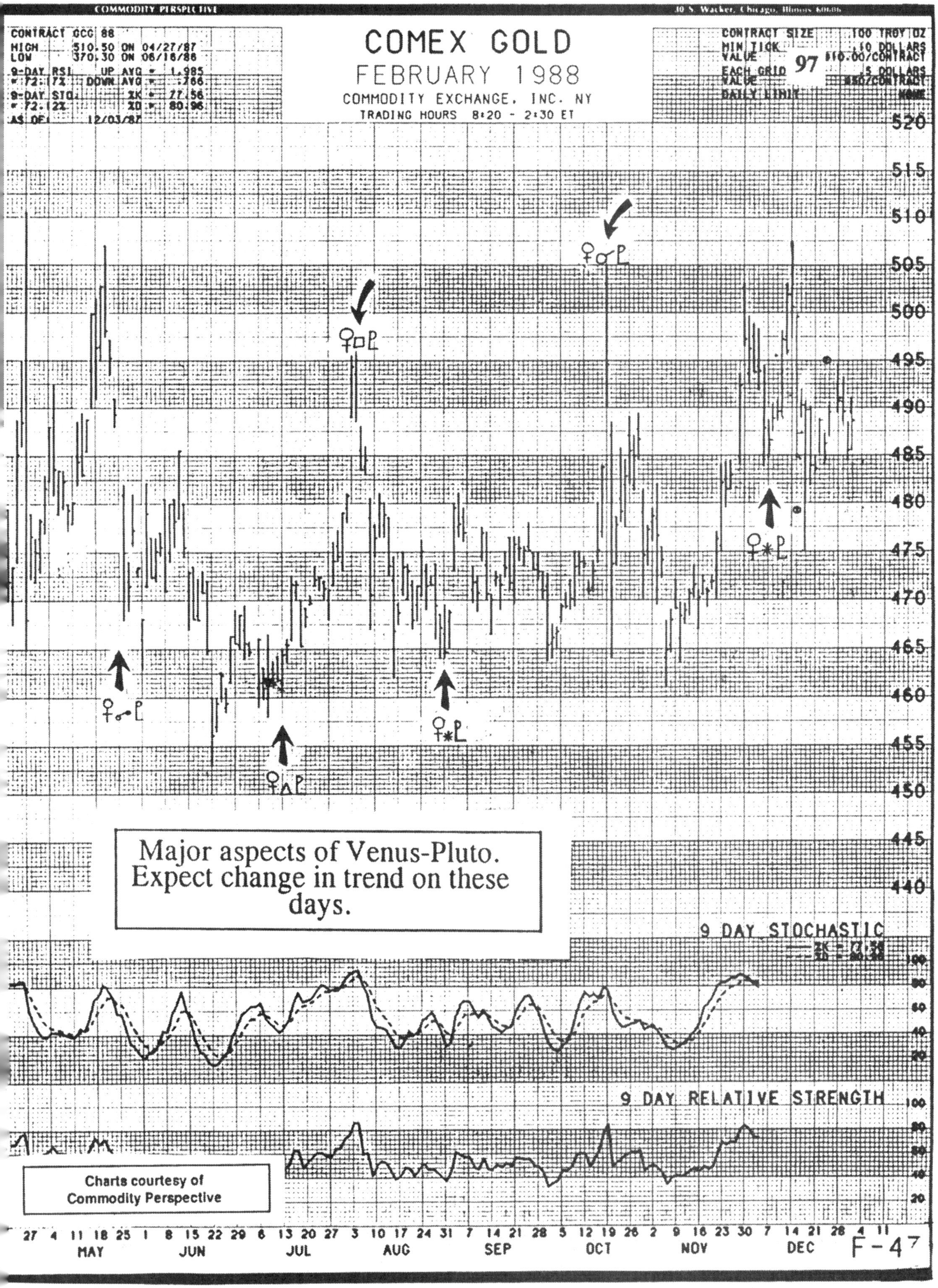
COMMODITY PERSPECTIVE
30 S. Wacker, Chicago, Illinois 60606
CONTRACT GCG 88
HIGH 510.50 ON 04/27/87
LOW 370.30 ON 06/16/86
AS OF: 12/03/87
COMEX GOLD
FEBRUARY 1988
COMMODITY EXCHANGE, INC. NY
TRADING HOURS 8:20 - 2:30 ET
CONTRACT SIZE 100 TROY OZ
EACH GRID 97
Major aspects of Venus-Pluto. Expect change in trend on these days.
9 DAY STOCHASTIC
9 DAY RELATIVE STRENGTH
Charts courtesy of Commodity Perspective
MAY
JUN
JUL
AUG
SEP
OCT
NOV
DEC

GOLD (N.Y.)

98
DECEMBER 1982

Commodity Exchange, Inc. N.Y.

COMMODITY PERSPECTIVE/CHICAGO, ILLINOIS

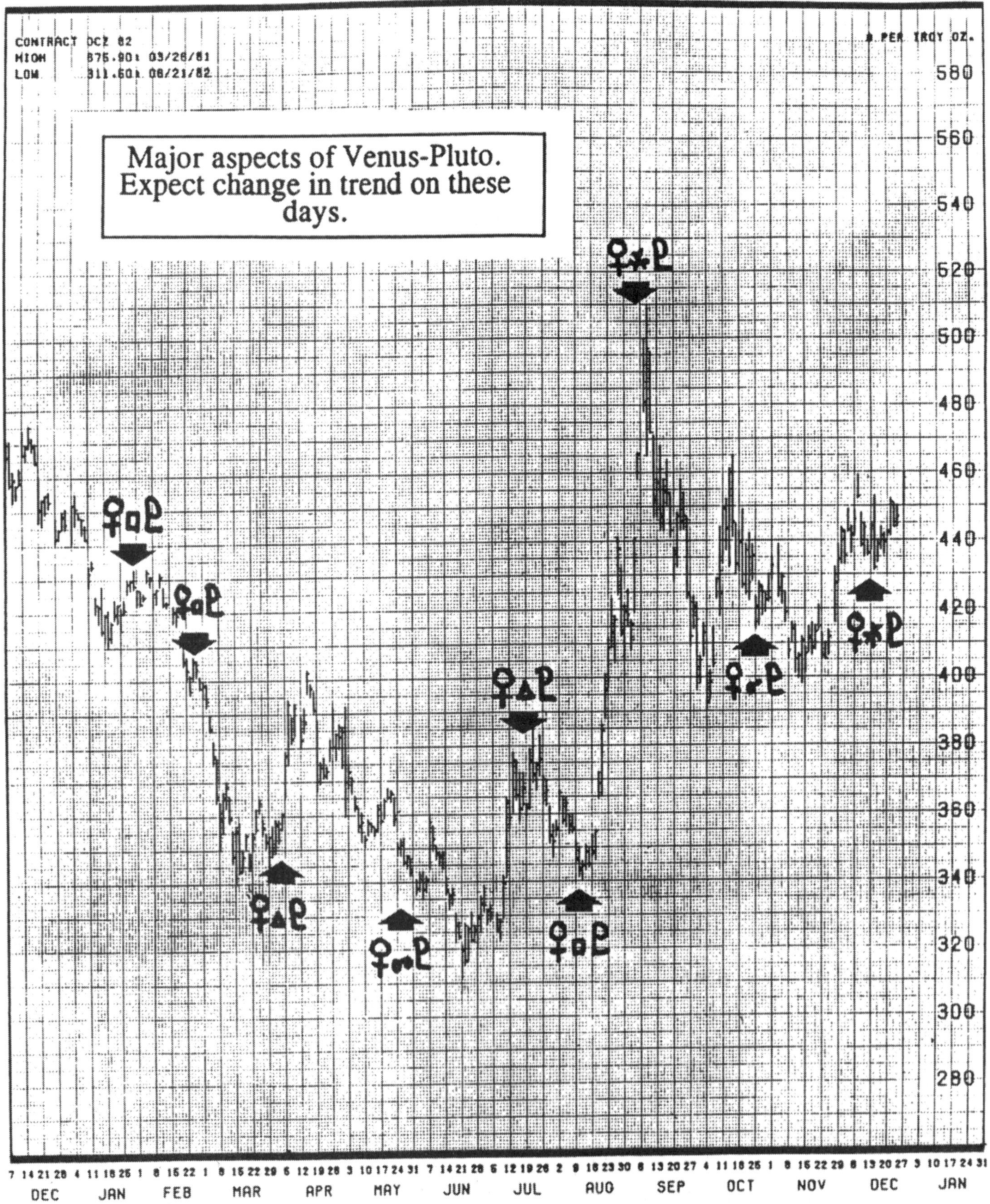

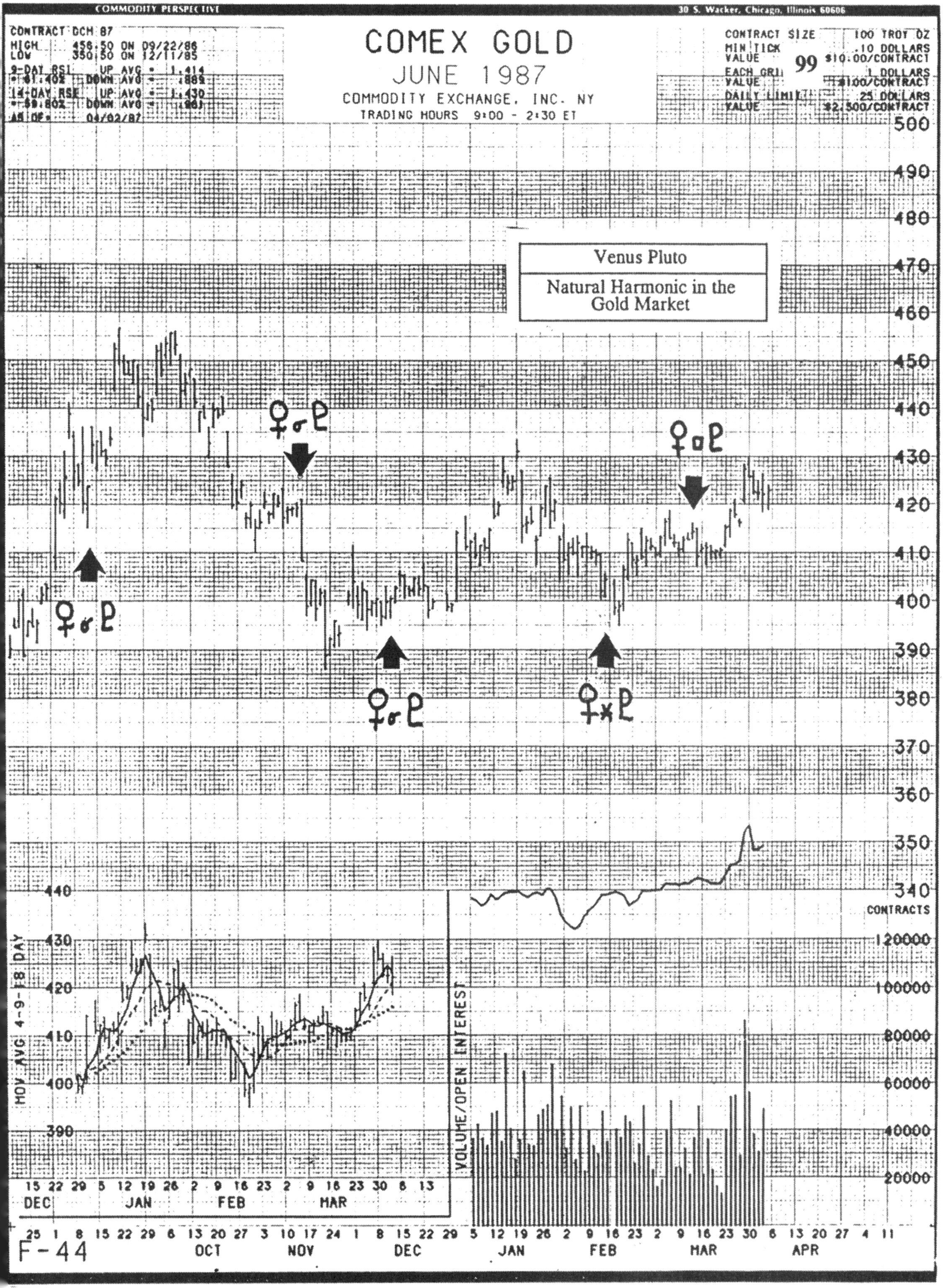
COMMODITY PERSPECTIVE
30 S. Wacker, Chicago, Illinois 60606
COMEX GOLD
JUNE 1987
COMMODITY EXCHANGE, INC. NY
TRADING HOURS 9:00 - 2:30 ET
Venus Pluto
Natural Harmonic in the Gold Market
VOLUME/OPEN INTEREST
MOV AVG 4-9-18 DAY
CONTRACTS
OCT
NOV
DEC
JAN
FEB
MAR
APR

GOLD (N.Y.)

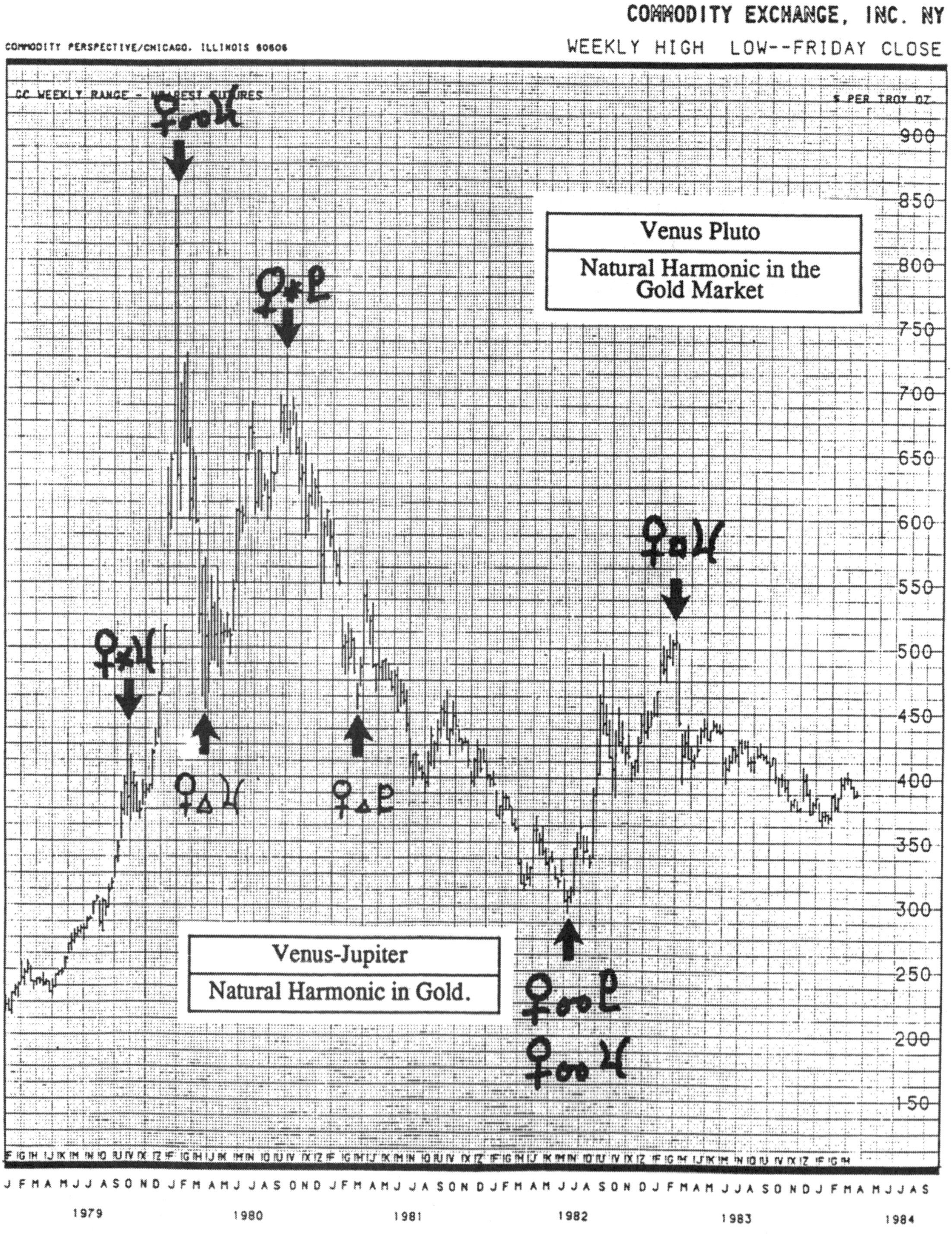
COMMODITY EXCHANGE, INC. NY
COMMODITY PERSPECTIVE/CHICAGO, ILLINOIS 60606
WEEKLY HIGH LOW--FRIDAY CLOSE
$ PER TROY OZ.
Venus Pluto
Natural Harmonic in the Gold Market
Venus-Jupiter
Natural Harmonic in Gold.
900
850
800
750
700
650
600
550
500
450
400
350
300
250
200
150
J F M A M J J A S O N D J F M A M J J A S O N D J F M A M J J A S O N D J F M A M J J A S O N D J F M A M J J A S O N D J F M A M J J A S
1979
1980
1981
1982
1983
1984

Mars-Jupiter

Mars makes its revolution around the Sun in 1.91 years. Jupiter completes its revolution in 11.8 years. Together their synodic period from conjunction (0°) to conjunction (0°) is 2.23 years. Every other conjunction of Mars-Jupiter is 4 1/3 years or 233 weeks--another Fibonacci number. The Mars-Jupiter aspects are very powerful and extremely accurate. The August 9th, 1982 bottom in the stock market occurred at Mars conjunction Jupiter. There are numerous examples of the accuracy of these aspects and they work consistently year after year!

Mars-Jupiter aspects of conjunction, sextile, square, opposition, and time may be used in timing stock and **BOND** market trades. These aspects usually work within 3 to 5 days of accuracy and last for 7 to 21 days. It is best to use lunar phenomena to pinpoint entry as the Mars-Jupiter aspect approaches.

S&P 500 INDEX

Charts courtesy of Commodity Perspective

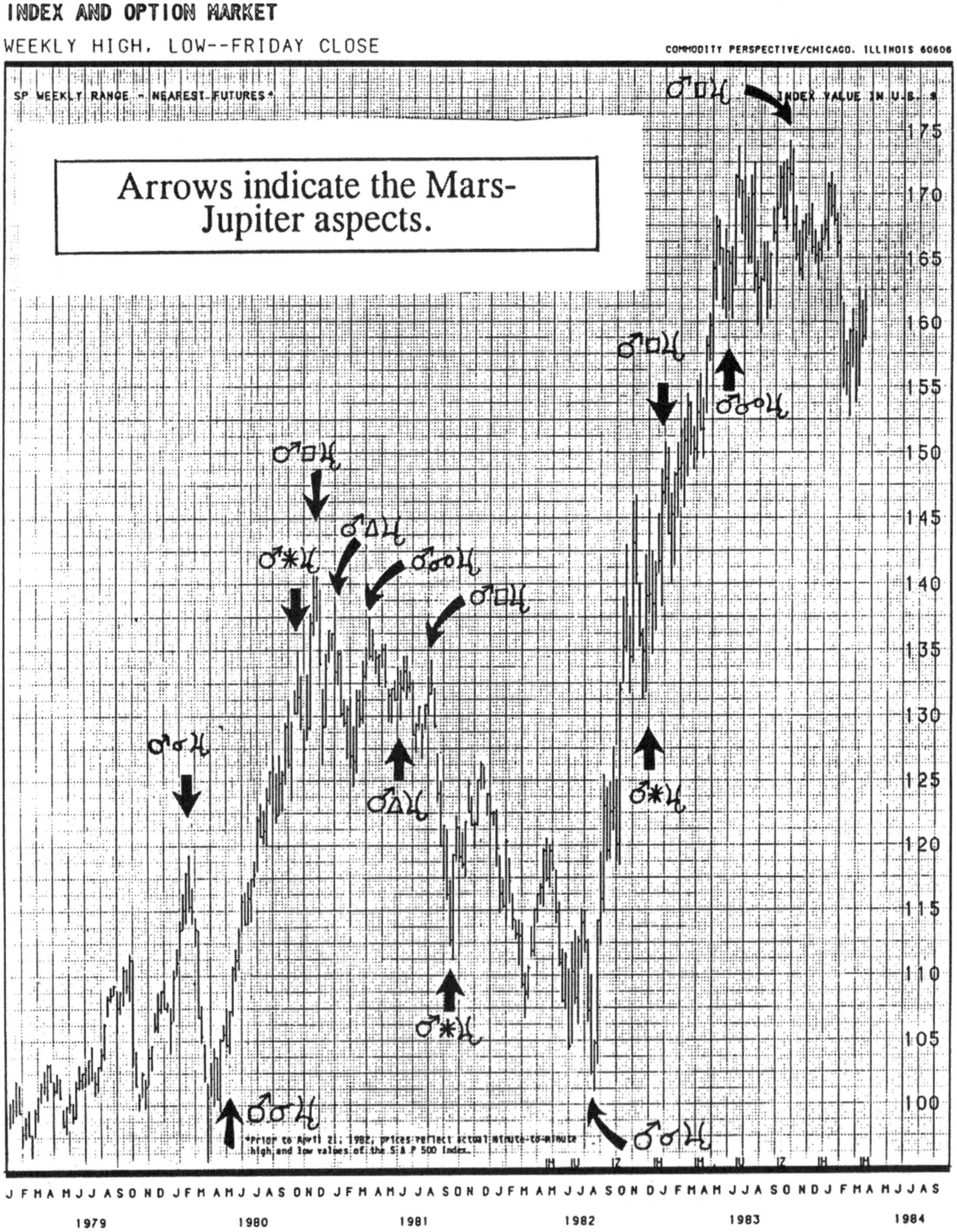

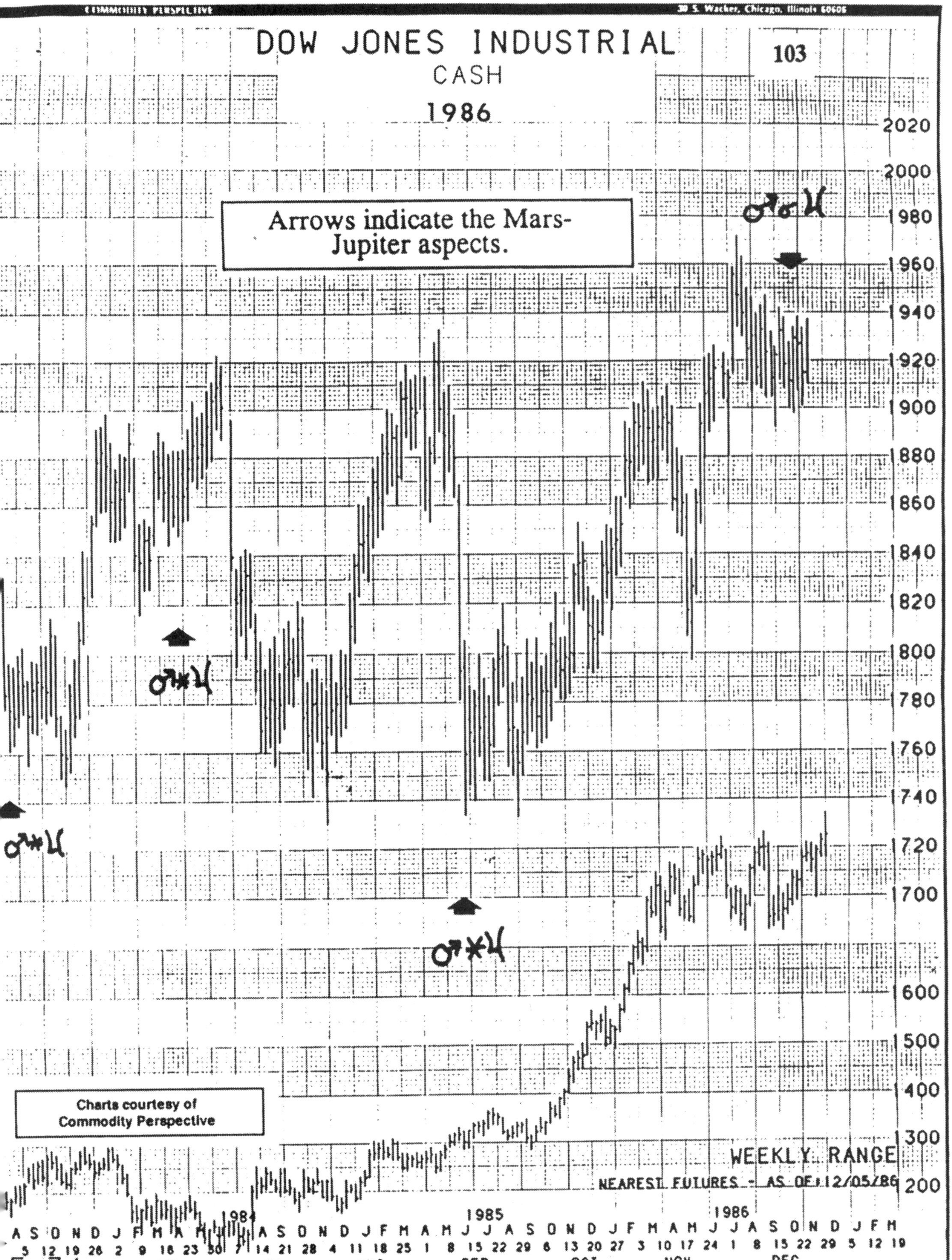
COMMODITY PERSPECTIVE
30 S. Wacker, Chicago, Illinois 60606
DOW JONES INDUSTRIAL
CASH
1986
103
Arrows indicate the Mars-Jupiter aspects.
♂☌♃
♂✶♃
♂✶♃
♂✶♃
Charts courtesy of Commodity Perspective
WEEKLY RANGE
NEAREST FUTURES - AS OF 12/05/86
1984
1985
1986
A S O N D J F M A M J J A S O N D J F M A M J J A S O N D J F M
5 12 19 26 2 9 16 23 30 7 14 21 28 4 11 18 25 1 8 15 22 29 6 13 20 27 3 10 17 24 1 8 15 22 29 5 12 19
JUN JUL AUG SEP OCT NOV DEC
2020
2000
1980
1960
1940
1920
1900
1880
1860
1840
1820
1800
1780
1760
1740
1720
1700
1600
1500
1400
1300
1200

F-34

Venus-Jupiter

The synodic period of Venus-Jupiter is .64 years or 233 days; another Fibonacci number! This combination has a very strong relationship to the Gold market. Venus is associated with sensitivity and touch. Jupiter is the expansive planet and the "money" planet. As you will see, the Gold market acts quite accurately to the Venus-Jupiter aspects of conjunctions, sextiles, trines, squares, and oppositions. Watch for trend change days when these aspects are present. This is especially true at the time of maximum lunar declination or true node change. It is an accurate short-term indicator for stocks.

The Sun also rules Gold. Two of the most consistent winners are to buy Gold when the Sun enters Leo (July 22) and short Gold when the Sun enters Aquarius (Jan 21). This is the equivalent of an *Astro-Seasonal tendency*. These moves usually last about three weeks and have a probability of success above 80%.

GOLD

MARCH 1983

International Monetary Market

COMMODITY PERSPECTIVE/CHICAGO, ILLINOIS 60604

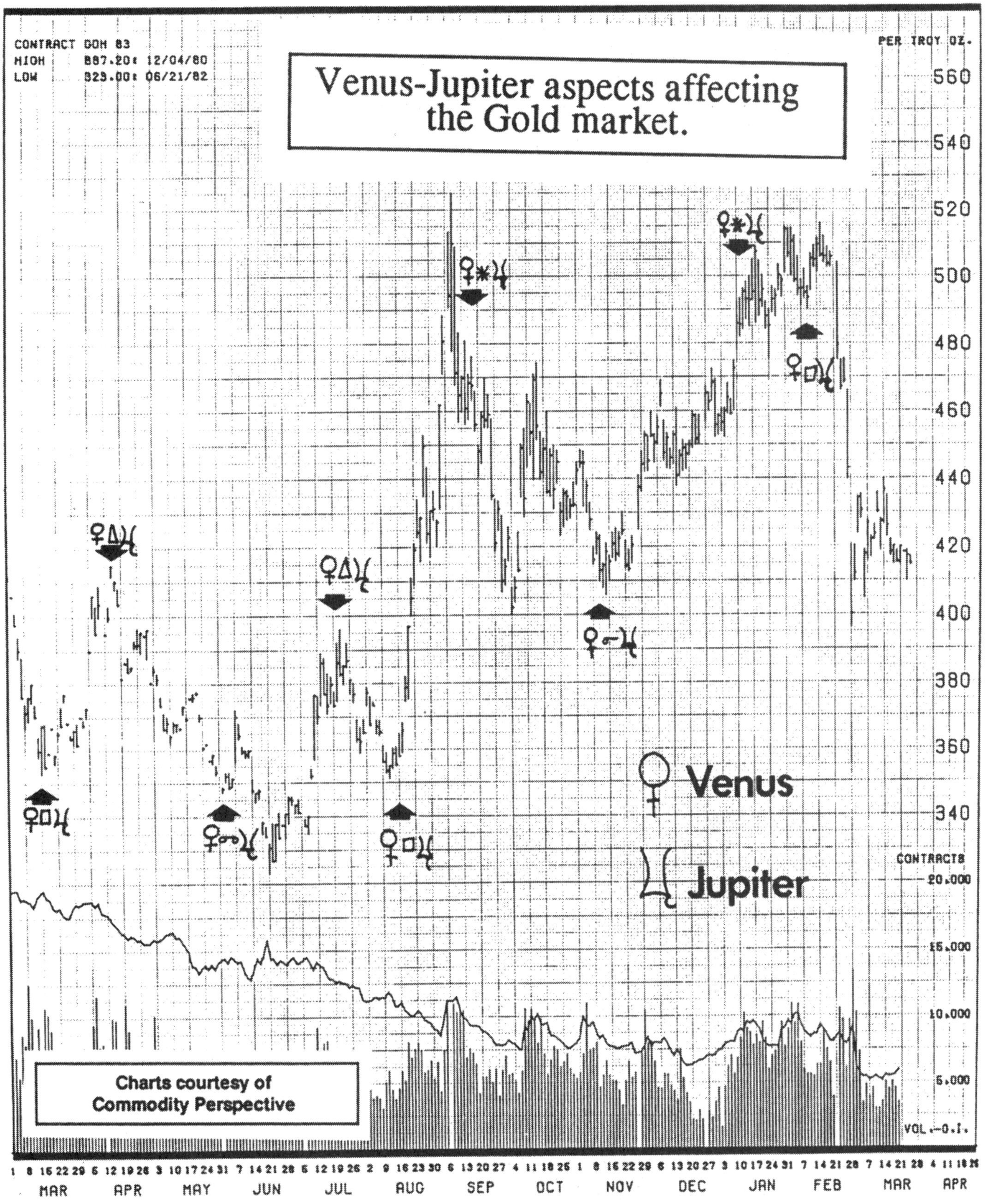

GOLD (N.Y.)

COMMODITY EXCHANGE, INC. NY

COMMODITY PERSPECTIVE/CHICAGO, ILLINOIS 60606

WEEKLY HIGH LOW--FRIDAY CLOSE

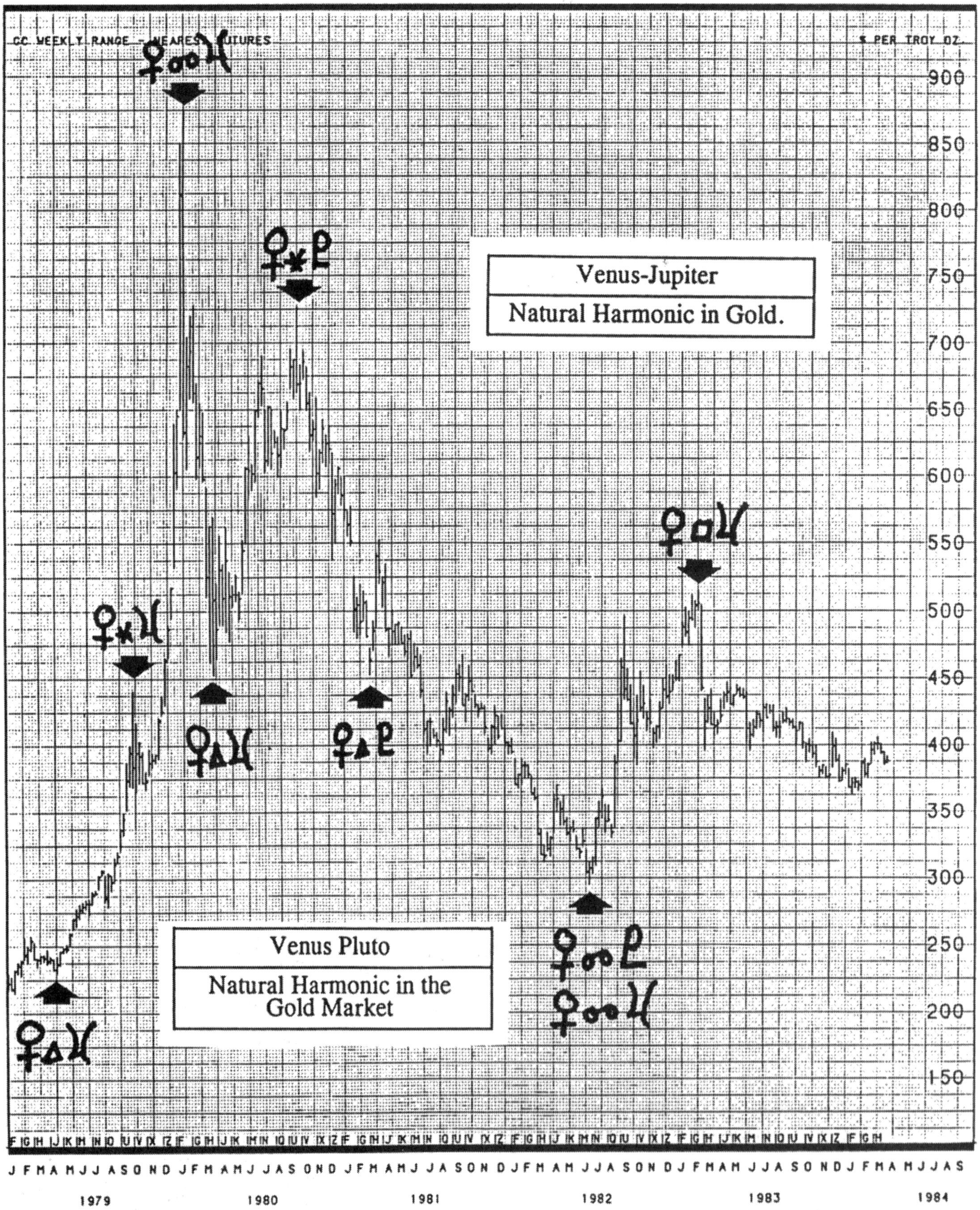

Saturn-Uranus: The Major Economic Cycle

The synodic period for the Saturn-Uranus combination is 45 years. That is the length of time necessary to travel from conjunction (0°) through the other aspects and back to conjunction again. Uranus is known as the "market" planet. Saturn is related to "change." A great deal of publicity has been made regarding the Nostradamus prediction of a great earthquake in the *New City; When Saturn and Uranus are in Capricorn in May 1988*. This quote is paraphrased from one of the translations of his quatrains. One must remember that Nostradamas was not infallible. Not all of his predictions came true--**at least not yet!** Part of the problem lies in the translation of his quatrains. Was Los Angeles the New City? I only bring this to your attention to alert you to the use of astrology in your daily life, if in fact you use it at all. It is my opinion that it is a guideline for decisions and nothing more. People should not rely on anyone's interpretation of the stars to rule their lives. Many factors control our destiny! The stars impel--they don't compel!

Uranus makes a complete cycle (revolution around the sun) in 84 years; Saturn makes the revolution in 29 years. The difference is 55 years! Can this be the "Kondratieff" cycle? The cycle is so long that a large sample size is not possible at this time. We do know that the economic conditions that prevail near the major aspects of Saturn-Uranus correlate to a "Bullish" or "Bearish" scenario. For example, the period of 22 1/2 years is a half-cycle of Saturn-Uranus or opposition (180°). If we look at the time frame of this opposition, November 8, 1966, it correlates to the

"October Massacre" of that year. When you add the twenty two and one half years back into the cycle you come out to 1987-1988 which is very close to the Saturn-Uranus conjunction. Will anyone argue that October 1987 was a "Massacre"? These planets move so slowly that the event will not be triggered on the exact day of the aspect. Remember, W.D. Gann said the "faster moving planets are the key," and Saturn and Uranus move very slowly.

Louise McWhirter spent a great deal of time researching the Saturn-Uranus aspects. In *McWhirter Theory of Stock Market Forecasting*, the author examines the economic correlations at the time of the Saturn-Uranus aspects. She claimed that the Saturn-Uranus conjunction and oppositions were responsible for economic prosperity or recession.

James Mars Langham referred to the Saturn-Uranus cycle as the single most accurate barometer of economic activity. Both McWhirter and Langham wrote their books in the late 30's and did not have the advantage of seeing their hypotheses fulfilled. Their ideas have been substantiated over the past fifty years as longer cycles of prosperity and recession correspond to aspects of Saturn-Uranus. Cmdr. David Williams completed a 200 year study of the major aspects of Saturn-Uranus and found them to be an accurate predictor of business activity in 7 out of 10 cases. This material is published in his book *Financial Astrology*.

As an investor it would be beneficial to keep in mind the Saturn-Uranus cycle! If the effects of Saturn-Uranus in conjunction (0^{0}), that occurred in February 1988, begin to unfold it would indicate a severe economic contraction is upon us. There

are several factors that may "trigger" the event in my opinion. **First;** the Japanese stock market has not experienced a prolonged "Bear" Market since it opened 45 years ago (There is that number 45 again). Most of the trader investors are inexperienced and will not know how to handle a "bear" market. **The Japanese stock market does not allow short selling.** Short selling acts as a buffer when stocks go down because shorts buy back their borrowed stock, thus supporting prices. Short selling also prevents stocks from rising too rapidly. Second, an unexpected economic down turn could come from "nature" (i.e. earthquake, drought, flood, disease etc.).

Economic contraction does not have to be associated with personal financial adversity. Money can be made by knowing how to sell short and how to use option strategies. Clearance sales will abound in real estate, art, vacation spots and many luxury items if a severe recession appears.

Keep in mind that the use of astrology should not be viewed with a "fatalistic" outlook on life. Opportunity always presents itself--even in adversity. "Diamonds are polished by grit, man by adversity." Those of you reading this book are fortunate enough to live in a free and prosperous world.

Jupiter-Uranus

Jupiter is the largest planet in our solar system. It takes approximately 11.8 years to revolve around the sun. In contrast, the planet Uranus takes 84 years to complete the cycle. Together they combine into the most "researched" of all astro-economic cycles. The synodic period of Jupiter-Uranus is **13.8 years**. Squares (90°), conjunctions (0°), and oppositions (180°) occur at intervals of **3.4** years. Do the numbers 13.8 and 34 make the student of Fibonacci numbers increase his interest in this cycle?

Jupiter is referred to as the "money" planet and Uranus as the "market" planet. This combination is the reason for the popularity of the 41 month cycle. **All serious** students of astrology have examined this cycle and have determined its ability to predict business activity. Over 250 different types of economic data respond to this 41 month cycle phenomenon.

The Jupiter-Uranus aspects should be followed closely by the trader because of their importance to business activity. However, it is **not** to be used as a short term trading mechanism. I have found that after studying over 70 years of these aspects, it may take as long as 2 months for their effect to take hold because the two planets are moving so slowly. One of the reasons for the strong bullish move in 1987 was the positive trine aspect (120°) in June of 1987. After studying the past results of the Jupiter-Uranus aspects, the astute trader will mark these aspects on his charts for future reference. The dates are listed in the Appendix.

The Foundation for the Study of Cycles has done an excellent job at analyzing the 40 month cycle phenomenon.

S&P 500 INDEX

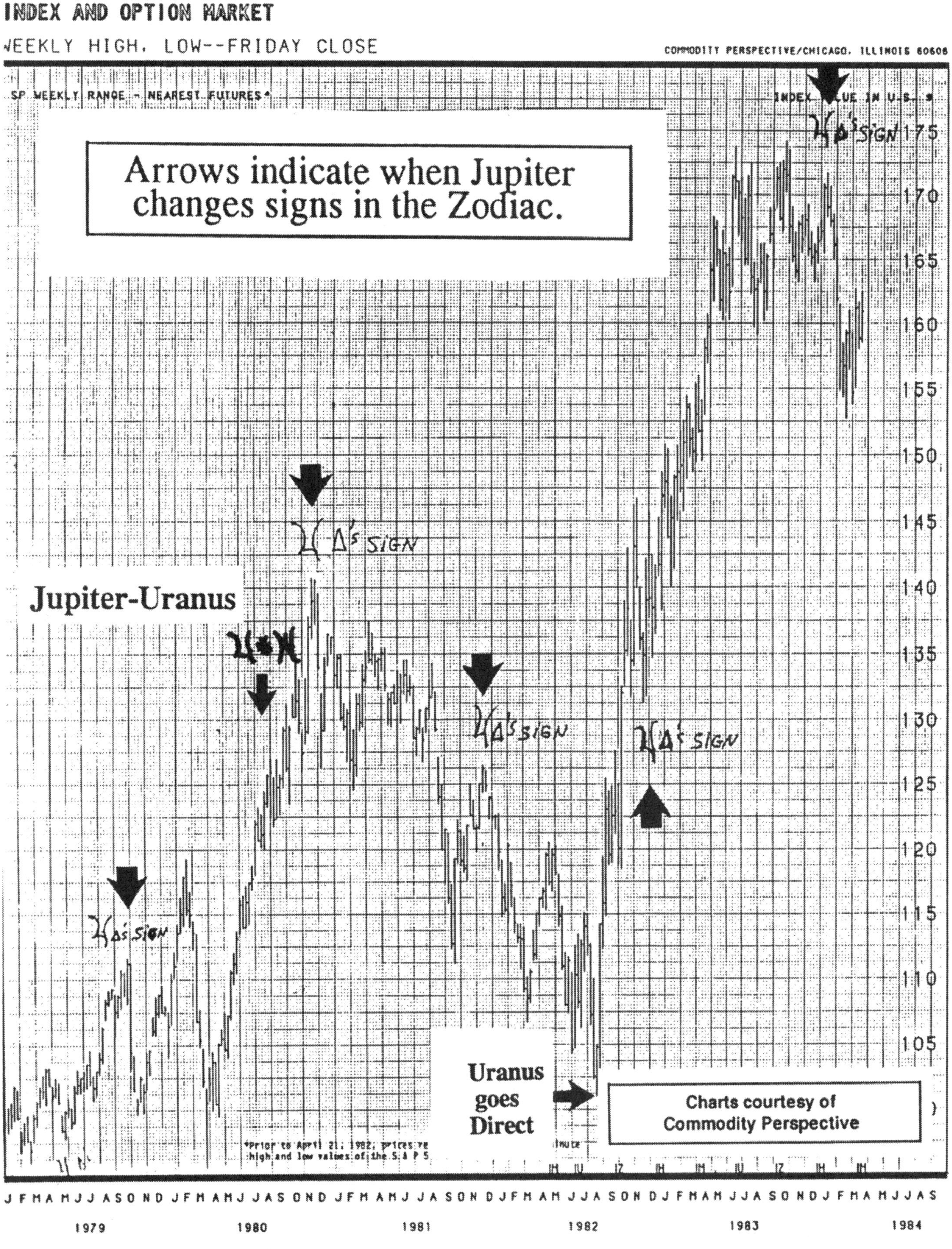
INDEX AND OPTION MARKET
WEEKLY HIGH, LOW--FRIDAY CLOSE
COMMODITY PERSPECTIVE/CHICAGO, ILLINOIS 60606
SP WEEKLY RANGE - NEAREST FUTURES*
Arrows indicate when Jupiter changes signs in the Zodiac.
Jupiter-Uranus
Uranus goes Direct
Charts courtesy of Commodity Perspective
175
170
165
160
155
150
145
140
135
130
125
120
115
110
105
J F M A M J J A S O N D J F M A M J J A S O N D J F M A M J J A S O N D J F M A M J J A S O N D J F M A M J J A S O N D J F M A M J J A S
1979
1980
1981
1982
1983
1984

Mars-Uranus

The planet Mars and the planet Uranus have a synodic period of 1.9 years. It takes that long for the two planets to start at conjunction 0° and complete one cycle. In sidereal time in terms of tropical years, Mars revolves around the Sun in 1.8 years and Uranus 84 years. As Mars is moving much faster, this cycle would be classified as an intermediate term trading cycle. Once you study the aspects of Mars-Uranus at conjunction 0°, sextile 60°, square 90°, trine 120° and opposition 180° and place these times on the Swiss Franc, Deutche Mark, Japanese Yen and S&P 500 you will see the accuracy of this combination. Trend changes at Mars-Uranus aspects are quite sudden and usually last several weeks. This should not be surprising to the student of astrology because Uranus is "the financial" planet and Mars is the planet for "energy, activity, and strength."

W.D. Gann left a very sparse legacy in his writings and teaching on the subject of astrology. Only a few brief hand written sentences were found. One of these sentences referred to Mars as the <u>Key</u> to timing. In addition, his last published work *The Magic Word* was also a book filled with the summation of his philosophical ideas. At that time in his life, Gann had studied Pythagorean mathematics, the Kabala and the Bible quite extensively. It is my opinion that this is why he mentioned Mars on his charts, because it is thought to be the Biblical planet.

The relationships of the aspects is the same for Mars-Uranus as it is for the others--conjunctions, sextiles, and trines are positive and squares and oppositions are negative. One must

constantly keep in mind that although these aspects are associated with positive or negative bias, they can reverse their roles. It is at this time that the trader should be prepared to act the opposite of the norm. For example, conjunctions are usually positive, but if the currencies are dropping into a low as the conjunction is forming between Mars-Uranus, one should look for a buying opportunity.

The timing effect of the Mars-Uranus aspect most often occurs within a two to three day period. There have been occurrences where the aspects take seven days to trigger a trend change.

James Mars Langham in *Cyclical Market Forecasting of Stocks and Grain* referred to the Mars-Uranus aspect "as the little wheel (Mars) within the big wheel (Uranus)." Langham thought that this was a significant combination and the statistics substantiate this fact. Mars-Uranus is an excellent market forecaster approximately 80% of the time. A close examination of the currency charts in this book will give credibility to the accuracy of the Mars-Uranus aspect as a timing mechanism.

SWISS FRANC

INTERNATIONAL MONETARY MARKET

WEEKLY HIGH, LOW--FRIDAY CLOSE

COMMODITY PERSPECTIVE/CHICAGO, ILLINOIS 60606

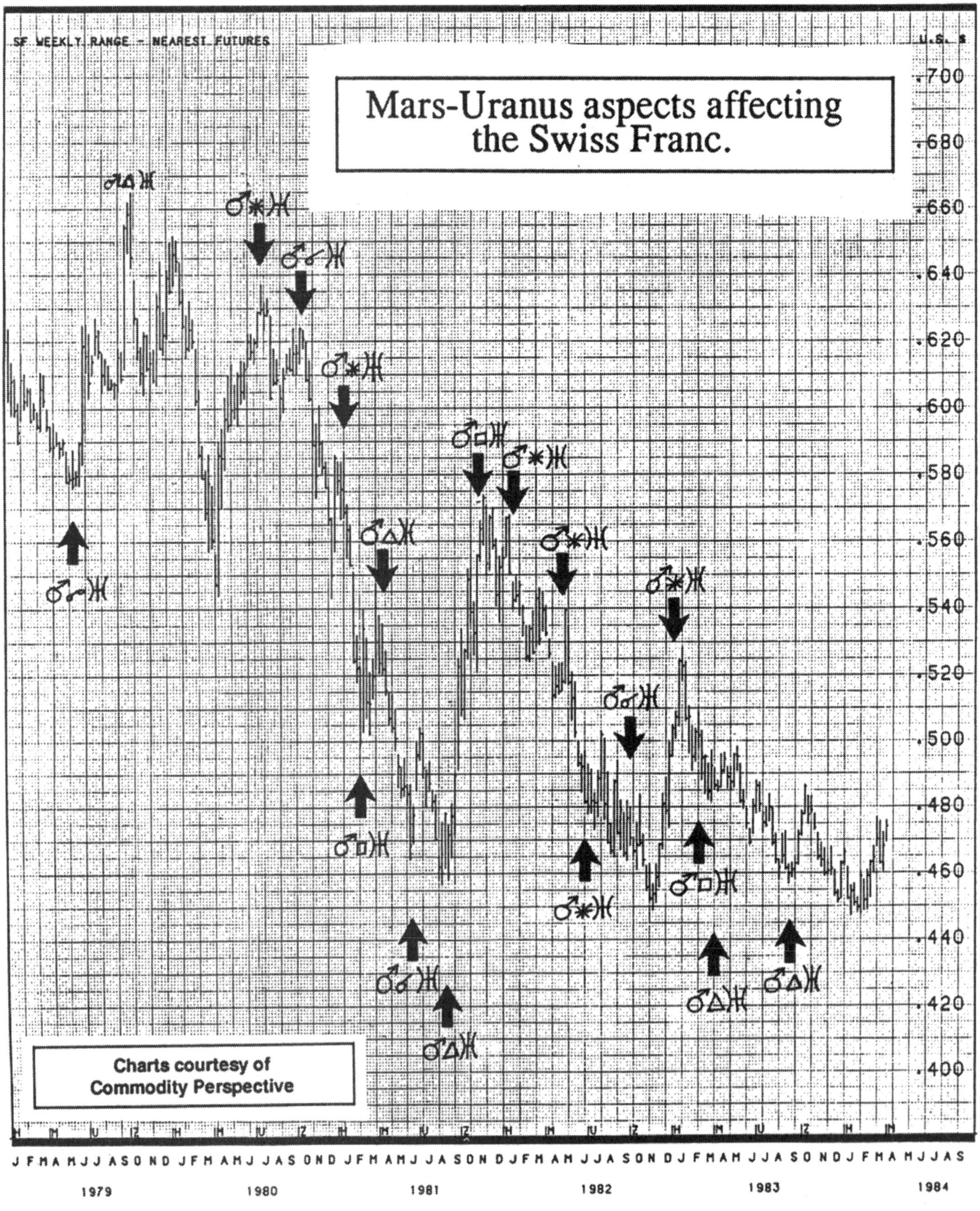

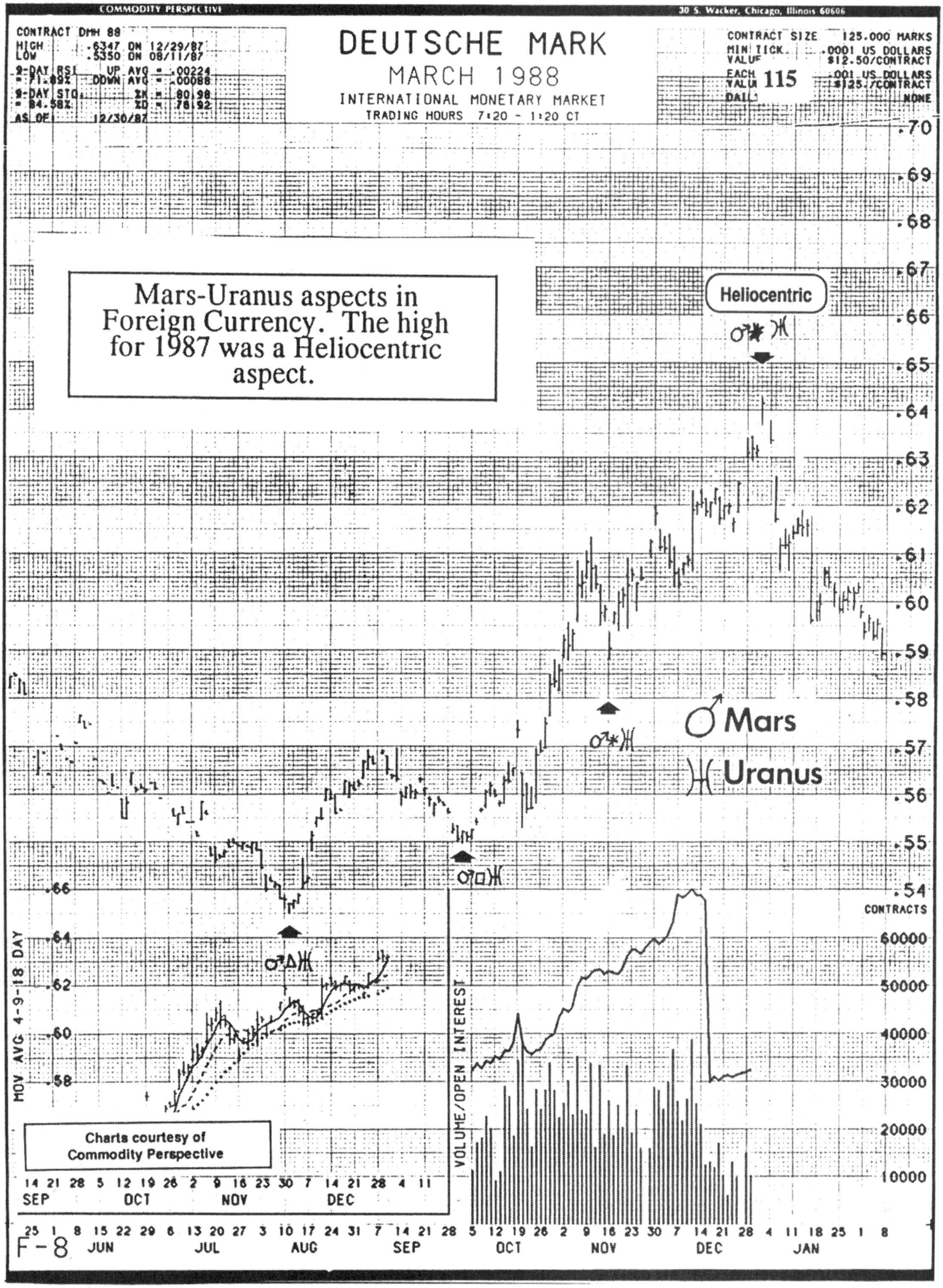
COMMODITY PERSPECTIVE
30 S. Wacker, Chicago, Illinois 60606
CONTRACT DMH 88
HIGH .6347 ON 12/29/87
LOW .5350 ON 08/11/87
9-DAY RSI = 71.89% UP AVG = .00224 DOWN AVG = .00088
9-DAY STO. = 84.58% %K = 80.98 %D = 78.92
AS OF 12/30/87
DEUTSCHE MARK
MARCH 1988
INTERNATIONAL MONETARY MARKET
TRADING HOURS 7:20 - 1:20 CT
CONTRACT SIZE 125.000 MARKS
MIN TICK. VALUE .0001 US DOLLARS $12.50/CONTRACT
EACH VALU 115 .001 US DOLLARS $125./CONTRACT
DAIL NONE
Mars-Uranus aspects in Foreign Currency. The high for 1987 was a Heliocentric aspect.
Heliocentric
♂ Mars
♅ Uranus
CONTRACTS
MOV AVG 4-9-18 DAY
VOLUME/OPEN INTEREST
Charts courtesy of Commodity Perspective
SEP OCT NOV DEC
JUN JUL AUG SEP OCT NOV DEC JAN
F-8

Mars-Saturn

This discovery was found quite by accident. A few years ago I was talking to Rich Anderson about the gestation and life cycles in cattle. Rich is a commodity broker, speculator, and cattleman from Minneapolis and South Dakota. I've never figured out which hat he wears the most. After talking to him, I programmed "Blue Star" to pull out all of the combinations relating to cattle and the planet Saturn. Within a short time it was apparent that the Mars-Saturn relationship was very important to the timing of Live Cattle futures. It does not work in Pork Bellies. The only thing I've found astrologically that works in Pork Bellies is a "broken" crystal ball. If you find one please call me.

The synodic period of Mars-Saturn is approximately 2 years, plus or minus a few days. This is about the time cattle need to gain weight from birth to slaughter. This two year synodic period in Mars-Saturn was "accidently" spotted by Blue Star.

The Mars-Saturn aspects also have a profound effect on the Foreign Currencies (i.e. the U.S. dollar). It is most probably due to the influence of Mars. Regardless of why it happens, the trader should be aware of the Mars-Saturn aspects when trading Foreign Currency.

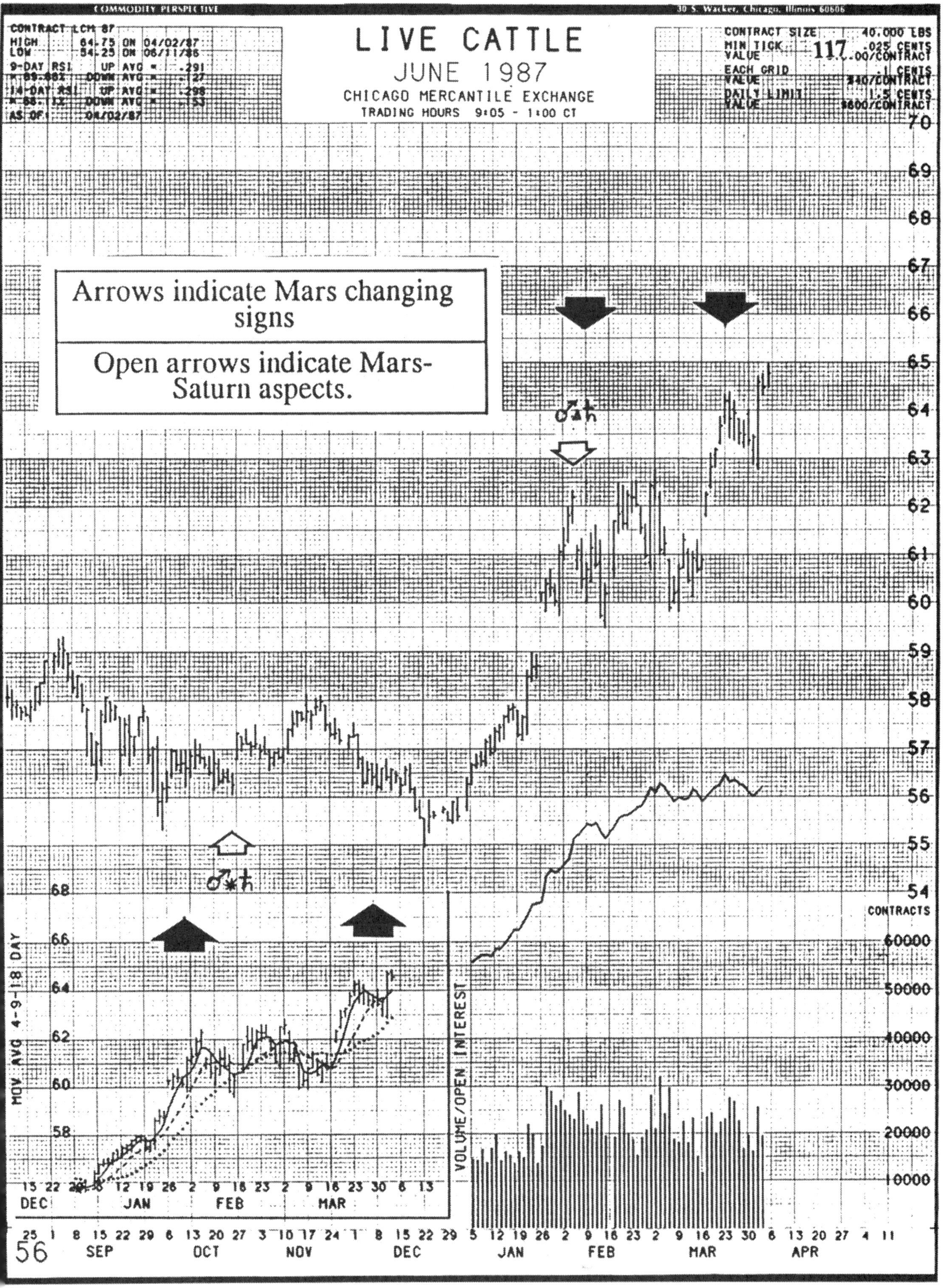
COMMODITY PERSPECTIVE
30 S. Wacker, Chicago, Illinois 60606
LIVE CATTLE
JUNE 1987
CHICAGO MERCANTILE EXCHANGE
TRADING HOURS 9:05 - 1:00 CT
CONTRACT SIZE 40,000 LBS
Arrows indicate Mars changing signs
Open arrows indicate Mars-Saturn aspects.
MOV AVG 4-9-18 DAY
VOLUME/OPEN INTEREST
CONTRACTS
DEC
JAN
FEB
MAR
SEP
OCT
NOV
DEC
JAN
FEB
MAR
APR

CATTLE

118
DECEMBER 1975

Chicago Mercantile Exchange

COMMODITY PERSPECTIVE/CHICAGO, ILLINOIS 60604

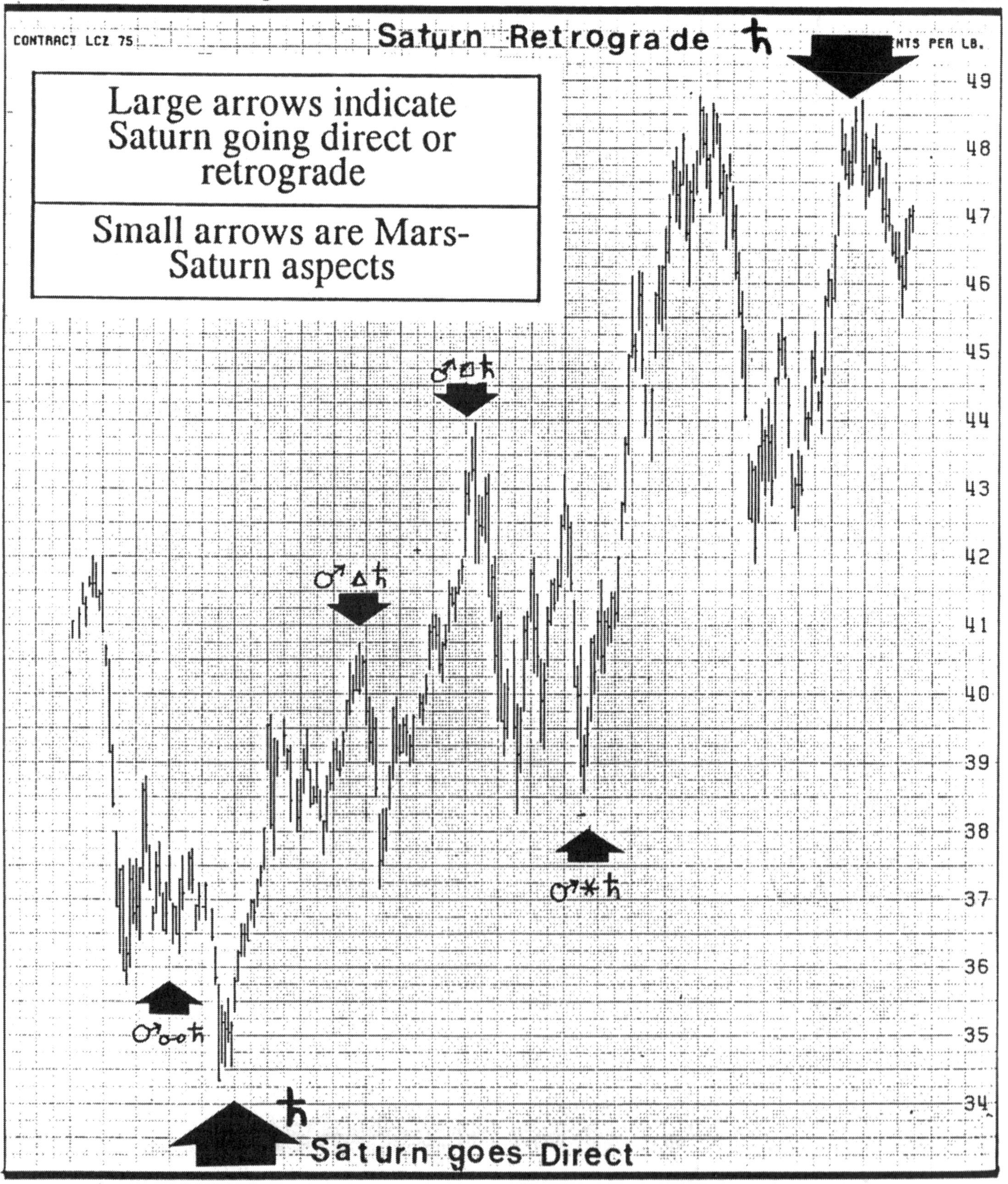

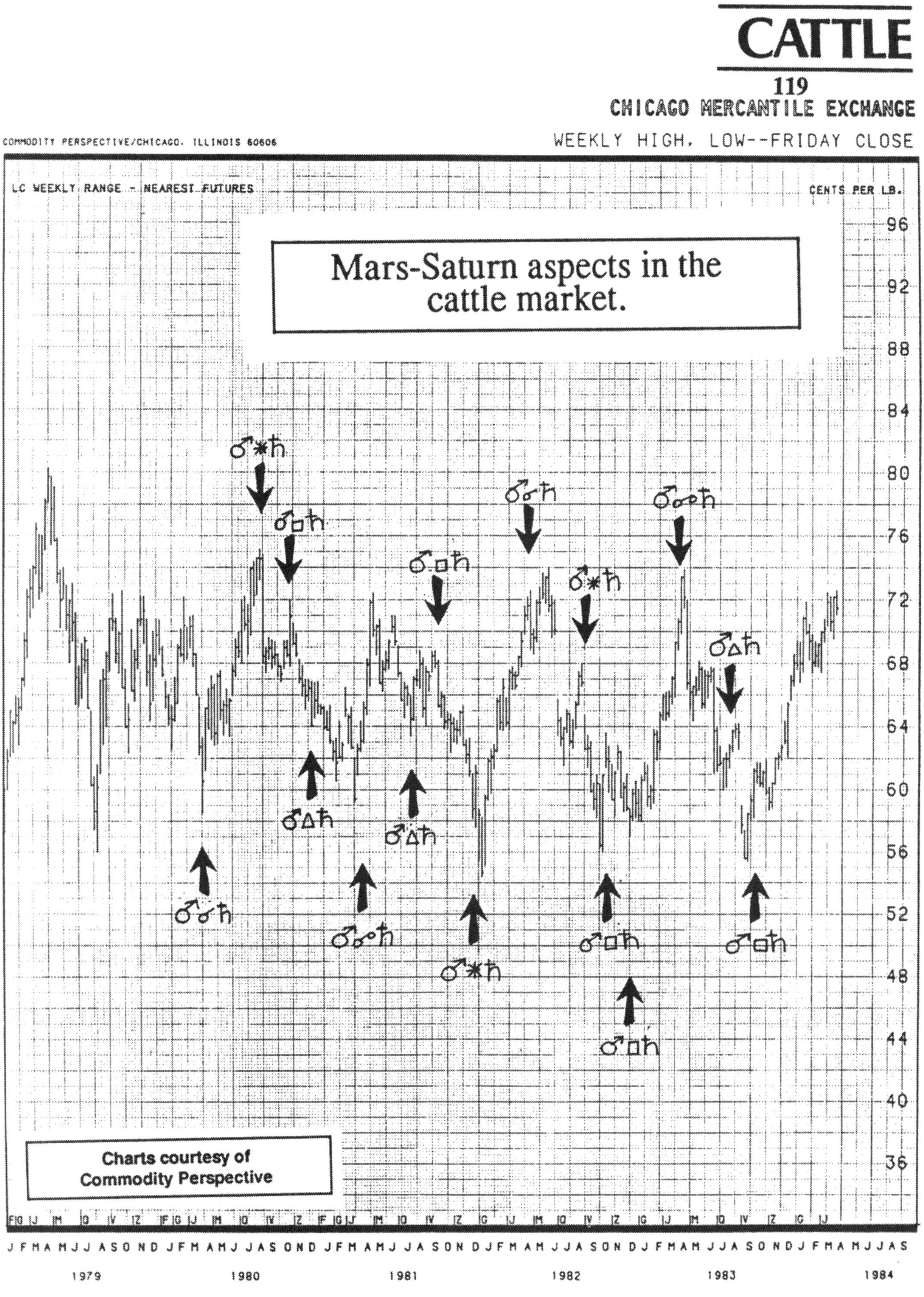

Mars-Saturn aspects in the cattle market.

Charts courtesy of Commodity Perspective

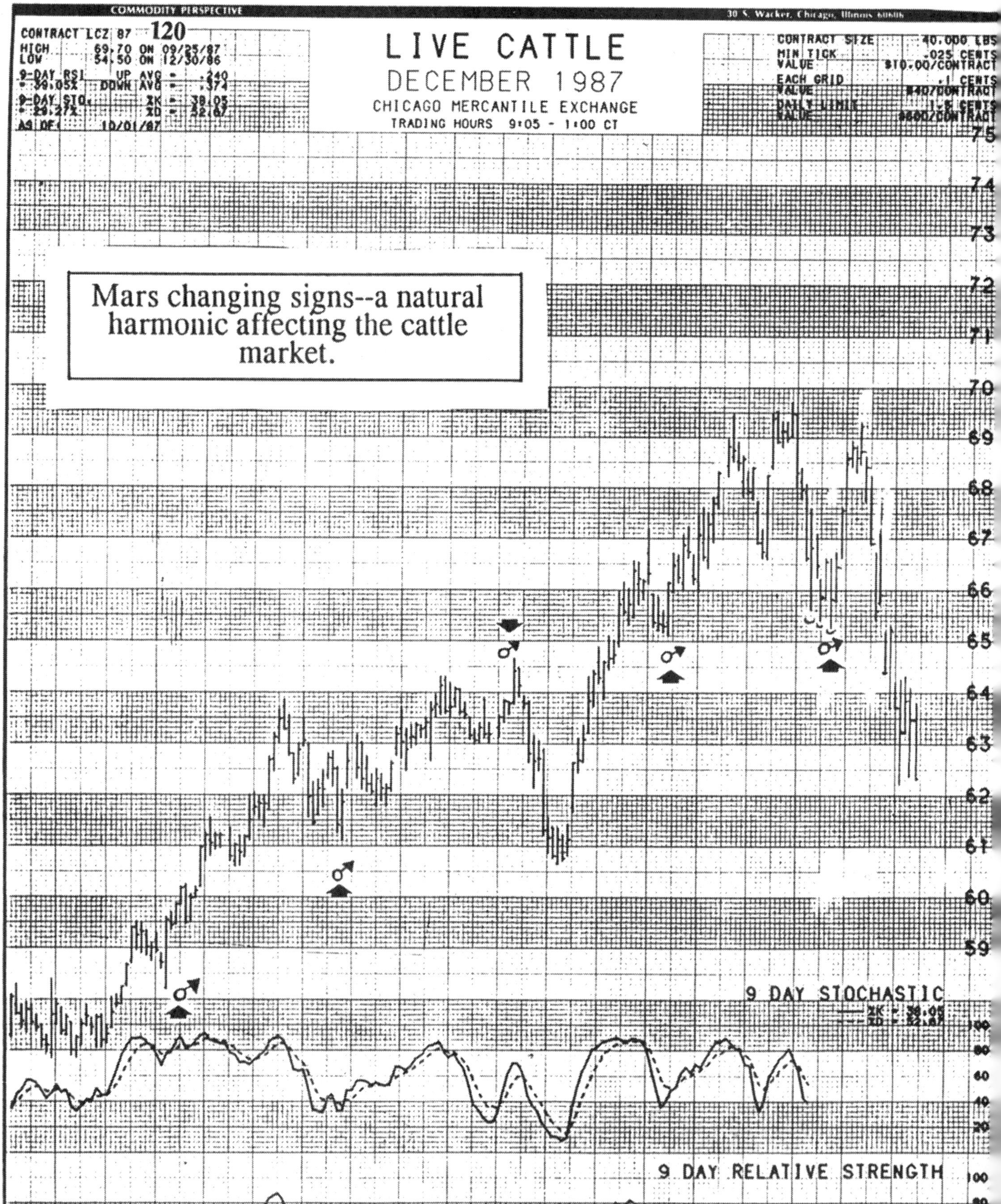
COMMODITY PERSPECTIVE
30 S. Wacker, Chicago, Illinois 60606
CONTRACT LCZ 87 120
HIGH 69.70 ON 09/25/87
LOW 54.50 ON 12/30/86
AS OF 10/01/87
LIVE CATTLE
DECEMBER 1987
CHICAGO MERCANTILE EXCHANGE
TRADING HOURS 9:05 - 1:00 CT
CONTRACT SIZE 40,000 LBS
MIN TICK .025 CENTS
VALUE $10.00/CONTRACT
EACH GRID .1 CENTS
VALUE $40/CONTRACT
Mars changing signs--a natural harmonic affecting the cattle market.
9 DAY STOCHASTIC
9 DAY RELATIVE STRENGTH
Charts courtesy of Commodity Perspective
MAR
APR
MAY
JUN
JUL
AUG
SEP
OCT

Wheat

There is an interesting astrological phenomenon regarding the trading of Wheat. It is based on the heliocentric positions of the planets Mercury, Jupiter and Saturn. You must use a Heliocentric Ephemeris to find the date that planetary aspects occur. For your convenience, the Appendix in the back of the book lists these important dates for trend changes in Wheat.

The original research of the Mercury-Jupiter aspects and Mercury-Saturn aspects was done by George Bayer. He is referred to in Section One.

When the planet Mercury makes an opposition (180°) or conjunction (0°) with Jupiter (heliocentrically), you should expect a top in Wheat. If Mercury makes an opposition (180°) or conjunction (0°) with Saturn (heliocentrically), you should expect a bottom in Wheat. The timing of this trade is plus or minus two days. There are a series of events when occurring at the same time usually lead to dramatic price changes in Wheat:

1. Mercury conjunction or opposition Saturn or Jupiter (Heliocentric)
2. Mercury retrograde (Geo)
3. Moon crossing the equator at 0° (Geo)

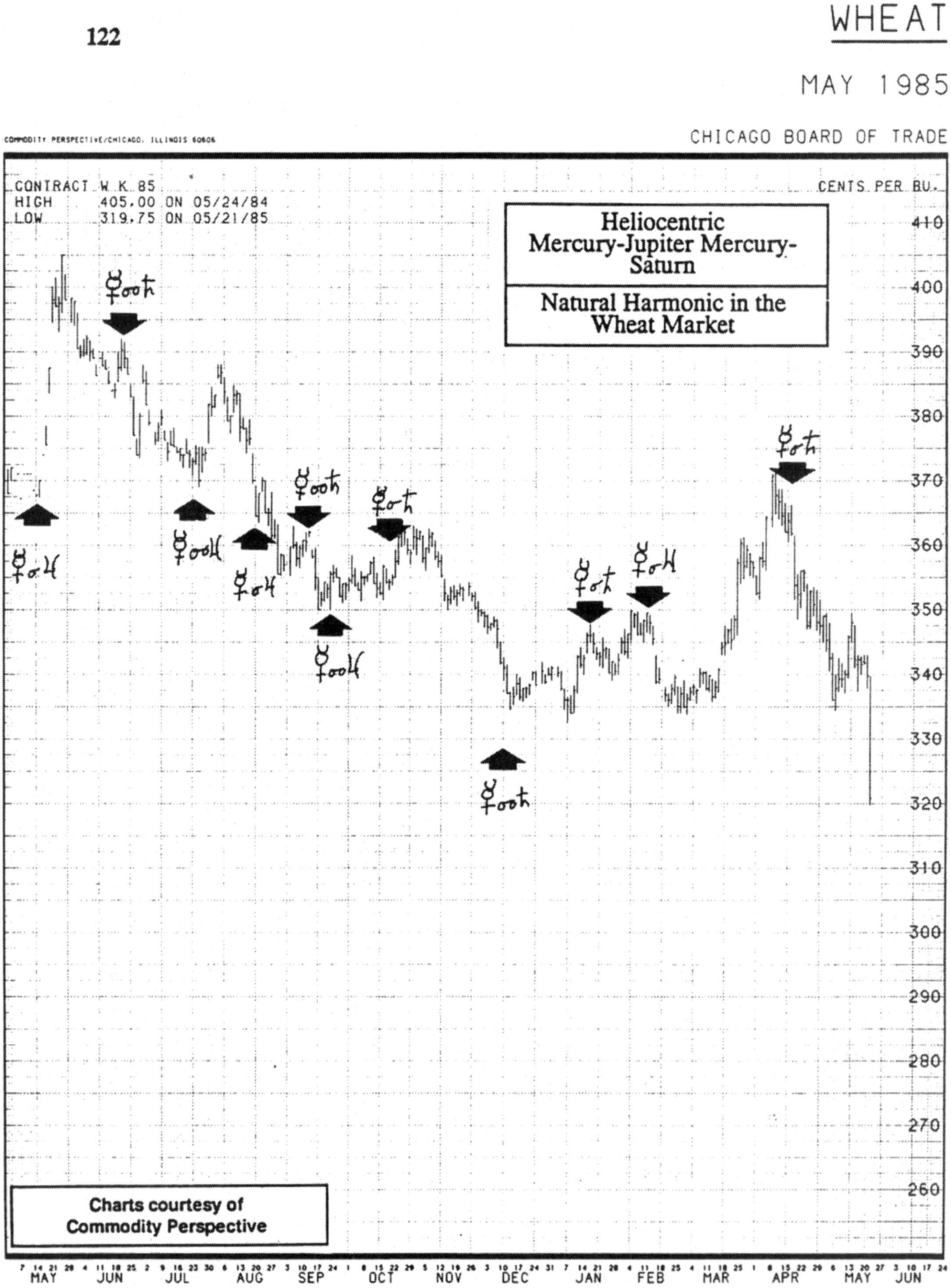
WHEAT
MAY 1985
COMMODITY PERSPECTIVE/CHICAGO, ILLINOIS 60606
CHICAGO BOARD OF TRADE
CONTRACT W K 85
HIGH 405.00 ON 05/24/84
LOW 319.75 ON 05/21/85
CENTS PER BU.
Heliocentric
Mercury-Jupiter Mercury-Saturn
Natural Harmonic in the Wheat Market
410
400
390
380
370
360
350
340
330
320
310
300
290
280
270
260
Charts courtesy of
Commodity Perspective
MAY
JUN
JUL
AUG
SEP
OCT
NOV
DEC
JAN
FEB
MAR
APR
MAY
JUN

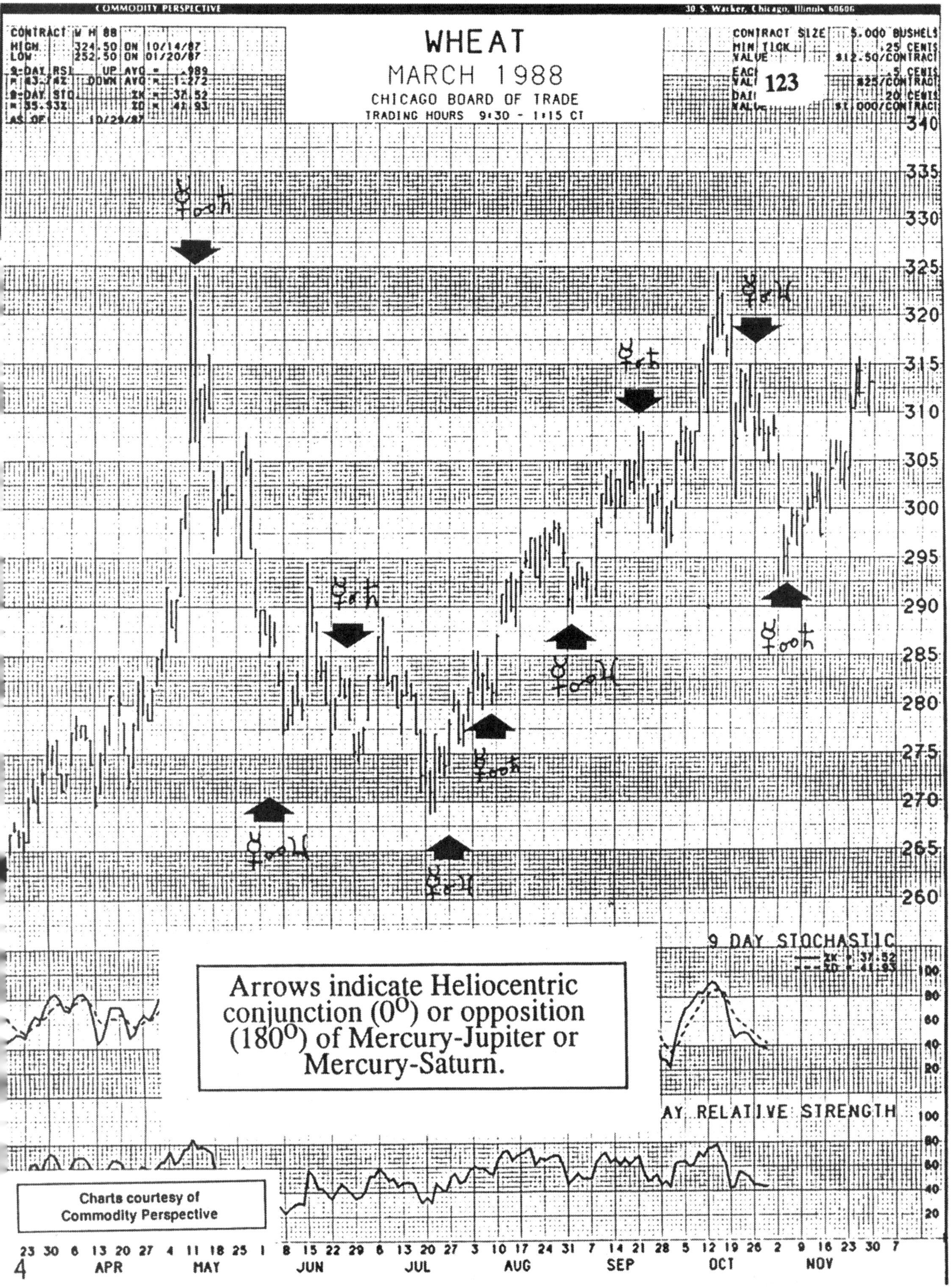
COMMODITY PERSPECTIVE
30 S. Wacker, Chicago, Illinois 60606
WHEAT
MARCH 1988
CHICAGO BOARD OF TRADE
TRADING HOURS 9:30 - 1:15 CT
123
CONTRACT SIZE 5,000 BUSHELS
9 DAY STOCHASTIC
RELATIVE STRENGTH
Arrows indicate Heliocentric conjunction (0°) or opposition (180°) of Mercury-Jupiter or Mercury-Saturn.
Charts courtesy of Commodity Perspective
APR
MAY
JUN
JUL
AUG
SEP
OCT
NOV

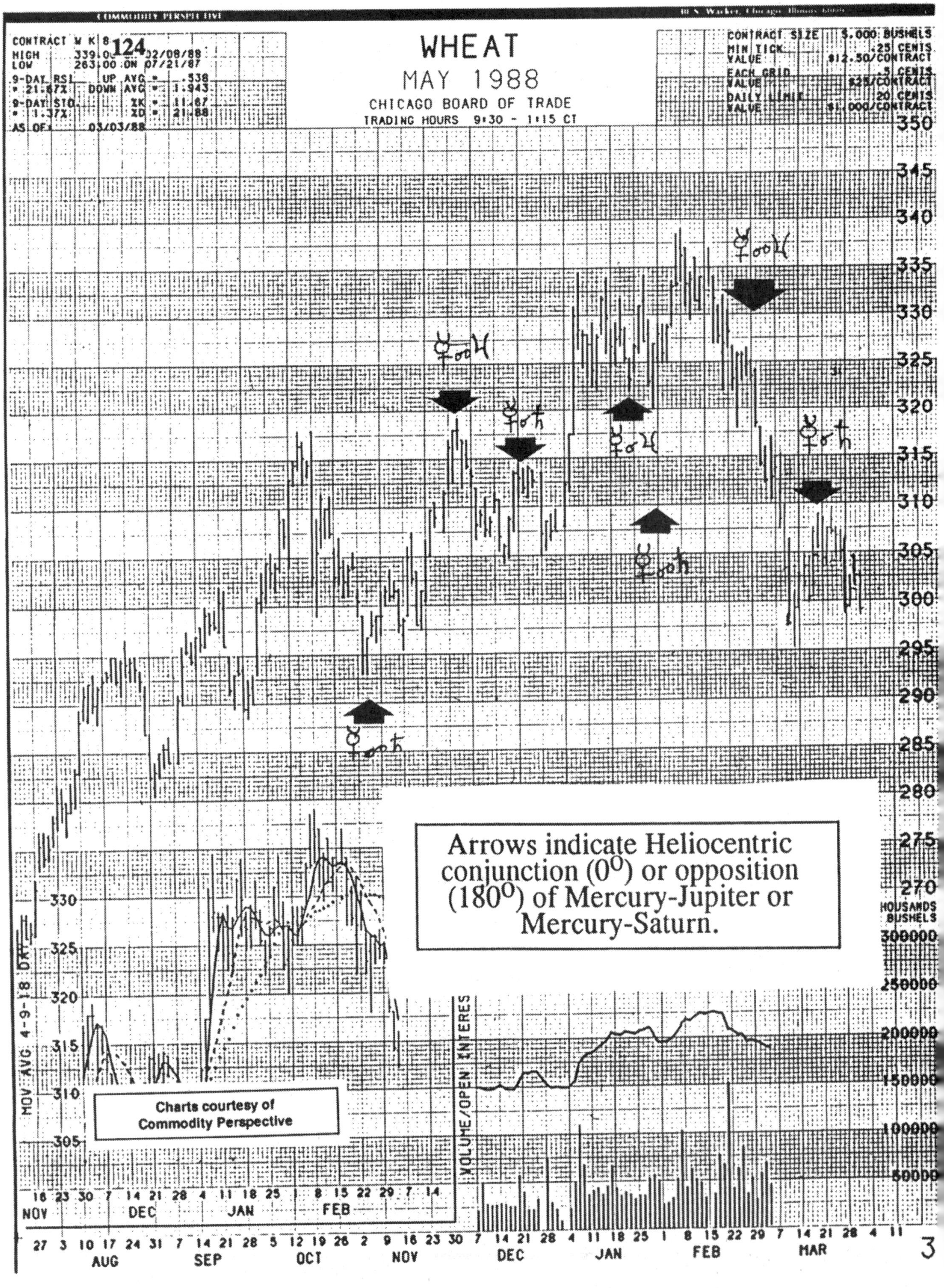

Arrows indicate Heliocentric conjunction (0°) or opposition (180°) of Mercury-Jupiter or Mercury-Saturn.

DECEMBER 1978

Chicago Board of Trade

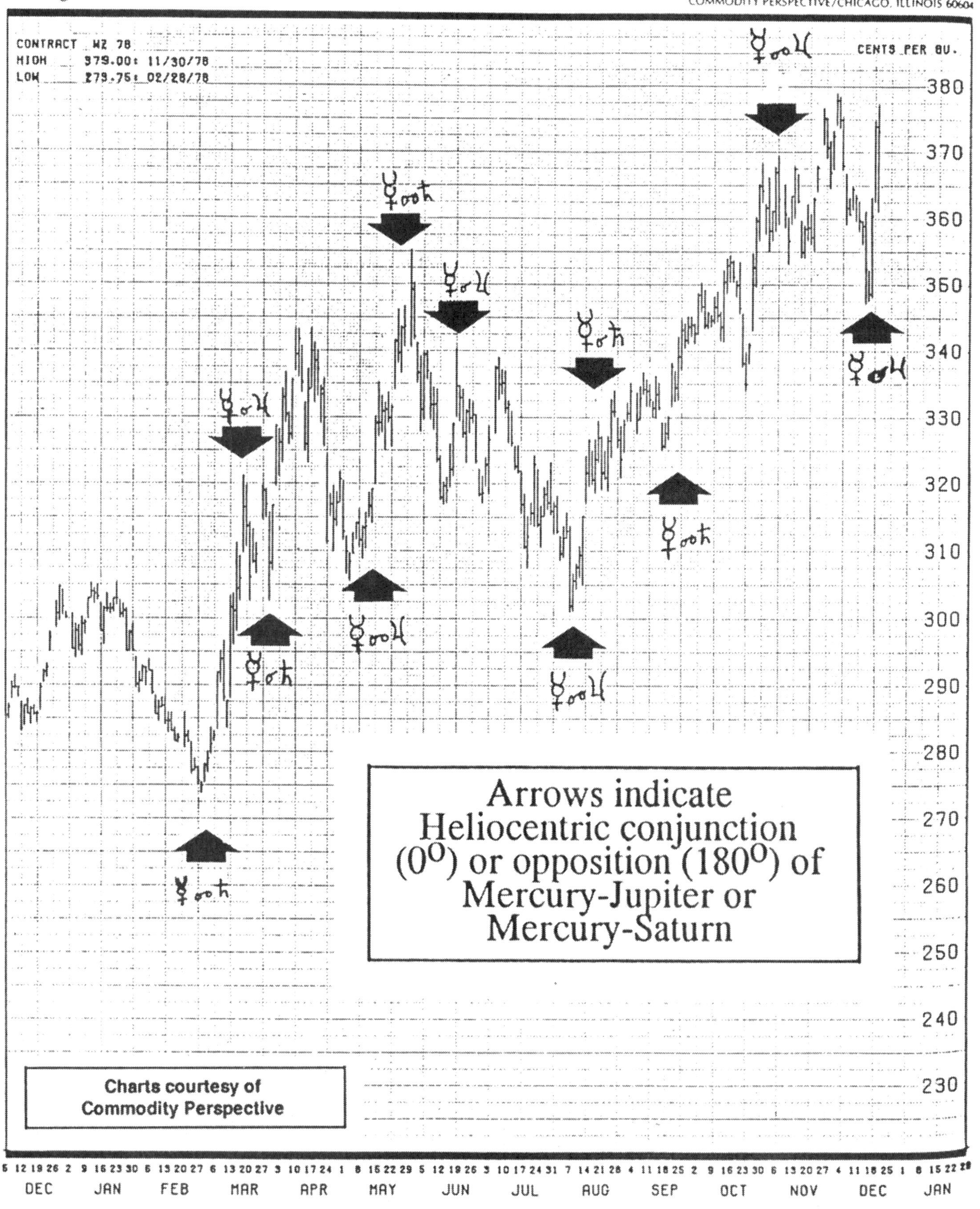

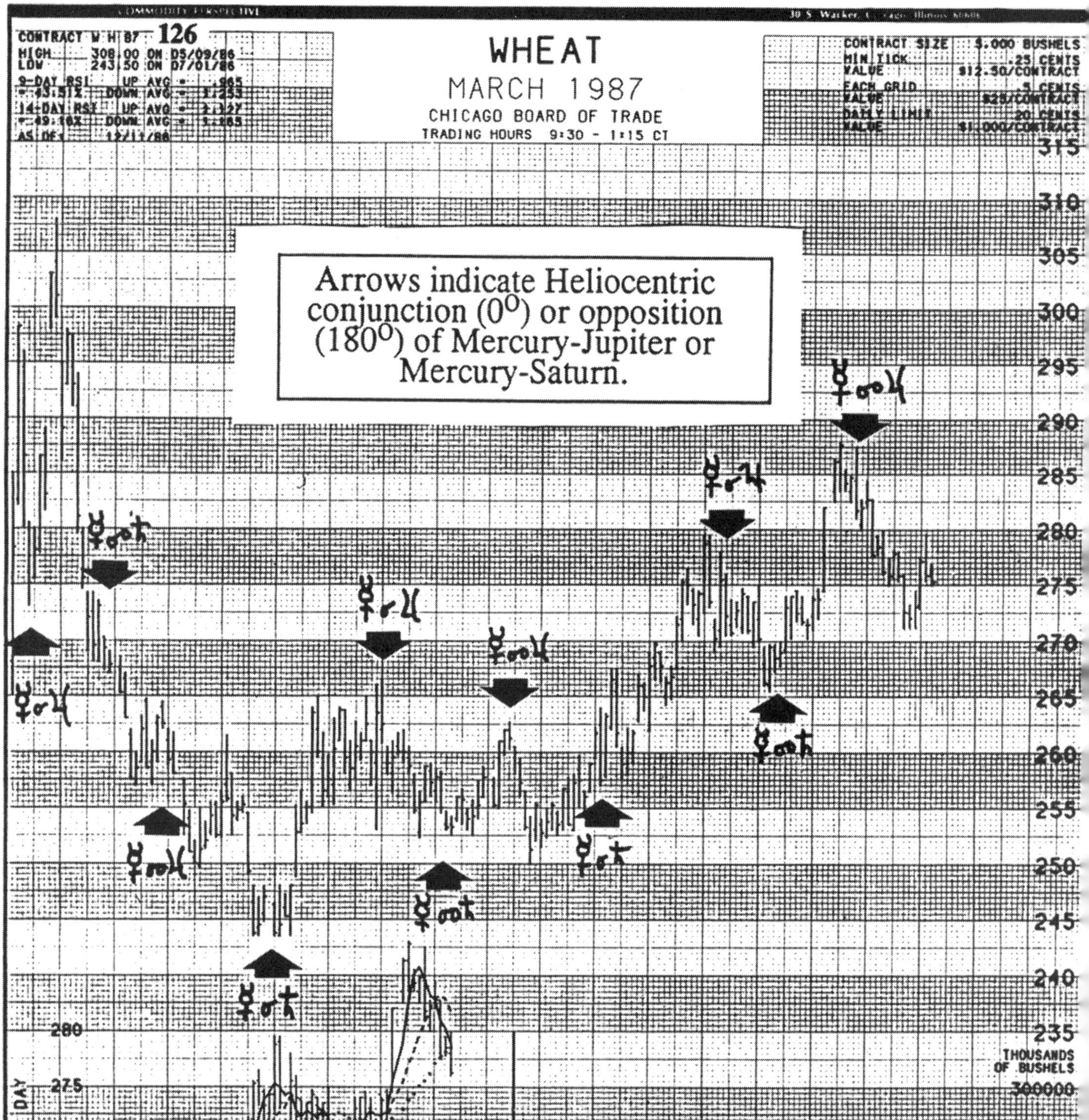
COMMODITY PERSPECTIVE
WHEAT
MARCH 1987
CHICAGO BOARD OF TRADE
TRADING HOURS 9:30 - 1:15 CT
CONTRACT W H 87 126
HIGH 308.00 ON 05/09/86
LOW 243.50 ON 07/01/86
AS OF: 12/11/86
CONTRACT SIZE 5,000 BUSHELS
MIN. TICK .25 CENTS
VALUE $12.50/CONTRACT
EACH GRID .5 CENTS
VALUE $25/CONTRACT
DAILY LIMIT 20 CENTS
VALUE $1,000/CONTRACT
Arrows indicate Heliocentric conjunction (0°) or opposition (180°) of Mercury-Jupiter or Mercury-Saturn.
MOV AVG 4-9-18 DAY
VOLUME/OPEN INTEREST
THOUSANDS OF BUSHELS
Charts courtesy of Commodity Perspective
MAY
JUN
JUL
AUG
SEP
OCT
NOV
DEC
3

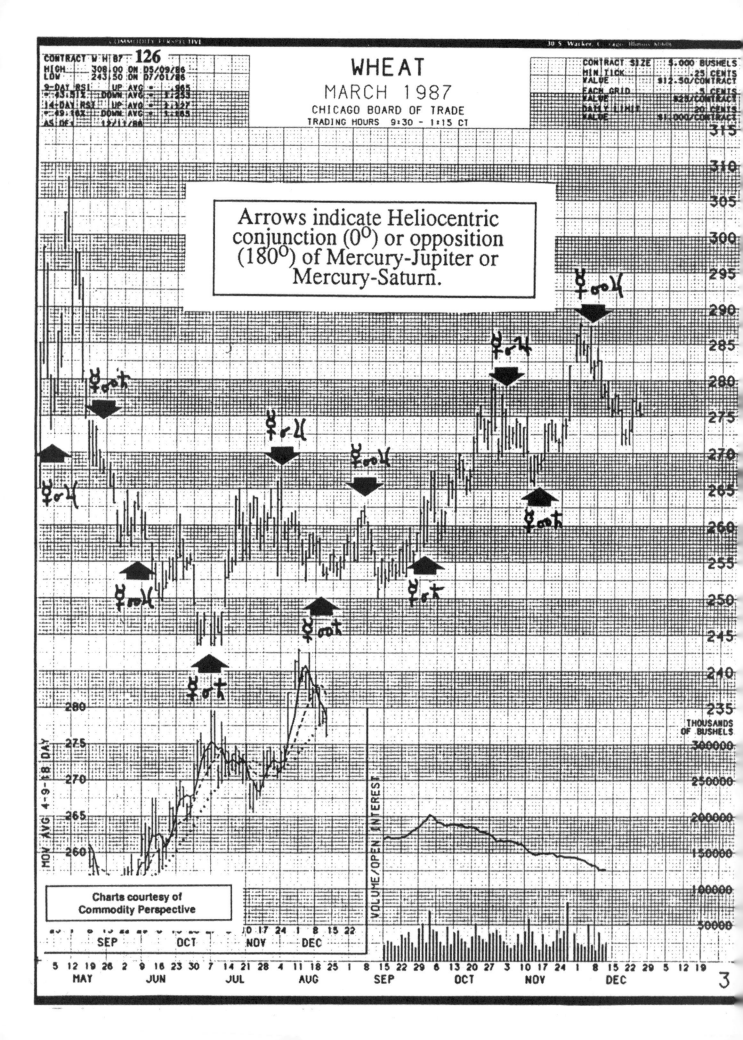

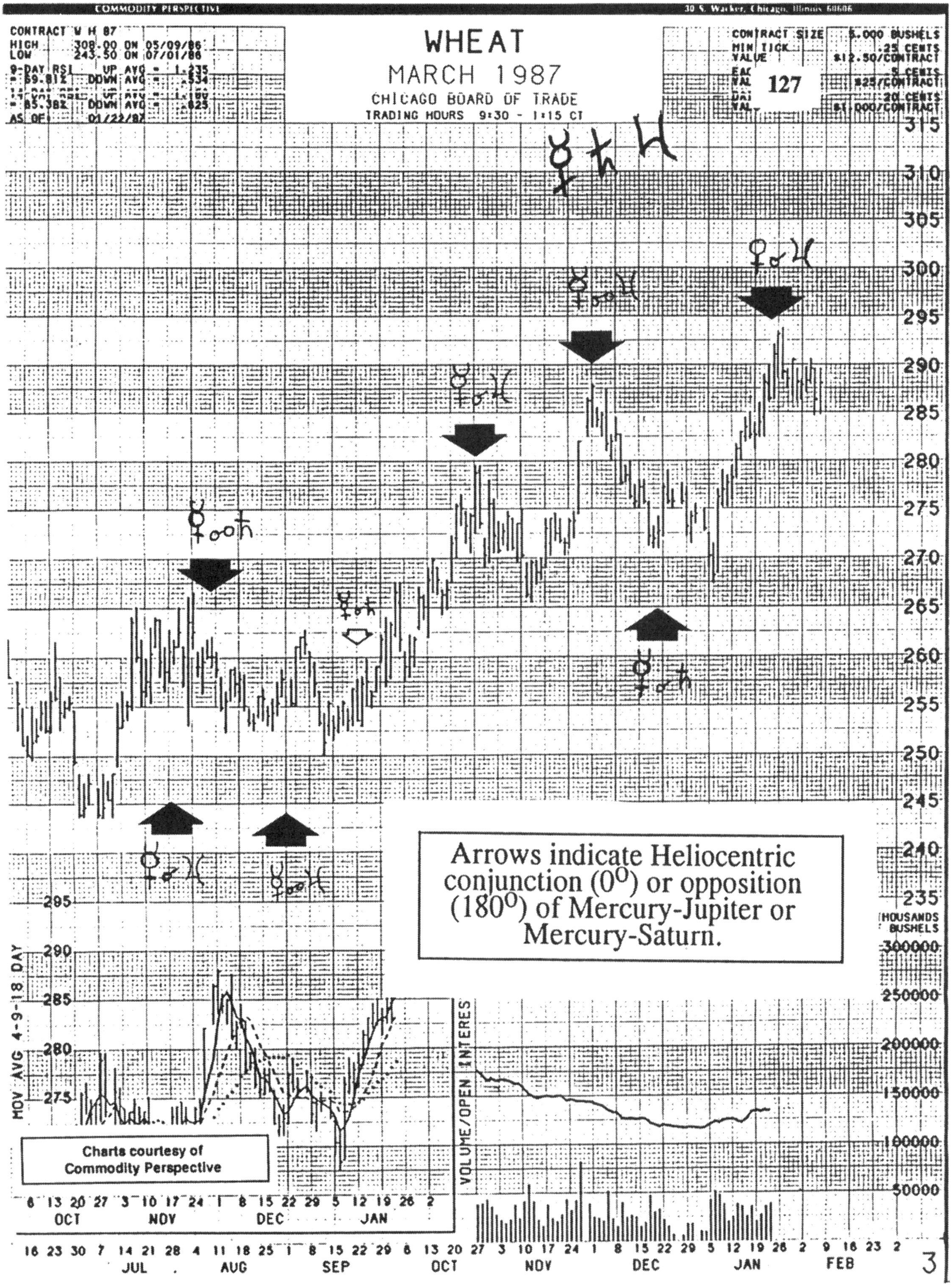

Arrows indicate Heliocentric conjunction (0^0) or opposition (180^0) of Mercury-Jupiter or Mercury-Saturn.

'Combust'

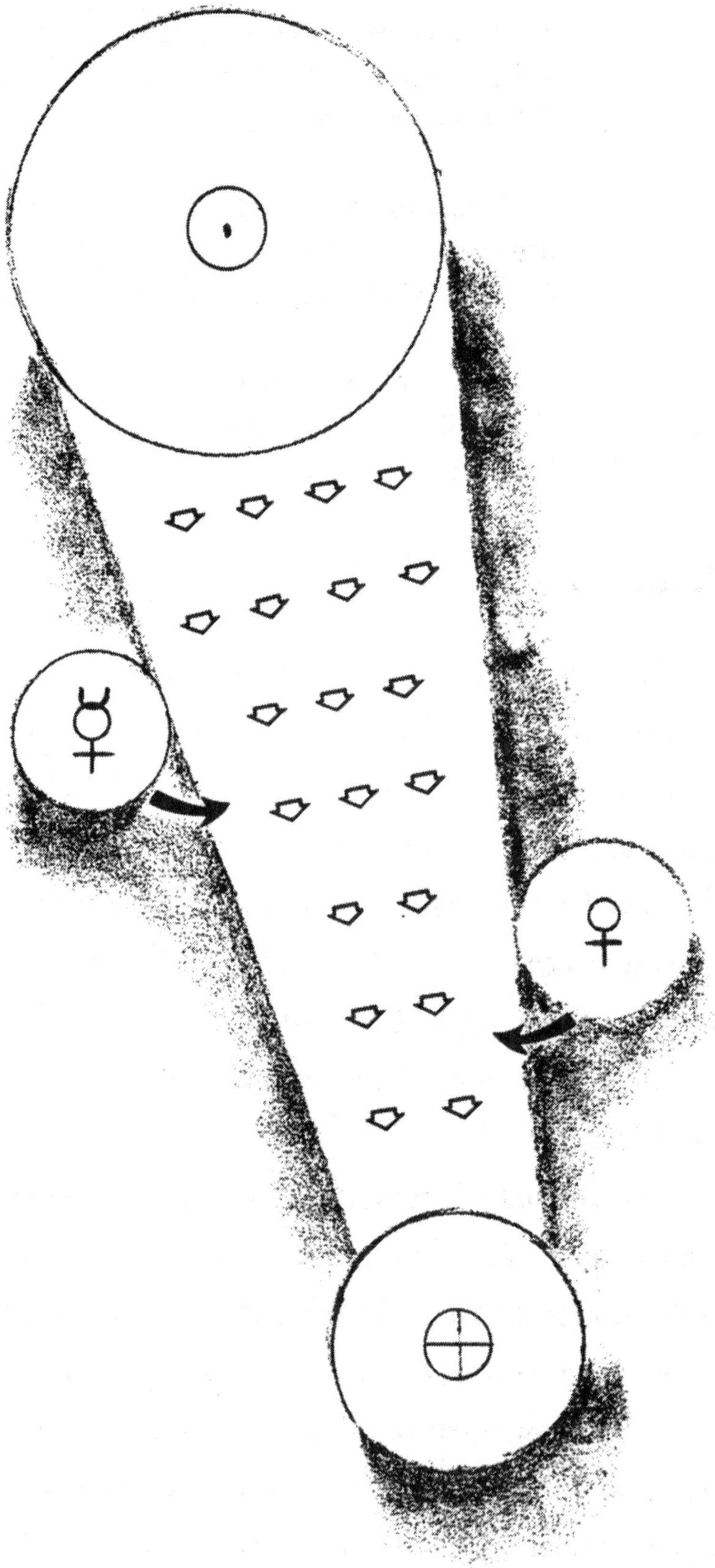

We have researched this phenomenon and determined the following:

1. The time period between Entry, Exact and Leaving is usually one complete price swing as measured by Elliott Wave enthusiasts.

2. Timing of price trend changes involving "combust" **must** be associated with one or more lunar phases (i.e. Full Moon at Apogee or Maximum Declination).

3. Entry and Leaving exhibit the greatest thrust! Again, it is usually necessary to have an associated lunar phase present at the time of **Entry or Leaving.**

Combust

The planets Mercury and Venus are the closest to the Sun. They travel quite rapidly around the Sun, Mercury in 88 days and Venus in 225 days. Combust is the conjunction (0°) of Mercury and Venus with a 13° orb for Mercury and an 8° orb for Venus. This was described by T.G. Butaney in *Forecasting Prices.* There is an artist's conception of how "combust" appears from the Earth on the following page. The Appendix shows 1988 and 1989 as periods of "combust." Three phases are shown: **Entry, Exact, and Leaving**.

Mercury and Venus must have a tremendous effect on the bombardment of solar rays on the earth. As they move back and forth between the Sun and Earth it makes sense that Mercury and Venus affect weather patterns and growing conditions on earth. These rays must affect the psychology of traders! Butaney was very adamant concerning these conditions! As a grain and soybean trader you must be aware when "combust" is in effect.

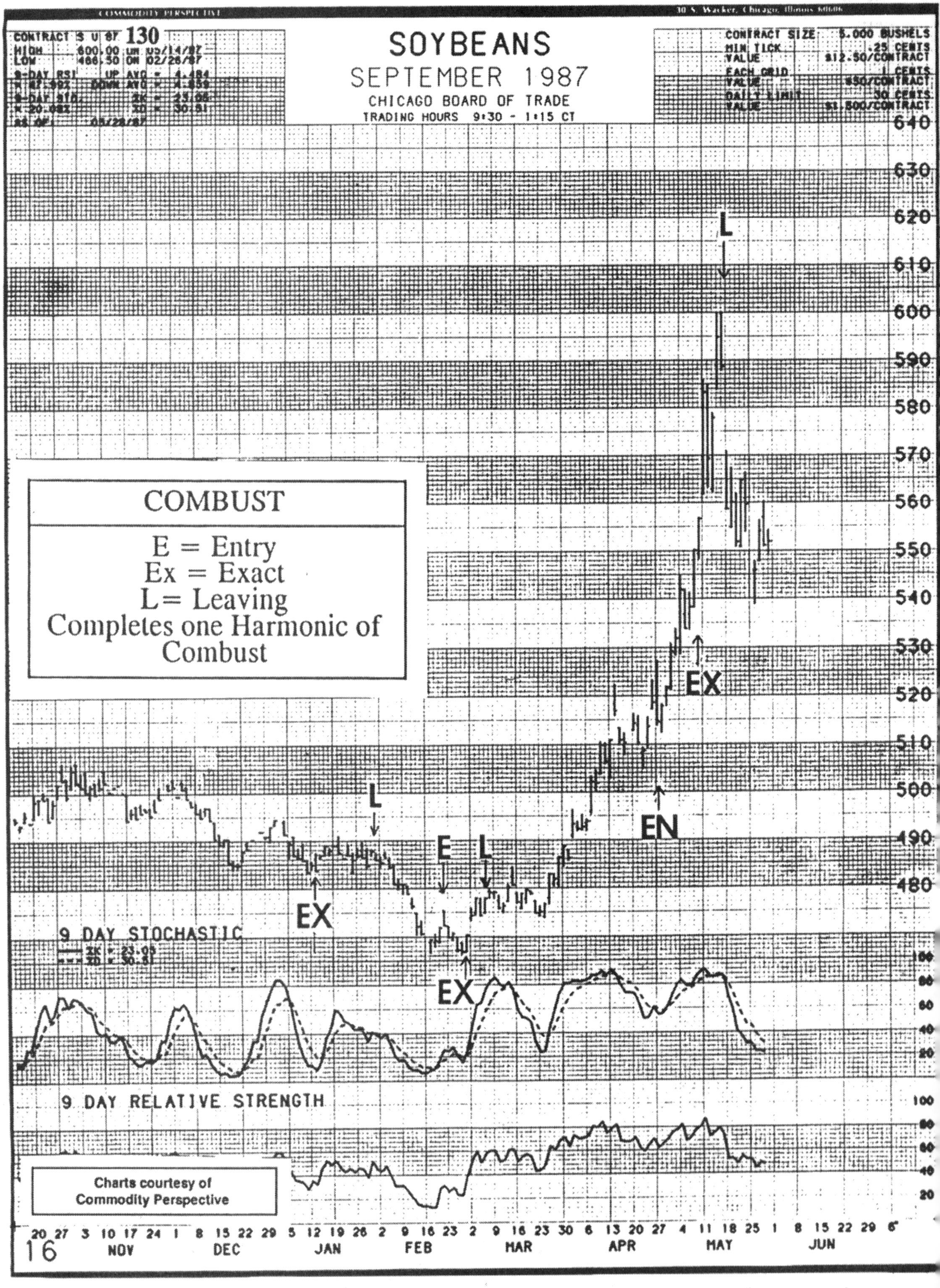
COMMODITY PERSPECTIVE
30 S. Wacker, Chicago, Illinois 60606
SOYBEANS
SEPTEMBER 1987
CHICAGO BOARD OF TRADE
TRADING HOURS 9:30 - 1:15 CT
CONTRACT S U 87 130
HIGH 600.00 ON 05/14/87
LOW 466.50 ON 02/26/87
CONTRACT SIZE 5,000 BUSHELS
MIN TICK .25 CENTS
VALUE $12.50/CONTRACT
EACH GRID 1 CENTS
VALUE $50/CONTRACT
DAILY LIMIT 30 CENTS
VALUE $1,500/CONTRACT
COMBUST
E = Entry
Ex = Exact
L= Leaving
Completes one Harmonic of Combust
L
EX
EN
E
9 DAY STOCHASTIC
9 DAY RELATIVE STRENGTH
Charts courtesy of Commodity Perspective
NOV
DEC
JAN
FEB
MAR
APR
MAY
JUN
16

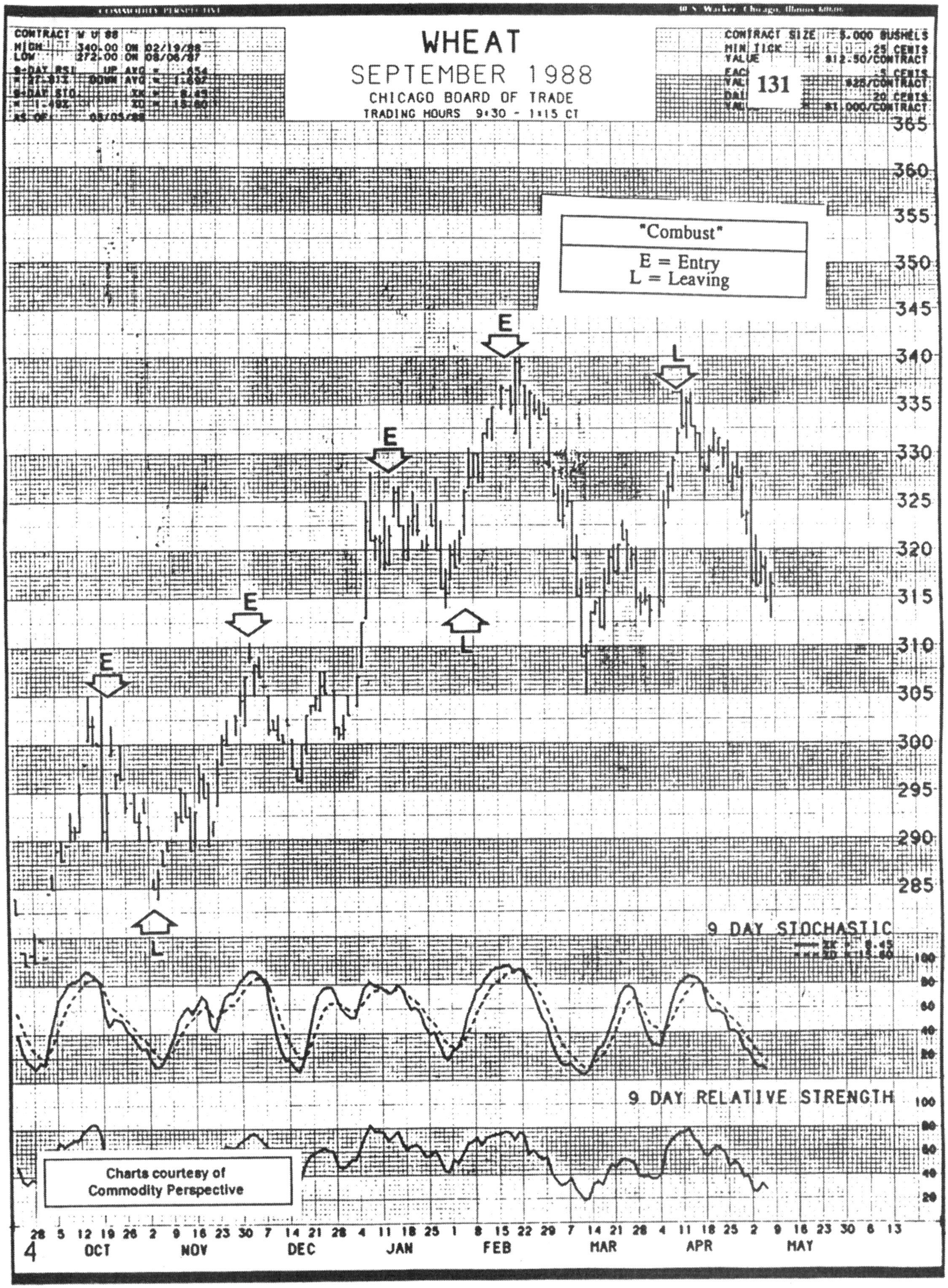
WHEAT
SEPTEMBER 1988
CHICAGO BOARD OF TRADE
TRADING HOURS 9:30 - 1:15 CT
131
"Combust"
E = Entry
L = Leaving
E
E
E
E
L
L
L
L
9 DAY STOCHASTIC
9 DAY RELATIVE STRENGTH
Charts courtesy of
Commodity Perspective
OCT
NOV
DEC
JAN
FEB
MAR
APR
MAY

SECTION FOUR:

THE STOCK MARKET
1987-1989

Section Four:

The Stock Market 1987-1989

The 1987 Top in the Stock Market

The stock market in 1987 was a wonderful example of how astrology provides "warning" signs of impending problems. The market started the year with the most explosive upmove ever experienced in the stock market. Was it a coincidence that the United States experienced the highest water tides in 100 years on December 31, 1986? Jupiter and Uranus were forming a major bullish aspect (trine 120°) June 21st, 1987, and the market went uninterrupted for eight months.

As August was approaching the financial astrologer would have been excited about the plethora of ominous signs that were occurring near the same time. What really puzzled me was that the publicity about these events was covered extensively in the press. Reporters described the phenomenon as "Harmonic Convergence." However, I know of only two who were adamant about this as being the "Final" top, Mason Sexton of *Harmonic Research* and myself. I knew that I was right because it was so difficult to convince people even though the facts were there.

"Harmonic Convergence" was referred to by the Mayan calendar and the Hopi Indian calendar. It is the formation of six planets all in conjunction (0°) within days of one another:

Mercury	conjunction	Venus
Sun	conjunction	Mercury
Mercury	conjunction	Mars
Sun	conjunction	Venus
Venus	conjunction	Mars
Sun	conjunction	Mars

In addition, Mars was trine (120°) Jupiter adding further bullish sentiment. In addition, four of these planets were in the same zodiac sign of Leo--which is associated with power. The market began to roll over on the New Moon of August 24th and finished at the crossing of the Moon's true node at the ecliptic on August 27th.

The only time I have seen this many conjunctions in one week was the low in October 1974. What was even more remarkable was the symmetry that the market was revealing (illustrated in the following table):

LOWS---TO---HIGHS
1932 to 1987 = 55 years
1966 to 1987 = 21 years
1974 to 1987 = 13 years
1979 to 1987 = 8 years
1982 to 1987 = 5 years
1984 to 1987 = 3 years

THAT IS ABOUT AS PERFECT A SEQUENCE OF FIBONACCI NUMBERS AS ONE COULD EXPECT.

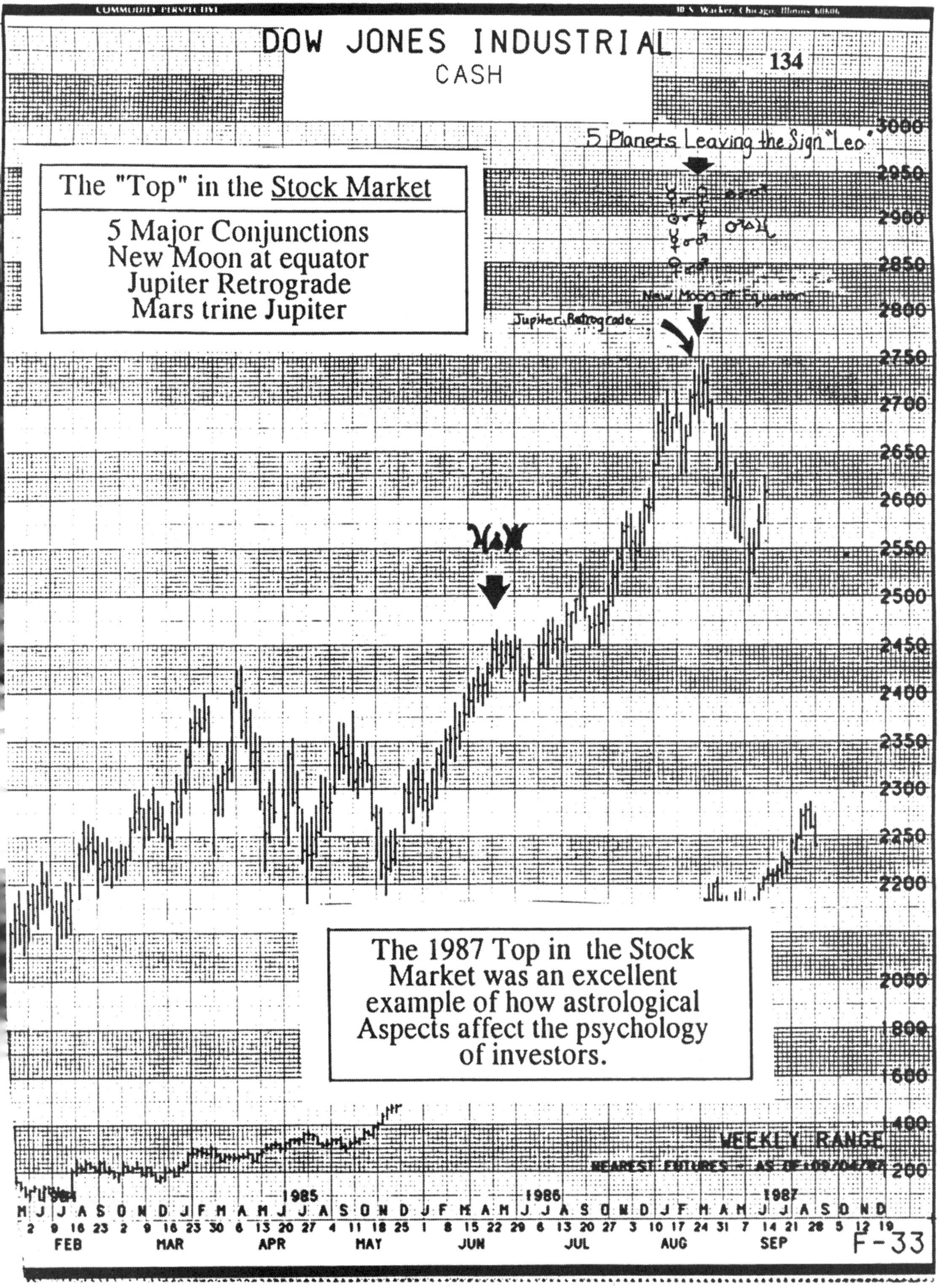
COMMODITY PERSPECTIVE
30 S. Wacker, Chicago, Illinois 60606
DOW JONES INDUSTRIAL
CASH
134
5 Planets Leaving the Sign "Leo"
The "Top" in the Stock Market
5 Major Conjunctions
New Moon at equator
Jupiter Retrograde
Mars trine Jupiter
New Moon at Equator
Jupiter Retrograde
The 1987 Top in the Stock Market was an excellent example of how astrological Aspects affect the psychology of investors.
WEEKLY RANGE
NEAREST FUTURES - AS OF 09/04/87
1984
1985
1986
1987
M J J A S O N D J F M A M J J A S O N D J F M A M J J A S O N D J F M A M J J A S O N D
2 9 16 23 2 9 16 23 30 6 13 20 27 4 11 18 25 1 8 15 22 29 6 13 20 27 3 10 17 24 31 7 14 21 28 5 12 19
FEB
MAR
APR
MAY
JUN
JUL
AUG
SEP
3000
2950
2900
2850
2800
2750
2700
2650
2600
2550
2500
2450
2400
2350
2300
2250
2200
2000
1800
1600
1400
1200
F-33

DOW JONES INDUSTRIALS – 1974

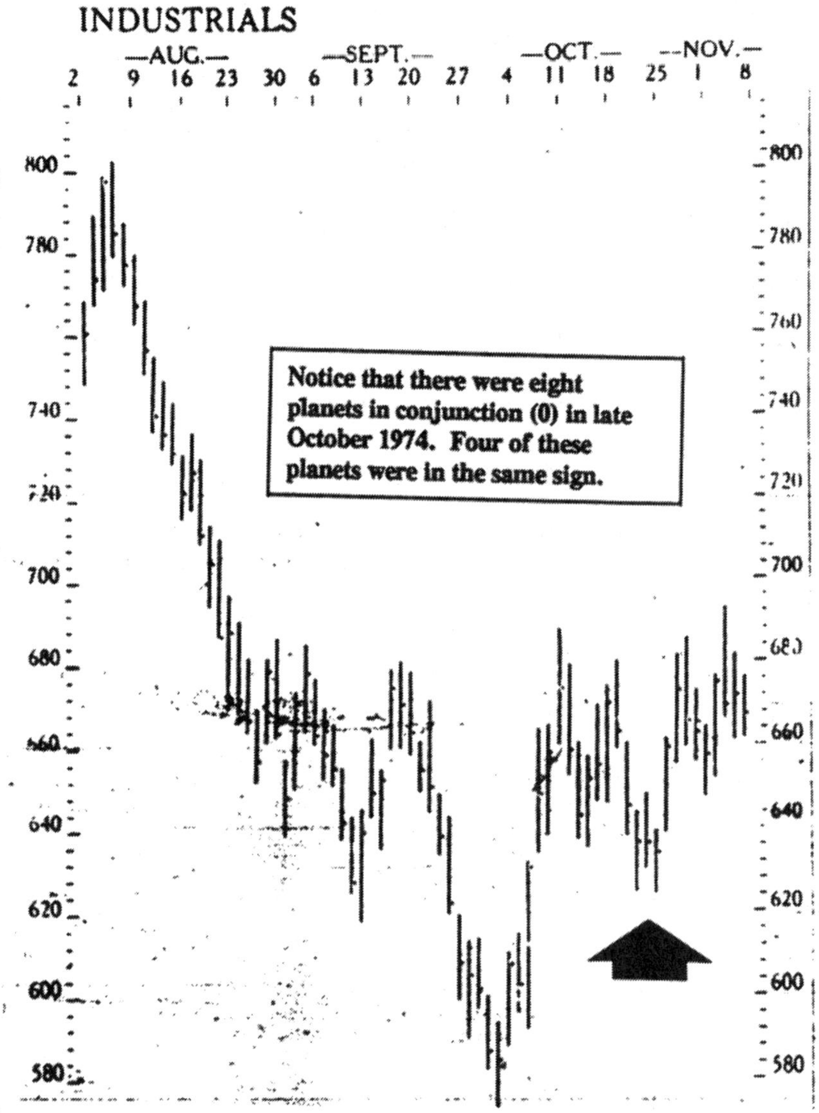

ASPECTS, 1974 MAIN

	DATE	TIME	EX	JOB	#	P1 POS.	HS	P2 POS.	HS
⊙ ——— ☌ ♅	21OCT74	02:22 PM	X	TR-TR	01	28♎08	01	28♎08	01
♀ ——— ☌ ♂	24OCT74	06:59 AM	X	TR-TR	01	27♎32	01	27♎32	01
♀ ——— ☌ ♅		10:39 PM	X	TR-TR	01	28♎21	01	28♎21	01
☿ ——— ☌ ⊙	25OCT74	05:27 AM	X	TR-TR	01	01♏45R	01	01♏45	01
♂ ——— ☌ ♅		01:39 PM	X	TR-TR	01	28♎23	01	28♎23	01
☿ ——— ☌ ♀	26OCT74	10:43 AM	X	TR-TR	01	00♏14R	01	00♏14	01
☿ ——— ☌ ♂	27OCT74	02:49 AM	X	TR-TR	01	29♎26R	01	29♎26	01
♃ ——— □ ♆		04:42 AM	X	TR-TR	01	08♓04R	05	08♐04	02
☿ ——— ☌ ♅		09:50 PM	X	TR-TR	01	28♎32R	01	28♎32	01
⊙ ——— △ ♃	31OCT74	11:36 AM	X	TR-TR	01	08♏00	01	08♓00R	05

Venus In 1988

(The following three sections concerning the astrological effect of Venus in 1988 is from *Valliere's Natural Cycles Almanac 1988* and is reprinted with their permission.)

Normally, each summer Venus reaches its maximum north declination for the year at from 23 to 25 degrees north. This means that it rises and sets far north on the horizon, and is above the horizon each day much longer than it is below.

In early May, 1988, however, Venus reaches $27^{o}44'$ north, the maximum in an eight-year declination cycle. In 1987, Venus rose and set north of the equator from March 12 to August 7--a total of 149 days. In 1988 it will do so from February 11 to November 1--a total of 264 days.

The table below lists Venus' north declination maximums since 1796. As you can see,this effect has been slowly getting more extreme over the past few hundred years.

VENUS, MAXIMUM NORTH DECLINATION
Eight-Year Declination Cycle

5/1796	26n14	5/1868	26n42	5/1940	27n20
5/1804	26n17	5/1876	26n46	5/1948	27n24
5/1812	26n20	5/1884	26n50	5/1956	27n29
5/1820	26n23	5/1892	26n54	5/1964	27n33
5/1828	26n26	5/1900	26n58	5/1972	27n37
5/1836	26n29	5/1908	27n02	5/1980	27n41
5/1844	26n33	5/1916	27n07	5/1988	27n44
5/1852	26n33	5/1924	27n11	5/1996	27n47
5/1860	26n39	5/1932	27n15		

Source: Valliere's Almanac

A Venus declination maximum adds yet another factor to the total tidal pull, which is already strong near a major lunar standstill. At a declination maximum, a planet slows down, stops and changes direction, which means it spends a longer-than-average time near its degree of maximum declination. In late spring and early summer, 1988, the maximum declination of the moon will be within a degree of Venus' declination. Thus each month it will be spending a longer-than-usual period in parallel or contra-parallel to Venus.

The coincidence of both the Moon and Venus at such high declinations has happened in only five years since 1800, as shown in the following table. As you can see, this table shows a correlation between Moon/Venus declination peaks and economic cycles in the U.S. The dates and durations of the depression years are from Sachs-Thorp (Encyclopedia of American History, ed. Richard B. Morris New York: Harper, 1965, p. 536). Sachs-Thorp shows 17 depressions since 1800, averaging 30 months duration. For the next table I have selected the five longest depressions since 1800.

Coincidence of Moon and Venus Maximum North Declinations and Economic Depressions Over 40 Months Long, Since 1800.

Moon Max.	Venus Max.	Depression	Durations
1820	1820	Depression 1815-21	71 months
1838	1836	Depression 1837-43	72 months
1876	1876	Depression 1873-78	66 months
1892	1894	Depression 1893-97	48 months
1932	1932	Depression 1929-33	42 months
1987	1988	?	?

Source: Valliere's Natural Cycles Almanac 1988

Other Planets in 1988

Saturn also reaches a declination maximum during 1988. After reaching aphelion (its farthest distance from the sun) on September 11 1988, Saturn goes on in November and December to attain 22°40' south declination.

As mentioned earlier, in 1988, there is also a series of conjunctions between Saturn and Uranus taking place on February 12, June 26, and October 17.

A Replay of the Great Crash

In 1988, we are near a sunspot minimum and a lunar major standstill. Venus and Saturn reach maximum declination, Saturn reaches aphelion, and there are major hard aspects between Saturn

and Uranus. What does this signify? The following table shows the results of a search of 20th century celestial combinations.

PARALLEL CELESTIAL EVENTS, 1929-33 and 1986-88

1/1929 through 8/1933		9/1986 through 11/1988	
11/1929	Saturn aphelion	9/1986	Sunspot minimum
12/1929	Saturn max. decl.	9/1987	Moon max. decl.
1/1931	Saturn Uranus sq. (geo and helio)	5/1988	Venus max. decl.
		6/1988	Saturn-Uranus conj. (geo and helio)
3/1932	Moon max. decl.		
5/1932	Venus max. decl.	11/1988	Saturn aphelion
8/1933	Sunspot in minimum	11/1988	Saturn max. decl.

Source: Valliere's Almanac

There are striking parallels between the period 1986-1988 and 1929-1933. Both periods were bounded by a sunspot minimum and a Saturn maximum south declination. The main difference is that in 1929-1933 the Saturn declination maximum began the period and the sunspot minimum ended it, whereas in the present period it's the other way around. Also, in 1988, the Saturn-Uranus aspect is a conjunction instead of a square, and and additional factor is Pluto reaching zero declination on February 27, the first time since 1863.

From 1929 to 1933, American society was halted and forced to retreat during the Great Depression. In terms of planetary symbolism,the changes were sudden (Uranus) and difficult (Saturn). As in the present period, the Sun, Moon and Venus were at extreme points in their cycles, and there were dramatic trend reversals such as

SECTION FIVE:

TRADING WITH ASTRO-CYCLES

we have already begun seeing. For 1988, the main celestial events are obviously again saying "beware."

Source: Valliere's Almanac

BE PREPARED!

Section Five:

Trading with Astro-cycles

The Ten Rules of Trading

1. Never add to a losing position.
2. If the position is showing a loss at the end of the 2nd day--liquidate it!
3. When in doubt--stay out.
4. Never risk more than 10% of your capital!
5. Stops are placed for protection--use them!
6. Never spread a loss.
7. Never allow a substantial profit to become a loss.
8. Plan your trading and follow the plan.
9. The only true facts in commodity trading are fear and greed.
10. Take equity out for enjoyment and "rainy days."

The Gartley "222" Entry Technique

H.M. Gartley wrote *Profits in the Stock Market* in 1935. Originally there were only 1000 copies sold for about $1500 each. This was at the time of the greatest depression in our country's history. One could have purchased three brand new Ford automobiles with that much money!. This is the best book on the technical aspects of the stock market that I have ever found. It is interesting that it was written before R.N. Elliott was popularizd by Charles Collins.

On page "222" of this book is a time and price pattern that is **THE** best technical trade I have ever found. It has everything that the speculator could ask for in a trade:

1. **Control of Risk**--you place your stop above (below) the old high (low).
2. Trading in the direction of the short term trend--you are not picking a top.
3. The Profit to Loss ratio is better than 4 to 1.
4. Three out of four (75%) of the trades will be profitable.

Profits in the Stock Market contains cycles, extensive price wave analysis, and the best pattern recognition formations.. You will find several examples of Gartley's "222" in the chart section. Basically the pattern is depicted by the following diagram:

Gartley 222

1. A-B-C Correction
2. Price at Fibonacci Level at Pt. C (.618 retrace)
3. Risk-Reward Level excellent
4. Stop Protection quantified at Pt. A

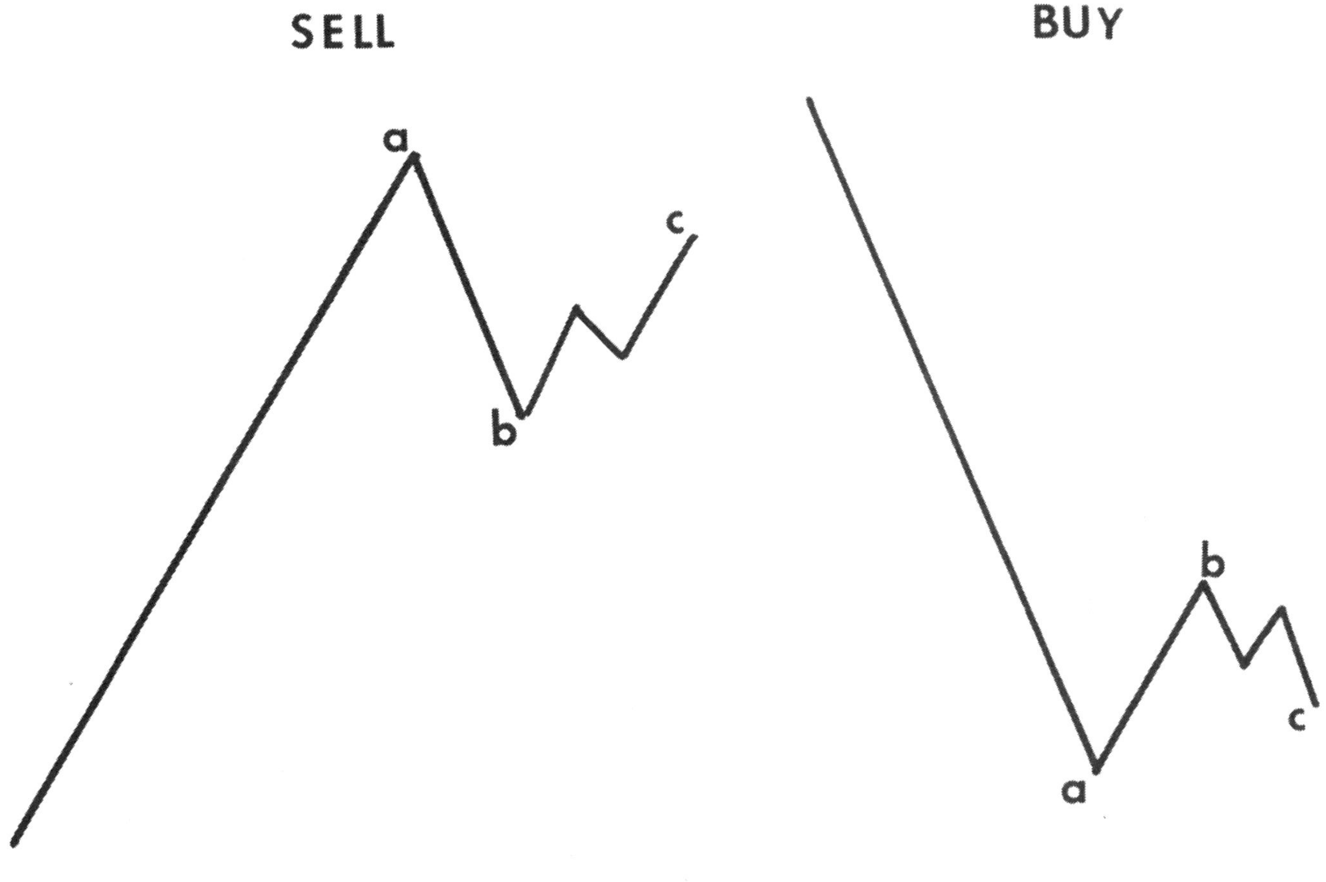

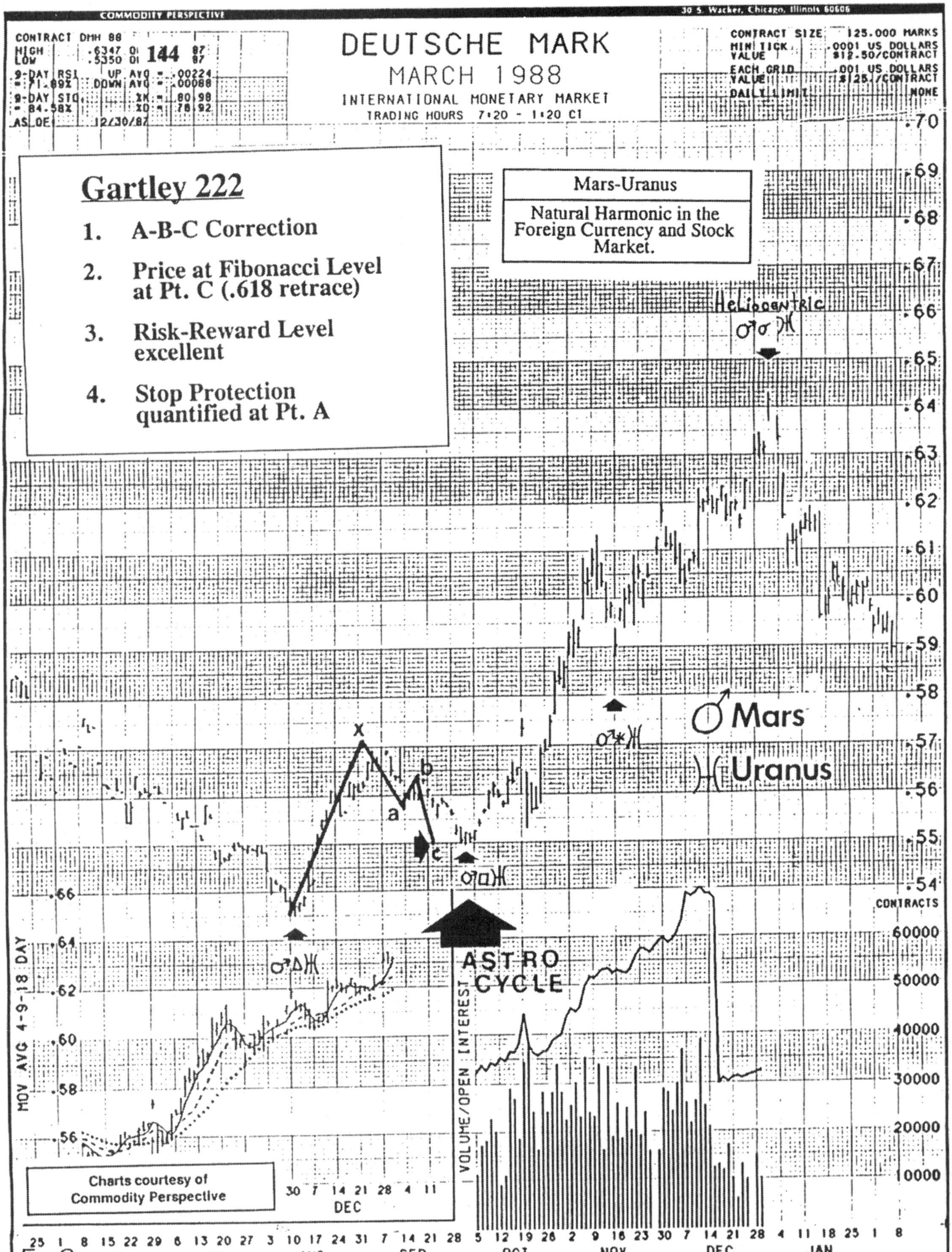
COMMODITY PERSPECTIVE
30 S. Wacker, Chicago, Illinois 60606
DEUTSCHE MARK
MARCH 1988
INTERNATIONAL MONETARY MARKET
TRADING HOURS 7:20 - 1:20 CT
CONTRACT SIZE 125.000 MARKS
MIN TICK VALUE .0001 US DOLLARS $12.50/CONTRACT
EACH GRID VALUE .001 US DOLLARS $25./CONTRACT
DAILY LIMIT NONE
Gartley 222
1. A-B-C Correction
2. Price at Fibonacci Level at Pt. C (.618 retrace)
3. Risk-Reward Level excellent
4. Stop Protection quantified at Pt. A
Mars-Uranus
Natural Harmonic in the Foreign Currency and Stock Market.
Heliocentric
Mars
Uranus
x
a
b
c
ASTRO CYCLE
MOV AVG 4-9-18 DAY
VOLUME/OPEN INTEREST
CONTRACTS
Charts courtesy of Commodity Perspective
JUN
JUL
AUG
SEP
OCT
NOV
DEC
JAN

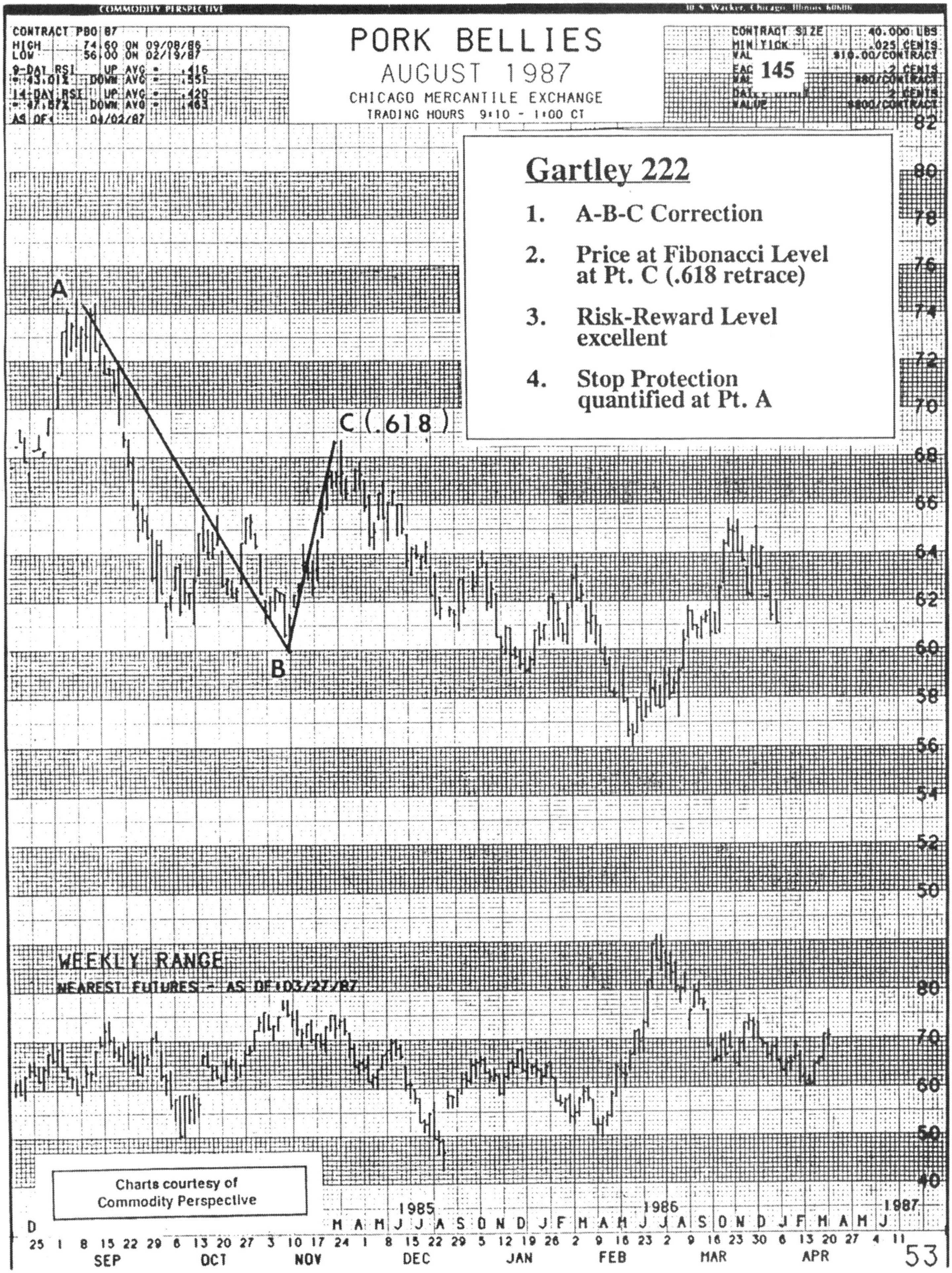

COMMODITY PERSPECTIVE
PORK BELLIES
AUGUST 1987
CHICAGO MERCANTILE EXCHANGE
TRADING HOURS 9:10 - 1:00 CT
CONTRACT PBO 87
HIGH 74.60 ON 09/08/86
LOW 56.00 ON 02/19/87
CONTRACT SIZE 40,000 LBS
145
Gartley 222
1. A-B-C Correction
2. Price at Fibonacci Level at Pt. C (.618 retrace)
3. Risk-Reward Level excellent
4. Stop Protection quantified at Pt. A
A
B
C (.618)
WEEKLY RANGE
NEAREST FUTURES - AS OF 03/27/87
Charts courtesy of Commodity Perspective
SEP
OCT
NOV
DEC
JAN
FEB
MAR
APR
1985
1986
1987
53

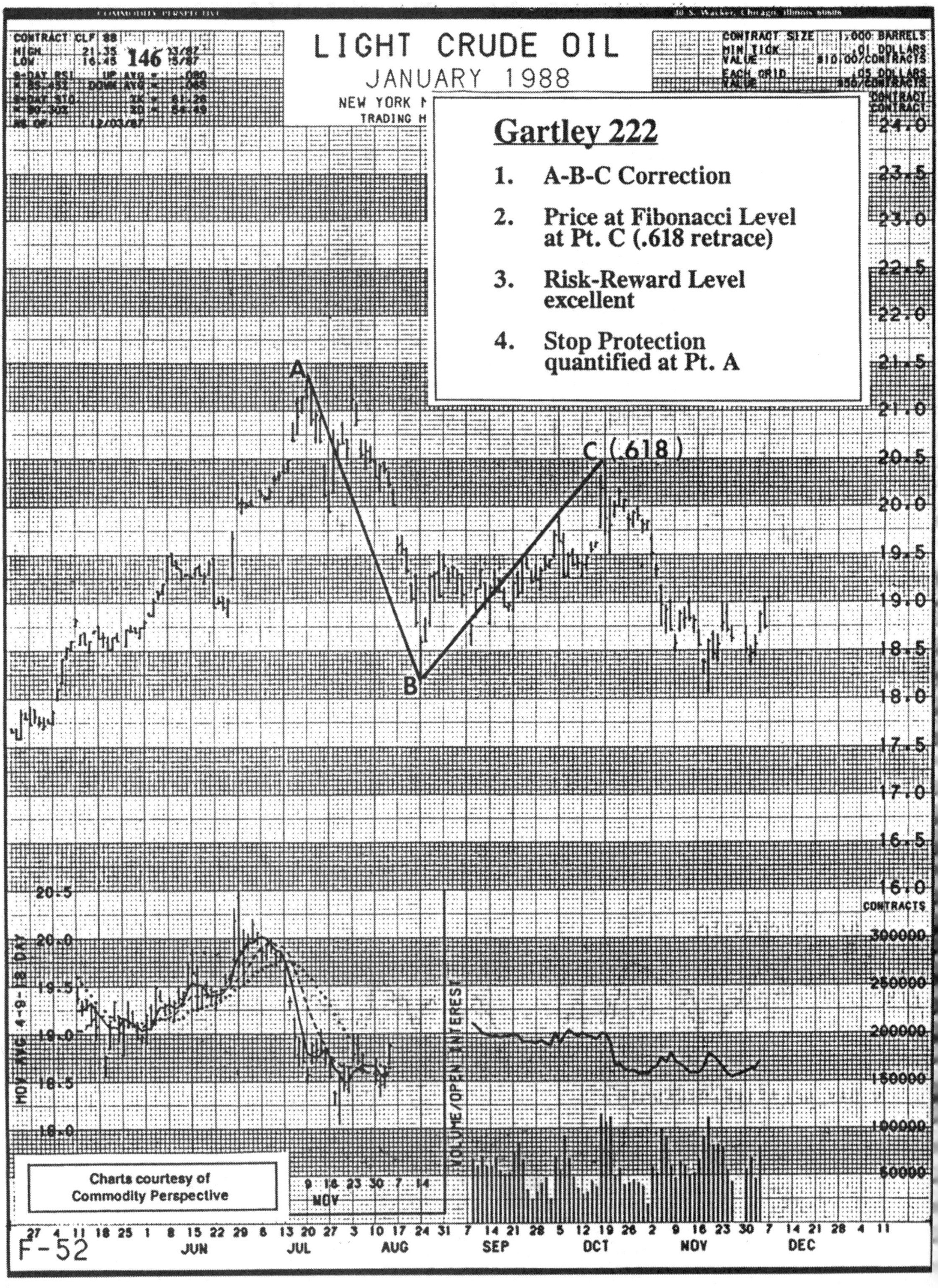
LIGHT CRUDE OIL
JANUARY 1988
Gartley 222
1. A-B-C Correction
2. Price at Fibonacci Level at Pt. C (.618 retrace)
3. Risk-Reward Level excellent
4. Stop Protection quantified at Pt. A
A
B
C (.618)
Charts courtesy of Commodity Perspective
VOLUME/OPEN INTEREST
JUN
JUL
AUG
SEP
OCT
NOV
DEC
F-52

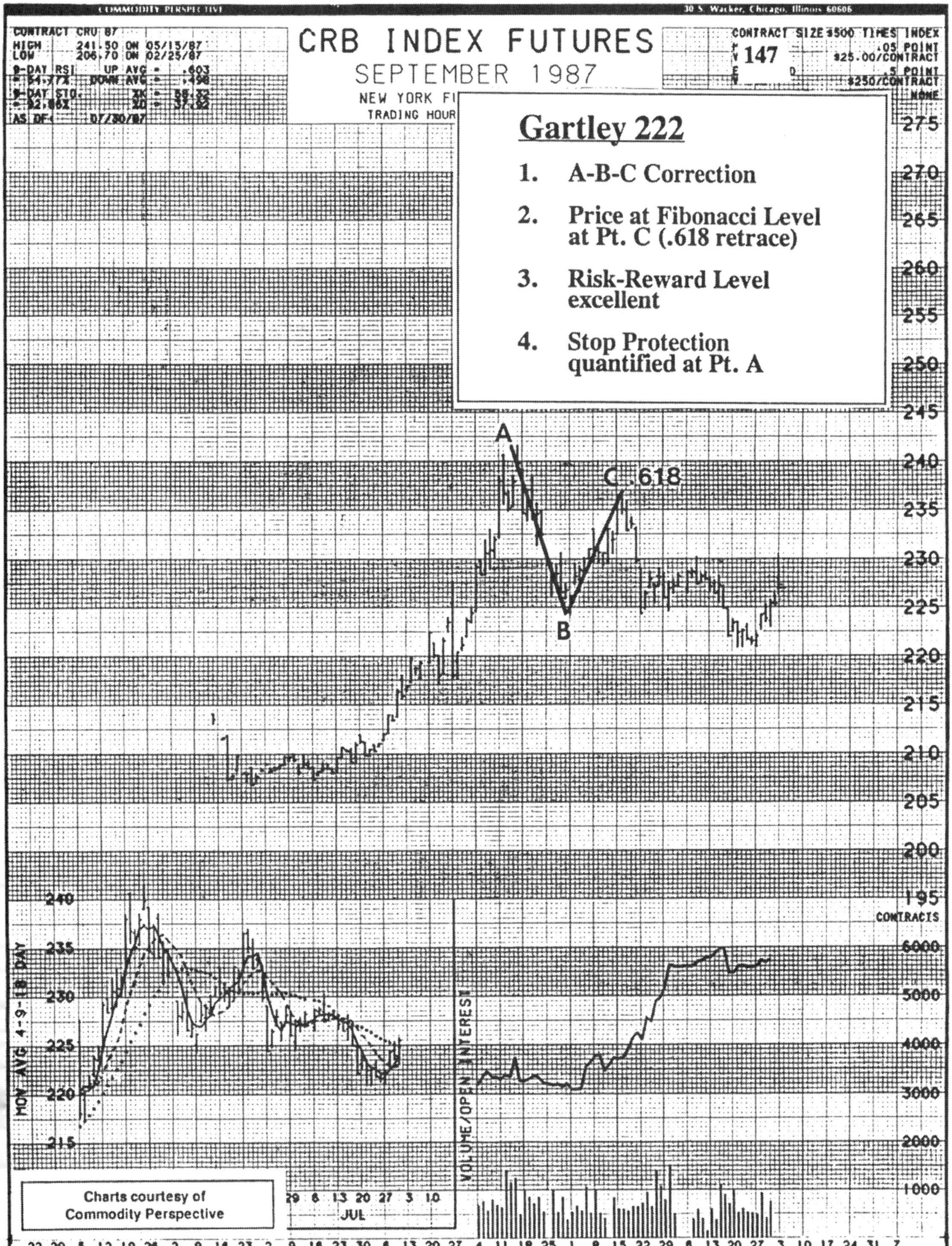
CRB INDEX FUTURES
SEPTEMBER 1987
Gartley 222
1. A-B-C Correction
2. Price at Fibonacci Level at Pt. C (.618 retrace)
3. Risk-Reward Level excellent
4. Stop Protection quantified at Pt. A
A
B
C .618
Charts courtesy of Commodity Perspective
JAN FEB MAR APR MAY JUN JUL AUG
MOV AVG 4-9-18 DAY
VOLUME/OPEN INTEREST
CONTRACTS

The 1-3-5 Entry Technique

The Gartley "222" trading entry is the best I have ever found in 20 years of research. Further research into excellent entry techniques uncovered a variation of the Gartley method. I call it the 1-3-5 because of the use of the Fibonacci number sequence.

Standard technical analysis warns of the difficulty in picking the "exact" top or bottom in the market. Bernard Baruch stated it succinctly "Don't try to buy at the bottom or sell at the top. This can't be done--except by liars." As traders we are faced with the decision as to how to control risk. We already know that we can not control the market action. The control of risk is of paramount importance to the successful trader. **"He who knows not what he risks--risks all!"** (Chinese proverb)

The 1-3-5 signal incorporates the following parameters:

1. A previous top or bottom has been formed.
2. The price action is now moving toward the old top or bottom at the Fibonacci retracement point of .618!
3. There are no limit moves in the last three weeks.
4. Astro cycle aspects or lunar phenomena are present. Once these parameters have been completed the entry rules are as follows:

1. Enter the market at the .618 retracement.
2. Place stop above the old high (low).
3. Determine the amount of profit you expect.

1-3-5 BUY SIGNAL

1. Enter market at .618 retracement.
2. Place stop below old low.
3. Determine the profit objective

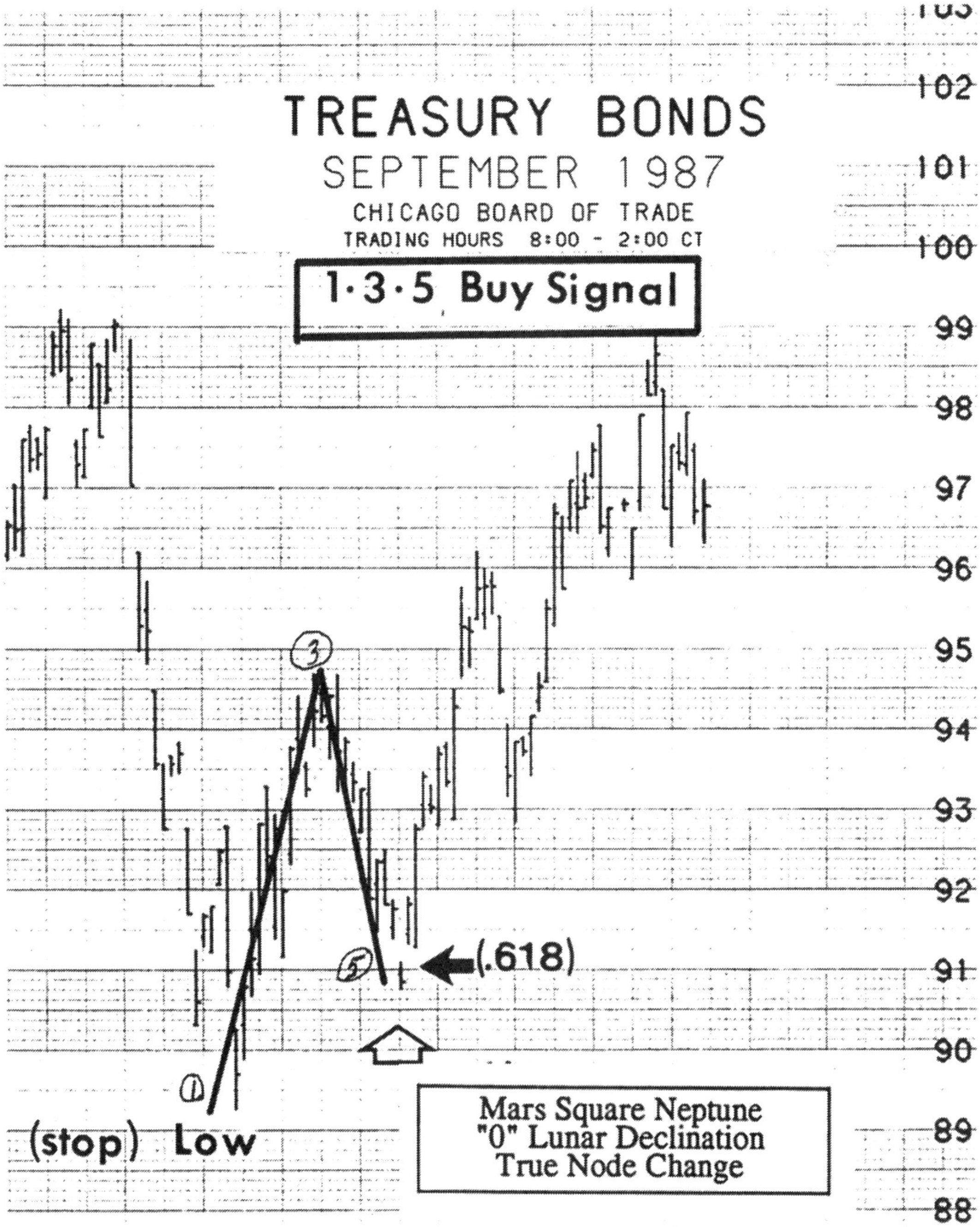

1-3-5 SELL SIGNAL

1. Enter market at .618 retracement.
2. Place stop above old high.
3. Determine the profit objective.

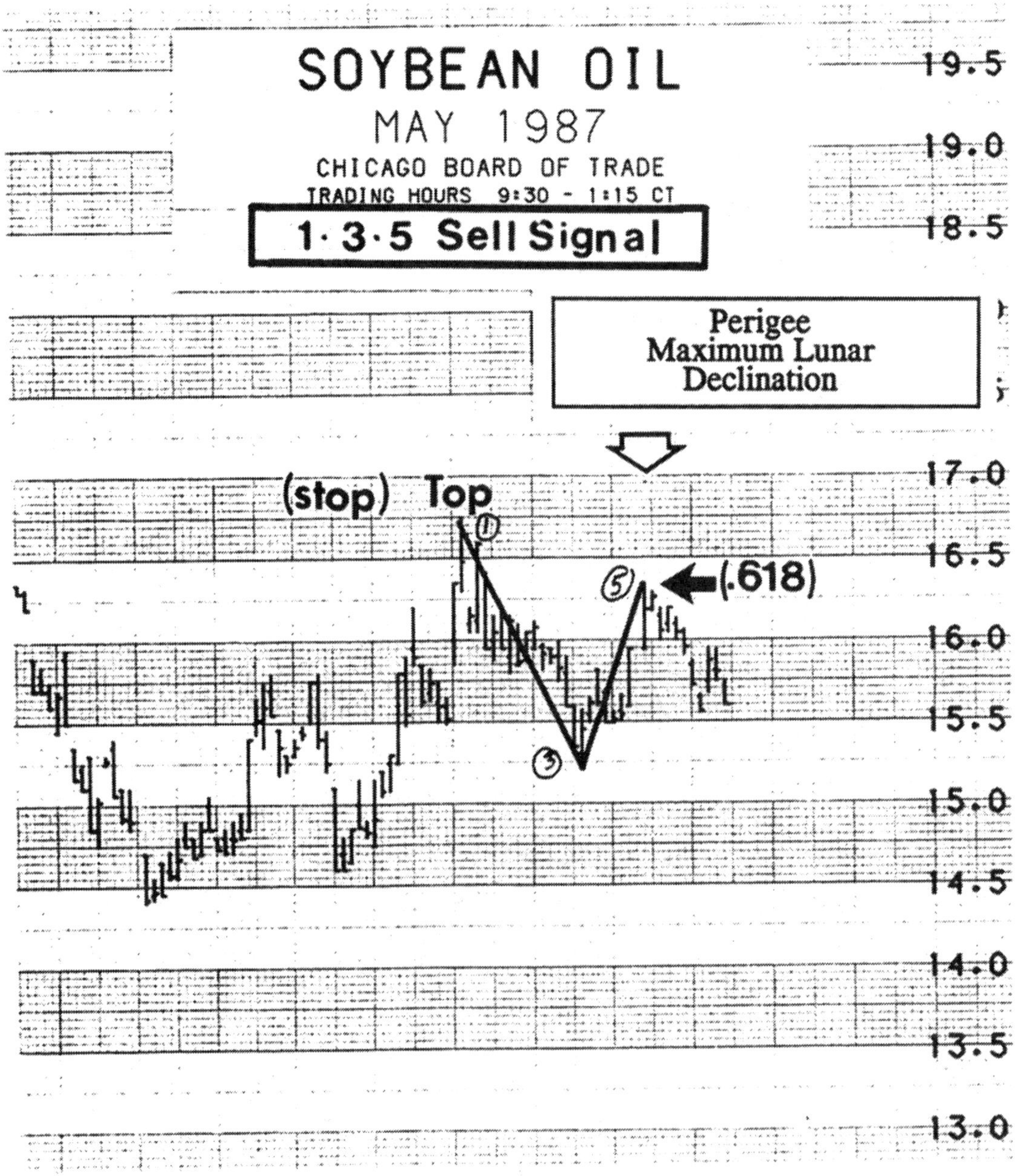

Astro Cycle--Timing Analysis Sheet

1. **CHECK FOR MAJOR ASPECTS FOR EACH COMMODITY.**
   (i.e. Venus-Uranus for the stock market or Venus & Pluto for the gold market.)
   a. Conjunction
   b. Sextile
   c. Square
   d. Trine
   e. Opposition

2. **CHECK LUNAR PHENOMENON**
   a. Maximum or Zero Declination
   b. True node going D or R
   c. Apogee or Perigee
   d. Full or New Moon

3. **CHECK NUMBER OF ASPECTS**
   a. Four or less aspects
   b. More than twelve

4. **CHECK THE ZODIAC SIGN CHANGES OF EACH PLANET**
   a. Which planets are changing signs?
   b. Are there more than 2 planets in the same sign?
   c. Retrograde motion of a "key" planet.

5. **CHECK PATTERN RECOGNITION PROFILE**
   a. Gartley 222
   b. 1-3-5

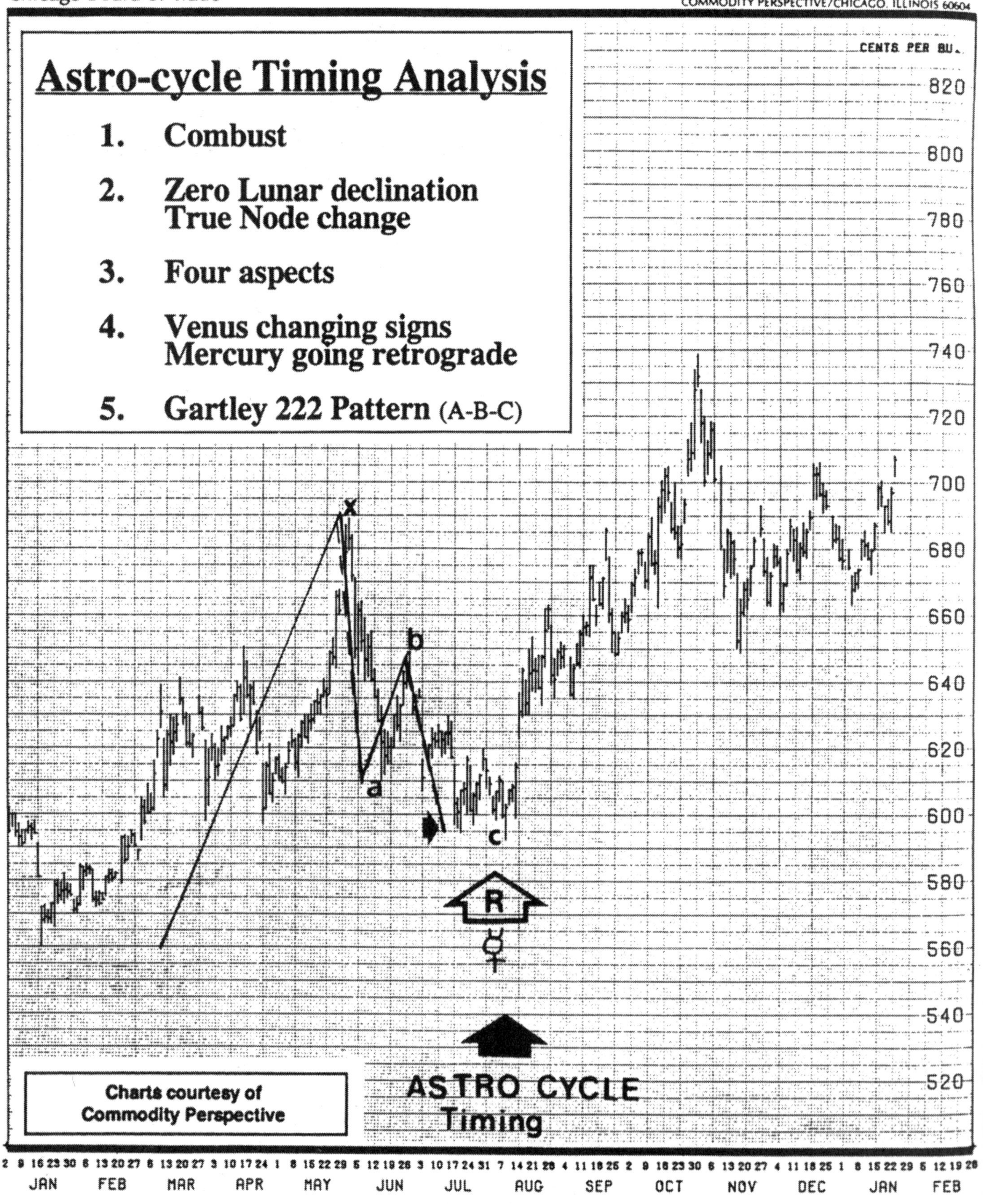
SOYBEANS
152
JANUARY 1979
Chicago Board of Trade
COMMODITY PERSPECTIVE/CHICAGO, ILLINOIS 60604
Astro-cycle Timing Analysis
1. Combust
2. Zero Lunar declination
True Node change
3. Four aspects
4. Venus changing signs
Mercury going retrograde
5. Gartley 222 Pattern (A-B-C)
CENTS PER BU.
820
800
780
760
740
720
700
680
660
640
620
600
580
560
540
520
x
a
b
c
R
Charts courtesy of
Commodity Perspective
ASTRO CYCLE
Timing
JAN
FEB
MAR
APR
MAY
JUN
JUL
AUG
SEP
OCT
NOV
DEC
JAN
FEB

Danger Signs When Using Astro Cycles

There are three signs that most major market moves exhibit just before they start accelerating:

1. Gap in the price action--prices move sharply on the opening and continue throughout the day.
2. Several days of wide price ranges that are considerably more than the normal range. An example: the average daily range for the S&P 500 is 200 points per day, then suddenly the daily trading range expands to 500 points per day.
3. The market closes at the high (or low) of the trading range each day. This is referred to by technicians as a "tail" close because it closes at the extreme of the range. Usually 3 tail closes signal acceleration.

When the events occur at astrological events you must respect them. "Markets are never wrong--men often are!" There are several examples of these moves in the book and they are listed as such.

SECTION SIX:

APPENDIX

Section Six:

Appendix--Astro-cycle Dates

Mars-Jupiter
Mars-Uranus

Natural Harmonic effecting the Stock Market and Treasury Bonds

	DATE	TIME	E X	JOE			
♂———— ⚹ ♅	18APR82	00:51 AM	X	TR-[illegible]			
♂———— ⚹ ♅	29MAY82	11:29 PM	X	TR-TR	02 | 02 ♎22	08 | 02 ♐22R	08
♂———— ☌ ♃	08AUG82	07:58 AM	X	TR-TR	01 | 02 ♏55	07 | 02 ♏55	07
♂———— ☌ ♅	21SEP82	08:48 PM	X	TR-TR	02 | 01 ♐23	08 | 01 ♐23	08
♂———— ⚹ ♃	04DEC82	04:15 AM	X	TR-TR	01 | 25 ♑26	10 | 25 ♏26	08
♂———— ⚹ ♅	17DEC82	10:26 PM	X	TR-TR	02 | 06 ♒09	11 | 06 ♐09	08
♂———— □ ♃	24JAN83	04:54 AM	X	TR-TR	01 | 05 ♓23	12 | 05 ♐23	08
♂———— □ ♅	27JAN83	07:06 PM	X	TR-TR	02 | 08 ♓12	12 | 08 ♐12	08
♂———— △ ♅	08MAR83	03:39 PM	X	TR-TR	02 | 09 ♈06	12 | 09 ♐06	08
♂———— △ ♃	10MAR83	10:27 AM	X	TR-TR	01 | 10 ♈27	12 | 10 ♐27	08
♂———— ☍ ♃	25MAY83	03:56 PM	X	TR-TR	01 | 06 ♊19	02 | 06 ♐19R	08
♂———— ☍ ♅	26MAY83	09:39 PM	X	TR-TR	02 | 07 ♊11	02 | 07 ♐11R	08
♂———— △ ♃	15AUG83	09:27 PM	X	TR-TR	01 | 01 ♌33	05 | 01 ♐33	08
♂———— △ ♅	21AUG83	09:31 AM	X	TR-TR	02 | 05 ♌06	05 | 05 ♐06	08
♂———— □ ♅	10OCT83	03:54 AM	X	TR-TR	02 | 06 ♍25	06 | 06 ♐25	08
♂———— □ ♃	14OCT83	09:43 AM	X	TR-TR	01 | 09 ♍01	06 | 09 ♐01	08
♂———— ⚹ ♅	04DEC83	01:56 PM	X	TR-TR	02 | 09 ♎31	06 | 09 ♐31	08
♂———— ⚹ ♃	04JAN84	07:59 PM	X	TR-TR	01 | 26 ♎49	07 | 26 ♐49	09
♂———— ☌ ♅	03SEP84	03:59 PM	X	TR-TR	02 | 09 ♐39	08 | 09 ♐39	08
♂———— ☌ ♃	13OCT84	09:49 PM	X	TR-TR	01 | 06 ♑11	10 | 06 ♑11	10
♂———— ⚹ ♅	03DEC84	04:07 PM	X	TR-TR	02 | 13 ♒41	11 | 13 ♐41	08
♂———— □ ♅	15JAN85	05:23 AM	X	TR-TR	02 | 16 ♓09	12 | 16 ♐09	09
♂———— ⚹ ♃	31JAN85	06:53 PM	X	TR-TR	01 | 28 ♓42	12 | 28 ♑42	10
♂———— △ ♅	26FEB85	06:05 AM	X	TR-TR	02 | 17 ♈43	01 | 17 ♐43	09
♂———— □ ♃	29MAR85	03:51 PM	X	TR-TR	01 | 10 ♉35	01 | 10 ♒35	11
♂———— △ ♃	20MAY85	07:35 AM	X	TR-TR	01 | 16 ♊35	03 | 16 ♒35	11
♂———— ☍ ♅		10:44 AM	X	TR-TR	02 | 16 ♊41	03 | 16 ♐41R	09
♂———— ☍ ♃	11AUG85	06:04 AM	X	TR-TR	01 | 11 ♌08	05 | 11 ♒08R	11
♂———— △ ♅	15AUG85	05:00 PM	X	TR-TR	02 | 13 ♌59	05 | 13 ♐59R	08
♂———— □ ♅	03OCT85	01:35 AM	X	TR-TR	02 | 14 ♍41	06 | 14 ♐41	09
♂———— △ ♃	11NOV85	06:34 PM	X	TR-TR	01 | 09 ♎36	06 | 09 ♒36	11
♂———— ⚹ ♅	23NOV85	11:28 PM	X	TR-TR	02 | 17 ♎13	07 | 17 ♐13	09
♂———— □ ♃	20JAN86	08:39 PM	X	TR-TR	01 | 22 ♏44	08 | 22 ♒44	11
♂———— ☌ ♅	13MAR86	05:28 AM	X	TR-TR	02 | 22 ♐17	09 | 22 ♐17	09
♂———— ⚹ ♃	02MAY86	06:21 AM	X	TR-TR	01 | 15 ♑37	10 | 15 ♓37	12
♂———— ⚹ ♃	21JUN86	07:18 AM	X	TR-TR	01 | 22 ♑08R	10 | 22 ♓08	12
♂———— ⚹ ♃	12SEP86	08:54 AM	X	TR-TR	01 | 17 ♑38	10 | 17 ♓38R	12
♂———— ⚹ ♅	11NOV86	07:42 PM	X	TR-TR	02 | 20 ♒39	11 | 20 ♐39	09
♂———— ☌ ♃	18DEC86	05:12 PM	X	TR-TR	01 | 15 ♓39	12 | 15 ♓39	12
♂———— □ ♅	29DEC86	11:47 PM	X	TR-TR	02 | 23 ♓30	12 | 23 ♐30	09
♂———— △ ♅	14FEB87	09:11 AM	X	TR-TR	02 | 25 ♈50	01 | 25 ♐50	09
♂———— ⚹ ♃	24APR87	01:12 PM	X	TR-TR	01 | 12 ♊42	02 | 12 ♈42	01
♂———— ☍ ♅	14MAY87	05:35 PM	X	TR-TR	02 | 25 ♊58	03 | 25 ♐58R	09
♂———— □ ♃	29JUN87	10:37 PM	X	TR-TR	01 | 25 ♋49	04 | 25 ♈49	01
♂———— △ ♅	11AUG87	10:55 AM	X	TR-TR	02 | 22 ♌54	05 | 22 ♐54R	09
♂———— △ ♃	22AUG87	04:18 AM	X	TR-TR	01 | 29 ♌43	05 | 29 ♈43R	01
♂———— □ ♅	27SEP87	04:49 PM	X	TR-TR	02 | 23 ♍01	06 | 23 ♐01	09
♂———— ☍ ♃	11NOV87	04:25 AM	X	TR-TR	01 | 21 ♎42	07 | 21 ♈42R	01
♂———— ⚹ ♅	16NOV87	05:40 AM	X	TR-TR	02 | 24 ♎59	07 | 24 ♐59	09
♂———— △ ♃	16FEB88	02:11 AM	X	TR-TR	01 | 25 ♐52	09 | 25 ♈52	01
♂———— ☌ ♅	22FEB88	03:48 PM	X	TR-TR	02 | 00 ♑18	09 | 00 ♑18	09

MARS-JUP-URANUS,GEO EST

Aspect	DATE	TIME	EX	JOB	#	P1 POS.	HS	P2 POS.	HS
♂———————— □ ♃	21APR88	03:54 PM	X	TR-TR	01	10 ♒ 02	11	10 ♉ 02	01
♂———————— ⚹ ♅	22MAY88	08:37 AM	X	TR-TR	02	00 ♓ 09	11	00 ♑ 09R	09
♂———————— ⚹ ♃	08JUL88	01:46 PM	X	TR-TR	01	27 ♓ 35	12	27 ♉ 35	02
♂———————— □ ♅	09JUL88	10:46 PM	X	TR-TR	02	28 ♓ 16	12	28 ♐ 16R	09
♂———————— ⚹ ♃	24SEP88	09:07 PM	X	TR-TR	01	10 ♈ 01R	12	06 ♊ 08R	02
♂———————— ⚹ ♃	15NOV88	02:35 PM	X	TR-TR	01	08 ♈ 53R	12	02 ♊ 02R	02

Mars-Jupiter
Mars-Uranus

Natural Harmonic effecting the Stock Market and Treasury Bonds

EST.GEO MARS JUPITER

Mars-Jupiter

Natural Harmonic in the Stock Market

	DATE	TIME	EX	JO				
♂----------☍ ♃	25JAN79	11:43 AM	X	TR-TR 01	03 ♒ 54	02	03 ♌ 54R	08
♂----------△ ♃	05APR79	07:27 PM	X	TR-TR 01	29 ♓ 12	03	29 ♋ 12	08
♂----------□ ♃	20MAY79	02:07 PM	X	TR-TR 01	03 ♉ 28	05	03 ♌ 28	08
♂----------⚹ ♃	15JUL79	12:49 PM	X	TR-TR 01	13 ♊ 49	06	13 ♌ 49	08
♂----------☌ ♃	15DEC79	06:16 PM	X	TR-TR 01	10 ♍ 04	09	10 ♍ 04	09
♂----------☌ ♃	27FEB80	03:18 AM	X	TR-TR 01	04 ♍ 57R	09	04 ♍ 57R	09
♂----------☌ ♃	05MAY80	05:08 AM	X	TR-TR 01	00 ♍ 22	09	00 ♍ 22	09
♂----------⚹ ♃	05OCT80	09:15 PM	X	TR-TR 01	25 ♏ 38	12	25 ♍ 38	09
♂----------□ ♃	29NOV80	01:22 PM	X	TR-TR 01	05 ♑ 51	01	05 ♎ 51	09
♂----------△ ♃	12JAN81	03:38 PM	X	TR-TR 01	10 ♒ 10	02	10 ♎ 10	10
♂----------☍ ♃	24MAR81	06:25 AM	X	TR-TR 01	05 ♈ 43	03	05 ♎ 43R	09
♂----------△ ♃	05JUN81	07:46 PM	X	TR-TR 01	00 ♊ 34	06	00 ♎ 34	09
♂----------□ ♃	25JUL81	10:01 PM	X	TR-TR 01	05 ♋ 13	07	05 ♎ 13	09
♂----------⚹ ♃	30SEP81	11:59 AM	X	TR-TR 01	17 ♌ 50	09	17 ♎ 50	10
♂----------☌ ♃	08AUG82	07:55 AM	X	TR-TR 01	02 ♏ 55	11	02 ♏ 55	11
♂----------⚹ ♃	04DEC82	04:17 AM	X	TR-TR 01	25 ♑ 26	02	25 ♏ 26	12
♂----------□ ♃	24JAN83	04:53 AM	X	TR-TR 01	05 ♓ 23	03	05 ♐ 23	12
♂----------△ ♃	10MAR83	10:25 AM	X	TR-TR 01	10 ♈ 27	04	10 ♐ 27	12
♂----------☍ ♃	25MAY83	03:55 PM	X	TR-TR 01	06 ♊ 19	06	06 ♐ 19R	12
♂----------△ ♃	15AUG83	09:29 PM	X	TR-TR 01	01 ♌ 33	08	01 ♐ 33	12
♂----------□ ♃	14OCT83	09:40 AM	X	TR-TR 01	09 ♍ 01	09	09 ♐ 01	12
♂----------⚹ ♃	04JAN84	08:01 PM	X	TR-TR 01	26 ♎ 49	10	26 ♐ 49	01
♂----------☌ ♃	13OCT84	09:48 PM	X	TR-TR 01	06 ♑ 11	01	06 ♑ 11	01
♂----------⚹ ♃	31JAN85	06:50 PM	X	TR-TR 01	28 ♓ 42	03	28 ♑ 42	02
♂----------□ ♃	29MAR85	03:53 PM	X	TR-TR 01	10 ♉ 35	05	10 ♒ 35	02
♂----------△ ♃	20MAY85	07:33 AM	X	TR-TR 01	16 ♊ 35	07	16 ♒ 35	02
♂----------☍ ♃	11AUG85	06:04 AM	X	TR-TR 01	11 ♌ 08	08	11 ♒ 08R	02
♂----------△ ♃	11NOV85	06:33 PM	X	TR-TR 01	09 ♎ 36	10	09 ♒ 36	02
♂----------□ ♃	20JAN86	08:40 PM	X	TR-TR 01	22 ♏ 44	12	22 ♒ 44	03
♂----------⚹ ♃	02MAY86	06:36 AM	X	TR-TR 01	15 ♑ 38	02	15 ♓ 38	03
♂----------⚹ ♃	21JUN86	06:40 AM	X	TR-TR 01	22 ♑ 08R	02	22 ♓ 08	03
♂----------⚹ ♃	12SEP86	08:47 AM	X	TR-TR 01	17 ♑ 38	02	17 ♓ 38R	03
♂----------☌ ♃	18DEC86	05:14 PM	X	TR-TR 01	15 ♓ 39	03	15 ♓ 39	03
♂----------⚹ ♃	24APR87	01:12 PM	X	TR-TR 01	12 ♊ 42	06	12 ♈ 42	04
♂----------□ ♃	29JUN87	10:35 PM	X	TR-TR 01	25 ♋ 49	08	25 ♈ 49	04
♂----------△ ♃	22AUG87	04:20 AM	X	TR-TR 01	29 ♌ 43	09	29 ♈ 43R	04
♂----------☍ ♃	11NOV87	04:25 AM	X	TR-TR 01	21 ♎ 42	10	21 ♈ 42R	04
♂----------△ ♃	16FEB88	02:14 AM	X	TR-TR 01	25 ♐ 52	01	25 ♈ 52	04
♂----------□ ♃	21APR88	03:54 PM	X	TR-TR 01	10 ♒ 02	02	10 ♉ 02	05
♂----------⚹ ♃	08JUL88	01:57 PM	X	TR-TR 01	27 ♓ 36	03	27 ♉ 36	06
♂----------⚹ ♃	24SEP88	09:19 PM	X	TR-TR 01	22 ♓ 06R	03	06 ♊ 08R	06
♂----------⚹ ♃	15NOV88	02:42 PM	X	TR-TR 01	27 ♓ 49	03	02 ♊ 02R	06

MARS/URANUS,GEO EST

Mars-Uranus

Natural Harmonic in the Foreign Currency and Stock Market.

	DATE	TIME	E X	JC		
♂ ——— ⚹ ♅	25JUN80	03:51 PM	X	TR-TR 01	21 ♍ 59 03	21 ♏ 59R 04
♂ ——— ☌ ♅	02OCT80	09:26 AM	X	TR-TR 01	23 ♏ 11 04	23 ♏ 11 04
♂ ——— ⚹ ♅	28DEC80	11:40 AM	X	TR-TR 01	28 ♑ 15 07	28 ♏ 15 05
♂ ——— □ ♅	06FEB81	11:41 AM	X	TR-TR 01	29 ♒ 48 08	29 ♏ 48 05
♂ ——— △ ♅	16MAR81	11:08 PM	X	TR-TR 01	00 ♈ 03 09	00 ♐ 03R 05
♂ ——— ☍ ♅	01JUN81	02:11 PM	X	TR-TR 01	27 ♉ 33 11	27 ♏ 33R 05
♂ ——— △ ♅	27AUG81	00:59 AM	X	TR-TR 01	26 ♋ 17 01	26 ♏ 17 05
♂ ——— □ ♅	17OCT81	10:30 PM	X	TR-TR 01	28 ♌ 17 02	28 ♏ 17 05
♂ ——— ⚹ ♅	20DEC81	05:52 AM	X	TR-TR 01	02 ♎ 03 03	02 ♐ 03 05
♂ ——— ⚹ ♅	18APR82	01:04 AM	X	TR-TR 01	03 ♎ 59R 03	03 ♐ 59R 05
♂ ——— ⚹ ♅	29MAY82	11:17 PM	X	TR-TR 01	02 ♎ 22 03	02 ♐ 22R 05
♂ ——— ☌ ♅	21SEP82	08:49 PM	X	TR-TR 01	01 ♐ 23 05	01 ♐ 23 05
♂ ——— ⚹ ♅	17DEC82	10:26 PM	X	TR-TR 01	06 ♒ 09 07	06 ♐ 09 05
♂ ——— □ ♅	27JAN83	07:04 PM	X	TR-TR 01	08 ♓ 12 08	08 ♐ 12 05
♂ ——— △ ♅	08MAR83	03:38 PM	X	TR-TR 01	09 ♈ 06 10	09 ♐ 06 05
♂ ——— ☍ ♅	26MAY83	09:40 PM	X	TR-TR 01	07 ♊ 11 11	07 ♐ 11R 05
♂ ——— △ ♅	21AUG83	09:32 AM	X	TR-TR 01	05 ♌ 06 01	05 ♐ 06 05
♂ ——— □ ♅	10OCT83	03:52 AM	X	TR-TR 01	06 ♍ 25 02	06 ♐ 25 05
♂ ——— ⚹ ♅	04DEC83	01:59 PM	X	TR-TR 01	09 ♎ 31 04	09 ♐ 31 05
♂ ——— ☌ ♅	03SEP84	03:58 PM	X	TR-TR 01	09 ♐ 39 05	09 ♐ 39 05
♂ ——— ⚹ ♅	03DEC84	04:08 PM	X	TR-TR 01	13 ♒ 41 07	13 ♐ 41 05
♂ ——— □ ♅	15JAN85	05:25 AM	X	TR-TR 01	16 ♓ 09 09	16 ♐ 09 05
♂ ——— △ ♅	26FEB85	06:05 AM	X	TR-TR 01	17 ♈ 43 10	17 ♐ 43 05
♂ ——— ☍ ♅	20MAY85	10:42 AM	X	TR-TR 01	16 ♊ 41 11	16 ♐ 41R 05
♂ ——— △ ♅	15AUG85	05:02 PM	X	TR-TR 01	13 ♌ 59 01	13 ♐ 59R 05
♂ ——— □ ♅	03OCT85	01:35 AM	X	TR-TR 01	14 ♍ 41 03	14 ♐ 41 05
♂ ——— ⚹ ♅	23NOV85	11:28 PM	X	TR-TR 01	17 ♎ 13 04	17 ♐ 13 05
♂ ——— ☌ ♅	13MAR86	05:29 AM	X	TR-TR 01	22 ♐ 17 05	22 ♐ 17 05
♂ ——— ⚹ ♅	11NOV86	07:42 PM	X	TR-TR 01	20 ♒ 39 08	20 ♐ 39 05
♂ ——— □ ♅	29DEC86	11:44 PM	X	TR-TR 01	23 ♓ 30 09	23 ♐ 30 05
♂ ——— △ ♅	14FEB87	09:13 AM	X	TR-TR 01	25 ♈ 50 10	25 ♐ 50 05
♂ ——— ☍ ♅	14MAY87	05:34 PM	X	TR-TR 01	25 ♊ 58 11	25 ♐ 58R 05
♂ ——— △ ♅	11AUG87	10:55 AM	X	TR-TR 01	22 ♌ 54 02	22 ♐ 54R 05
♂ ——— □ ♅	27SEP87	04:50 PM	X	TR-TR 01	23 ♍ 01 03	23 ♐ 01 05
♂ ——— ⚹ ♅	16NOV87	05:39 AM	X	TR-TR 01	24 ♎ 59 04	24 ♐ 59 05
♂ ——— ☌ ♅	22FEB88	03:48 PM	X	TR-TR 01	00 ♑ 18 06	00 ♑ 18 06
♂ ——— ⚹ ♅	22MAY88	08:37 AM	X	TR-TR 01	00 ♓ 09 08	00 ♑ 09R 06
♂ ——— □ ♅	09JUL88	10:52 PM	X	TR-TR 01	28 ♓ 16 09	28 ♐ 16R 05
♂ ——— △ ♅	24JAN89	04:57 PM	X	TR-TR 01	03 ♉ 07 10	03 ♑ 07 06
♂ ——— ☍ ♅	07MAY89	02:07 AM	X	TR-TR 01	05 ♋ 01 12	05 ♑ 01R 06
♂ ——— △ ♅	06AUG89	05:48 AM	X	TR-TR 01	01 ♍ 49 02	01 ♑ 49R 06
♂ ——— □ ♅	21SEP89	01:23 PM	X	TR-TR 01	01 ♎ 24 03	01 ♑ 24 06
♂ ——— ⚹ ♅	08NOV89	03:37 AM	X	TR-TR 01	02 ♏ 46 04	02 ♑ 46 06
♂ ——— ☌ ♅	09FEB90	09:22 AM	X	TR-TR 01	07 ♑ 57 06	07 ♑ 57 06
♂ ——— ⚹ ♅	03MAY90	07:56 AM	X	TR-TR 01	09 ♓ 26 08	09 ♑ 26R 06
♂ ——— □ ♅	11JUN90	12:03 PM	X	TR-TR 01	08 ♈ 19 10	08 ♑ 19R 06
♂ ——— △ ♅	22JUL90	11:32 AM	X	TR-TR 01	06 ♉ 42 10	06 ♑ 42R 06

JUP/SAT/URANUS,GEO EST

Jupiter-Saturn
Jupiter-Uranus

Natural Harmonic in the Stock Market

Aspect	DATE	TIME	EX	JOB					
♃ ☌ ♅	18FEB83	05:41 PM	X	TR-TR					
♃ ☌ ♅	14MAY83	03:43 PM	X	TR-TR					
♃ ☌ ♅	25SEP83	08:55 AM	X	TR-TR					
♃ ⚹ ♄	05MAY84	10:43 AM	X	TR-TR	01	12 ♑ 54R	11	12 ♏ 54R	08
♃ ⚹ ♄	08JUN84	06:10 AM	X	TR-TR	01	10 ♑ 39R	11	10 ♏ 39R	08
♃ ⚹ ♄	22JAN85	12:24 PM	X	TR-TR	01	26 ♑ 32	11	26 ♏ 32	09
♃ ⚹ ♅	21MAY85	10:05 AM	X	TR-TR	01	16 ♒ 39	12	16 ♐ 39R	10
♃ ⚹ ♅	14JUL85	04:30 PM	X	TR-TR	01	14 ♒ 34R	12	14 ♐ 34R	10
♃ ⚹ ♅	08JAN86	01:12 PM	X	TR-TR	01	19 ♒ 56	12	19 ♐ 56	10
♃ □ ♄	02APR86	07:48 AM	X	TR-TR	01	09 ♓ 32	01	09 ♐ 32R	09
♃ □ ♅	04JUN86	07:08 PM	X	TR-TR	01	20 ♓ 39	01	20 ♐ 39R	10
♃ □ ♅	06SEP86	02:57 PM	X	TR-TR	01	18 ♓ 24R	01	18 ♐ 24	10
♃ □ ♅	12FEB87	02:55 AM	X	TR-TR	01	25 ♓ 45	01	25 ♐ 45	10
♃ △ ♄	23MAY87	07:25 AM	X	TR-TR	01	19 ♈ 05	02	19 ♐ 05R	10
♃ △ ♅	21JUN87	11:46 AM	X	TR-TR	01	24 ♈ 31	02	24 ♐ 31R	10
♃ △ ♅	24OCT87	08:11 AM	X	TR-TR	01	23 ♈ 52R	02	23 ♐ 52	10
♃ △ ♄	21NOV87	08:49 AM	X	TR-TR	01	20 ♈ 44R	02	20 ♐ 44	10
♄ ☌ ♅	12FEB88	07:47 PM	X	TR-TR	01	29 ♐ 55	10	29 ♐ 55	10
♃ △ ♅	12MAR88	07:12 AM	X	TR-TR	01	00 ♉ 49	02	00 ♑ 49	10
♃ △ ♄	18MAR88	05:53 AM	X	TR-TR	01	02 ♉ 06	02	02 ♑ 06	10
♄ ☌ ♅	26JUN88	12:20 PM	X	TR-TR	01	28 ♐ 47R	10	28 ♐ 47R	10
♄ ☌ ♅	18OCT88	08:18 AM	X	TR-TR	01	27 ♐ 49	10	27 ♐ 49	10
♃ ☍ ♅	08AUG89	02:18 PM	X	TR-TR	01	01 ♋ 45	04	01 ♑ 45R	10
♃ ☍ ♄	10SEP89	11:16 AM	X	TR-TR	01	07 ♋ 18	05	07 ♑ 18R	11
♃ ☍ ♄	14NOV89	01:36 AM	X	TR-TR	01	10 ♋ 26R	05	10 ♑ 26	11
♃ ☍ ♅	29DEC89	00:54 AM	X	TR-TR	01	05 ♋ 35R	05	05 ♑ 35	11
♃ ☍ ♅	13MAY90	02:28 PM	X	TR-TR	01	09 ♋ 13	05	09 ♑ 13R	11
♃ ☍ ♄	13JUL90	07:52 AM	X	TR-TR	01	22 ♋ 07	05	22 ♑ 07R	11
♃ ☍ ♄	15MAR91	08:31 PM	X	TR-TR	01	03 ♌ 53R	06	03 ♒ 53	12
♃ ☍ ♄	16MAY91	08:21 PM	X	TR-TR	01	06 ♌ 51	06	06 ♒ 51	12
♃ △ ♅	11NOV91	05:42 AM	X	TR-TR	01	11 ♍ 00	07	11 ♑ 00	11
♃ △ ♅	12JAN92	08:16 AM	X	TR-TR	01	14 ♍ 22R	07	14 ♑ 22	11
♃ △ ♅	31JUL92	02:46 PM	X	TR-TR	01	15 ♍ 06	07	15 ♑ 06R	11

Jupiter-Saturn
Jupiter-Uranus

Natural Harmonic in the Stock Market

Aspect	DATE	TIME	EX	JOB					
♃ □ ♅	16FEB24	01:07 PM	X	TR-TR					
♃ □ ♅	17APR24	01:17 PM	X	TR-TR	01	19 ♐ 41R	10	19 ♓ 41	01
♃ □ ♅	23OCT24	03:45 AM	X	TR-TR	01	18 ♐ 05	10	18 ♓ 05R	01
♃ ⚹ ♄	21FEB25	11:32 PM	X	TR-TR	01	14 ♑ 19	11	14 ♏ 19R	08
♃ ⚹ ♅	27NOV25	11:48 PM	X	TR-TR	01	21 ♑ 34	11	21 ♓ 34R	01
♄ △ ♅	20DEC25	08:07 PM	X	TR-TR	01	21 ♏ 43	09	21 ♓ 43	01
♄ △ ♅	23MAR26	12:30 PM	X	TR-TR	01	25 ♏ 49R	09	25 ♓ 49	01
♃ □ ♄	29APR26	11:40 PM	X	TR-TR	01	23 ♒ 49	12	23 ♏ 49R	09
♃ □ ♄	29AUG26	09:29 AM	X	TR-TR	01	20 ♒ 27R	12	20 ♏ 27	09
♄ △ ♅	30OCT26	05:42 AM	X	TR-TR	01	26 ♏ 03	09	26 ♓ 03R	01
♃ □ ♄	17FEB27	07:25 AM	X	TR-TR	01	06 ♓ 59	01	06 ♐ 59	09
♄ △ ♅	12JUN27	02:19 PM	X	TR-TR	01	03 ♐ 08R	09	03 ♈ 08	01
♃ △ ♄	26JUN27	04:14 AM	X	TR-TR	01	02 ♈ 16	01	02 ♐ 16R	09
♃ ☌ ♅	15JUL27	04:09 PM	X	TR-TR	01	03 ♈ 24	01	03 ♈ 24R	01
♃ ☌ ♅	11AUG27	06:20 AM	X	TR-TR	01	03 ♈ 00R	01	03 ♈ 00R	01
♃ △ ♄	29AUG27	09:51 AM	X	TR-TR	01	01 ♈ 29R	01	01 ♐ 29	09
♄ △ ♅	10SEP27	03:38 AM	X	TR-TR	01	02 ♐ 02	09	02 ♈ 02R	01
♃ ☌ ♅	25JAN28	01:46 AM	X	TR-TR	01	00 ♈ 24	01	00 ♈ 24	01
♃ △ ♄	15APR28	11:23 PM	X	TR-TR	01	18 ♈ 51	02	18 ♐ 51R	10
♃ ⚹ ♅	07AUG29	04:38 AM	X	TR-TR	01	11 ♊ 12	03	11 ♈ 12R	02
♃ ⚹ ♅	03JAN30	10:32 PM	X	TR-TR	01	07 ♊ 35R	03	07 ♈ 35	01
♄ □ ♅	22FEB30	03:09 AM	X	TR-TR	01	09 ♑ 15	11	09 ♈ 15	01
♃ ⚹ ♅	27MAR30	01:52 PM	X	TR-TR	01	11 ♊ 03	03	11 ♈ 03	02
♄ □ ♅	09APR30	00:49 AM	X	TR-TR	01	11 ♑ 45	11	11 ♈ 45	02
♃ ☍ ♄	26JUL30	10:54 PM	X	TR-TR	01	06 ♋ 46	05	06 ♑ 46R	11
♃ □ ♅	05SEP30	03:08 AM	X	TR-TR	01	14 ♋ 35	05	14 ♈ 35R	02
♄ □ ♅	12DEC30	01:45 PM	X	TR-TR	01	11 ♑ 28	11	11 ♈ 28R	02
♃ ☍ ♄	10JAN31	07:02 PM	X	TR-TR	01	14 ♋ 53R	05	14 ♑ 53	11
♃ □ ♅	01FEB31	10:16 PM	X	TR-TR	01	12 ♋ 12R	05	12 ♈ 12	02
♃ □ ♅	17MAY31	04:28 PM	X	TR-TR	01	17 ♋ 35	05	17 ♈ 35	02
♃ ☍ ♄	10JUN31	03:12 PM	X	TR-TR	01	22 ♋ 09	05	22 ♑ 09R	11
♄ □ ♅	21JUL31	03:33 AM	X	TR-TR	01	19 ♑ 22R	11	19 ♈ 22	02
♃ △ ♅	10OCT31	03:12 PM	X	TR-TR	01	17 ♌ 25	06	17 ♈ 25R	02
♄ □ ♅	16OCT31	07:36 PM	X	TR-TR	01	17 ♑ 10	11	17 ♈ 10R	02
♃ △ ♅	15FEB32	03:15 PM	X	TR-TR	01	16 ♌ 34R	06	16 ♈ 34	02
♃ △ ♅	09JUL32	09:34 AM	X	TR-TR	01	23 ♌ 14	06	23 ♈ 14	02
♃ △ ♄	25OCT33	08:36 PM	X	TR-TR	01	09 ♎ 50	07	09 ♒ 50	12

EST.GEO COMBUST MERC 13

Mercury Combust

Natural Harmonic effecting the grain and soybean market.

	DATE	TIME	E X	JOB	#	POS.		POS.	
☿ ---- ☌ ☉	21SEP86	10:23 PM	L	TR-TR	01	11♎50	10	28♍50	09
☿ ---- ☌ ☉	06NOV86	09:26 PM	E	TR-TR	01	27♏23R	12	14♏23	11
☿ ---- ☌ ☉	12NOV86	11:17 PM	X	TR-TR	01	20♏29R	11	20♏29	11
☿ ---- ☌ ☉	19NOV86	07:22 AM	L	TR-TR	01	13♏52R	11	26♏52	12
☿ ---- ☌ ☉	19DEC86	11:25 PM	E	TR-TR	01	14♐59	12	27♐59	01
☿ ---- ☌ ☉	12JAN87	12:07 PM	X	TR-TR	01	21♑57	02	21♑57	02
☿ ---- ☌ ☉	31JAN87	10:09 AM	L	TR-TR	01	24♒12	03	11♒12	02
☿ ---- ☌ ☉	20FEB87	05:15 AM	E	TR-TR	01	14♓14R	03	01♓14	03
☿ ---- ☌ ☉	27FEB87	12:43 PM	X	TR-TR	01	08♓36R	03	08♓36	03
☿ ---- ☌ ☉	06MAR87	04:05 AM	L	TR-TR	01	02♓15R	03	15♓15	03
☿ ---- ☌ ☉	25APR87	04:06 AM	E	TR-TR	01	21♈38	04	04♉38	05
☿ ---- ☌ ☉	07MAY87	05:25 AM	X	TR-TR	01	16♉21	05	16♉21	05
☿ ---- ☌ ☉	18MAY87	11:11 AM	L	TR-TR	01	10♊12	06	27♉12	06
☿ ---- ☌ ☉	25JUN87	01:26 AM	E	TR-TR	01	16♋11R	08	03♋11	07
☿ ---- ☌ ☉	03JUL87	11:04 PM	X	TR-TR	01	11♋41R	07	11♋41	07
☿ ---- ☌ ☉	13JUL87	06:26 AM	L	TR-TR	01	07♋33R	07	20♋33	08
☿ ---- ☌ ☉	07AUG87	03:13 PM	E	TR-TR	01	01♌47	08	14♌47	08
☿ ---- ☌ ☉	20AUG87	00:30 AM	X	TR-TR	01	26♌41	09	26♌41	09
☿ ---- ☌ ☉	03SEP87	03:25 PM	L	TR-TR	01	23♍48	09	10♍48	09
☿ ---- ☌ ☉	21OCT87	10:08 PM	E	TR-TR	01	11♏11R	11	28♎11	10
☿ ---- ☌ ☉	28OCT87	02:51 AM	X	TR-TR	01	04♏21R	11	04♏21	11
☿ ---- ☌ ☉	03NOV87	05:18 PM	L	TR-TR	01	27♎57R	10	10♏57	11
☿ ---- ☌ ☉	29NOV87	07:40 AM	E	TR-TR	01	23♏45	12	06♐45	12
☿ ---- ☌ ☉	23DEC87	02:53 AM	X	TR-TR	01	00♑56	01	00♑56	01
☿ ---- ☌ ☉	13JAN88	11:41 AM	L	TR-TR	01	05♒43	02	22♑43	02
☿ ---- ☌ ☉	04FEB88	02:06 AM	E	TR-TR	01	27♒41R	03	14♒41	02
☿ ---- ☌ ☉	10FEB88	11:25 PM	X	TR-TR	01	21♒39R	03	21♒39	03
☿ ---- ☌ ☉	17FEB88	07:04 AM	L	TR-TR	01	15♒03R	02	28♒03	03
☿ ---- ☌ ☉	07APR88	01:38 PM	E	TR-TR	01	05♈09	03	18♈09	04
☿ ---- ☌ ☉	20APR88	10:14 AM	X	TR-TR	01	00♉45	05	00♉45	05
☿ ---- ☌ ☉	02MAY88	00:03 AM	L	TR-TR	01	25♉01	06	12♉01	05
☿ ---- ☌ ☉	03JUN88	03:52 PM	E	TR-TR	01	26♊28R	07	13♊28	06
☿ ---- ☌ ☉	12JUN88	10:56 PM	X	TR-TR	01	22♊22R	07	22♊22	07
☿ ---- ☌ ☉	22JUN88	09:11 AM	L	TR-TR	01	18♊22R	07	01♋22	07
☿ ---- ☌ ☉	22JUL88	04:32 AM	E	TR-TR	01	16♋47	08	29♋47	08
☿ ---- ☌ ☉	02AUG88	10:30 PM	X	TR-TR	01	11♌01	08	11♌01	08
☿ ---- ☌ ☉	16AUG88	05:24 AM	L	TR-TR	01	06♍46	09	23♌46	09
☿ ---- ☌ ☉	04OCT88	04:11 PM	E	TR-TR	01	24♎51R	10	11♎51	10
☿ ---- ☌ ☉	11OCT88	01:34 AM	X	TR-TR	01	18♎10R	10	18♎10	10
☿ ---- ☌ ☉	17OCT88	11:48 PM	L	TR-TR	01	12♎02R	10	25♎02	10
☿ ---- ☌ ☉	08NOV88	09:12 PM	E	TR-TR	01	03♏54	11	16♏54	11
☿ ---- ☌ ☉	01DEC88	04:24 AM	X	TR-TR	01	09♐25	12	09♐25	12
☿ ---- ☌ ☉	24DEC88	11:44 AM	L	TR-TR	01	16♑06	02	03♑06	01
☿ ---- ☌ ☉	18JAN89	06:01 AM	E	TR-TR	01	11♒20R	02	28♑20	02
☿ ---- ☌ ☉	24JAN89	07:12 PM	X	TR-TR	01	05♒00R	02	05♒00	02
☿ ---- ☌ ☉	30JAN89	09:49 PM	L	TR-TR	01	28♑13R	02	11♒13	02
☿ ---- ☌ ☉	21MAR89	08:29 AM	E	TR-TR	01	17♓55	03	00♈55	03
☿ ---- ☌ ☉	04APR89	08:37 AM	X	TR-TR	01	14♈45	04	14♈45	04
☿ ---- ☌ ☉	16APR89	11:48 AM	L	TR-TR	01	09♉40	05	26♈40	04
☿ ---- ☌ ☉	14MAY89	07:39 AM	E	TR-TR	01	06♊41R	06	23♉41	06

:ST.GEO COMBUST MERC 13

Mercury Combust

Natural Harmonic effecting the grain and soybean market.

	DATE	TIME	E X	JOB		
☿----☌ ☉	06JAN84	02:18 AM	L	TR-TR 01	02♑09R 01	15♑09 02
☿----☌ ☉	20FEB84	07:20 PM	E	TR-TR 01	18♒33 03	01♓33 03
☿----☌ ☉	08MAR84	12:33 PM	X	TR-TR 01	18♓20 03	18♓20 03
☿----☌ ☉	22MAR84	01:46 AM	L	TR-TR 01	14♈50 04	01♈50 03
☿----☌ ☉	13APR84	03:05 AM	E	TR-TR 01	06♉35R 05	23♈35 04
☿----☌ ☉	21APR84	11:51 PM	X	TR-TR 01	02♉15R 05	02♉15 05
☿----☌ ☉	30APR84	06:54 AM	L	TR-TR 01	27♈19R 04	10♉19 05
☿----☌ ☉	11JUN84	06:32 PM	E	TR-TR 01	08♊11 06	21♊11 07
☿----☌ ☉	22JUN84	09:25 PM	X	TR-TR 01	01♋48 07	01♋48 07
☿----☌ ☉	04JUL84	07:45 AM	L	TR-TR 01	25♋42 08	12♋42 08
☿----☌ ☉	21AUG84	02:44 AM	E	TR-TR 01	11♍25R 09	28♌25 09
☿----☌ ☉	28AUG84	09:33 AM	X	TR-TR 01	05♍27R 09	05♍27 09
☿----☌ ☉	05SEP84	09:47 AM	L	TR-TR 01	00♍12R 09	13♍12 09
☿----☌ ☉	24SEP84	05:36 AM	E	TR-TR 01	18♍33 09	01♎33 09
☿----☌ ☉	10OCT84	12:37 PM	X	TR-TR 01	17♎35 10	17♎35 10
☿----☌ ☉	31OCT84	04:45 PM	L	TR-TR 01	21♏39 11	08♏39 11
☿----☌ ☉	08DEC84	07:39 AM	E	TR-TR 01	29♐37R 01	16♐37 01
☿----☌ ☉	14DEC84	09:31 AM	X	TR-TR 01	22♐48R 01	22♐48 01
☿----☌ ☉	20DEC84	10:02 AM	L	TR-TR 01	15♐55R 01	28♐55 01
☿----☌ ☉	31JAN85	01:15 AM	E	TR-TR 01	28♑19 02	11♒19 02
☿----☌ ☉	19FEB85	02:50 AM	X	TR-TR 01	00♓37 03	00♓37 03
☿----☌ ☉	06MAR85	00:23 AM	L	TR-TR 01	28♓35 03	15♓35 03
☿----☌ ☉	26MAR85	00:54 AM	E	TR-TR 01	18♈31R 04	05♈31 03
☿----☌ ☉	03APR85	09:06 AM	X	TR-TR 01	13♈46R 04	13♈46 04
☿----☌ ☉	11APR85	00:36 AM	L	TR-TR 01	08♈17R 03	21♈17 04
☿----☌ ☉	27MAY85	03:51 AM	E	TR-TR 01	23♉01 06	06♊01 06
☿----☌ ☉	07JUN85	09:11 AM	X	TR-TR 01	16♊46 07	16♊46 07
☿----☌ ☉	18JUN85	01:09 PM	L	TR-TR 01	10♋26 07	27♊26 07
☿----☌ ☉	02AUG85	10:21 PM	E	TR-TR 01	23♌44R 09	10♌44 08
☿----☌ ☉	10AUG85	05:09 PM	X	TR-TR 01	18♌12R 09	18♌12 09
☿----☌ ☉	19AUG85	04:55 AM	L	TR-TR 01	13♌22R 08	26♌22 09
☿----☌ ☉	08SEP85	00:48 AM	E	TR-TR 01	02♍31 09	15♍31 09
☿----☌ ☉	22SEP85	02:50 PM	X	TR-TR 01	29♍45 09	29♍45 09
☿----☌ ☉	11OCT85	06:57 AM	L	TR-TR 01	01♏07 11	18♎07 10
☿----☌ ☉	22NOV85	04:07 PM	E	TR-TR 01	13♐31R 12	00♐31 12
☿----☌ ☉	28NOV85	04:58 PM	X	TR-TR 01	06♐37R 12	06♐37 12
☿----☌ ☉	04DEC85	08:15 PM	L	TR-TR 01	29♏50R 12	12♐50 12
☿----☌ ☉	10JAN86	05:24 AM	E	TR-TR 01	06♑53 01	19♑53 02
☿----☌ ☉	31JAN86	08:12 PM	X	TR-TR 01	11♒52 02	11♒52 02
☿----☌ ☉	17FEB86	12:36 PM	L	TR-TR 01	11♓46 03	28♒46 03
☿----☌ ☉	08MAR86	07:18 PM	E	TR-TR 01	01♈08R 03	18♓08 03
☿----☌ ☉	16MAR86	02:36 PM	X	TR-TR 01	27♈41 04	27♈41 04
☿----☌ ☉	23MAR86	04:35 PM	L	TR-TR 01	19♓57R 03	02♈57 03
☿----☌ ☉	11MAY86	07:48 AM	E	TR-TR 01	07♉32 05	20♉32 05
☿----☌ ☉	22MAY86	08:25 PM	X	TR-TR 01	01♊38 06	01♊38 06
☿----☌ ☉	02JUN86	10:55 PM	L	TR-TR 01	25♊18 07	12♊18 06
☿----☌ ☉	14JUL86	09:51 PM	E	TR-TR 01	05♌21R 08	22♋21 08
☿----☌ ☉	23JUL86	06:11 AM	X	TR-TR 01	00♌19R 08	00♌19 08
☿----☌ ☉	01AUG86	05:01 AM	L	TR-TR 01	25♋52R 08	08♌52 08
☿----☌ ☉	23AUG86	05:07 AM	E	TR-TR 01	16♌59 08	29♌59 09
☿----☌ ☉	05SEP86	12:33 PM	X	TR-TR 01	12♍51 09	12♍51 09

ƎST,GEO COMBUST MERC 13

Mercury Combust

Natural Harmonic effecting the grain and soybean market.

	DATE	TIME	E X	JOB		
☿ ---- ☌ ☉	23MAY89	04:37 PM	X	TR-TR 01	02 ♊ 43R 06	02 ♊ 43 06
☿ ---- ☌ ☉	01JUN89	09:19 PM	L	TR-TR 01	28 ♉ 32R 06	11 ♊ 32 06
☿ ---- ☌ ☉	06JUL89	06:59 PM	E	TR-TR 01	01 ♋ 52 07	14 ♋ 52 08
☿ ---- ☌ ☉	18JUL89	03:18 AM	X	TR-TR 01	25 ♋ 41 08	25 ♋ 41 08
☿ ---- ☌ ☉	30JUL89	11:16 AM	L	TR-TR 01	20 ♌ 28 09	07 ♌ 28 08
☿ ---- ☌ ☉	18SEP89	01:10 AM	E	TR-TR 01	08 ♎ 19R 09	25 ♍ 19 09
☿ ---- ☌ ☉	24SEP89	05:11 PM	X	TR-TR 01	01 ♎ 50R 09	01 ♎ 50 09
☿ ---- ☌ ☉	02OCT89	00:43 AM	L	TR-TR 01	26 ♍ 01R 09	09 ♎ 01 10
☿ ---- ☌ ☉	21OCT89	04:33 PM	E	TR-TR 01	15 ♎ 28 10	28 ♎ 28 10
☿ ---- ☌ ☉	10NOV89	01:57 PM	X	TR-TR 01	18 ♏ 22 11	18 ♏ 22 11
☿ ---- ☌ ☉	04DEC89	08:22 AM	L	TR-TR 01	25 ♐ 23 01	12 ♐ 23 12

NEPTUNE, GEO EST VENUS

T. Bonds

	DATE	TIME	EX	JOB	#	P1 POS.	HS	P2 POS.	HS
♇ ------- ☌ ♆	25JAN84	06:24 PM	X	TR-TR	01	00 ♑ 14	10	00 ♑ 14	10
♇ ------- ⚹ ♆	15MAR84	09:35 AM	X	TR-TR	01	01 ♓ 20	12	01 ♑ 20	10
♇ ------- □ ♆	08APR84	06:48 PM	X	TR-TR	01	01 ♈ 25	01	01 ♑ 25R	10
♇ ------- △ ♆	02MAY84	10:57 PM	X	TR-TR	01	01 ♉ 11	02	01 ♑ 11R	10
♇ ------- ☍ ♆	19JUN84	09:26 PM	X	TR-TR	01	00 ♋ 05	04	00 ♑ 05R	10
♇ ------- △ ♆	06AUG84	06:17 PM	X	TR-TR	01	28 ♌ 57	06	28 ♐ 57R	10
♇ ------- □ ♆	30AUG84	10:24 PM	X	TR-TR	01	28 ♍ 41	07	28 ♐ 41R	10
♇ ------- ⚹ ♆	24SEP84	09:56 AM	X	TR-TR	01	28 ♎ 43	08	28 ♐ 43	10
♇ ------- ☌ ♆	13NOV84	01:56 PM	X	TR-TR	01	29 ♐ 45	10	29 ♐ 45	10
♇ ------- ⚹ ♆	05JAN85	01:31 PM	X	TR-TR	01	01 ♓ 40	12	01 ♑ 40	10
♇ ------- □ ♆	05FEB85	03:04 AM	X	TR-TR	01	02 ♈ 42	01	02 ♑ 42	10
♇ ------- △ ♆	09JUN85	00:36 AM	X	TR-TR	01	02 ♉ 38	02	02 ♑ 38R	10
♇ ------- ☍ ♆	03AUG85	06:32 AM	X	TR-TR	01	01 ♋ 15	04	01 ♑ 15R	10
♇ ------- △ ♆	22SEP85	03:16 PM	X	TR-TR	01	00 ♍ 53	06	00 ♑ 53	10
♇ ------- □ ♆	17OCT85	07:03 AM	X	TR-TR	01	01 ♎ 11	07	01 ♑ 11	10
♇ ------- ⚹ ♆	10NOV85	08:23 PM	X	TR-TR	01	01 ♏ 47	08	01 ♑ 47	10
♇ ------- ☌ ♆	29DEC85	11:27 PM	X	TR-TR	01	03 ♑ 31	10	03 ♑ 31	10
♇ ------- ⚹ ♆	17FEB86	00:58 AM	X	TR-TR	01	05 ♓ 09	12	05 ♑ 09	10
♇ ------- □ ♆	13MAR86	11:21 AM	X	TR-TR	01	05 ♈ 38	01	05 ♑ 38	10
♇ ------- △ ♆	06APR86	08:31 PM	X	TR-TR	01	05 ♉ 49	02	05 ♑ 49	10
♇ ------- ☍ ♆	25MAY86	05:25 PM	X	TR-TR	01	05 ♋ 14	04	05 ♑ 14R	10
♇ ------- △ ♆	14JUL86	10:45 PM	X	TR-TR	01	03 ♍ 56	06	03 ♑ 56R	10
♇ ------- □ ♆	10AUG86	08:00 PM	X	TR-TR	01	03 ♎ 21	07	03 ♑ 21R	10
♇ ------- ⚹ ♆	10SEP86	07:12 PM	X	TR-TR	01	03 ♏ 03	08	03 ♑ 03R	10
♇ ------- ☌ ♆	11FEB87	06:29 AM	X	TR-TR	01	07 ♑ 07	10	07 ♑ 07	10
♇ ------- ⚹ ♆	04APR87	03:47 AM	X	TR-TR	01	08 ♓ 00	12	08 ♑ 00	10
♇ ------- □ ♆	29APR87	00:26 AM	X	TR-TR	01	07 ♈ 54	01	07 ♑ 54R	10
♇ ------- △ ♆	23MAY87	11:57 AM	X	TR-TR	01	07 ♉ 31	02	07 ♑ 31R	10
♇ ------- ☍ ♆	10JUL87	06:29 PM	X	TR-TR	01	06 ♋ 18	04	06 ♑ 18R	10
♇ ------- △ ♆	27AUG87	04:32 PM	X	TR-TR	01	05 ♍ 21	06	05 ♑ 21R	10
♇ ------- □ ♆	20SEP87	06:16 PM	X	TR-TR	01	05 ♎ 14	07	05 ♑ 14	10
♇ ------- ⚹ ♆	15OCT87	00:49 AM	X	TR-TR	01	05 ♏ 27	08	05 ♑ 27	10
♇ ------- ☌ ♆	03DEC87	07:01 AM	X	TR-TR	01	06 ♑ 44	10	06 ♑ 44	10

GEO JUPITER/URANUS

Jupiter Uranus

Natural Harmonic in the Stock Market.

	DATE	TIME	EX	JOB					
♃ ✶ ♅	28SEP57	04:26 AM	X	TR-TR					
♃ □ ♅	24NOV58	06:23 AM	X	TR-TR	01	16♏22	08	16♌22R	06
♃ △ ♅	08JAN60	01:04 AM	X	TR-TR	01	20♐18	10	20♌18R	06
♃ ☍ ♅	14MAR62	07:00 AM	X	TR-TR	01	27♒27	12	27♌27R	06
♃ ☍ ♅	08OCT62	09:03 AM	X	TR-TR	01	03♓33R	01	03♍33	07
♃ ☍ ♅	07DEC62	06:11 AM	X	TR-TR	01	05♓18	01	05♍18	07
♃ △ ♅	06MAY64	08:33 PM	X	TR-TR	01	05♉56	02	05♍56R	07
♃ □ ♅	08JUN65	04:32 PM	X	TR-TR	01	10♊54	03	10♍54	07
♃ ✶ ♅	22JUL66	07:03 PM	X	TR-TR	01	17♋00	05	17♍00	07
♃ ☌ ♅	11DEC68	09:58 AM	X	TR-TR	01	03♎39	07	03♎39	07
♃ ☌ ♅	11MAR69	02:32 PM	X	TR-TR	01	02♎27R	07	02♎27R	07
♃ ☌ ♅	20JUL69	03:01 AM	X	TR-TR	01	00♎40	07	00♎40	07
♃ ✶ ♅	09DEC71	10:47 PM	X	TR-TR	01	17♐26	10	17♎26	08
♃ □ ♅	23JAN73	05:53 AM	X	TR-TR	01	23♑03	11	23♎03	08
♃ △ ♅	25FEB74	05:03 PM	X	TR-TR	01	27♒30	12	27♎30R	08
♃ ☍ ♅	18APR76	05:15 AM	X	TR-TR	01	05♉24	02	05♏24R	08
♃ △ ♅	17JUN78	04:52 PM	X	TR-TR	01	12♋47	05	12♏47R	08
♃ □ ♅	29JUL79	11:05 PM	X	TR-TR	01	16♌56	06	16♏56	08
♃ ✶ ♅	22SEP80	06:22 AM	X	TR-TR	01	22♍43	07	22♏43	09
♃ ☌ ♅	18FEB83	05:41 PM	X	TR-TR	01	08♐52	09	08♐52	09
♃ ☌ ♅	14MAY83	03:36 PM	X	TR-TR	01	07♐41R	09	07♐41R	09
♃ ☌ ♅	25SEP83	08:53 AM	X	TR-TR	01	05♐49	09	05♐49	09
♃ ✶ ♅	21MAY85	10:02 AM	X	TR-TR	01	16♒39	12	16♐39R	10
♃ ✶ ♅	14JUL85	04:32 PM	X	TR-TR	01	14♒34R	12	14♐34R	09
♃ ✶ ♅	08JAN86	01:11 PM	X	TR-TR	01	19♒56	12	19♐56	10
♃ □ ♅	04JUN86	07:08 PM	X	TR-TR	01	20♓39	01	20♐39R	10
♃ □ ♅	06SEP86	02:59 PM	X	TR-TR	01	18♓24R	01	18♐24	10
♃ □ ♅	12FEB87	02:55 AM	X	TR-TR	01	25♓45	01	25♐45	10
♃ △ ♅	21JUN87	11:47 AM	X	TR-TR	01	24♈31	02	24♐31R	10
♃ △ ♅	24OCT87	08:16 AM	X	TR-TR	01	23♈52R	02	23♐52	10
♃ △ ♅	12MAR88	07:14 AM	X	TR-TR	01	00♉49	02	00♑49	10
♃ ☍ ♅	08AUG89	02:15 PM	X	TR-TR	01	01♋45	04	01♑45R	10
♃ ☍ ♅	29DEC89	00:54 AM	X	TR-TR	01	05♋35R	05	05♑35	11
♃ ☍ ♅	13MAY90	02:28 PM	X	TR-TR	01	09♋13	05	09♑13R	11
♃ △ ♅	11NOV91	05:48 AM	X	TR-TR	01	11♍00	07	11♑00	11
♃ △ ♅	12JAN92	08:18 AM	X	TR-TR	01	14♍22R	07	14♑22	11
♃ △ ♅	31JUL92	02:47 PM	X	TR-TR	01	15♍06	07	15♑06R	11

Retrograde

Uranus-Saturn effects stocks
Jupiter effects stocks
Neptune effects bonds
Pluto effects gold

		DATE	TIME	EX	JOB					
♄	SR	06JAN80	03:50 PM	X	TR-TR					
♇	SR	24JAN80	08:06 AM	X	TR-TR					
♅	SR	29FEB80	00:34 AM	X	TR-TR	01	25♏34	09	25♏34	09
♆	SR	24MAR80	07:57 AM	X	TR-TR	01	22♐41	10	22♐41	10
♃	SD	26APR80	02:19 AM	X	TR-TR	01	00♍14	06	00♍14	06
♄	SD	22MAY80	04:58 AM	X	TR-TR	01	20♍12	07	20♍12	07
♇	SD	28JUN80	11:58 AM	X	TR-TR	01	18♎58	08	18♎58	08
♅	SD	30JUL80	03:15 AM	X	TR-TR	01	21♏30	09	21♏30	09
♆	SD	31AUG80	02:18 PM	X	TR-TR	01	19♐54	10	19♐54	10
♄	SR	18JAN81	11:01 AM	X	TR-TR	01	09♎47	07	09♎47	07
♃	SR	24JAN81	01:06 PM	X	TR-TR	01	10♎23	07	10♎23	07
♇	SR	26JAN81	03:38 AM	X	TR-TR	01	24♎21	08	24♎21	08
♅	SR	04MAR81	05:40 PM	X	TR-TR	01	00♐07	09	00♐07	09
♆	SR	26MAR81	09:31 PM	X	TR-TR	01	24♐52	10	24♐52	10
♃	SD	27MAY81	01:19 PM	X	TR-TR	01	00♎27	07	00♎27	07
♄	SD	04JUN81	08:44 PM	X	TR-TR	01	03♎00	07	03♎00	07
♇	SD	01JUL81	09:40 AM	X	TR-TR	01	21♎32	08	21♎32	08
♅	SD	04AUG81	03:27 AM	X	TR-TR	01	26♏03	09	26♏03	09
♆	SD	03SEP81	00:54 AM	X	TR-TR	01	22♐05	10	22♐05	10
♇	SR	29JAN82	01:17 AM	X	TR-TR	01	26♎56	08	26♎56	08
♄	SR	30JAN82	11:01 PM	X	TR-TR	01	22♎15	08	22♎15	08
♃	SR	23FEB82	11:28 PM	X	TR-TR	01	10♏20	08	10♏20	08
♅	SR	09MAR82	02:11 PM	X	TR-TR	01	04♐38	09	04♐38	09
♆	SR	29MAR82	06:54 AM	X	TR-TR	01	27♐03	10	27♐03	10
♄	SD	18JUN82	05:24 AM	X	TR-TR	01	15♎30	08	15♎30	08
♃	SD	27JUN82	12:15 PM	X	TR-TR	01	00♏26	08	00♏26	08
♇	SD	04JUL82	04:29 AM	X	TR-TR	01	24♎07	08	24♎07	08
♅	SD	09AUG82	00:52 AM	X	TR-TR	01	00♐35	09	00♐35	09
♆	SD	05SEP82	12:49 PM	X	TR-TR	01	24♐17	10	24♐17	10
♇	SR	31JAN83	08:52 PM	X	TR-TR	01	29♎32	08	29♎32	08
♄	SR	12FEB83	04:59 AM	X	TR-TR	01	04♏26	08	04♏26	08
♅	SR	14MAR83	05:36 AM	X	TR-TR	01	09♐07	09	09♐07	09
♃	SR	27MAR83	07:44 PM	X	TR-TR	01	10♐55	09	10♐55	09
♆	SR	31MAR83	08:06 PM	X	TR-TR	01	29♐14	10	29♐14	10
♄	SD	01JUL83	06:23 AM	X	TR-TR	01	27♎43	08	27♎43	08
♇	SD	07JUL83	04:06 AM	X	TR-TR	01	26♎43	08	26♎43	08
♃	SD	29JUL83	00:32 AM	X	TR-TR	01	01♐04	09	01♐04	09
♅	SD	14AUG83	00:15 AM	X	TR-TR	01	05♐04	09	05♐04	09
♆	SD	08SEP83	00:21 AM	X	TR-TR	01	26♐28	10	26♐28	10
♇	SR	03FEB84	06:54 PM	X	TR-TR	01	02♏08	08	02♏08	08
♄	SR	24FEB84	06:47 AM	X	TR-TR	01	16♏23	08	16♏23	08
♅	SR	17MAR84	11:49 PM	X	TR-TR	01	13♐34	09	13♐34	09
♆	SR	02APR84	05:44 AM	X	TR-TR	01	01♑26	10	01♑26	10
♃	SR	29APR84	12:06 PM	X	TR-TR	01	12♑58	11	12♑58	11
♇	SD	08JUL84	11:54 PM	X	TR-TR	01	29♎19	08	29♎19	08
♄	SD	13JUL84	00:07 AM	X	TR-TR	01	09♏42	08	09♏42	08
♅	SD	17AUG84	08:48 PM	X	TR-TR	01	09♐32	09	09♐32	09
♃	SD	29AUG84	06:09 PM	X	TR-TR	01	03♑08	10	03♑08	10
♆	SD	09SEP84	11:32 AM	X	TR-TR	01	28♐39	10	28♐39	10
♇	SR	05FEB85	02:08 PM	X	TR-TR	01	04♏45	08	04♏45	08
♄	SR	07MAR85	06:14 AM	X	TR-TR	01	28♏08	09	28♏08	09

GEO MARS/SATURN

Mars-Saturn

Natural Harmonic in the Live Cattle Market

	DATE	TIME	EX	JOB					
♂----------☌ ♄	23JUN80	09:58 PM	X	TR-TR					
♂----------✱ ♄	16OCT80	08:58 AM	X	TR-TR	01	03♐05	09	03♎05	07
♂----------□ ♄	02DEC80	04:15 AM	X	TR-TR	01	07♑51	11	07♎51	07
♂----------△ ♄	12JAN81	02:58 AM	X	TR-TR	01	09♒45	12	09♎45	07
♂----------☍ ♄	25MAR81	08:41 AM	X	TR-TR	01	06♈34	01	06♎34R	07
♂----------△ ♄	09JUN81	05:52 AM	X	TR-TR	01	03♊01	03	03♎01	07
♂----------□ ♄	25JUL81	04:31 PM	X	TR-TR	01	05♋04	04	05♎04	07
♂----------✱ ♄	18SEP81	11:57 PM	X	TR-TR	01	10♌46	06	10♎46	07
♂----------☌ ♄	07JUL82	01:09 AM	X	TR-TR	01	15♎47	08	15♎47	08
♂----------✱ ♄	26OCT82	12:37 PM	X	TR-TR	01	26♐07	10	26♎07	08
♂----------□ ♄	11DEC82	03:34 PM	X	TR-TR	01	01♒14	11	01♏14	08
♂----------△ ♄	22JAN83	12:18 PM	X	TR-TR	01	04♓04	12	04♏04	08
♂----------☍ ♄	08APR83	05:48 AM	X	TR-TR	01	02♉08	02	02♏08R	08
♂----------△ ♄	25JUN83	05:58 PM	X	TR-TR	01	27♊45	04	27♎45R	08
♂----------□ ♄	12AUG83	03:21 AM	X	TR-TR	01	29♋07	05	29♎07	08
♂----------✱ ♄	06OCT83	07:56 PM	X	TR-TR	01	04♍22	06	04♏22	08
♂----------☌ ♄	14FEB84	05:46 PM	X	TR-TR	01	16♏18	08	16♏18	08
♂----------✱ ♄	29OCT84	07:12 PM	X	TR-TR	01	17♑36	11	17♏36	08
♂----------□ ♄	16DEC84	01:42 AM	X	TR-TR	01	23♒08	12	23♏08	09
♂----------△ ♄	29JAN85	12:40 PM	X	TR-TR	01	27♓00	01	27♏00	09
♂----------☍ ♄	21APR85	05:53 AM	X	TR-TR	01	26♉34	03	26♏34R	09
♂----------△ ♄	12JUL85	01:02 AM	X	TR-TR	01	21♋37	05	21♏37R	09
♂----------□ ♄	28AUG85	09:39 PM	X	TR-TR	01	22♌24	06	22♏24	09
♂----------✱ ♄	22OCT85	07:44 PM	X	TR-TR	01	27♍07	07	27♏07	09
♂----------☌ ♄	17FEB86	09:58 AM	X	TR-TR	01	08♐58	09	08♐58	09
♂----------✱ ♄	21OCT86	12:08 PM	X	TR-TR	01	07♒16	12	07♐16	09
♂----------□ ♄	15DEC86	03:50 PM	X	TR-TR	01	13♓32	01	13♐32	09
♂----------△ ♄	04FEB87	05:04 AM	X	TR-TR	01	18♈47	02	18♐47	10
♂----------☍ ♄	05MAY87	08:42 PM	X	TR-TR	01	20♊09	04	20♐09R	10
♂----------△ ♄	29JUL87	07:31 PM	X	TR-TR	01	14♌52	06	14♐52R	09
♂----------□ ♄	15SEP87	08:54 AM	X	TR-TR	01	15♍08	07	15♐08	09
♂----------✱ ♄	07NOV87	09:05 AM	X	TR-TR	01	19♎13	08	19♐13	10
♂----------☌ ♄	23FEB88	08:00 AM	X	TR-TR	01	00♑45	10	00♑45	10
♂----------✱ ♄	23MAY88	09:50 PM	X	TR-TR	01	01♓09	12	01♑09R	10
♂----------□ ♄	09JUL88	04:38 AM	X	TR-TR	01	27♓54	01	27♐54R	10
♂----------△ ♄	04FEB89	08:59 PM	X	TR-TR	01	09♉32	02	09♑32	11
♂----------☍ ♄	20MAY89	12:05 PM	X	TR-TR	01	13♋19	05	13♑19R	11
♂----------△ ♄	15AUG89	06:46 PM	X	TR-TR	01	07♍51	07	07♑51R	11
♂----------□ ♄	01OCT89	03:37 AM	X	TR-TR	01	07♎38	07	07♑38	11
♂----------✱ ♄	20NOV89	09:13 AM	X	TR-TR	01	11♏02	08	11♑02	11
♂----------☌ ♄	28FEB90	06:15 PM	X	TR-TR	01	22♑07	11	22♑07	11
♂----------✱ ♄	24MAY90	08:08 AM	X	TR-TR	01	25♓02	01	25♑02R	11
♂----------□ ♄	02JUL90	02:13 AM	X	TR-TR	01	22♈56	02	22♑56R	11
♂----------△ ♄	12AUG90	09:42 PM	X	TR-TR	01	20♉00	02	20♑00R	11
♂----------☍ ♄	06JUN91	08:56 AM	X	TR-TR	01	06♌31	06	06♒31R	12
♂----------△ ♄	02SEP91	03:40 PM	X	TR-TR	01	01♎01	07	01♒01R	11
♂----------□ ♄	17OCT91	01:20 AM	X	TR-TR	01	00♏19	08	00♒19	11
♂----------✱ ♄	03DEC91	01:01 AM	X	TR-TR	01	02♐57	09	02♒57	12

EST.GEO MERCURY R & D

Mercury Retrograde or Direct

Natural Harmonic in Grains and Soybeans.

	DATE	TIME	E X	JO		
☿----SD	10JAN84	10:40 PM	X	TR-TR 01	00♑23 02	00♑23 02
☿----SR	11APR84	02:59 PM	X	TR-TR 01	06♉42 05	06♉42 05
☿----SD	05MAY84	09:09 AM	X	TR-TR 01	26♈18 05	26♈18 05
☿----SR	14AUG84	02:17 PM	X	TR-TR 01	13♍24 09	13♍24 09
☿----SD	06SEP84	10:34 PM	X	TR-TR 01	00♍02 09	00♍02 09
☿----SR	04DEC84	03:46 PM	X	TR-TR 01	00♑49 02	00♑49 02
☿----SD	24DEC84	01:18 PM	X	TR-TR 01	14♐30 01	14♐30 01
☿----SR	24MAR85	04:56 PM	X	TR-TR 01	18♈39 05	18♈39 05
☿----SD	16APR85	11:56 PM	X	TR-TR 01	06♈43 04	06♈43 04
☿----SR	27JUL85	07:26 PM	X	TR-TR 01	25♌19 09	25♌19 09
☿----SD	20AUG85	05:35 PM	X	TR-TR 01	13♌13 09	13♌13 09
☿----SR	18NOV85	10:33 AM	X	TR-TR 01	15♐00 01	15♐00 01
☿----SD	08DEC85	06:50 AM	X	TR-TR 01	28♏46 12	28♏46 12
☿----SR	07MAR86	09:40 AM	X	TR-TR 01	01♈19 04	01♈19 04
☿----SD	30MAR86	03:23 AM	X	TR-TR 01	17♓56 03	17♓56 03
☿----SR	09JUL86	03:19 PM	X	TR-TR 01	06♌25 09	06♌25 09
☿----SD	02AUG86	07:31 PM	X	TR-TR 01	25♋44 08	25♋44 08
☿----SR	02NOV86	01:27 AM	X	TR-TR 01	29♏10 12	29♏10 12
☿----SD	22NOV86	02:54 AM	X	TR-TR 01	13♏05 12	13♏05 12
☿----SR	18FEB87	01:05 PM	X	TR-TR 01	14♓30 03	14♓30 03
☿----SD	12MAR87	04:35 PM	X	TR-TR 01	29♒57 03	29♒57 03
☿----SR	20JUN87	10:40 PM	X	TR-TR 01	16♋49 08	16♋49 08
☿----SD	15JUL87	02:43 AM	X	TR-TR 01	07♋24 08	07♋24 08
☿----SR	16OCT87	11:31 AM	X	TR-TR 01	13♏13 12	13♏13 12
☿----SD	06NOV87	00:55 AM	X	TR-TR 01	27♎24 11	27♎24 11
☿----SR	02FEB88	01:22 AM	X	TR-TR 01	28♒04 03	28♒04 03
☿----SD	23FEB88	01:22 PM	X	TR-TR 01	12♒41 03	12♒41 03
☿----SR	31MAY88	04:43 PM	X	TR-TR 01	26♊47 07	26♊47 07
☿----SD	24JUN88	05:58 PM	X	TR-TR 01	18♊09 07	18♊09 07
☿----SR	28SEP88	04:15 PM	X	TR-TR 01	27♎04 11	27♎04 11
☿----SD	19OCT88	10:56 PM	X	TR-TR 01	11♎39 10	11♎39 10
☿----SR	15JAN89	07:49 PM	X	TR-TR 01	11♒54 03	11♒54 03
☿----SD	05FEB89	04:54 PM	X	TR-TR 01	25♑59 02	25♑59 02
☿----SR	12MAY89	05:14 AM	X	TR-TR 01	06♊51 07	06♊51 07
☿----SD	05JUN89	02:59 AM	X	TR-TR 01	28♉09 06	28♉09 06
☿----SR	11SEP89	03:32 PM	X	TR-TR 01	10♎34 10	10♎34 10
☿----SD	03OCT89	05:52 PM	X	TR-TR 01	25♍45 10	25♍45 10
☿----SR	30DEC89	05:26 PM	X	TR-TR 01	25♑54 02	25♑54 02

Mars changing signs

Natural harmonic in Cattle and Treasury Bonds

	DATE	TIME	EX	JOB	#	P1 POS.	HS	P2 POS.	HS
♂-----------CNJSA	02FEB86	01:28 AM	X	TR-TR	01	00 ♐ 00	01	00 ♐ 00	01
♂-----------CNJCP	27MAR86	10:44 PM	X	TR-TR	01	00 ♑ 00	02	00 ♑ 00	02
♂-----------CNJAQ	08OCT86	07:58 PM	X	TR-TR	01	00 ♒ 00	03	00 ♒ 00	03
♂-----------CNJPI	25NOV86	09:35 PM	X	TR-TR	01	00 ♓ 00	03	00 ♓ 00	03
♂-----------CNJAR	08JAN87	07:24 AM	X	TR-TR	01	00 ♈ 00	04	00 ♈ 00	04
♂-----------CNJTA	20FEB87	09:45 AM	X	TR-TR	01	00 ♉ 00	06	00 ♉ 00	06
♂-----------CNJGE	05APR87	11:38 AM	X	TR-TR	01	00 ♊ 00	07	00 ♊ 00	07
♂-----------CNJCA	20MAY87	10:00 PM	X	TR-TR	01	00 ♋ 00	08	00 ♋ 00	08
♂-----------CNJLE	06JUL87	11:49 AM	X	TR-TR	01	00 ♌ 00	09	00 ♌ 00	09
♂-----------CNJVI	22AUG87	02:53 PM	X	TR-TR	01	00 ♍ 00	09	00 ♍ 00	09
♂-----------CNJLI	08OCT87	02:27 PM	X	TR-TR	01	00 ♎ 00	10	00 ♎ 00	10
♂-----------CNJSC	23NOV87	10:22 PM	X	TR-TR	01	00 ♏ 00	12	00 ♏ 00	12
♂-----------CNJSA	08JAN88	10:25 AM	X	TR-TR	01	00 ♐ 00	01	00 ♐ 00	01
♂-----------CNJCP	22FEB88	05:17 AM	X	TR-TR	01	00 ♑ 00	02	00 ♑ 00	02
♂-----------CNJAQ	06APR88	04:42 PM	X	TR-TR	01	00 ♒ 00	03	00 ♒ 00	03
♂-----------CNJPI	22MAY88	02:45 AM	X	TR-TR	01	00 ♓ 00	03	00 ♓ 00	03
♂-----------CNJAR	13JUL88	03:05 PM	X	TR-TR	01	00 ♈ 00	04	00 ♈ 00	04
♂-----------CNJAR	23OCT88	04:17 PM	X	TR-TR	01	00 ♈ 00	04	00 ♈ 00	04
♂-----------CNJAR	01NOV88	09:37 AM	X	TR-TR	01	00 ♈ 00	04	00 ♈ 00	04
♂-----------CNJTA	19JAN89	03:15 AM	X	TR-TR	01	00 ♉ 00	06	00 ♉ 00	06
♂-----------CNJGE	11MAR89	03:50 AM	X	TR-TR	01	00 ♊ 00	07	00 ♊ 00	07
♂-----------CNJCA	28APR89	11:39 PM	X	TR-TR	01	00 ♋ 00	08	00 ♋ 00	08
♂-----------CNJLE	16JUN89	09:12 AM	X	TR-TR	01	00 ♌ 00	09	00 ♌ 00	09
♂-----------CNJVI	03AUG89	08:36 AM	X	TR-TR	01	00 ♍ 00	09	00 ♍ 00	09
♂-----------CNJLI	19SEP89	09:39 AM	X	TR-TR	01	00 ♎ 00	10	00 ♎ 00	10
♂-----------CNJSC	04NOV89	00:32 AM	X	TR-TR	01	00 ♏ 00	12	00 ♏ 00	12
♂-----------CNJSA	17DEC89	11:56 PM	X	TR-TR	01	00 ♐ 00	01	00 ♐ 00	01
♂-----------CNJCP	29JAN90	09:12 AM	X	TR-TR	01	00 ♑ 00	02	00 ♑ 00	02
♂-----------CNJAQ	11MAR90	10:54 AM	X	TR-TR	01	00 ♒ 00	03	00 ♒ 00	03
♂-----------CNJPI	20APR90	05:11 PM	X	TR-TR	01	00 ♓ 00	03	00 ♓ 00	03
♂-----------CNJAR	31MAY90	02:14 AM	X	TR-TR	01	00 ♈ 00	04	00 ♈ 00	04
♂-----------CNJTA	12JUL90	09:43 AM	X	TR-TR	01	00 ♉ 00	06	00 ♉ 00	06
♂-----------CNJGE	31AUG90	06:33 AM	X	TR-TR	01	00 ♊ 00	07	00 ♊ 00	07
♂-----------CNJGE	14DEC90	02:50 AM	X	TR-TR	01	00 ♊ 00	07	00 ♊ 00	07

UPITER.GEO EST VENUS

Venus-Jupiter

Natural Harmonic in Gold.

	DATE	TIME	E X	JOB					
♀------☌ ♃	26JAN84	08:30 PM	X	TR-TR	01	01♑34	02	01♑34	02
♀------⚹ ♃	23MAR84	02:32 AM	X	TR-TR	01	10♓51	03	10♑51	02
♀------□ ♃	17APR84	11:37 PM	X	TR-TR	01	12♈45	04	12♑45	02
♀------△ ♃	12MAY84	07:55 AM	X	TR-TR	01	12♉42	06	12♑42R	02
♀------☍ ♃	26JUN84	04:30 PM	X	TR-TR	01	08♋26	08	08♑26R	02
♀------△ ♃	10AUG84	02:49 PM	X	TR-TR	01	03♍42	09	03♑42R	02
♀------□ ♃	03SEP84	01:55 PM	X	TR-TR	01	03♎10	10	03♑10	02
♀------⚹ ♃	29SEP84	04:21 AM	X	TR-TR	01	04♏33	11	04♑33	02
♀------☌ ♃	24NOV84	09:16 PM	X	TR-TR	01	13♑19	02	13♑19	02
♀------⚹ ♃	31JAN85	05:31 PM	X	TR-TR	01	28♓41	04	28♑41	02
♀------⚹ ♃	07APR85	02:30 AM	X	TR-TR	01	11♈58R	04	11♒58	03
♀------⚹ ♃	20MAY85	07:06 PM	X	TR-TR	01	16♈37	05	16♒37	03
♀------□ ♃	23JUN85	03:26 AM	X	TR-TR	01	16♉26	06	16♒26R	03
♀------△ ♃	19JUL85	00:40 AM	X	TR-TR	01	14♊05	07	14♒05R	03
♀------☍ ♃	04SEP85	01:25 AM	X	TR-TR	01	08♌28	09	08♒28R	03
♀------△ ♃	22OCT85	01:48 PM	X	TR-TR	01	07♎44	10	07♒44	03
♀------□ ♃	17NOV85	04:43 PM	X	TR-TR	01	10♏22	12	10♒22	03
♀------⚹ ♃	15DEC85	04:07 AM	X	TR-TR	01	14♐53	01	14♒53	03
♀------☌ ♃	11FEB86	03:19 AM	X	TR-TR	01	27♒46	03	27♒46	03
♀------⚹ ♃	11APR86	11:50 AM	X	TR-TR	01	11♉31	06	11♓31	03
♀------□ ♃	10MAY86	03:55 PM	X	TR-TR	01	17♊06	07	17♓06	03
♀------△ ♃	07JUN86	10:50 PM	X	TR-TR	01	20♋59	08	20♓59	04
♀------☍ ♃	31JUL86	11:27 AM	X	TR-TR	01	22♍17	10	22♓17R	04
♀------△ ♃	28SEP86	05:45 PM	X	TR-TR	01	15♏34	12	15♓34R	03
♀------△ ♃	04NOV86	05:56 PM	X	TR-TR	01	12♏59R	12	12♓59R	03
♀------△ ♃	22DEC86	01:12 AM	X	TR-TR	01	16♏05	12	16♓05	03
♀------□ ♃	29JAN87	08:44 AM	X	TR-TR	01	22♐47	01	22♓47	04
♀------⚹ ♃	03MAR87	06:19 AM	X	TR-TR	01	00♒10	02	00♈10	04
♀------☌ ♃	04MAY87	11:11 PM	X	TR-TR	01	15♈05	05	15♈05	05
♀------⚹ ♃	02JUL87	11:41 AM	X	TR-TR	01	26♊10	07	26♈10	05
♀------□ ♃	29JUL87	06:05 AM	X	TR-TR	01	28♋59	08	28♈59	05
♀------△ ♃	23AUG87	03:25 AM	X	TR-TR	01	29♌43	09	29♈43R	05
♀------☍ ♃	07OCT87	01:04 PM	X	TR-TR	01	26♎07	11	26♈07R	05
♀------△ ♃	20NOV87	11:31 AM	X	TR-TR	01	20♐49	01	20♈49R	05
♀------□ ♃	13DEC87	07:08 PM	X	TR-TR	01	19♑46	02	19♈46R	05
♀------⚹ ♃	07JAN88	08:58 PM	X	TR-TR	01	20♒43	03	20♈43	05
♀------☌ ♃	05MAR88	05:22 PM	X	TR-TR	01	29♈26	05	29♈26	05
♀------⚹ ♃	12SEP88	07:21 PM	X	TR-TR	01	05♌54	09	05♊54	07
♀------□ ♃	09OCT88	07:31 AM	X	TR-TR	01	05♍45	09	05♊45R	07
♀------△ ♃	01NOV88	09:14 PM	X	TR-TR	01	03♎46	10	03♊46R	07
♀------☍ ♃	16DEC88	00:39 AM	X	TR-TR	01	28♏07	12	28♉07R	06
♀------△ ♃	31JAN89	01:40 PM	X	TR-TR	01	26♑19	02	26♉19	06
♀------□ ♃	26FEB89	03:53 AM	X	TR-TR	01	28♒20	03	28♉20	06
♀------⚹ ♃	25MAR89	10:24 AM	X	TR-TR	01	02♈19	04	02♊19	07
♀------☌ ♃	22MAY89	08:58 PM	X	TR-TR	01	14♊31	07	14♊31	07
♀------⚹ ♃	22JUL89	09:44 AM	X	TR-TR	01	28♌15	09	28♊15	08
♀------□ ♃	21AUG89	08:08 AM	X	TR-TR	01	04♎07	10	04♋07	08
♀------△ ♃	19SEP89	02:19 PM	X	TR-TR	01	08♏28	12	08♋28	08
♀------☍ ♃	15NOV89	04:13 PM	X	TR-TR	01	10♑21	02	10♋21R	08

Mars-Saturn
Mars-Uranus

Natural Harmonic effecting the Treasury Bonds, Stock Market and Currencies.

		DATE	TIME	E X	JC					
♂———△	♅	31MAR76	03:50 PM	X	TR-					
♂———☌	♄	12MAY76	09:49 AM	X	TR-					
♂———□	♅	23MAY76	08:12 AM	X	TR-TR	01	03 ♌ 59	04	03 ♏ 59R	07
♄———□	♅	01JUL76	10:20 PM	X	TR-TR	01	03 ♌ 04	04	03 ♏ 04R	07
♂———⚹	♅	11JUL76	06:44 PM	X	TR-TR	01	03 ♍ 02	05	03 ♏ 02	07
♂———⚹	♄	11SEP76	02:14 PM	X	TR-TR	01	12 ♎ 00	06	12 ♌ 00	05
♂———☌	♅	18OCT76	12:33 PM	X	TR-TR	01	06 ♏ 44	07	06 ♏ 44	07
♂———□	♄	01NOV76	06:46 AM	X	TR-TR	01	16 ♏ 14	07	16 ♌ 14	05
♂———△	♄	13DEC76	06:30 PM	X	TR-TR	01	16 ♐ 38	08	16 ♌ 38R	05
♂———⚹	♅	15JAN77	10:46 PM	X	TR-TR	01	11 ♑ 23	10	11 ♏ 23	07
♄———□	♅	23FEB77	07:04 PM	X	TR-TR	01	11 ♌ 45R	05	11 ♏ 45R	07
♂———☍	♄	24FEB77	09:51 AM	X	TR-TR	01	11 ♒ 42	11	11 ♌ 42R	05
♂———□	♅		11:01 AM	X	TR-TR	01	11 ♒ 45	11	11 ♏ 45R	07
♂———△	♅	02APR77	07:23 PM	X	TR-TR	01	10 ♓ 52	12	10 ♏ 52R	07
♄———□	♅	22APR77	05:27 PM	X	TR-TR	01	10 ♌ 05	05	10 ♏ 05R	07
♂———△	♄	11MAY77	11:09 AM	X	TR-TR	01	10 ♈ 46	12	10 ♌ 46	05
♂———☍	♅	16JUN77	07:05 PM	X	TR-TR	01	08 ♉ 03	01	08 ♏ 03R	07
♂———□	♄	25JUN77	04:19 PM	X	TR-TR	01	14 ♉ 32	01	14 ♌ 32	05
♂———⚹	♄	17AUG77	01:20 PM	X	TR-TR	01	20 ♊ 58	03	20 ♌ 58	05
♂———△	♅	16SEP77	05:42 AM	X	TR-TR	01	09 ♋ 17	04	09 ♏ 17	07
♂———□	♅	13MAY78	10:04 PM	X	TR-TR	01	14 ♌ 01	05	14 ♏ 01R	07
♂———☌	♄	04JUN78	05:14 PM	X	TR-TR	01	25 ♌ 03	05	25 ♌ 03	05
♂———⚹	♅	05JUL78	09:14 PM	X	TR-TR	01	12 ♍ 25	06	12 ♏ 25R	07
♂———⚹	♄	01OCT78	11:37 PM	X	TR-TR	01	08 ♏ 21	07	08 ♍ 21	06
♂———☌	♅	11OCT78	02:05 PM	X	TR-TR	01	14 ♏ 59	07	14 ♏ 59	07
♂———□	♄	19NOV78	11:58 AM	X	TR-TR	01	12 ♐ 49	08	12 ♍ 49	06
♂———△	♄	30DEC78	06:05 PM	X	TR-TR	01	13 ♑ 54	10	13 ♍ 54R	06
♂———⚹	♅	07JAN79	03:19 PM	X	TR-TR	01	20 ♑ 00	10	20 ♏ 00	07
♂———□	♅	16FEB79	04:48 AM	X	TR-TR	01	20 ♒ 58	11	20 ♏ 58	07
♂———☍	♄	11MAR79	11:12 PM	X	TR-TR	01	09 ♓ 43	12	09 ♍ 43R	06
♂———△	♅	25MAR79	08:07 PM	X	TR-TR	01	20 ♓ 37	12	20 ♏ 37R	07
♂———△	♄	25MAY79	05:52 PM	X	TR-TR	01	07 ♉ 18	01	07 ♍ 18	05
♂———☍	♅	08JUN79	11:34 PM	X	TR-TR	01	17 ♉ 48	01	17 ♏ 48R	07
♂———□	♄	10JUL79	06:07 AM	X	TR-TR	01	10 ♊ 09	02	10 ♍ 09	06
♂———⚹	♄	02SEP79	09:04 AM	X	TR-TR	01	16 ♋ 15	04	16 ♍ 15	06
♂———△	♅	04SEP79	12:46 PM	X	TR-TR	01	17 ♋ 37	04	17 ♏ 37	07
♄———⚹	♅	17SEP79	00:12 AM	X	TR-TR	01	18 ♍ 05	06	18 ♏ 05	07
♂———□	♅	31OCT79	01:01 AM	X	TR-TR	01	20 ♌ 26	05	20 ♏ 26	07
♄———⚹	♅	17FEB80	09:58 PM	X	TR-TR	01	25 ♍ 31R	06	25 ♏ 31	08
♂———☌	♄	23JUN80	10:01 PM	X	TR-TR	01	21 ♍ 05	06	21 ♍ 05	06
♂———⚹	♅	25JUN80	03:54 PM	X	TR-TR	01	21 ♍ 59	06	21 ♏ 59R	07
♄———⚹	♅	04JUL80	11:17 PM	X	TR-TR	01	21 ♍ 46	06	21 ♏ 46R	07
♂———☌	♅	02OCT80	09:26 AM	X	TR-TR	01	23 ♏ 11	08	23 ♏ 11	08
♂———⚹	♄	16OCT80	08:59 AM	X	TR-TR	01	03 ♐ 05	08	03 ♎ 05	06
♂———□	♄	02DEC80	04:14 AM	X	TR-TR	01	07 ♑ 51	09	07 ♎ 51	06
♂———⚹	♅	28DEC80	11:41 AM	X	TR-TR	01	28 ♑ 15	10	28 ♏ 15	08
♂———△	♄	12JAN81	02:57 AM	X	TR-TR	01	09 ♒ 45	11	09 ♎ 45	06
♂———□	♅	06FEB81	11:41 AM	X	TR-TR	01	29 ♒ 48	11	29 ♏ 48	08
♂———△	♅	16MAR81	11:07 PM	X	TR-TR	01	00 ♈ 03	12	00 ♐ 03R	08
♂———☍	♄	25MAR81	08:40 AM	X	TR-TR	01	06 ♈ 34	12	06 ♎ 34R	06
♂———☍	♅	01JUN81	02:09 PM	X	TR-TR	01	27 ♉ 33	02	27 ♏ 33R	08

Natural Harmonic effecting the Treasury Bonds, Stock Market and Currencies.

Aspect		DATE	TIME		E X	J					
♂———————△	♄	09JUN81	05:51	AM	X	TR	[illegible]	[illegible]♊01	[illegible]	[illegible]♎01	[illegible]
♂———————□	♄	25JUL81	04:33	PM	X	TR-TR	01	05♋04	03	05♎04	06
♂———————△	♅	27AUG81	01:01	AM	X	TR-TR	01	26♋17	04	26♏17	08
♂——————— ✶	♄	18SEP81	11:53	PM	X	TR-TR	01	10♌46	05	10♎46	06
♂———————□	♅	17OCT81	10:28	PM	X	TR-TR	01	28♌17	05	28♏17	08
♂——————— ✶	♅	20DEC81	05:56	AM	X	TR-TR	01	02♎03	06	02♐03	08
♂——————— ✶	♅	18APR82	00:51	AM	X	TR-TR	01	03♎59R	06	03♐59R	08
♂——————— ✶	♅	29MAY82	11.29	PM	X	TR-TR	01	02♎22	06	02♐22R	08
♂——————— ☌	♄	07JUL82	01:10	AM	X	TR-TR	01	15♎47	06	15♎47	06
♂——————— ☌	♅	21SEP82	08:48	PM	X	TR-TR	01	01♐23	08	01♐23	08
♂——————— ✶	♄	26OCT82	12:35	PM	X	TR-TR	01	26♐07	09	26♎07	07
♂———————□	♄	11DEC82	03:33	PM	X	TR-TR	01	01♒14	10	01♏14	07
♂——————— ✶	♅	17DEC82	10:26	PM	X	TR-TR	01	06♒09	11	06♐09	08
♂———————△	♄	22JAN83	12:19	PM	X	TR-TR	01	04♓04	11	04♏04	07
♂———————□	♅	27JAN83	07:06	PM	X	TR-TR	01	08♓12	11	08♐12	08
♂———————△	♅	08MAR83	03:39	PM	X	TR-TR	01	09♈06	12	09♐06	08
♂——————— ☍	♄	08APR83	05:50	AM	X	TR-TR	01	02♉08	01	02♏08R	07
♂——————— ☍	♅	26MAY83	09:39	PM	X	TR-TR	01	07♊11	02	07♐11R	08
♂———————△	♄	25JUN83	05:59	PM	X	TR-TR	01	27♊45	03	27♎45R	07
♂———————□	♄	12AUG83	03:20	AM	X	TR-TR	01	29♋07	04	29♎07	07
♂———————△	♅	21AUG83	09:31	AM	X	TR-TR	01	05♌06	05	05♐06	08
♂——————— ✶	♄	06OCT83	07:58	PM	X	TR-TR	01	04♍22	05	04♏22	07
♂———————□	♅	10OCT83	03:54	AM	X	TR-TR	01	06♍25	05	06♐25	08
♂——————— ✶	♅	04DEC83	01:56	PM	X	TR-TR	01	09♎31	06	09♐31	08
♂——————— ☌	♄	14FEB84	05:41	PM	X	TR-TR	01	16♏18	07	16♏18	07
♂——————— ☌	♅	03SEP84	03:59	PM	X	TR-TR	01	09♐39	08	09♐39	08
♂——————— ✶	♄	29OCT84	07:10	PM	X	TR-TR	01	17♑36	10	17♏36	07
♂——————— ✶	♅	03DEC84	04:07	PM	X	TR-TR	01	13♒41	11	13♐41	08
♂———————□	♄	16DEC84	01:42	AM	X	TR-TR	01	23♒08	11	23♏08	08
♂———————□	♅	15JAN85	05:23	AM	X	TR-TR	01	16♓09	12	16♐09	08
♂———————△	♄	29JAN85	12:42	PM	X	TR-TR	01	27♓00	12	27♏00	08
♂———————△	♅	26FEB85	06:05	AM	X	TR-TR	01	17♈43	12	17♐43	08
♂——————— ☍	♄	21APR85	05:52	AM	X	TR-TR	01	26♉34	02	26♏34R	08
♂——————— ☍	♅	20MAY85	10:44	AM	X	TR-TR	01	16♊41	02	16♐41R	08
♂———————△	♄	12JUL85	00:59	AM	X	TR-TR	01	21♋37	04	21♏37R	07
♂———————△	♅	15AUG85	05:00	PM	X	TR-TR	01	13♌59	05	13♐59R	08
♂———————□	♄	28AUG85	09:40	PM	X	TR-TR	01	22♌24	05	22♏24	07
♂———————□	♅	03OCT85	01:35	AM	X	TR-TR	01	14♍41	06	14♐41	08
♂——————— ✶	♄	22OCT85	07:43	PM	X	TR-TR	01	27♍07	06	27♏07	09
♂——————— ✶	♅	23NOV85	11:28	PM	X	TR-TR	01	17♎13	06	17♐13	08
♂——————— ☌	♄	17FEB86	09:56	AM	X	TR-TR	01	08♐58	08	08♐58	08
♂——————— ☌	♅	13MAR86	05:28	AM	X	TR-TR	01	22♐17	09	22♐17	09
♂——————— ✶	♄	21OCT86	12:11	PM	X	TR-TR	01	07♒16	11	07♐16	08
♂——————— ✶	♅	11NOV86	07:42	PM	X	TR-TR	01	20♒39	11	20♐39	09
♂———————□	♄	15DEC86	03:49	PM	X	TR-TR	01	13♓32	12	13♐32	08
♂———————□	♅	29DEC86	11:47	PM	X	TR-TR	01	23♓30	12	23♐30	09
♂———————△	♄	04FEB87	05:06	AM	X	TR-TR	01	18♈47	01	18♐47	08
♂———————△	♅	14FEB87	09:11	AM	X	TR-TR	01	25♈50	01	25♐50	09
♂——————— ☍	♄	05MAY87	08:41	PM	X	TR-TR	01	20♊09	03	20♐09R	09
♂——————— ☍	♅	14MAY87	05:35	PM	X	TR-TR	01	25♊58	03	25♐58R	09

Mars-Saturn
Mars-Uranus

Natural Harmonic effecting the Treasury Bonds, Stock Market and Currencies.

Aspect	DATE	TIME	EX	JC					
♂ △ ♄	29JUL87	07:33 PM	X	TR-					
♂ △ ♅	11AUG87	10:55 AM	X	TR-TR	01	22 ♌ 04	09	22 ♐ 04R	09
♂ □ ♄	15SEP87	08:54 AM	X	TR-TR	01	15 ♏ 08	06	15 ♐ 08	08
♂ □ ♅	27SEP87	04:49 PM	X	TR-TR	01	23 ♏ 01	06	23 ♐ 01	09
♂ ⚹ ♄	07NOV87	09:05 AM	X	TR-TR	01	19 ♎ 13	07	19 ♐ 13	09
♂ ⚹ ♅	16NOV87	05:40 AM	X	TR-TR	01	24 ♎ 59	07	24 ♐ 59	09
♄ ☌ ♅	12FEB88	07:47 PM	X	TR-TR	01	29 ♐ 55	09	29 ♐ 55	09
♂ ☌ ♅	22FEB88	03:48 PM	X	TR-TR	01	00 ♑ 18	09	00 ♑ 18	09
♂ ☌ ♄	23FEB86	08:01 AM	X	TR-TR	01	00 ♑ 45	09	00 ♑ 45	09
♂ ⚹ ♅	22MAY88	08:37 AM	X	TR-TR	01	00 ♓ 09	11	00 ♑ 09R	09
♂ ⚹ ♄	23MAY88	09:49 PM	X	TR-TR	01	01 ♓ 09	11	01 ♑ 09R	09
♄ ☌ ♅	26JUN88	12:20 PM	X	TR-TR	01	28 ♐ 47R	09	28 ♐ 47R	09
♂ □ ♄	09JUL88	04:32 AM	X	TR-TR	01	27 ♓ 54	12	27 ♐ 54R	09
♂ □ ♅		10:46 PM	X	TR-TR	01	28 ♓ 16	12	28 ♐ 16R	09
♄ ☌ ♅	18OCT88	08:18 AM	X	TR-TR	01	27 ♐ 49	09	27 ♐ 49	09

EST RETRO

Venus-Uranus

Important Stock Market indicator

	DATE	TIME	EX	JOB					
♅------------------SD	24APR60	00:00 AM	X	TR-TR					
♅------------------SR	30NOV60	09:40 PM	X	TR-TR	01	25♌48	12	25♌48	12
♀-------SR	20MAR61	03:24 PM	X	TR-TR	01	29♈06	08	29♈06	08
♅------------------SD	28APR61	11:03 PM	X	TR-TR	01	21♌39	12	21♌39	12
♀-------SD	01MAY61	11:10 PM	X	TR-TR	01	12♈44	08	12♈44	08
♅------------------SR	05DEC61	08:20 PM	X	TR-TR	01	00♍33	12	00♍33	12
♅------------------SD	04MAY62	01:57 AM	X	TR-TR	01	26♌24	12	26♌24	12
♀-------SR	22OCT62	11:58 PM	X	TR-TR	01	27♏38	03	27♏38	03
♀-------SD	03DEC62	07:36 AM	X	TR-TR	01	12♏13	03	12♏13	03
♅------------------SR	10DEC62	08:19 PM	X	TR-TR	01	05♍18	12	05♍18	12
♅------------------SD	09MAY63	02:28 AM	X	TR-TR	01	01♍09	12	01♍09	12
♅------------------SR	15DEC63	09:35 PM	X	TR-TR	01	10♍04	12	10♍04	12
♅------------------SD	13MAY64	04:38 AM	X	TR-TR	01	05♍55	12	05♍55	12
♀-------SR	29MAY64	04:52 AM	X	TR-TR	01	06♋52	10	06♋52	10
♀-------SD	11JUL64	08:30 AM	X	TR-TR	01	20♊21	10	20♊21	10
♅------------------SR	19DEC64	08:53 PM	X	TR-TR	01	14♍51	01	14♍51	01
♅------------------SD	18MAY65	08:33 AM	X	TR-TR	01	10♍42	12	10♍42	12
♅------------------SR	24DEC65	10:44 PM	X	TR-TR	01	19♍38	01	19♍38	01
♀-------SR	05JAN66	10:12 AM	X	TR-TR	01	13♒50	05	13♒50	05
♀-------SD	15FEB66	01:04 PM	X	TR-TR	01	28♑14	05	28♑14	05
♅------------------SD	23MAY66	09:26 AM	X	TR-TR	01	15♍29	01	15♍29	01
♅------------------SR	29DEC66	10:58 PM	X	TR-TR	01	24♍26	01	24♍26	01
♅------------------SD	28MAY67	03:27 PM	X	TR-TR	01	20♍17	01	20♍17	01
♀-------SR	08AUG67	10:05 AM	X	TR-TR	01	13♍54	01	13♍54	01
♀-------SD	20SEP67	04:41 AM	X	TR-TR	01	27♌38	12	27♌38	12
♅------------------SR	03JAN68	10:42 PM	X	TR-TR	01	29♍13	01	29♍13	01
♅------------------SD	01JUN68	05:12 PM	X	TR-TR	01	25♍04	01	25♍04	01
♅------------------SR	08JAN69	00:45 AM	X	TR-TR	01	04♎01	01	04♎01	01
♀-------SR	18MAR69	07:41 AM	X	TR-TR	01	26♈50	08	26♈50	08
♀-------SD	29APR69	03:03 PM	X	TR-TR	01	10♈30	07	10♈30	07
♅------------------SD	06JUN69	10:04 PM	X	TR-TR	01	29♍52	01	29♍52	01
♅------------------SR	12JAN70	10:25 PM	X	TR-TR	01	08♎48	01	08♎48	01
♅------------------SD	12JUN70	02:39 AM	X	TR-TR	01	04♎39	01	04♎39	01
♀-------SR	20OCT70	10:49 AM	X	TR-TR	01	25♏13	03	25♏13	03
♀-------SD	30NOV70	07:36 PM	X	TR-TR	01	09♏47	02	09♏47	02
♅------------------SR	18JAN71	00:19 AM	X	TR-TR	01	13♎34	02	13♎34	02
♅------------------SD	17JUN71	05:42 AM	X	TR-TR	01	09♎26	01	09♎26	01
♅------------------SR	22JAN72	10:10 PM	X	TR-TR	01	18♎19	02	18♎19	02
♀-------SR	26MAY72	09:07 PM	X	TR-TR	01	04♋45	10	04♋45	10
♅------------------SD	21JUN72	11:22 AM	X	TR-TR	01	14♎12	02	14♎12	02
♀-------SD	08JUL72	11:39 PM	X	TR-TR	01	18♊13	10	18♊13	10
♅------------------SR	26JAN73	09:14 PM	X	TR-TR	01	23♎04	02	23♎04	02
♅------------------SD	26JUN73	02:22 PM	X	TR-TR	01	18♎56	02	18♎56	02
♀-------SR	03JAN74	00:08 AM	X	TR-TR	01	11♒22	05	11♒22	05
♅------------------SR	31JAN74	08:03 PM	X	TR-TR	01	27♎47	02	27♎47	02
♀-------SD	13FEB74	01:51 AM	X	TR-TR	01	25♑48	05	25♑48	05
♅------------------SD	01JUL74	05:45 PM	X	TR-TR	01	23♎40	02	23♎40	02
♅------------------SR	05FEB75	04:25 PM	X	TR-TR	01	02♏28	02	02♏28	02
♅------------------SD	06JUL75	09:47 PM	X	TR-TR	01	28♎21	02	28♎21	02
♀-------SR	06AUG75	01:30 AM	X	TR-TR	01	11♍43	12	11♍43	12
♀-------SD	17SEP75	09:39 PM	X	TR-TR	01	25♌26	12	25♌26	12

EST RETRO

Venus-Uranus

Important Stock Market indicator

	DATE	TIME	EX	JOB					
♅ SR	10FEB76	03:20 PM	X	TR-TR					
♅ SD	10JUL76	10:36 PM	X	TR-TR	01	03♏02	02	03♏02	02
♅ SR	14FEB77	11:06 AM	X	TR-TR	01	11♏47	03	11♏47	03
♀ SR	15MAR77	10:56 PM	X	TR-TR	01	24♈34	08	24♈34	08
♀ SD	27APR77	05:59 AM	X	TR-TR	01	08♈15	07	08♈15	07
♅ SD	16JUL77	02:14 AM	X	TR-TR	01	07♏41	02	07♏41	02
♅ SR	19FEB78	08:15 AM	X	TR-TR	01	16♏24	03	16♏24	03
♅ SD	21JUL78	02:26 AM	X	TR-TR	01	12♏19	03	12♏19	03
♀ SR	17OCT78	10:04 PM	X	TR-TR	01	22♏48	03	22♏48	03
♀ SD	28NOV78	07:47 AM	X	TR-TR	01	07♏20	02	07♏20	02
♅ SR	24FEB79	04:37 AM	X	TR-TR	01	21♏00	03	21♏00	03
♅ SD	26JUL79	03:05 AM	X	TR-TR	01	16♏55	03	16♏55	03
♅ SR	28FEB80	10:56 PM	X	TR-TR	01	25♏34	03	25♏34	03
♀ SR	24MAY80	02:18 PM	X	TR-TR	01	02♋35	10	02♋35	10
♀ SD	06JUL80	03:34 PM	X	TR-TR	01	16♊03	10	16♊03	10
♅ SD	30JUL80	04:11 AM	X	TR-TR	01	21♏30	03	21♏30	03
♅ SR	04MAR81	07:21 PM	X	TR-TR	01	00♐07	03	00♐07	03
♅ SD	04AUG81	01:30 AM	X	TR-TR	01	26♏03	03	26♏03	03
♀ SR	31DEC81	02:32 PM	X	TR-TR	01	08♒54	05	08♒54	05
♀ SD	10FEB82	03:35 PM	X	TR-TR	01	23♑22	05	23♑22	05
♅ SR	09MAR82	12:27 PM	X	TR-TR	01	04♐38	03	04♐38	03
♅ SD	09AUG82	02:49 AM	X	TR-TR	01	00♐35	03	00♐35	03
♅ SR	14MAR83	06:50 AM	X	TR-TR	01	09♐07	03	09♐07	03
♀ SR	03AUG83	03:46 PM	X	TR-TR	01	09♍30	12	09♍30	12
♅ SD	13AUG83	10:43 PM	X	TR-TR	01	05♐04	03	05♐04	03
♀ SD	15SEP83	01:30 PM	X	TR-TR	01	23♌12	12	23♌12	12
♅ SR	18MAR84	00:05 AM	X	TR-TR	01	13♐34	04	13♐34	04
♅ SD	17AUG84	09:34 PM	X	TR-TR	01	09♐32	04	09♐32	04
♀ SR	13MAR85	01:38 PM	X	TR-TR	01	22♈18	08	22♈18	08
♅ SR	22MAR85	02:55 PM	X	TR-TR	01	17♐59	04	17♐59	04
♀ SD	24APR85	08:07 PM	X	TR-TR	01	06♈00	07	06♈00	07
♅ SD	22AUG85	05:57 PM	X	TR-TR	01	13♐58	04	13♐58	04
♅ SR	27MAR86	08:21 AM	X	TR-TR	01	22♐22	04	22♐22	04
♅ SD	27AUG86	12:51 PM	X	TR-TR	01	18♐21	04	18♐21	04
♀ SR	15OCT86	10:30 AM	X	TR-TR	01	20♏24	03	20♏24	03
♀ SD	25NOV86	08:47 PM	X	TR-TR	01	04♏54	02	04♏54	02
♅ SR	31MAR87	08:16 PM	X	TR-TR	01	26♐44	04	26♐44	04
♅ SD	01SEP87	08:50 AM	X	TR-TR	01	22♐43	04	22♐43	04
♅ SR	04APR88	12:38 PM	X	TR-TR	01	01♑03	04	01♑03	04
♀ SR	22MAY88	08:19 AM	X	TR-TR	01	00♋27	10	00♋27	10
♀ SD	04JUL88	08:35 AM	X	TR-TR	01	13♊56	10	13♊56	10
♅ SD	05SEP88	01:21 AM	X	TR-TR	01	27♐03	04	27♐03	04
♅ SR	09APR89	00:40 AM	X	TR-TR	01	05♑20	04	05♑20	04
♅ SD	09SEP89	07:01 PM	X	TR-TR	01	01♑20	04	01♑20	04
♀ SR	29DEC89	04:29 AM	X	TR-TR	01	06♒25	05	06♒25	05
♀ SD	08FEB90	04:59 AM	X	TR-TR	01	20♑55	05	20♑55	05
♅ SR	13APR90	02:04 PM	X	TR-TR	01	09♑35	04	09♑35	04
♅ SD	14SEP90	10:49 AM	X	TR-TR	01	05♑36	04	05♑36	04

Venus-Uranus

Important Stock Market indicator

	DATE	TIME	E X	JOB					
♀------□ ♅	11JAN80	11:16 AM	X	TR-TR	01	24 ♒ 31	06	24 ♏ 31	03
♀------△ ♅	05FEB80	08:38 PM	X	TR-TR	01	25 ♓ 19	07	25 ♏ 19	03
♀------☍ ♅	29MAR80	08:24 PM	X	TR-TR	01	25 ♉ 11	09	25 ♏ 11R	03
♀------△ ♅	30AUG80	03:54 PM	X	TR-TR	01	21 ♋ 55	11	21 ♏ 55	03
♀------□ ♅	28SEP80	02:43 PM	X	TR-TR	01	23 ♌ 00	12	23 ♏ 00	03
♀------⚹ ♅	25OCT80	02:20 PM	X	TR-TR	01	24 ♍ 27	01	24 ♏ 27	03
♀------☌ ♅	16DEC80	02:30 AM	X	TR-TR	01	27 ♏ 34	03	27 ♏ 34	03
♀------⚹ ♅	03FEB81	07:59 PM	X	TR-TR	01	29 ♑ 44	05	29 ♏ 44	03
♀------□ ♅	28FEB81	02:59 AM	X	TR-TR	01	00 ♓ 06	06	00 ♐ 06	03
♀------△ ♅	24MAR81	01:45 AM	X	TR-TR	01	29 ♓ 57R	07	29 ♏ 57R	03
♀------☍ ♅	10MAY81	08:46 AM	X	TR-TR	01	28 ♉ 28	09	28 ♏ 28R	03
♀------△ ♅	26JUN81	09:13 PM	X	TR-TR	01	26 ♋ 39	11	26 ♏ 39R	03
♀------□ ♅	21JUL81	04:18 AM	X	TR-TR	01	26 ♌ 08	12	26 ♏ 08R	03
♀------⚹ ♅	15AUG81	02:23 AM	X	TR-TR	01	26 ♍ 06	01	26 ♏ 06	03
♀------☌ ♅	06OCT81	06:22 PM	X	TR-TR	01	27 ♏ 42	03	27 ♏ 42	03
♀------⚹ ♅	10DEC81	10:29 PM	X	TR-TR	01	01 ♒ 31	05	01 ♐ 31	03
♀------⚹ ♅	17JAN82	04:47 AM	X	TR-TR	01	03 ♒ 28R	05	03 ♐ 28	03
♀------⚹ ♅	09MAR82	02:32 AM	X	TR-TR	01	04 ♒ 38	05	04 ♐ 38	03
♀------□ ♅	10APR82	09:42 AM	X	TR-TR	01	04 ♓ 12	06	04 ♐ 12R	03
♀------△ ♅	07MAY82	06:21 AM	X	TR-TR	01	03 ♈ 18	07	03 ♐ 18R	03
♀------☍ ♅	26JUN82	10:19 AM	X	TR-TR	01	01 ♊ 20	09	01 ♐ 20R	03
♀------△ ♅	14AUG82	05:46 PM	X	TR-TR	01	00 ♌ 35	11	00 ♐ 35	03
♀------□ ♅	08SEP82	11:27 AM	X	TR-TR	01	00 ♍ 58	12	00 ♐ 58	03
♀------⚹ ♅	03OCT82	07:56 AM	X	TR-TR	01	01 ♎ 50	01	01 ♐ 50	03
♀------☌ ♅	22NOV82	09:48 AM	X	TR-TR	01	04 ♐ 35	03	04 ♐ 35	03
♀------⚹ ♅	11JAN83	12:21 PM	X	TR-TR	01	07 ♒ 29	05	07 ♐ 29	03
♀------□ ♅	05FEB83	08:23 AM	X	TR-TR	01	08 ♓ 30	06	08 ♐ 30	03
♀------△ ♅	02MAR83	00:50 AM	X	TR-TR	01	09 ♈ 02	07	09 ♐ 02	03
♀------☍ ♅	20APR83	01:01 PM	X	TR-TR	01	08 ♊ 32	09	08 ♐ 32R	03
♀------△ ♅	12JUN83	01:04 PM	X	TR-TR	01	06 ♌ 30	11	06 ♐ 30R	03
♀------□ ♅	19JUL83	00:46 AM	X	TR-TR	01	05 ♍ 21	12	05 ♐ 21R	03
♀------□ ♅	18AUG83	08:09 PM	X	TR-TR	01	05 ♍ 05R	12	05 ♐ 05	03
♀------□ ♅	15OCT83	01:08 AM	X	TR-TR	01	06 ♍ 38	12	06 ♐ 38	03
♀------⚹ ♅	17NOV83	05:45 AM	X	TR-TR	01	08 ♎ 28	01	08 ♐ 28	03
♀------☌ ♅	10JAN84	12:44 PM	X	TR-TR	01	11 ♐ 40	04	11 ♐ 40	04
♀------⚹ ♅	29FEB84	09:21 PM	X	TR-TR	01	13 ♒ 26	05	13 ♐ 26	04
♀------□ ♅	25MAR84	06:59 AM	X	TR-TR	01	13 ♓ 32	07	13 ♐ 32R	04
♀------△ ♅	18APR84	07:28 AM	X	TR-TR	01	13 ♈ 09	08	13 ♐ 09R	04
♀------☍ ♅	04JUN84	05:12 PM	X	TR-TR	01	11 ♊ 27	10	11 ♐ 27R	04
♀------△ ♅	22JUL84	05:17 AM	X	TR-TR	01	09 ♌ 50	11	09 ♐ 50R	03
♀------□ ♅	15AUG84	08:42 AM	X	TR-TR	01	09 ♍ 32	12	09 ♐ 32R	03
♀------⚹ ♅	08SEP84	10:27 PM	X	TR-TR	01	09 ♎ 44	01	09 ♐ 44	03
♀------☌ ♅	29OCT84	02:28 PM	X	TR-TR	01	11 ♐ 38	04	11 ♐ 38	04
♀------⚹ ♅	21DEC84	02:43 PM	X	TR-TR	01	14 ♒ 46	06	14 ♐ 46	04
♀------□ ♅	19JAN85	06:16 AM	X	TR-TR	01	16 ♓ 21	07	16 ♐ 21	04
♀------△ ♅	25FEB85	01:46 PM	X	TR-TR	01	17 ♈ 42	08	17 ♐ 42	04
♀------△ ♅	28MAR85	06:54 AM	X	TR-TR	01	17 ♈ 58R	08	17 ♐ 58R	04
♀------△ ♅	20MAY85	08:47 PM	X	TR-TR	01	16 ♈ 40	08	16 ♐ 40R	04
♀------☍ ♅	19JUL85	08:32 AM	X	TR-TR	01	14 ♊ 27	10	14 ♐ 27R	04
♀------△ ♅	08SEP85	06:00 PM	X	TR-TR	01	14 ♌ 05	11	14 ♐ 05	04
♀------□ ♅	03OCT85	10:39 PM	X	TR-TR	01	14 ♍ 42	01	14 ♐ 42	04

Venus-Uranus

Important Stock Market indicator

		DATE	TIME	E X	JOB		
♀------⚹	♅	29OCT85	00:57 AM	X	TR-TR		
♀------☌	♅	18DEC85	04:35 AM	X	TR-TR 01	18♐41 04	18♐41 04
♀------⚹	♅	06FEB86	00:16 AM	X	TR-TR 01	21♒20 06	21♐20 04
♀------□	♅	02MAR86	02:30 PM	X	TR-TR 01	22♓06 07	22♐06 04
♀------△	♅	26MAR86	11:09 PM	X	TR-TR 01	22♈22 08	22♐22 04
♀------☍	♅	14MAY86	06:47 AM	X	TR-TR 01	21♊28 10	21♐28R 04
♀------△	♅	02JUL86	08:22 AM	X	TR-TR 01	19♌33 12	19♐33R 04
♀------□	♅	28JUL86	05:32 AM	X	TR-TR 01	18♏44 01	18♐44R 04
♀------⚹	♅	25AUG86	03:13 PM	X	TR-TR 01	18♎22 02	18♐22R 04

EST.HELIO MERC/JUP/SAT

Heliocentric Mercury-Jupiter Mercury-Saturn

Natural Harmonic in the Wheat Market

		DATE	TIME	EX	J					
☿----☌	♄	27JAN84	12:53 PM	X	TR					
☿----☌	♃	13FEB84	03:52 AM	X	TR					
☿----☍	♄	18MAR84	08:08 PM	X	TR-TR	01	11 ♉ 40	06	11 ♏ 40	12
☿----☍	♃	26MAR84	04:17 PM	X	TR-TR	01	00 ♋ 19	08	00 ♑ 19	02
☿----☌	♄	25APR84	10:25 AM	X	TR-TR	01	12 ♏ 50	12	12 ♏ 50	12
☿----☌	♃	13MAY84	06:25 PM	X	TR-TR	01	04 ♑ 15	02	04 ♑ 15	02
☿----☍	♄	15JUN84	06:36 AM	X	TR-TR	01	14 ♉ 26	06	14 ♏ 26	12
☿----☍	♃	23JUN84	07:31 PM	X	TR-TR	01	07 ♋ 37	08	07 ♑ 37	02
☿----☌	♄	23JUL84	08:10 AM	X	TR-TR	01	15 ♏ 38	12	15 ♏ 38	12
☿----☌	♃	12AUG84	08:22 AM	X	TR-TR	01	11 ♑ 42	02	11 ♑ 42	02
☿----☍	♄	11SEP84	04:55 PM	X	TR-TR	01	17 ♉ 12	06	17 ♏ 12	12
☿----☍	♃	20SEP84	11:29 PM	X	TR-TR	01	15 ♋ 00	08	15 ♑ 00	02
☿----☌	♄	20OCT84	06:08 AM	X	TR-TR	01	18 ♏ 24	12	18 ♏ 24	12
☿----☌	♃	10NOV84	09:14 PM	X	TR-TR	01	19 ♑ 15	02	19 ♑ 15	02
☿----☍	♄	09DEC84	03:07 AM	X	TR-TR	'01	19 ♉ 57	06	19 ♏ 57	12
☿----☍	♃	19DEC84	04:26 AM	X	TR-TR	01	22 ♋ 29	08	22 ♑ 29	02
☿----☌	♄	17JAN85	04:17 AM	X	TR-TR	01	21 ♏ 10	12	21 ♏ 10	12
☿----☌	♃	09FEB85	08:36 AM	X	TR-TR	01	26 ♑ 54	02	26 ♑ 54	02
☿----☍	♄	07MAR85	01:11 PM	X	TR-TR	01	22 ♉ 42	06	22 ♏ 42	12
☿----☍	♃	18MAR85	10:31 AM	X	TR-TR	01	00 ♌ 03	09	00 ♒ 03	03
☿----☌	♄	16APR85	02:36 AM	X	TR-TR	01	23 ♏ 55	12	23 ♏ 55	12
☿----☌	♃	10MAY85	06:08 PM	X	TR-TR	01	04 ♒ 38	03	04 ♒ 38	03
☿----☍	♄	03JUN85	11:09 PM	X	TR-TR	01	25 ♉ 26	06	25 ♏ 26	12
☿----☍	♃	15JUN85	05:58 PM	X	TR-TR	01	07 ♌ 44	09	07 ♒ 44	03
☿----☌	♄	14JUL85	01:02 AM	X	TR-TR	01	26 ♏ 40	12	26 ♏ 40	12
☿----☌	♃	09AUG85	01:32 AM	X	TR-TR	01	12 ♒ 27	03	12 ♒ 27	03
☿----☍	♄	31AUG85	08:59 AM	X	TR-TR	01	28 ♉ 09	06	28 ♏ 09	12
☿----☍	♃	13SEP85	03:04 AM	X	TR-TR	01	15 ♌ 31	09	15 ♒ 31	03
☿----☌	♄	10OCT85	11:36 PM	X	TR-TR	01	29 ♏ 24	01	29 ♏ 24	01
☿----☌	♃	07NOV85	06:37 AM	X	TR-TR	01	20 ♒ 21	03	20 ♒ 21	03
☿----☍	♄	27NOV85	06:45 PM	X	TR-TR	01	00 ♊ 52	07	00 ♐ 52	01
☿----☍	♃	11DEC85	02:03 PM	X	TR-TR	01	23 ♌ 23	09	23 ♒ 23	03
☿----☌	♄	07JAN86	10:16 PM	X	TR-TR	01	02 ♐ 08	01	02 ♐ 08	01
☿----☌	♃	05FEB86	09:18 AM	X	TR-TR	01	28 ♒ 20	03	28 ♒ 20	03
☿----☍	♄	24FEB86	04:25 AM	X	TR-TR	01	03 ♊ 35	07	03 ♐ 35	01
☿----☍	♃	11MAR86	03:14 AM	X	TR-TR	01	01 ♍ 20	09	01 ♓ 20	03
☿----☌	♄	06APR86	09:01 PM	X	TR-TR	01	04 ♐ 51	01	04 ♐ 51	01
☿----☌	♃	06MAY86	09:34 AM	X	TR-TR	01	06 ♓ 22	03	06 ♓ 22	03
☿----☍	♄	23MAY86	02:02 PM	X	TR-TR	01	06 ♊ 17	07	06 ♐ 17	01
☿----☍	♃	08JUN86	06:53 PM	X	TR-TR	01	09 ♍ 23	09	09 ♓ 23	03
☿----☌	♄	04JUL86	07:49 PM	X	TR-TR	01	07 ♐ 34	01	07 ♐ 34	01
☿----☌	♃	04AUG86	07:25 AM	X	TR-TR	01	14 ♓ 29	03	14 ♓ 29	03
☿----☍	♄	19AUG86	11:34 PM	X	TR-TR	01	08 ♊ 59	07	08 ♐ 59	01
☿----☍	♃	06SEP86	01:16 PM	X	TR-TR	01	17 ♍ 29	10	17 ♓ 29	04
☿----☌	♄	01OCT86	06:38 PM	X	TR-TR	01	10 ♐ 17	01	10 ♐ 17	01
☿----☌	♃	02NOV86	02:56 AM	X	TR-TR	01	22 ♓ 38	04	22 ♓ 38	04
☿----☍	♄	16NOV86	09:03 AM	X	TR-TR	01	11 ♊ 40	07	11 ♐ 40	01
☿----☍	♃	05DEC86	10:39 AM	X	TR-TR	01	25 ♍ 40	10	25 ♓ 40	04
☿----☌	♄	29DEC86	05:28 PM	X	TR-TR	01	12 ♐ 59	01	12 ♐ 59	01
☿----☌	♃	30JAN87	08:15 PM	X	TR-TR	01	00 ♈ 49	04	00 ♈ 49	04
☿----☍	♄	12FEB87	06:30 PM	X	TR-TR	01	14 ♊ 21	07	14 ♐ 21	01

:EST.HELIO MERC/JUP/SAT

Heliocentric Mercury-Jupiter Mercury-Saturn

Natural Harmonic in the Wheat Market

		DATE	TIME	E X	J		
☿ ----☍	♃	05MAR87	11:18 AM	X	TF		
☿ ----☌	♄	28MAR87	04:17 PM	X	TF		
☿ ----☌	♃	30APR87	11:32 AM	X	TR-TR 01	09♈01 04	09♈01 04
☿ ----☍	♄	12MAY87	03:56 AM	X	TR-TR 01	17♊01 07	17♐01 01
☿ ----☍	♃	03JUN87	03:21 PM	X	TR-TR 01	12♎09 11	12♈09 05
☿ ----☌	♄	25JUN87	03:04 PM	X	TR-TR 01	18♐22 01	18♐22 01
☿ ----☌	♃	29JUL87	00:56 AM	X	TR-TR 01	17♈13 05	17♈13 05
☿ ----☍	♄	08AUG87	01:20 PM	X	TR-TR 01	19♊42 07	19♐42 01
☿ ----☍	♃	01SEP87	10:50 PM	X	TR-TR 01	20♎25 11	20♈25 05
☿ ----☌	♄	22SEP87	01:47 PM	X	TR-TR 01	21♐04 01	21♐04 01
☿ ----☌	♃	26OCT87	12:37 PM	X	TR-TR 01	25♈25 05	25♈25 05
☿ ----☍	♄	04NOV87	10:43 PM	X	TR-TR 01	22♊22 07	22♐22 01
☿ ----☍	♃	01DEC87	09:42 AM	X	TR-TR 01	28♎42 11	28♈42 05
☿ ----☌	♄	20DEC87	12:25 PM	X	TR-TR 01	23♐45 01	23♐45 01
☿ ----☌	♃	23JAN88	10:46 PM	X	TR-TR 01	03♉35 05	03♉35 05
☿ ----☍	♄	01FEB88	08:06 AM	X	TR-TR 01	25♊02 08	25♐02 02
☿ ----☍	♃	29FEB88	11:43 PM	X	TR-TR 01	06♏58 12	06♉58 06
☿ ----☌	♄	18MAR88	10:57 AM	X	TR-TR 01	26♐26 02	26♐26 02
☿ ----☌	♃	22APR88	07:35 AM	X	TR-TR 01	11♉44 06	11♉44 06
☿ ----☍	♄	29APR88	05:30 PM	X	TR-TR 01	27♊42 08	27♐42 02
☿ ----☍	♃	30MAY88	04:29 PM	X	TR-TR 01	15♏12 12	15♉12 06
☿ ----☌	♄	15JUN88	09:21 AM	X	TR-TR 01	29♐06 02	29♐06 02
☿ ----☌	♃	20JUL88	03:16 PM	X	TR-TR 01	19♉49 06	19♉49 06
☿ ----☍	♄	27JUL88	02:56 AM	X	TR-TR 01	00♋22 08	00♑22 02
☿ ----☍	♃	29AUG88	11:25 AM	X	TR-TR 01	23♏24 12	23♉24 06
☿ ----☌	♄	12SEP88	07:37 AM	X	TR-TR 01	01♑47 02	01♑47 02
☿ ----☌	♃	17OCT88	09:58 PM	X	TR-TR 01	27♉50 06	27♉50 06
☿ ----☍	♄	23OCT88	12:22 PM	X	TR-TR 01	03♋02 08	03♑02 02
☿ ----☍	♃	28NOV88	07:49 AM	X	TR-TR 01	01♐32 01	01♊32 07
☿ ----☌	♄	10DEC88	05:43 AM	X	TR-TR 01	04♑28 02	04♑28 02
☿ ----☌	♃	15JAN89	03:51 AM	X	TR-TR 01	05♊47 07	05♊47 07
☿ ----☍	♄	19JAN89	09:50 PM	X	TR-TR 01	05♋41 08	05♑41 02
☿ ----☍	♃	27FEB89	04:53 AM	X	TR-TR 01	09♐35 01	09♊35 07
☿ ----☌	♄	09MAR89	03:38 AM	X	TR-TR 01	07♑09 02	07♑09 02
☿ ----☌	♃	14APR89	09:06 AM	X	TR-TR 01	13♊39 07	13♊39 07
☿ ----☍	♄	18APR89	07:22 AM	X	TR-TR 01	08♋21 08	08♑21 02
☿ ----☍	♃	29MAY89	01:46 AM	X	TR-TR 01	17♐33 01	17♊33 07
☿ ----☌	♄	06JUN89	01:22 AM	X	TR-TR 01	09♑49 02	09♑49 02
☿ ----☌	♃	12JUL89	01:54 PM	X	TR-TR 01	21♊25 07	21♊25 07
☿ ----☍	♄	15JUL89	04:57 PM	X	TR-TR 01	11♋01 08	11♑01 02
☿ ----☍	♃	27AUG89	09:40 PM	X	TR-TR 01	25♐26 02	25♊26 08
☿ ----☌	♄	02SEP89	10:53 PM	X	TR-TR 01	12♑30 02	12♑30 02
☿ ----☌	♃	09OCT89	06:24 PM	X	TR-TR 01	29♊07 08	29♊07 08
☿ ----☍	♄	12OCT89	02:36 AM	X	TR-TR 01	13♋41 08	13♑41 02
☿ ----☍	♃	26NOV89	03:51 PM	X	TR-TR 01	03♑12 02	03♋12 08
☿ ----☌	♄	30NOV89	08:11 PM	X	TR-TR 01	15♑11 02	15♑11 02

		DATE	TIME		EX	JO					
♇-------□	E	28JAN82	08:03	AM	X	TR-TR	01	26 ♑ 56R	01	26 ♎ 56	09
♇-------□	E	24FEB82	05:30	AM	X	TR-TR	01	26 ♑ 44	01	26 ♎ 44R	09
♇-------△	E	02APR82	05:38	AM	X	TR-TR	01	25 ♒ 56	02	25 ♎ 56R	09
♇-------☍	E	25MAY82	10:21	PM	X	TR-TR	01	24 ♈ 32	03	24 ♎ 32R	09
♇-------△	E	15JUL82	02:27	PM	X	TR-TR	01	24 ♊ 09	06	24 ♎ 09	09
♇-------□	E	09AUG82	05:34	PM	X	TR-TR	01	24 ♋ 29	07	24 ♎ 29	09
♇-------✶	E	03SEP82	06:00	PM	X	TR-TR	01	25 ♌ 08	08	25 ♎ 08	09
♇-------☌	E	23OCT82	10:37	AM	X	TR-TR	01	26 ♎ 59	09	26 ♎ 59	09
♇-------✶	E	11DEC82	03:42	PM	X	TR-TR	01	28 ♐ 46	12	28 ♎ 46	09
♇-------□	E	04JAN83	11:49	PM	X	TR-TR	01	29 ♑ 19	01	29 ♎ 19	09
♇-------△	E	29JAN83	03:30	AM	X	TR-TR	01	29 ♒ 32	02	29 ♎ 32	09
♇-------☍	E	18MAR83	08:31	AM	X	TR-TR	01	28 ♈ 58	03	28 ♎ 58R	09
♇-------△	E	07MAY83	03:40	AM	X	TR-TR	01	27 ♊ 38	06	27 ♎ 38R	09
♇-------□	E	03JUN83	03:40	AM	X	TR-TR	01	27 ♋ 02	07	27 ♎ 02R	09
♇-------✶	E	05JUL83	10:43	AM	X	TR-TR	01	26 ♌ 43	08	26 ♎ 43R	09
♇-------✶	E	31AUG83	11:44	AM	X	TR-TR	01	27 ♌ 33R	08	27 ♎ 33	09
♇-------✶	E	03OCT83	08:40	AM	X	TR-TR	01	28 ♌ 41	08	28 ♎ 41	09
♇-------☌	E	07DEC83	11:19	AM	X	TR-TR	01	01 ♏ 09	09	01 ♏ 09	09
♇-------✶	E	27JAN84	07:30	AM	X	TR-TR	01	02 ♑ 07	12	02 ♏ 07	09
♇-------□	E	20FEB84	03:59	PM	X	TR-TR	01	02 ♒ 04	01	02 ♏ 03R	09
♇-------△	E	15MAR84	04:16	PM	X	TR-TR	01	01 ♓ 41	02	01 ♏ 41R	09
♇-------☍	E	02MAY84	08:08	AM	X	TR-TR	01	00 ♉ 25	03	00 ♏ 25R	09
♇-------△	E	19JUN84	08:38	AM	X	TR-TR	01	29 ♊ 26	06	29 ♎ 26R	09
♇-------□	E	13JUL94	04:20	PM	X	TR-TR	01	29 ♋ 19	07	29 ♎ 19	09
♇-------✶	E	07AUG84	06:03	AM	X	TR-TR	01	29 ♌ 33	08	29 ♎ 33	09
♇-------☌	E	26SEP84	05:34	AM	X	TR-TR	01	00 ♏ 57	09	00 ♏ 57	09
♇-------✶	E	16NOV84	05:48	AM	X	TR-TR	01	02 ♑ 57	12	02 ♏ 57	09
♇-------□	E	12DEC84	05:19	AM	X	TR-TR	01	03 ♒ 51	01	03 ♏ 51	09
♇-------△	E	08JAN85	03:35	AM	X	TR-TR	01	04 ♓ 30	02	04 ♏ 30	09
♇-------☍	E	08JUN85	02:18	PM	X	TR-TR	01	02 ♉ 14	03	02 ♏ 14R	09
♇-------△	E	03AUG85	11:49	PM	X	TR-TR	01	02 ♋ 05	06	02 ♏ 05	09
♇-------□	E	30AUG85	03:11	AM	X	TR-TR	01	02 ♌ 36	07	02 ♏ 36	09
♇-------✶	E	24SEP85	04:48	PM	X	TR-TR	01	03 ♍ 24	08	03 ♏ 24	09
♇-------☌	E	13NOV85	04:50	PM	X	TR-TR	01	05 ♏ 21	09	05 ♏ 21	09
♇-------✶	E	01JAN86	04:38	PM	X	TR-TR	01	06 ♑ 56	12	06 ♏ 56	09
♇-------□	E	25JAN86	08:15	PM	X	TR-TR	01	07 ♒ 19	01	07 ♏ 19	10
♇-------△	E	18FEB86	06:51	PM	X	TR-TR	01	07 ♓ 20	02	07 ♏ 20R	10
♇-------☍	E	07APR86	09:55	AM	X	TR-TR	01	06 ♉ 30	03	06 ♏ 30R	09
♇-------△	E	25MAY86	04:41	PM	X	TR-TR	01	05 ♋ 12	06	05 ♏ 12R	09
♇-------□	E	19JUN86	02:20	PM	X	TR-TR	01	04 ♌ 43	07	04 ♏ 43R	09
♇-------✶	E	15JUL86	11:36	AM	X	TR-TR	01	04 ♍ 33	08	04 ♏ 33	09
♇-------☌	E	13SEP86	09:07	PM	X	TR-TR	01	05 ♏ 33	09	05 ♏ 33	09
♇-------☌	E	13NOV86	07:59	PM	X	TR-TR	01	07 ♏ 52R	10	07 ♏ 52	10
♇-------☌	E	10DEC86	03:25	PM	X	TR-TR	01	08 ♏ 51	10	08 ♏ 51	10
♇-------✶	E	13FEB87	06:59	PM	X	TR-TR	01	09 ♑ 59	12	09 ♏ 59R	10
♇-------□	E	11MAR87	10:18	AM	X	TR-TR	01	09 ♒ 45	01	09 ♏ 45R	10
♇-------△	E	05APR87	04:47	AM	X	TR-TR	01	09 ♓ 15	02	09 ♏ 15R	10
♇-------☍	E	23MAY87	07:53	PM	X	TR-TR	01	07 ♉ 55	04	07 ♏ 55R	10
♇-------△	E	11JUL97	11:27	AM	X	TR-TR	01	07 ♋ 10	06	07 ♏ 10R	09
♇-------□	E	04AUG87	11:03	PM	X	TR-TR	01	07 ♌ 15	07	07 ♏ 15	09
♇-------✶	E	29AUG87	01:25	PM	X	TR-TR	01	07 ♍ 40	08	07 ♏ 40	10

VENUS/PLUT,GEO EST GOLD

Venus Pluto

Natural Harmonic in the Gold Market

	DATE	TIME	EX	JOB #	POS. HS	POS. HS
♀------☌ E	18OCT87	02:49 AM	X	TR-TR 01	09♏17 10	09♏17 10
♀------⚹ E	06DEC87	10:05 PM	X	TR-TR 01	11♑14 01	11♏14 10

Retrograde
Uranus-Saturn effects stocks Jupiter effects stocks Neptune effects bonds Pluto effects gold

RETROGRADE,ESY GEO

		DATE	TIME		E X	J					
♇	SR	11JAN75	06:56	AM	X	TR-TR	01	09♎15	05	09♎15	05
♅	SR	05FEB75	06:21	PM	X	TR-TR	01	02♏28	06	02♏28	06
♄	SD	16MAR75	02:11	AM	X	TR-TR	01	11♋57	02	11♋57	02
♆	SR		03:19	AM	X	TR-TR	01	11♐48	07	11♐48	07
♇	SD	15JUN75	07:05	PM	X	TR-TR	01	06♎29	05	06♎29	05
♅	SD	06JUL75	08:18	PM	X	TR-TR	01	28♎21	06	28♎21	06
♃	SR	14AUG75	01:08	PM	X	TR-TR	01	24♈42	12	24♈42	12
♆	SD	21AUG75	04:43	AM	X	TR-TR	01	09♐01	07	09♐01	07
♄	SR	14NOV75	02:38	PM	X	TR-TR	01	02♌59	04	02♌59	04
♃	SD	10DEC75	08:13	AM	X	TR-TR	01	14♈45	11	14♈45	11
♇	SR	14JAN76	01:55	AM	X	TR-TR	01	11♎43	05	11♎43	05
♅	SR	10FEB76	02:01	PM	X	TR-TR	01	07♏09	06	07♏09	06
♆	SR	15MAR76	12:51	PM	X	TR-TR	01	13♐58	07	13♐58	07
♄	SD	27MAR76	01:57	PM	X	TR-TR	01	26♋02	03	26♋02	03
♇	SD	18JUN76	10:48	AM	X	TR-TR	01	08♎56	05	08♎56	05
♅	SD	11JUL76	00:37	AM	X	TR-TR	01	03♏02	06	03♏02	06
♆	SD	22AUG76	04:37	PM	X	TR-TR	01	11♐12	07	11♐12	07
♃	SR	19SEP76	01:36	PM	X	TR-TR	01	01♊12	01	01♊12	01
♄	SR	27NOV76	01:56	PM	X	TR-TR	01	16♌53	04	16♌53	04
♃	SD	15JAN77	04:11	AM	X	TR-TR	01	21♉10	12	21♉10	12
♇	SR		07:34	PM	X	TR-TR	01	14♎11	05	14♎11	05
♅	SR	14FEB77	11:44	AM	X	TR-TR	01	11♏47	06	11♏47	06
♆	SR	18MAR77	00:32	AM	X	TR-TR	01	16♐09	07	16♐09	07
♄	SD	11APR77	00:07	AM	X	TR-TR	01	09♌57	04	09♌57	04
♇	SD	21JUN77	04:56	AM	X	TR-TR	01	11♎24	05	11♎24	05
♅	SD	16JUL77	00:39	AM	X	TR-TR	01	07♏41	06	07♏41	06
♆	SD	25AUG77	04:10	AM	X	TR-TR	01	13♐22	07	13♐22	07
♃	SR	24OCT77	04:13	AM	X	TR-TR	01	06♋09	02	06♋09	02
♄	SR	11DEC77	05:46	AM	X	TR-TR	01	00♍33	04	00♍33	04
♇	SR	18JAN78	04:13	PM	X	TR-TR	01	16♎42	05	16♎42	05
♅	SR	19FEB78	08:26	AM	X	TR-TR	01	16♏24	06	16♏24	06
♃	SD		08:59	PM	X	TR-TR	01	26♊04	02	26♊04	02
♆	SR	20MAR78	10:20	AM	X	TR-TR	01	18♐19	07	18♐19	07
♄	SD	25APR78	06:26	AM	X	TR-TR	01	23♌39	04	23♌39	04
♇	SD	23JUN78	09:40	PM	X	TR-TR	01	13♎54	05	13♎54	05
♅	SD	21JUL78	02:53	AM	X	TR-TR	01	12♏19	06	12♏19	06
♆	SD	27AUG78	03:26	PM	X	TR-TR	01	15♐33	07	15♐33	07
♃	SR	25NOV78	02:52	PM	X	TR-TR	01	09♌04	04	09♌04	04
♄	SR	24DEC78	02:05	PM	X	TR-TR	01	13♍56	05	13♍56	05
♇	SR	21JAN79	10:47	AM	X	TR-TR	01	19♎14	05	19♎14	05
♅	SR	24FEB79	03:15	AM	X	TR-TR	01	21♏00	06	21♏00	06
♆	SR	22MAR79	10:14	PM	X	TR-TR	01	20♐30	07	20♐30	07
♃	SD	25MAR79	06:02	PM	X	TR-TR	01	29♋00	03	29♋00	03
♄	SD	09MAY79	08:04	AM	X	TR-TR	01	07♍05	05	07♍05	05
♇	SD	26JUN79	05:46	PM	X	TR-TR	01	16♎25	05	16♎25	05
♅	SD	26JUL79	03:26	AM	X	TR-TR	01	16♏55	06	16♏55	06
♆	SD	30AUG79	02:45	AM	X	TR-TR	01	17♐43	07	17♐43	07
♃	SR	26DEC79	10:33	AM	X	TR-TR	01	10♍15	05	10♍15	05
♄	SR	06JAN80	03:28	PM	X	TR-TR	01	27♍01	05	27♍01	05
♇	SR	24JAN80	08:22	AM	X	TR-TR	01	21♎47	06	21♎47	06
♅	SR	29FEB80	00:43	AM	X	TR-TR	01	25♏34	06	25♏34	06

Retrograde

Uranus-Saturn effects stocks
Jupiter effects stocks
Neptune effects bonds
Pluto effects gold

	DATE	TIME	EX	JOB					
♅ SR	22MAR85	03:51 PM	X	TR-TR					
♆ SR	04APR85	06:30 PM	X	TR-TR	01	03 ♑ 37	10	03 ♑ 37	10
♃ SR	04JUN85	05:10 PM	X	TR-TR	01	16 ♒ 58	12	16 ♒ 58	12
♇ SD	12JUL85	00:37 AM	X	TR-TR	01	01 ♏ 56	08	01 ♏ 56	08
♄ SD	25JUL85	12:36 PM	X	TR-TR	01	21 ♏ 28	09	21 ♏ 28	09
♅ SD	22AUG85	05:14 PM	X	TR-TR	01	13 ♐ 58	09	13 ♐ 58	09
♆ SD	12SEP85	00:03 AM	X	TR-TR	01	00 ♑ 51	10	00 ♑ 51	10
♃ SD	03OCT85	01:37 AM	X	TR-TR	01	07 ♒ 07	12	07 ♒ 07	12
♇ SR	08FEB86	11:58 AM	X	TR-TR	01	07 ♏ 22	08	07 ♏ 22	08
♄ SR	19MAR86	03:56 AM	X	TR-TR	01	09 ♐ 42	09	09 ♐ 42	09
♅ SR	27MAR86	06:39 AM	X	TR-TR	01	22 ♐ 22	10	22 ♐ 22	10
♆ SR	07APR86	05:04 AM	X	TR-TR	01	05 ♑ 49	11	05 ♑ 49	11
♃ SR	12JUL86	10:56 AM	X	TR-TR	01	22 ♓ 51	01	22 ♓ 51	01
♇ SD	14JUL86	08:52 PM	X	TR-TR	01	04 ♏ 33	08	04 ♏ 33	08
♄ SD	06AUG86	10:09 PM	X	TR-TR	01	03 ♐ 04	09	03 ♐ 04	09
♅ SD	27AUG86	02:28 PM	X	TR-TR	01	18 ♐ 21	10	18 ♐ 21	10
♆ SD	14SEP86	10:31 AM	X	TR-TR	01	03 ♑ 02	10	03 ♑ 02	10
♃ SD	08NOV86	05:22 AM	X	TR-TR	01	12 ♓ 58	01	12 ♓ 58	01
♇ SR	11FEB87	06:50 AM	X	TR-TR	01	09 ♏ 59	08	09 ♏ 59	08
♄ SR	30MAR87	11:50 PM	X	TR-TR	01	21 ♐ 10	10	21 ♐ 10	10
♅ SR	31MAR87	10:27 PM	X	TR-TR	01	26 ♐ 44	10	26 ♐ 44	10
♆ SR	09APR87	04:33 PM	X	TR-TR	01	08 ♑ 00	11	08 ♑ 00	11
♇ SD	17JUL87	09:18 PM	X	TR-TR	01	07 ♏ 09	08	07 ♏ 09	08
♄ SD	19AUG87	03:36 AM	X	TR-TR	01	14 ♐ 32	09	14 ♐ 32	09
♃ SR		04:11 PM	X	TR-TR	01	29 ♈ 44	02	29 ♈ 44	02
♅ SD	01SEP87	06:59 AM	X	TR-TR	01	22 ♐ 43	10	22 ♐ 43	10
♆ SD	17SEP87	00:20 AM	X	TR-TR	01	05 ♑ 14	10	05 ♑ 14	10
♃ SD	15DEC87	05:28 AM	X	TR-TR	01	19 ♈ 46	02	19 ♈ 46	02
♇ SR	14FEB88	04:32 AM	X	TR-TR	01	12 ♏ 36	08	12 ♏ 36	08
♅ SR	04APR88	11:01 AM	X	TR-TR	01	01 ♑ 03	10	01 ♑ 03	10
♄ SR	10APR88	07:14 PM	X	TR-TR	01	02 ♑ 33	10	02 ♑ 33	10
♆ SR	11APR88	03:59 AM	X	TR-TR	01	10 ♑ 12	11	10 ♑ 12	11
♇ SD	19JUL88	06:06 PM	X	TR-TR	01	09 ♏ 46	08	09 ♏ 46	08
♄ SD	30AUG88	04:07 AM	X	TR-TR	01	25 ♐ 56	10	25 ♐ 56	10
♅ SD	05SEP88	03:24 AM	X	TR-TR	01	27 ♐ 03	10	27 ♐ 03	10
♆ SD	18SEP88	09:50 AM	X	TR-TR	01	07 ♑ 25	11	07 ♑ 25	11
♃ SR	24SEP88	07:45 AM	X	TR-TR	01	06 ♊ 08	03	06 ♊ 08	03
♃ SD	20JAN89	02:22 AM	X	TR-TR	01	26 ♉ 05	03	26 ♉ 05	03
♇ SR	15FEB89	11:45 PM	X	TR-TR	01	15 ♏ 12	08	15 ♏ 12	08
♅ SR	09APR89	01:17 AM	X	TR-TR	01	05 ♑ 20	10	05 ♑ 20	10
♆ SR	13APR89	02:28 PM	X	TR-TR	01	12 ♑ 23	11	12 ♑ 23	11
♄ SR	22APR89	04:04 PM	X	TR-TR	01	13 ♑ 56	11	13 ♑ 56	11
♇ SD	22JUL89	06:03 PM	X	TR-TR	01	12 ♏ 22	08	12 ♏ 22	08
♅ SD	09SEP89	05:51 PM	X	TR-TR	01	01 ♑ 20	10	01 ♑ 20	10
♄ SD	11SEP89	00:59 AM	X	TR-TR	01	07 ♑ 18	11	07 ♑ 18	11
♆ SD	20SEP89	11:53 PM	X	TR-TR	01	09 ♑ 37	11	09 ♑ 37	11
♃ SR	28OCT89	07:27 PM	X	TR-TR	01	10 ♋ 53	05	10 ♋ 53	05
♇ SR	18FEB90	08:54 PM	X	TR-TR	01	17 ♏ 48	08	17 ♏ 48	08
♃ SD	24FEB90	12:18 PM	X	TR-TR	01	00 ♋ 48	04	00 ♋ 48	04
♅ SR	13APR90	02:02 PM	X	TR-TR	01	09 ♑ 35	11	09 ♑ 35	11

CRASH.GEO PST 1929-32

	DATE	TIME	E X	JOB	#	P1 POS.	HS	P2 POS.	HS
♀ △ ♂	01JAN29	11:59 PM	X	TR-TR	01	25 ♒ 10	01	25 ♊ 10R	05
♂ ☍ ♄	05JAN29	03:44 AM	X	TR-TR	01	24 ♊ 13R	05	24 ♐ 13	11
♀ ⚹ ♃	06JAN29	06:20 PM	X	TR-TR	01	00 ♓ 41	01	00 ♉ 41	03
☿ □ ♃	08JAN29	11:23 AM	X	TR-TR	01	00 ♒ 46	12	00 ♉ 46	03
☿ ⚹ ♅	10JAN29	08:36 AM	X	TR-TR	01	03 ♒ 49	12	03 ♈ 49	02
☉ □ ♃	21JAN29	08:35 PM	X	TR-TR	01	01 ♒ 41	12	01 ♉ 41	03
☿ △ ♂	22JAN29	04:34 PM	X	TR-TR	01	21 ♒ 07	01	21 ♊ 07R	05
☉ ⚹ ♅	24JAN29	08:39 AM	X	TR-TR	01	04 ♒ 14	12	04 ♈ 14	02
♀ □ ♂		08:42 PM	X	TR-TR	01	21 ♓ 01	02	21 ♊ 01R	05
♀ □ ♄	30JAN29	07:26 AM	X	TR-TR	01	26 ♓ 53	02	26 ♐ 53	11
☿ △ ♂	03FEB29	05:24 PM	X	TR-TR	01	21 ♒ 20R	01	21 ♊ 20	05
☿ ☌ ☉	06FEB29	07:44 PM	X	TR-TR	01	17 ♒ 54R	01	17 ♒ 54	01
♀ ☌ ♅		09:34 PM	X	TR-TR	01	04 ♈ 46	02	04 ♈ 46	02
☉ △ ♂	11FEB29	04:27 AM	X	TR-TR	01	22 ♒ 19	01	22 ♊ 19	05
☿ ⚹ ♀	13FEB29	07:03 AM	X	TR-TR	01	11 ♒ 06R	01	11 ♈ 06	02
☉ ⚹ ♄	17FEB29	06:08 AM	X	TR-TR	01	28 ♒ 27	01	28 ♐ 27	11
☉ ⚹ ♃	25FEB29	00:52 AM	X	TR-TR	01	06 ♓ 17	01	06 ♉ 17	03
♀ ⚹ ♂	05MAR29	03:38 AM	X	TR-TR	01	28 ♈ 03	03	28 ♊ 03	05
♀ △ ♄	07MAR29	10:18 AM	X	TR-TR	01	29 ♈ 38	03	29 ♐ 38	.11
♂ ☍ ♄	09MAR29	11:48 PM	X	TR-TR	01	29 ♊ 46	05	29 ♐ 46	11
☿ ⚹ ♄	15MAR29	05:28 PM	X	TR-TR	01	00 ♓ 01	01	00 ♑ 01	11
☿ △ ♂	17MAR29	03:49 PM	X	TR-TR	01	02 ♓ 43	01	02 ♋ 43	05
☿ ⚹ ♀	20MAR29	02:53 AM	X	TR-TR	01	06 ♓ 17	01	06 ♉ 17	03
☉ □ ♄		11:38 PM	X	TR-TR	01	00 ♈ 13	02	00 ♑ 13	11
☿ ⚹ ♃	23MAR29	11:53 AM	X	TR-TR	01	11 ♓ 24	02	11 ♉ 24	03
☉ □ ♂	27MAR29	09:05 PM	X	TR-TR	01	07 ♈ 02	02	07 ♋ 02	05
☉ ☌ ♅	28MAR29	04:36 AM	X	TR-TR	01	07 ♈ 21	02	07 ♈ 21	02
♂ □ ♅		03:16 PM	X	TR-TR	01	07 ♋ 22	05	07 ♈ 22	02
♀ ⚹ ♂	30MAR29	03:14 AM	X	TR-TR	01	08 ♉ 02R	03	08 ♋ 02	06
☿ □ ♄	03APR29	07:53 PM	X	TR-TR	01	00 ♈ 30	02	00 ♑ 30	11
☿ ☌ ♅	07APR29	07:51 PM	X	TR-TR	01	07 ♈ 57	02	07 ♈ 57	02
☿ □ ♂	10APR29	03:07 PM	X	TR-TR	01	13 ♈ 24	02	13 ♋ 24	06
☿ ☌ ☉	17APR29	07:59 AM	X	TR-TR	01	27 ♈ 09	03	27 ♈ 09	03
♂ ⚹ ♃	18APR29	03:01 AM	X	TR-TR	01	17 ♋ 06	06	17 ♉ 06	03
☿ △ ♄		09:25 PM	X	TR-TR	01	00 ♉ 27	03	00 ♑ 27R	11
☿ ☌ ♀		10:17 PM	X	TR-TR	01	00 ♉ 31	03	00 ♉ 31R	03
♀ △ ♄	19APR29	01:14 AM	X	TR-TR	01	00 ♉ 26R	03	00 ♑ 26R	11
♀ ☌ ☉	20APR29	01:24 AM	X	TR-TR	01	29 ♈ 48R	03	29 ♈ 48	03
☉ △ ♄		04:22 PM	X	TR-TR	01	00 ♉ 25	03	00 ♑ 25R	11
☿ ☌ ♃	27APR29	10:05 PM	X	TR-TR	01	19 ♉ 23	03	19 ♉ 23	03
☿ ⚹ ♂	29APR29	07:09 PM	X	TR-TR	01	23 ♉ 04	03	23 ♋ 04	06
♀ □ ♂	01MAY29	01:28 AM	X	TR-TR	01	23 ♈ 44R	03	23 ♋ 44	06
☿ ⚹ ♅	09MAY29	06:25 PM	X	TR-TR	01	09 ♊ 38	04	09 ♈ 38	02
☉ ☌ ♃	14MAY29	04:59 AM	X	TR-TR	01	23 ♉ 14	03	23 ♉ 14	03
♀ △ ♄	31MAY29	05:02 PM	X	TR-TR	01	28 ♈ 31	03	28 ♐ 31R	11
♂ △ ♅		05:46 PM	X	TR-TR	01	10 ♌ 33	07	10 ♈ 33	02
☉ ⚹ ♅	01JUN29	05:57 AM	X	TR-TR	01	10 ♊ 34	04	10 ♈ 34	02
☉ ⚹ ♂		10:30 PM	X	TR-TR	01	11 ♊ 13	04	11 ♌ 13	07
☿ ☌ ☉	09JUN29	03:04 AM	X	TR-TR	01	18 ♊ 06R	05	18 ♊ 06	05
☿ ⚹ ♂	11JUN29	02:03 PM	X	TR-TR	01	16 ♊ 45R	05	16 ♌ 45	07
☉ ☍ ♄	18JUN29	04:05 PM	X	TR-TR	01	27 ♊ 13	05	27 ♐ 13R	11

	DATE	TIME	EX	JOB	#	P1 POS.	HS	P2 POS.	HS
♂ △ ♄	28JUN29	05:51 AM	X	TR-TR	01	26 ♌ 31	07	26 ♐ 31R	11
☉ □ ♅	03JUL29	10:38 AM	X	TR-TR	01	11 ♋ 18	06	11 ♈ 18	02
☿ ☍ ♄	08JUL29	02:13 PM	X	TR-TR	01	25 ♊ 48	05	25 ♐ 48R	11
♀ □ ♂	13JUL29	00:56 AM	X	TR-TR	01	05 ♊ 24	04	05 ♍ 24	07
♀ ☌ ♃	14JUL29	01:04 PM	X	TR-TR	01	06 ♊ 57	04	06 ♊ 57	04
☿ ⚹ ♂	15JUL29	08:15 PM	X	TR-TR	01	07 ♋ 06	05	07 ♍ 06	07
♂ □ ♃	16JUL29	02:47 AM	X	TR-TR	01	07 ♍ 16	07	07 ♊ 16	04
☿ □ ♅	18JUL29	04:09 AM	X	TR-TR	01	11 ♋ 23	06	11 ♈ 23R	02
♀ ⚹ ♅		06:26 PM	X	TR-TR	01	11 ♊ 23	04	11 ♈ 23R	02
☿ ☌ ☉	30JUL29	08:25 PM	X	TR-TR	01	07 ♌ 28	07	07 ♌ 28	07
♀ ☍ ♄		11:10 PM	X	TR-TR	01	24 ♊ 32	05	24 ♐ 32R	11
☿ ⚹ ♃	01AUG29	04:17 AM	X	TR-TR	01	10 ♌ 13	07	10 ♊ 13	04
☿ △ ♅		04:36 PM	X	TR-TR	01	11 ♌ 17	07	11 ♈ 17R	02
☉ ⚹ ♃	03AUG29	01:37 AM	X	TR-TR	01	10 ♌ 33	07	10 ♊ 33	04
☉ △ ♅		07:22 PM	X	TR-TR	01	11 ♌ 15	07	11 ♈ 15R	02
♃ ⚹ ♅	07AUG29	01:40 AM	X	TR-TR	01	11 ♊ 12	04	11 ♈ 12R	02
☿ △ ♄	08AUG29	04:50 AM	X	TR-TR	01	24 ♌ 14	07	24 ♐ 14R	11
♂ □ ♄	12AUG29	07:02 AM	X	TR-TR	01	24 ♍ 06	08	24 ♐ 06R	11
♀ □ ♅	14AUG29	05:31 PM	X	TR-TR	01	11 ♋ 03	06	11 ♈ 03R	02
☉ △ ♄	17AUG29	02:09 AM	X	TR-TR	01	24 ♌ 00	07	24 ♐ 00R	11
☿ □ ♃	18AUG29	04:59 PM	X	TR-TR	01	12 ♍ 56	08	12 ♊ 56	04
☿ ⚹ ♀	24AUG29	09:46 PM	X	TR-TR	01	22 ♍ 44	08	22 ♋ 44	06
☿ □ ♄	25AUG29	04:22 PM	X	TR-TR	01	23 ♍ 54	08	23 ♐ 54R	11
♂ ☍ ♅	06SEP29	04:34 PM	X	TR-TR	01	10 ♎ 24	08	10 ♈ 24R	02
☿ ☍ ♅	07SEP29	00:25 AM	X	TR-TR	01	10 ♎ 23	08	10 ♈ 23R	02
☿ ☌ ♂		11:06 AM	X	TR-TR	01	10 ♎ 54	08	10 ♎ 54	08
☉ □ ♃	08SEP29	01:07 AM	X	TR-TR	01	15 ♍ 13	08	15 ♊ 13	05
♀ △ ♅		09:38 PM	X	TR-TR	01	10 ♌ 19	07	10 ♈ 19R	02
♀ ⚹ ♂	11SEP29	06:17 PM	X	TR-TR	01	13 ♌ 43	07	13 ♎ 43	08
☿ △ ♃		06:29 PM	X	TR-TR	01	15 ♎ 31	08	15 ♊ 31	05
♀ ⚹ ♃	13SEP29	08:59 AM	X	TR-TR	01	15 ♌ 38	07	15 ♊ 38	05
♂ △ ♃	14SEP29	07:57 PM	X	TR-TR	01	15 ♎ 44	08	15 ♊ 44	05
☿ ⚹ ♀	17SEP29	03:06 AM	X	TR-TR	01	20 ♎ 07	09	20 ♌ 07	07
☉ □ ♄		06:33 AM	X	TR-TR	01	24 ♍ 12	08	24 ♐ 12	11
♀ △ ♄	20SEP29	03:08 PM	X	TR-TR	01	24 ♌ 19	07	24 ♐ 19	11
☿ ☌ ♂	26SEP29	06:26 AM	X	TR-TR	01	23 ♎ 19R	09	23 ♎ 19	09
♂ ⚹ ♄	28SEP29	05:44 AM	X	TR-TR	01	24 ♎ 39	09	24 ♐ 39	11
☉ ☍ ♅	02OCT29	06:23 PM	X	TR-TR	01	09 ♎ 24	08	09 ♈ 24R	02
☿ △ ♃	06OCT29	06:53 AM	X	TR-TR	01	16 ♎ 24R	08	16 ♊ 24R	05
☿ ☌ ☉	07OCT29	10:13 PM	X	TR-TR	01	14 ♎ 29R	08	14 ♎ 29	08
♀ □ ♃	08OCT29	07:21 PM	X	TR-TR	01	16 ♍ 23	08	16 ♊ 23R	05
☉ △ ♃	09OCT29	08:01 PM	X	TR-TR	01	16 ♎ 22	08	16 ♊ 22R	05
☿ ☍ ♅	13OCT29	05:48 PM	X	TR-TR	01	08 ♎ 57R	08	08 ♈ 57R	02
♀ □ ♄	16OCT29	10:35 AM	X	TR-TR	01	25 ♍ 45	08	25 ♐ 45	11
☉ ⚹ ♄	19OCT29	12:57 PM	X	TR-TR	01	25 ♎ 59	09	25 ♐ 59	11
☿ ☍ ♅		03:52 PM	X	TR-TR	01	08 ♎ 43	08	08 ♈ 43R	02
♀ ☍ ♅	26OCT29	05:25 PM	X	TR-TR	01	08 ♎ 28	08	08 ♈ 28R	02
☿ △ ♃		09:24 PM	X	TR-TR	01	15 ♎ 37	08	15 ♊ 37R	05
♀ △ ♃	01NOV29	03:36 AM	X	TR-TR	01	15 ♎ 12	08	15 ♊ 12R	05
☿ ⚹ ♄	03NOV29	06:45 PM	X	TR-TR	01	27 ♎ 18	09	27 ♐ 18	11

CRASH,GEO PST 1929-32

	DATE	TIME	EX	JOB	#	P1 POS.	HS	P2 POS.	HS
♀ ⚹ ♄	11NOV29	10:51 AM	X	TR-TR	01	28♎02	09	28♐02	11
☿ ☌ ☉	27NOV29	06:03 AM	X	TR-TR	01	04♐51	10	04♐51	10
♂ △ ♅	28NOV29	06:13 PM	X	TR-TR	01	07♐36	10	07♈36R	02
☿ △ ♅		11:43 PM	X	TR-TR	01	07♐35	10	07♈35R	02
☿ ☌ ♂	29NOV29	04:32 AM	X	TR-TR	01	07♐54	10	07♐54	10
☉ △ ♅		10:23 PM	X	TR-TR	01	07♐34	10	07♈34R	02
☿ ☍ ♃	01DEC29	01:10 PM	X	TR-TR	01	11♐36	10	11♊36R	04
☉ ☌ ♂	02DEC29	11:12 PM	X	TR-TR	01	10♐39	10	10♐39	10
☉ ☍ ♃	03DEC29	03:03 PM	X	TR-TR	01	11♐19	10	11♊19R	04
♂ ☍ ♃		08:17 PM	X	TR-TR	01	11♐18	10	11♊18R	04
♀ △ ♅	12DEC29	09:34 PM	X	TR-TR	01	07♐28	10	07♈28R	02
☿ ☌ ♄	14DEC29	08:10 AM	X	TR-TR	01	01♑40	11	01♑40	11
♀ ☍ ♃		06:46 PM	X	TR-TR	01	09♐50	10	09♊50R	04
☿ □ ♅	18DEC29	00:34 AM	X	TR-TR	01	07♑27	11	07♈27	02
☉ ☌ ♄	24DEC29	08:21 PM	X	TR-TR	01	02♑54	11	02♑54	11
☉ □ ♅	29DEC29	08:59 AM	X	TR-TR	01	07♑31	12	07♈31	02
♀ ☌ ♂	02JAN30	08:37 AM	X	TR-TR	01	03♑11	11	03♑11	11
♀ ☌ ♄		11:46 PM	X	TR-TR	01	03♑59	11	03♑59	11
♂ ☌ ♄	03JAN30	11:47 AM	X	TR-TR	01	04♑03	11	04♑03	11
♃ ⚹ ♅		07:27 PM	X	TR-TR	01	07♊35R	04	07♈35	02
♀ □ ♅	05JAN30	09:13 PM	X	TR-TR	01	07♑37	12	07♈37	02
♂ □ ♅	08JAN30	06:53 AM	X	TR-TR	01	07♑40	12	07♈40	02
☿ △ ♃	09JAN30	05:38 AM	X	TR-TR	01	07♒09	01	07♊09R	04
☿ ⚹ ♅	10JAN30	07:17 AM	X	TR-TR	01	07♒43	01	07♈43	02
☿ ⚹ ♅	14JAN30	08:28 PM	X	TR-TR	01	07♒49R	01	07♈49	02
☿ △ ♃	16JAN30	05:28 PM	X	TR-TR	01	06♒42R	01	06♊42R	04
☿ ☌ ☉	21JAN30	04:43 PM	X	TR-TR	01	01♒17R	12	01♒17	12
☿ ☌ ♀	23JAN30	04:23 AM	X	TR-TR	01	29♑22R	12	29♑22	12
☉ △ ♃	26JAN30	05:10 PM	X	TR-TR	01	06♒23	01	06♊23R	04
☉ ⚹ ♅	28JAN30	12:28 PM	X	TR-TR	01	08♒13	01	08♈13	02
♀ △ ♃		05:51 PM	X	TR-TR	01	06♒22	01	06♊22R	04
☿ ☌ ♂	29JAN30	01:55 AM	X	TR-TR	01	23♑33R	12	23♑33	12
♀ ⚹ ♅	30JAN30	06:30 AM	X	TR-TR	01	08♒17	01	08♈17	02
♀ ☌ ☉	06FEB30	09:39 AM	X	TR-TR	01	17♒14	01	17♒14	01
♂ △ ♃	15FEB30	02:42 AM	X	TR-TR	01	06♒44	01	06♊44	04
♂ ⚹ ♅	18FEB30	02:31 AM	X	TR-TR	01	09♒04	01	09♈04	02
☿ △ ♃	21FEB30	01:36 PM	X	TR-TR	01	07♒07	01	07♊07	04
♄ □ ♅	22FEB30	00:07 AM	X	TR-TR	01	09♑15	12	09♈15	02
♀ □ ♃		07:47 AM	X	TR-TR	01	07♓11	01	07♊11	04
☿ ⚹ ♅	23FEB30	07:09 AM	X	TR-TR	01	09♒19	01	09♈19	02
♀ ⚹ ♄	24FEB30	02:54 AM	X	TR-TR	01	09♓25	01	09♑25	12
☉ □ ♃	26FEB30	11:56 AM	X	TR-TR	01	07♓30	01	07♊30	04
☉ ⚹ ♄	28FEB30	06:41 PM	X	TR-TR	01	09♓48	02	09♑48	12
☿ ☌ ♂	01MAR30	07:19 PM	X	TR-TR	01	18♒11	01	18♒11	01
☿ □ ♃	15MAR30	06:33 AM	X	TR-TR	01	09♓19	01	09♊19	04
☿ ⚹ ♄	16MAR30	03:54 AM	X	TR-TR	01	10♓50	02	10♑50	12
♀ ⚹ ♃	20MAR30	04:22 PM	X	TR-TR	01	10♈03	02	10♊03	04
♀ ☌ ♅	21MAR30	04:55 AM	X	TR-TR	01	10♈42	02	10♈42	02
♀ □ ♄		01:09 PM	X	TR-TR	01	11♈07	02	11♑07	12
♃ ⚹ ♅	27MAR30	10:54 AM	X	TR-TR	01	11♊03	04	11♈03	02

	DATE	TIME	EX	JOB	#	P1 POS.	HS	P2 POS.	HS
♂———— ⚹ ♄	31MAR30	03:52 PM	X	TR-TR	01	11♓32	02	11♑32	12
♂———— □ ♃		10:55 PM	X	TR-TR	01	11♓46	02	11♊46	04
☿ —— ☌ ☉	01APR30	05:01 AM	X	TR-TR	01	11♈04	02	11♈04	02
☿ —— ☌ ♅		07:58 AM	X	TR-TR	01	11♈20	02	11♈20	02
☿ —— □ ♄		10:45 AM	X	TR-TR	01	11♈34	02	11♑34	12
☉———— ☌ ♅		11:20 AM	X	TR-TR	01	11♈20	02	11♈20	02
☿ —— ⚹ ♃		02:23 PM	X	TR-TR	01	11♈52	02	11♊52	04
☉———— □ ♄		05:06 PM	X	TR-TR	01	11♈34	02	11♑34	12
☉———— ⚹ ♃	02APR30	02:26 AM	X	TR-TR	01	11♈57	02	11♊57	04
♄———— □ ♅	08APR30	09:46 PM	X	TR-TR	01	11♑45	12	11♈45	02
♀——— △ ♄	15APR30	09:43 AM	X	TR-TR	01	11♉51	03	11♑51	12
☿ —— △ ♄	16APR30	01:15 PM	X	TR-TR	01	11♉52	03	11♑52	12
☿ —— ☌ ♀	19APR30	02:57 PM	X	TR-TR	01	17♉02	03	17♉02	03
☿ —— ☌ ♀	29APR30	00:58 AM	X	TR-TR	01	28♉35	04	28♉35	04
☉———— △ ♄	02MAY30	02:39 PM	X	TR-TR	01	11♉47	03	11♑47R	12
♂———— □ ♄	09MAY30	11:43 AM	X	TR-TR	01	11♈37	02	11♑37R	12
♀——— ⚹ ♂	10MAY30	01:51 AM	X	TR-TR	01	12♊04	04	12♈04	02
♀——— ⚹ ♅	11MAY30	05:55 AM	X	TR-TR	01	13♊29	04	13♈29	02
♂———— ☌ ♅		11:43 PM	X	TR-TR	01	13♈32	02	13♈32	02
♀——— ☌ ♃	17MAY30	07:31 AM	X	TR-TR	01	20♊52	05	20♊52	05
☿ —— ☌ ☉	19MAY30	09:10 PM	X	TR-TR	01	28♉27R	04	28♉27	04
♂———— ⚹ ♃	23MAY30	10:21 AM	X	TR-TR	01	22♈13	03	22♊13	05
♀——— ☍ ♄	02JUN30	02:01 PM	X	TR-TR	01	10♋31	06	10♑31R	12
☉———— ⚹ ♅	05JUN30	03:51 PM	X	TR-TR	01	14♊33	04	14♈33	02
♀——— □ ♅		10:44 PM	X	TR-TR	01	14♋34	06	14♈34	02
♂———— △ ♄	15JUN30	08:40 PM	X	TR-TR	01	09♉40	03	09♑40R	12
☉———— ☌ ♃	20JUN30	07:34 AM	X	TR-TR	01	28♊33	05	28♊33	05
☿ —— ⚹ ♅	26JUN30	09:17 AM	X	TR-TR	01	15♊08	04	15♈08	02
☉———— ☍ ♄	30JUN30	07:39 PM	X	TR-TR	01	08♋35	06	08♑35R	12
♀——— △ ♅	01JUL30	05:13 PM	X	TR-TR	01	15♌13	07	15♈13	02
☿ —— ☌ ♃	05JUL30	02:36 PM	X	TR-TR	01	02♋03	05	02♋03	05
☉———— □ ♅	07JUL30	08:58 PM	X	TR-TR	01	15♋18	06	15♈18	02
☿ —— ☍ ♄	08JUL30	11:32 AM	X	TR-TR	01	08♋01	06	08♑01R	12
☿ —— □ ♅	11JUL30	09:47 PM	X	TR-TR	01	15♋20	06	15♈20	02
♀——— □ ♂	14JUL30	02:08 PM	X	TR-TR	01	00♍16	07	00♊16	04
☿ —— ☌ ☉	15JUL30	02:03 AM	X	TR-TR	01	22♋11	06	22♋11	06
♀——— ⚹ ♃	18JUL30	03:42 PM	X	TR-TR	01	04♍59	07	04♋59	05
♀——— △ ♄	20JUL30	01:18 PM	X	TR-TR	01	07♍10	07	07♑10R	11
☿ —— ⚹ ♂	21JUL30	02:53 AM	X	TR-TR	01	04♌49	07	04♊49	04
☿ —— △ ♅	26JUL30	12:09 PM	X	TR-TR	01	15♌22	07	15♈22R	02
♃———— ☍ ♄		07:56 PM	X	TR-TR	01	06♋46	05	06♑46R	11
♂———— ⚹ ♅	05AUG30	12:12 PM	X	TR-TR	01	15♊17	05	15♈17R	02
☿ —— △ ♄	07AUG30	02:05 PM	X	TR-TR	01	06♍06	07	06♑06R	11
☉———— △ ♅	08AUG30	05:10 AM	X	TR-TR	01	15♌15	07	15♈15R	02
☿ —— ⚹ ♃	09AUG30	11:18 PM	X	TR-TR	01	09♍44	08	09♋44	06
☉———— ⚹ ♂	14AUG30	08:26 AM	X	TR-TR	01	21♌08	07	21♊08	05
♀——— □ ♄		10:31 PM	X	TR-TR	01	05♎47	08	05♑47R	11
♀——— □ ♃	20AUG30	11:04 AM	X	TR-TR	01	11♎48	08	11♋48	06
☿ —— □ ♂	23AUG30	09:19 AM	X	TR-TR	01	26♍59	08	26♊59	05
♀——— ☍ ♅		09:25 AM	X	TR-TR	01	14♎57	08	14♈57R	02

Section Seven:

Bibliography

1. *Astrologer's Forecasting Workbook* by Lloyd Cope, American Federation of Astrologer.

2. *Astro Cycles in Speculative Markets*--L. Jensen (Lambert-Gann)

3. *Business Cycles Versus Planetary Movements* --J.M. Langham (Maghnal)

4. *Planetary Effects on Stock Market Prices*--J.M. Langham (Maghnal)

5. *Cyclical Market Forecasting: Stocks and Grains*--J.M. Langham (Maghnal)

6. *Cycles--The Science of Prediction*--Dewey Daiken (Foundation Study of Cycles)

7. *The Moon Sign Book*--Llewellyn George (Llewellyn Pub.)

8. *Astro-economic Interpretation*--L. Jensen. Lambert Gann.

9. *A to Z Horoscope Maker and Delineator*. L. George. Llewellyn Pub.

10. *Economic Cycles: Their Law and Course*. H. Moore. Macmillan.

11. *Divine Proportion*. Huntley. Dover Press

12. *Stock Market Prediction*. Bradley Llewellyn Pub.

13. Secret Teaching of All Ages. M.P. Hall. Philo. Society of L.A.

14. *Valliere's Natural Cycles Almanac*. Astrolabe.

15. Matrix Software. Blue Star. 1-800-Planets.

16. Astro Computing Services. P.O. Box 16297 San Diego, CA 92116

17. *Forecasting Prices*. T.G. Butaney. Pearl Printing.

18. *Tunnel through the Air*. W. D. Gann. Lambert-Gann.

SECTION SEVEN:

BIBLIOGRAPHY

19. *The Magic Word*. W.D. Gann. Lambert Gann

20. *Rocky Mountain Financial Workbook*. W. Foster. Box 1093, Reseda CA 91355

21. *Astro Geographic Determinism*. Stock Forecast 1988. J. Gillien

22. *The Kabala of Numbers*. Sepherial. Newcastle

23. *Profits in the Stock Market*. H.M. Gartley. Lambert Gann Publishing

24. *American Ephemeris* 1981-1990 ACS Publications

25. *Astro-Geographic Determinism* Forecast 1987. J. Gillen

26. *The Moons North Node: An Important Cycles Indicator*. George J. McCormack FAFA. June 1947 established.

27. *Stock and Commodity Market Trend Timing Using Advanced Technical Analysis* Commodity Research Institute. John R. Hill.

About the Author

Larry Pesavento is a "Leo" (July 28, 1941)! He has a B.S. in Chemistry and an M.B.A. in Finance from Indiana State University. He has been an active trader for over twenty years and during 1982-1983 was a member of the International Monetary Market (IMM) and made his living as a floor trader in T-Bills, Swiss Francs and Gold. During 1978 through 1982 he operated a successful commodity management company. This was sold when he moved to Chicago to trade as a local. He maintains an extensive library on the subjects of trading systems, trading philosophy and financial astrology, and is a member of the American Federation of Astrologers and The Foundation for the Study of Cycles.

He currently lives in Shell Beach, California, where he operates the *Astro-Cycles Newsletter*.